Chinese Buddhism and Traditional Culture

Since the first century, when Buddhism entered China, this foreign religion has influenced and been influenced in turn by traditional Chinese culture, and eventually became an important part of it. That is one of the great historical themes not only for China but also for East Asia.

This book explores the elements of Buddhism, including its classics, doctrines, system, and rituals, to reveal the basic connotation of Buddhism as a cultural entity. Regarding the development of Buddhism in China, it traces the spread in chronological order, from the introduction in the Han Dynasties (202 BC–220 AD), to the prosperity in the Sixteen Kingdoms (ca. 304–439 AD), and then to the decline since the Five Dynasties (907–ca. 960 AD). It is noteworthy that the Buddhist schools in the Southern and Northern Dynasties (420–589 AD) and the Buddhist sects in the Sui and Tang Dynasties (581–907 AD) contributed to the sinicization of Buddhism. This book also deals with the interesting question of the similarities and differences between Chinese Buddhism and Indian Buddhism, to examine the specific characteristics of the former in terms of thought and culture. In the last chapter, the external influence of Chinese Buddhism in East Asia is studied.

Scholars and students in Buddhism and Chinese culture studies, especially those in Buddhist countries, will benefit from the book. Also, it will appeal to readers interested in religion, Chinese culture, and ancient Chinese history.

Fang Litian is a former first-class professor and doctoral tutor of the Department of Religious Studies, School of Philosophy, Renmin University of China, Director of the Buddhism and Religious Theory Institute, and Director of the Institute for Advanced Study of Religion. He has served successively as the vice president and consultant of the China Religious Society, executive vice president of the China Philosophy History Association, chief editor of the journal *History of Chinese Philosophy*, member of the Social Science Council of the Ministry of Education, and librarian of the Central Research Institute of Culture and History. His monographs include *Treatise of Buddhism in Wei, Jin, Northern and Southern Dynasties*, *Buddhist Philosophy*, *Chinese Buddhism and Traditional Culture*, and *The Essential Meaning of Chinese Buddhist Philosophy* (Volumes 1 and 2), among which *Buddhist Philosophy* won the honorary award of the first China Book Award, and *The Essential Meaning of Chinese Buddhist Philosophy* won the sixth national book award.

China Perspectives

The *China Perspectives* series focuses on translating and publishing works by leading Chinese scholars, writing about both global topics and China-related themes. It covers humanities and social sciences, education, media and psychology, as well as many interdisciplinary themes.

This is the first time any of these books have been published in English for international readers. The series aims to put forward a Chinese perspective, give insights into cutting-edge academic thinking in China, and inspire researchers globally.

Titles in history currently include

Merchants and Society in Modern China
Rise of Merchant Groups
Tang Lixing

Merchants and Society in Modern China
From Guild to Chamber of Commerce
Tang Lixing

John Leighton Stuart's Missionary-Educator's Career in China
Hao Ping

John Leighton Stuart's Political Career in China
Hao Ping

Contemporary Studies on Modern Chinese History
Zeng Yeying

The History of Chinese Ancient Politics I
Wang Zengyu

The History of Chinese Ancient Politics II
Wang Zengyu

For more information, please visit www.routledge.com/series/CPH

Chinese Buddhism and Traditional Culture

Fang Litian

LONDON AND NEW YORK

This book is published with financial support from the Chinese Fund for the Humanities and Social Sciences.

First published 2019
by Routledge
2 Park Square, Milton Park, Abingdon, Oxon OX14 4RN

and by Routledge
52 Vanderbilt Avenue, New York, NY 10017

Routledge is an imprint of the Taylor & Francis Group, an informa business

© 2019 Fang Litian

The right of Fang Litian to be identified as author of this work has been asserted by him in accordance with sections 77 and 78 of the Copyright, Designs and Patents Act 1988.

All rights reserved. No part of this book may be reprinted or reproduced or utilised in any form or by any electronic, mechanical, or other means, now known or hereafter invented, including photocopying and recording, or in any information storage or retrieval system, without permission in writing from the publishers.

Trademark notice: Product or corporate names may be trademarks or registered trademarks, and are used only for identification and explanation without intent to infringe.

English version by permission of China Renmin University Press

The original-language version of this book was published by Shanghai People's Publishing House in 1988.

British Library Cataloguing-in-Publication Data
A catalogue record for this book is available from the British Library

Library of Congress Cataloging-in-Publication Data
Names: Fang, Litian, author. | Translation of: Fang, Litian. Zhongguo
  fo jiao yu chuan tong wen hua.
Title: Chinese Buddhism and traditional culture / Fang Litian.Other titles:
  Zhongguo fo jiao yu chuan tong wen hua. English
Description: New York : Routledge, 2019. | Series: China perspectives
Identifiers: LCCN 2018040161 (print) | LCCN 2018045638 (ebook) |
  ISBN 9781315720487 (ebook) | ISBN 9781138855199 (hardcover)
Subjects: LCSH: Buddhism—China—History. | China—Civilization—
  Buddhist influences.
Classification: LCC BQ628 (ebook) | LCC BQ628 .F3613 2019 (print) |
  DDC 294.30951—dc23
LC record available at https://lccn.loc.gov/2018040161

ISBN: 978-1-138-85519-9 (hbk)
ISBN: 978-1-315-72048-7 (ebk)

Typeset in Times New Roman
by Apex CoVantage, LLC

Contents

1	The creation, evolution, and dissemination of Indian Buddhism	1
2	Buddhism's introduction into China and its change and development	27
3	Various Buddhist classics	74
4	The basic doctrines of Buddhism	90
5	Buddhist system and ritual	115
6	The Buddhist temple hall	128
7	Buddhist monuments in China	147
8	The source of basic characteristics of Chinese Buddhism	183
9	The external influence of Chinese Buddhism	212
	Index	225

1 The creation, evolution, and dissemination of Indian Buddhism

Among the earliest religions in the world, Buddhism, Christianity, and Islam are known as the world's three major religions. Having been popular in Asia for a long time, Buddhism was introduced to Europe, America, Africa, and Oceania at the end of the nineteenth century. Now it has approximately 330 million followers.

Shakyamuni's creation of Buddhism and its early development

1 The historical background of Shakyamuni's creation of Buddhism

It was said that from about the sixth century BC to the fifth century BC, Shakyamuni, the son of King Suddhodana of Kapilavastu (now southern Nepal) in ancient northern India, founded Buddhism. The era in which Shakyamuni lived and created Buddhism was characterized by social turbulence, sharp ethnic conflicts, and class contradictions. It was also an era when society was in turmoil, old and new ideas collided, and religious life prevailed.

From 2000 BC to 1000 BC, ancient Aryans primarily living in Central Asia settled in the Ganges Valley in India from the east. They oppressed and exploited the indigenous inhabitants, the majority of whom became slaves. From the sixth century BC to the fifth century BC, the slavery economy of India grew rapidly. As a result, the handicraft industry was separated from agriculture, the commodity economy was developed, and big cities, such as Rajagriha, Varanasi, and Sravasti, came into being. According to the records of Buddhist scriptures, 16 city-centered powers were established along the upstream to downstream of the Ganges Valley (in areas of central India). The most powerful states were Magadha, located on the southern bank of the Ganges Valley, and Kosala, on the northwest bank. Kapilavastu was a small aristocratic republic in the northeast and was seized by Virudhaka, king of Kosala, due to frequent attacks and annexation between countries in Shakyamuni's later years.

At that time, the caste system dominated in the states of India. The word "caste", also referred to as "clan name", is used to translate the Sanskrit word "Varna". Its original meaning was "color" or "skin". Because "Aryans" are white-skinned people while aboriginals are black-skinned people, this system was used by Aryans to distinguish themselves ethnically from the conquered indigenous people according to two Varnas (castes): Arya and Dassa. In social and political life, Arya, as a dominant caste, ruled the Dassa. As two opposite classes, each caste had its own hereditary occupations and members of these classes were not permitted to intermarry. Subsequently, for class division and the development of labor division, Arya developed three castes: Brahman, Kshatriya, and Vaisya. With the addition of Dassa – the fourth caste, Sudra – there are four castes, which means the four social levels: the highest class, the most noble and prominent one, was Brahman, which was a class of priests who considered themselves representatives of "Brahma" (God) and administered religious rites. At that time, decisions of state affairs and even family life were made by holding certain religious ceremonies, which were be presided over by Brahmans. Otherwise, these decisions were illegal. Therefore, Brahmans made up the theocracy, presided over sacrifices, and were the rulers of people's spiritual life. The next caste was Ksatriyas – namely, warriors – who administered political and military affairs. They seized political and military power, and were secular rulers of ancient India. Monks and priests were the flamen nobilities and warriors were military nobilities. These two classes were noble slave-owner classes. The third caste was Vaisyas, composed of farmers, herdsmen, artisans, and merchants. The majority of them belonged to the exploited class, having to pay taxes and do corvée. And the fourth caste was Sudras, composed of slaves, laborers, and servants. They were obligated to farm the land and graze livestock for their owners, without any rights, and they were severely oppressed and exploited. The four castes were separated by a clear line of distinction and differed greatly in social status, rights, obligations, duties, and lifestyles, and customs werepassed from generation to generation.

In the era when Sakyamuni lived, with the strengthening of the state apparatus, Ksatriyas became more and more powerful politically and militarily. Increasingly dissatisfied with the privileges of Brahmans, they asked for expansion of their rights and supported various non-Brahman ideas. Thanks to the development of handicrafts, booming commerce, and accumulation of wealth, business owners desired to improve their social status and made a strong demand for political power. Meanwhile, the slaves fought against the slave owners by fleeing, destroying water conservancy projects, and murdering slave owners. The emergence and growth of these social powers weakened Brahmans' control over politics, culture, religion, and ideology. Reflected in the ideological domain, the complicated political struggle also promoted ideas representing various interests of all classes. Problems with society and human beings produced 100 schools of thought. According to Buddhist scriptures, there were 96 kinds of ideologies or religious sects in addition to Buddhism. Generally speaking, there were two major ideological trends: one was the school of orthodox Brahmanist thought, and the other was the innovative thought of Sramanas (oblates).

As the dominant religion then, Brahmanism enshrined Vedas as a book from heaven and worshiped Brahma, Vishnu, and Shiva as three major gods respectively symbolizing the "creation", "protection", and "destruction" of the universe.

Brahmanism also held three guiding principles: God-inspired Vedas, almighty sacrificial ritual, and Supreme Brahman. It also advocated that the whole universe was a unity in which the subjective and objective, the self and the world, the souls of the individuals and the universe were integrated. It noted that the world people knew had no inherent entity that belonged to the "divined self" – Brahma, the eternal existence, and the human soul were just one part of such existence. Brahmanism claimed that the four castes were all borne by Brahma: Brahmans derived from his mouth, Ksatriyas from his shoulders, Vaisyas from his navel, and Sudras from his feet. Thus, the social standing of the four castes, noble or humble, was decided according to this. Besides, Brahmanism boasted of superstitious ideas, such as the chain of cause and effect, the eternal cycle of birth and death, the immortality of the soul, and the form of reincarnation depending on whether one acted in accordance with the teachings of Brahmanism. Therefore, a devoted practitioner of Brahmanism would be reincarnated to heaven after death; otherwise, he or she would be turned into a beast and go to hell. It also stressed that only the first three castes were entitled to believe in religion, to hold the rites to offer sacrifices to ghosts and God, and to be reincarnated to heaven after death. Sudras were deprived of the right to conduct a religious ceremony, let alone ascend to God after death. In other words, Sudras could find no way out socially or religiously.

Among the anti-Brahmanic schools, the well-known school of Jainism believed in the relations of cause and effect, soul liberation, asceticism, and ethics about purity and contamination. According to this sect, people's present life was determined by "karma" (thought, speech, and behavior) in the previous life. Therefore, only by religious practice could the soul be liberated. Equal to its attached body, the soul was an omnipresent, semi-physical entity growing as the volume grows. People must purify themselves morally for the liberation of their soul. As stains on morality were caused by impure fine materials entering into the soul, it was necessary to block their entry to obtain moral purity and enable the soul to enter Nirvana and thus get liberated. To this end, Jainism, while opposing offering sacrifice, claimed strictly observation of disciplines and advocated the five precepts: refraining from killing, cheating, stealing, committing adultery, and accumulating private property. In addition, it encouraged going hungry, lying on a bed of nails, exposing oneself to the sun and fire, throwing oneself into rocks, pulling one's hair, smoking their nose, and other ascetic practices regarded as ways to realize liberation. For another example, Lokayatika, a famous materialistic school, denied the existence of Brahma. Instead, it believed that both humankind and the world were composed of four major elements: earth, water, fire, and wind, which would decompose and vanish after death, thereby denying the existence of an afterlife where happiness could be pursued. It was in favor of carnal desires and caste equality while condemning reincarnation, metempsychosis, sacrificial rites, and asceticism. This theory was the most fierce criticism and opposition against Brahmanism. An "intuitionism school" considered everything from the perspective of relativism without making a decisive conclusion. For instance, they thought that there might or might not be an afterlife and retribution. That's why the intuitionism school was described as being as intangible as the loach. However, it advocated concentration practices to obtain true wisdom. In addition, there were three similar theories. The first was the theory of "the Seven Elements", which held that the human body was composed of seven elements: earth, water, fire, wind, bitterness, joy, and soul (life). Once they dispersed, people died. These elements were not created by something else nor did they create anything else. Elements are eternal. The second was fatalism, which held that everything in life was determined by fate and could not be decided by individual will. Besides, it insisted that ethics made no sense, religious practice did not work, and retribution simply didn't exist. The last was fortuitism. According to this theory, everything in the world emerged and developed by accident. Therefore, it encouraged indulgence, which in essence was the theory of ethical skepticism and religious negativism. To sum up, by differing in viewpoints, these theories were consistent in objecting to the political and ideological domination of Brahmanism.

The foregoing is the social, political, ideological, and religious background and environment under which Shakyamuni founded Buddhism.

2 Shakyamuni's creation of Buddhism and its early development

Shakyamuni, the founder of Buddhism, had his given name, Siddharta, and his family name, Gotama. As he belonged to the Sakya clan, he was also called Shakyamuni. "Muni" means jewel in Sanskrit and is often compared to a saint. Therefore, Shakyamuni is a title of respect, meaning a sage of the Sakya clan. Having attained enlightenment, Shakyamuni is also called "Fo" in Chinese. "Fo" is the abbreviation for "Fotuo", which is used to translate the word "Buddha". Buddha means an enlightened person. The term "Buddha" has existed in India since the earliest times, but Buddhism attributes the three additional connotations to the term. They are as follows: (1) enlightenment; (2) perfect enlightenment; (3) supreme or paramount enlightenment. That means Buddha's wisdom and achievement have reached the highest and the most perfect sphere in enlightening both oneself and others, and the behavior of enlightening both oneself and others has reached an incomparable degree.

We cannot figure out the exact date of Shakyamuni's birth and death and there are different records in various Buddhist classics. It is generally accepted that he lived during 565 BC–486 BC, and was a contemporary of Confucius in the Spring and Autumn Period of China. As mentioned before, Shakyamuni was the son of King Suddhodana of Kapilavastu. It was said that after seven days of his birth, his mother, Queen Mahamaya, passed away, and his aunt Pajapati became the new queen and brought up the little prince. Decent and intelligent as Shakyamuni was, his father, Suddhodana, had great expectations of him. At that time, confronted with two great powers of Magadha and Kosala and threatened severely by the latter, Kapilavastu was in a tough and dangerous situation. Therefore, King Suddhodana hoped that his son would succeed to the throne and free Kapilavastu from the invasion of the neighboring states. So he cultivated his son strictly in a comprehensive way, expecting him to become the well-renowned Wheel-Turning King – namely, a universal ruler who can unify the whole world. Thanks to his father's care, Shakyamuni not only learned literature and arithmetic from Brahman scholars but also studied war and martial arts with warriors, becoming a man with broad knowledge and profound thought. So he was elected as the "prince". However, contrary to his father's expectation (being the "Wheel-Turning King"), Shakyamuni was devoted to academic achievements instead of becoming a political ruler. Eventually, after he renounced the family for study and practice, he created Buddhism by pioneering a unique system of doctrine.

The reason Shakyamuni chose to become a monk was also explained in Buddhist scriptures. It was said that at the age of 14, while going out, Shakyamuni observed that an exhausted farmer, though sweating and panting, was ploughing under the scorching sun. The cattle, with ropes around their necks, were being flogged and wounded and were bleeding. Insects from the field were pecked by the flying birds. However, the farmer did not take into account of the value of the animals' lives. Suddenly, Shakyamuni awakened to the cruelty of the world and the misery of life. Later, he witnessed weak and ugly old people, the moaning and suffering sick, and the stiff bodies of the dead. Being unhappy, disgusted, and fearful, he felt the pain and misery suffered by human beings, as well as the transience and impermanence of life. All these things made him ponder such problems as what causes the pain of life? How can the world be delivered from suffering? The knowledge he had acquired could not solve these problems. Then the prince was deeply anxious and sad. Afterwards, he met a monk from whom he learned that one could be freed from illness and death by renouncing the world and practicing according to a religious doctrine. Then the idea of becoming a monk came to his mind, which was rejected by his father. To stop his son, when Shakyamuni was only 16 years old, his father arranged for him to marry his cousin, Princess Yaasodhara, from a neighboring state. She bore him a son named Rahula. The king also built him three magnificent palaces, named for cold, hot, and warm seasons, surrounding him with worldly pleasures. What's more, he often tried to persuade his son not to renounce the family. But all his efforts were in vain. At the age of 29 after tonsure, Shakyamuni resolutely relinquished his throne and said farewell to his wife and son. He went on into the remote mountains and wilderness to visit famous scholars and learned from them with the aim of freeing himself from the sufferings of life.

After renouncing the family, Shakyamuni looked for masters in Magadha, where he learned from the religious mentors Alara Kalama and Uddaka Rampaputta about general concepts of faith and practice, such as meditating and living by religious discipline ("Vinaya"). However, what they taught couldn't satisfy his quest, and he left to wander about. Then he made up his mind to concentrate on practicing the most rigorous austerity. In other words, he sought to get enlightened and free his life from pain by self-restraint. Thus he began to use a variety of terrible methods, such as gradually reducing to eating only one grain of wheat per day or just one meal in seven days. He ate seeds, grass, and sometimes even feces for survival. He wore clothes woven with coarse wool or made of deerskin or bark, which stimulated his skin. He removed his hair and stood still and lay on thorns, deer manure, and cow dung. Without bathing, he looked like a withered tree. Moreover, he often went to a cemetery and slept beside the decaying corpses. Shakyamuni went through suffering and pain for six years, resulting only in fragility and weakness, but did not achieve enlightenment or unravel the mysteries of the world. Since it proved fruitless, he began to understand that austerity led to no avail: he had reached the extremes of self-restraint but it was in vain. Then he thought about another way to gain knowledge and eliminate pain. Looking back upon his youth, he remembered that once while sitting under a tree, he entered into so-called meditation, getting both physical and mental pleasure. He found that it was a way to become enlightened. He further realized that sitting meditation required a strong body, so he had to eat. Having changed his ideas, he went to take a bath in the Falgu River to clean off all the dirt from over the past six years. Then, after accepting the deer's milk offered by a herdswoman, his strength was restored afresh. He then went to a nearby pippala tree (later called the bodhi tree). Sitting down with his legs crossed and facing the east, he made great vows: "Now if I fail to attain supreme enlightenment, I would rather have my body decompose than rise from this seat". After contemplating in such a manner for seven days and seven nights (also said to be 49 days), he was improved greatly in spirit, surpassing his own sight and hearing limits beyond time and space. Calm and smooth as a mirror, he felt all his worries had disappeared and all his doubts had been clarified. All of a sudden, he awakened to the true nature of the universe and life – a system of karmic retribution and reincarnation. At the age of 35, Sakyamuni grasped truth and achieved complete enlightenment and thus was liberated. Afterward, people called him Buddha and honored him as a truly enlightened sage and wise man. Later, he was also revered by his followers as "the World's most Venerable", which means that he had enough merit and virtue to benefit the world and was unique in the world.

After Sakyamuni attained Buddhahood, he spread his theory. He vowed to awaken and save sentient beings from darkness. In the next 45 years, being constantly seeking, he never stopped preaching his doctrine. Centering on the states of Magadha, Kosala, and Vatsa, he left his footprints on both sides of the Ganges Valley. He spent 25 years living in Jata Grove Monastery in Savatthi, the capital of Kosala. From time to time, he also resided in Bamboo Grove Monastery in Rajagaha, the capital of Magadha. Traveling from east to west, from Campa to Mathura, he preached widely. Wherever he went, he seldom participated in political and worldly life. Instead, he was committed to preaching and teaching his disciples. He was good at choosing metaphors from animal husbandry, labor, production, and daily life to clarify his teachings. In addition, he attached great importance to the organization of sanghas and the building of monasteries. At the age of 80, he passed away (Nirvana in Sanskrit) in Balau trees outside the city of Kusinara in the state of Malla. After the Buddha's death, his body was cremated and the remains (Buddhist relics) were said to be partitioned by eight states and then enshrined and worshiped.

Sakyamuni's efforts to create Buddhism can be summed up in two aspects: creating and preaching his doctrine, and establishing the system of sangha life.

The gist of Sakyamuni's doctrine was to explicate the suffering of life, the cause and nirvana of suffering, and the method for nirvana of suffering, the key points of which included the following:

(I) Theory of suffering

The basic starting point of Sakyamuni's doctrine was to conclude that life was "painful". Birth, old age, sickness, and death were painful, having to be with the hated was painful, having to be separated from the loved was painful, not being able to get satisfied materially and mentally was painful, and so forth. He believed that the essence of life was "suffering", and the world in which people lived was "painful". Why was there "suffering"? Because there was "birth". Birth was the beginning of suffering, and the entity of suffering. Why was there "life"? This was determined by "karma". People had three karmas: body, mouth, and meaning, and their acts, words, and thought determined the result in the future. People cycled in the "Six Realms of Samsara" (Deva, Manusya, Asura, Tiryagyoni, Presta, and Naraka) according to the different natures of their karmas. Why did all living beings have "karma"? It was because of "avijja", which meant ignorance – ignorance of Buddhist doctrine. Why were all living beings "avijja"? Because there was greed and a desire to pursue pleasure. Therefore, to eliminate "suffering" required "anutpanna" ("ajati"); "anutpanna" required no "karma"; to eliminate "karma", people had to eradicate "avijja", and believe in Buddhist doctrine; to eradicate "avijja", people had to root out "greed" and "love". Only when people rooted out "greed", "love", and other desires could they believe in Buddhism and eliminate "avijja", then stop "karma" and "anutpanna", and finally eliminate "suffering" and get "relief".

Sakyamuni's doctrine involved the origin of humans and the world. He opposed the Brahman argument that God created humans and the world, inherited the theory of "samsara" created by the Kshatriya king and the theory of "karma" created by Brahmans, and further established Pratitya-samutpada. "Pratitya" refers to conditions and causality. He preached that "whenever there is A, there is B; whenever A rises, B rises". Everything and every phenomenon in the world interacted as conditions, cause, and effect. The phenomenon of life was a cycle interacting as both cause and effect, consisting of a series of different links from "avijja", "act" (bulesis), and even "birth", "jara-marana", and so on. Therefore, to eliminate the consequence, we must eradicate the cause. To eliminate the suffering of life, we cannot rely on sacrifice or worship of God, or blind torture of ourselves. Only when we take methods such as circumcising and abiding by moral norms to eliminate the causes that lead to suffering, such as "greed", "love", and "avijja", can we achieve our goals.

(II) Theory of relief

Eliminating the suffering of life is to achieve the goal of relief. Brahmanism believed that the ultimate goal of relief was to unify the "ego" of the individual soul and "Brahman", which dominated the universe – namely, the realm of "Brahma-atma-aikya". Sakyamuni objected to this claim, and he believed that a human was made up of material and spiritual factors. Without spiritual domination and soul, human had "anatta". He learned Jainism's doctrine of cleanliness and stain, abandoned Jainism's theory of the causes of stain and the proof of cleanliness, and advocated "nirvana" as the goal of relief. Nirvana was translated from Sanskrit. The original meaning of Nirvana was "extinguishment of fire". Nirvana as discussed by Sakyamuni was to extinguish the cycle of life and death to achieve the goal of relief through practice, which was the highest ideal of Buddhism. Specifically, Nirvana meant the spiritual realm where greed, avijja, and trouble were exterminated forever, which was the relieved realm beyond life and death. According to legend, during the *sambodhi* of Sakyamuni, he claimed that he had obtained real knowledge: life and death had been broken, and a higher life had been obtained; avijja had been broken, and knowledge had arisen; darkness had been broken, and brightness had risen. His mind went beyond the world, and was relieved.

(III) Theory of madhyamapratipad

As for the way to achieve Nirvana, Sakyamuni clearly pointed out according to his practical experience in his first sermon that "enjoyment" and "ascetic practice" were two kinds of excessive behaviors, which were not desirable and people should not learn, but only "abandon the two sides and take the middle way". It meant that only following the impartial madhyamapratipad was the reasonable and correct practice. He stressed that self-indulgence and self-abuse were two extremes: blind pursuit of carnal desire was despicable, self-abstinence and self-mutilation were crazy, and both were useless actions, not a normal religious life. Normal religious life should be correct meditation, learning, and action. Sakyamuni's theory of madhyamapratipad was different from both the theory of Lokayata, which advocated enjoyment, and Jainism, which promoted ascetic practice, and was established essentially based on choosing from these two factions and combining his own experience, and would certainly carry a strong reconciling and neutral color. The dialectics of history showed that it was precisely because Sakyamuni's theory of madhyamapratipad avoided extremes that it was adaptable and soon widely spread.

Sakyamuni was also engaged in the creation of the sangha system with great enthusiasm and energy. A sangha – namely, a Buddhist group – was a form of organization for monachal Buddhists. At that time, Brahmanism had not organized religious life, but Jainism was organized, and Buddhism also carried out organized practicing life. In addition to sanghas, there were also Buddhist believers who practiced at home, called "lay Buddhists". At first, Sakyamuni allowed only men to be monks; later he allowed women and even prostitutes to become monks. People who followed Sakyamuni to become monks were mostly Brahmans, and there were also businessmen, hunters, barbers, robbers, murderers, and so forth, while slaves were rejected. The fact that Sudras joined Buddhist sanghas was not mentioned in the biographies of Sakyamuni; in fact, it was also difficult for them to break the rules of slave owners and become monks. According to legend, Sakyamuni had 500 disciples, and it was also said that there were 1,250 people, among whom the famous ones were ten "chief disciples", such as Sariputra and Maudgalyayana (Meren) from the Brahman caste, who assisted Sakyamuni in leading the disciples, with great effort. The chief disciple Kasyapa (Mahakasyapa) also belonged to the Brahman caste, and according to legend, he later became the host of the first Buddhist council. For another example, the Sakyan Ananda was Sakyamuni's beloved follower, to whom Sakyamuni entrusted his last teaching before death. The barber of Sakyan, Upali, and Sakyamuni's own son Rahula were also chief disciples; Subhuti, Purana, Katyayana, and Aniruddha were also the main disciples of Sakyamuni.

At first, Sakyamuni did not develop any system for sanghas. The precepts of the sangha were formed on the basis of what happened. In the event of an incident and difficulty, the monks asked Sakyamuni to rule, so his decision was considered to be the "Dharma" of the matter – namely, the precept. The precept developed by Sakyamuni involved a series of taboos on personal conduct and covered various aspects of lifestyle, including clothing, food, and residence, constituting the religious practice of believers, and was also a powerful lever to maintain the organization and order of sanghas. Among these precepts, the most important ones were the five precepts, which had to be observed by believers who practiced at home or monachal ones: abstain from killing, stealing, debauchery (abstain from prostitution), lying, and drinking. The precepts for monks and nuns included a wide range of items that were very harsh. Once the important precept was enacted, it would not change. However, Sakyamuni did not force others to abide by them, nor did he ask people to swear or make intellectual sacrifices.

Sakyamuni also developed systems for the sanghas regarding wandering and mendicity, settlement in rainy seasons, confession, and so on. It was said that at first the disciples of Sakyamuni wandered outside all year round. They walked every day to human habitations to collect alms. They held a bowl, kept their eyes down and silent, and accepted any food put by other people into the bowl, including meat. Sometimes they also accepted the invitation of certain pious people to eat in their home, and ate when the owner put the prepared food into their bowl. In the afternoon, they carefully sat in meditation and did not eat any more. But soon after, Sakyamuni ordered his disciples to abide by the established practice of the monks, that they shall wander outside most of the year, and rest for three months in rainy seasons. The rainy season in India was from May to August, during which going outside was prohibited so as to avoid hurting grass and insects, and the disciples had to sit in meditation and practice in the temple, accepting support. This period was called the "settling period". When the settling period was about to end, and before the disciples were to travel to all parts of the country and wander for mendicity, a two-day confession rally would be held, known as "pravarana". They asked others to expose their own faults and mistakes, and they themselves reflected and confessed; at the same time, they also, with the will of others, reported others' faults and mistakes, so as to help correct and improve.

With the increase in the quantity of monks, rallies needed a certain location, especially for settling in the rainy season every year, and temples were established. When Sakyamuni was alive, with his growing prestige, his believers also gradually formed a custom, and specifically built houses for him to rest, live, sit in meditation, and give sermons. These buildings had the scale of temples. According to legend, there was a wealthy businessman in Savatthi, Kosala, called Anathapindika (Sudatta). After he converted to Sakyamuni, he wanted to invite Sakya to live in Savatthi for the settling period. He chose the garden of Prince Jeta, and bought it with money that could pave all over the garden after many negotiations. Prince Jeta sold the ground of the garden, and presented the trees in the garden to Sayka. So the garden was named after these two people, known as Jetavana Anathapindada-arama. Anathapindika built a living room, lounge, storage room, warehouse, hall, bathroom, pool, and so forth in the garden for Sakya to use. Jetavana Anathapindada-arama and Venuvana-vihara in Rajagraha were jointly known as the earliest two sublime abodes. Sakyamuni lived and preached there for 25 years.

Sakyamuni founded the Buddhist doctrine, and after 45 years of travel around the country, he widely preached, absorbed believers, and organized sanghas, which made Buddhism gradually accepted by the Indians. Sakyamuni was regarded as the leader by his disciples, and his osseous remains were regarded as sacred objects after he died, which were worshiped by his believers. The important places of his practice in his life also became sacred places for believers to worship, such as Kapilavastu, his birthplace, Bodh Gaya, the place where he became the Buddha, Deer Reserve, the place where he preached for the first time, and Kushinagar, the place of his Nirvana. While Sakyamuni was alive, he dictated his doctrine to his disciples. According to legend, in the year he died, his chief disciple Kasyapa convened a large number of monks in Rajagraha to recite the Buddhist scriptures – namely, the so-called first samgiti – in which the chief disciples Ananda and Upali respectively chanted Sutras and Vinaya. And later it was handed down and developed into the *Agama Sutra*. This sutra was the collection of basic Buddhist classics in early times. In the 100 years after Sakyamuni created Buddhism and died, Buddhism spread mainly in the middle reaches of the ancient Ganges River, and Buddhist sanghas were unified, all pursuing the doctrine of Sakya, and monks observed the precepts strictly, basically making a living by mendicity. In history this period is known as the period of "early Buddhism", or "initial Buddhism".

The creation of Buddhism by Sakyamuni was a major event in the history of eastern civilization. It affected not only various divisions of Indian religions and thoughts but also the development of Indian history later on, and because of its outward spread, it also affected changes and development of religion, ethics, philosophy, literature, art, and folklore in many Asian countries.

It should be certain that the last role of Buddhism is as a panacea for alleviating human suffering and overcoming social crises. The way of relief guided by it for the people can only lead them to blindly concentrate on personal practice, so as to achieve spiritual balance and pleasure, and thus separate from real social life and fiery struggle, ignoring the transformation of society. History shows that Buddhism tended to die out in its birthplace of India in the thirteenth century, and went downhill in China after the Tang Dynasty. But the emergence of Buddhism, after all, was a tortuous reflection of people's wishes and demands, and therefore there was a certain historical significance. As for the cultural development brought about by Buddhism, some of the results should be fully affirmed.

Sakyamuni founded Buddhism in an attempt to transform the world in accordance with Buddhist doctrine, to free the people from suffering, and get spiritual relief. But the sufferings of the working people and the exploiting classes were fundamentally different. The suffering of the majority of the people came mainly from oppression and exploitation by the exploiting classes, which were caused by the underdevelopment of science and technology. The correct way to get rid of suffering should be to eradicate the class roots that produced oppression and exploitation, raise the level of science and technology, develop the economy, and continuously improve people's lives. Sakyamuni stressed that the way to relieve suffering and achieve the ideal state was to become a monk, cut off desire and hope for the afterlife. This could lead people only to negative obedience and humiliation, and make them content with the status quo, give in to fate, obey, grin and bear it, and comfort and benumb themselves. Not only could this not alleviate and relieve the suffering of people but also it was conducive to the exploiting classes, acting as a tool for them to maintain dominance, thus further deepening the suffering of people.

From the social support of Sakyamuni's creation of Buddhism, Buddhism represented the interests of Kshatriyas and wealthy businessmen. When Buddhism was born, it was greatly supported by rulers like King Bimbisara (King Yingjian) of Magadha and his son, King Ajatasatru, King Prasenajit (King Shengjun) of Kosala and his wife, King Maha-naman of Sakya Tribe, and King Mathura of Avanti. For example, King Bimbisara supported Sakya and gave him a promotional place – Venuvana-vihara. In addition, the aforementioned wealthy businessmen, such as Sudatta, were the most powerful donors to Sakya. According to Buddhist records, when Sakyamuni had just become Buddha, he stood up under the bodhi tree, and two businessmen gave him food first. Among the disciples recruited by Sakya, at first there were five monks, followed by the merchant Yasa, who brought 60 people to be converted to Sakyamuni at one time. Listing "abstaining from stealing" among the "five precepts" of Buddhism played the role of protecting private property, which was very conducive to the promotion of business development at the time. Businessmen were also afraid of war, and listing "abstaining from killing" among the "five precepts" was also much supported by businessmen. Buddhists and businessmen belonged to the Sramana ideology system that advocated changes, and they were both unorthodox heresies and discriminated against by Brahmanism. The common points of economic interests, doctrine, and social psychology united the early Buddhism and businessmen. Therefore, Buddhism represented the interests of the wealthy class in the castes of Kshatriya and Vaisya, rather than the interests of the laborers. Although Buddhism did not directly represent the interests of the laborers, the mutual dependence and support between it, Kshatriyas, and businessmen were required by the development of social productive forces at that time, which was indirectly conducive to laborers.

The progressive significance of Sakyamuni creating Buddhism was mainly manifested in the opposition to Brahmanism. Brahmanism advocated that Brahmanic gods created the world, and advocated killing animals for sacrifice and implementing the unequal system of four castes. Buddhism opposed the statement that God created the world, and claimed that it did not recognize Brahmanism's theocracy or worship idols. Sakyamuni was also opposed to killing animals for sacrifice. Brahmans made worshiping a career, and sacrifice was held on a large scale, took a long time, and required a large number of cattle to be killed. Brahmans held an "abhiseca ceremony" for the king, and asked for a remuneration worth 100,000 or even 200,000 cattle. Buddhism not only condemned killing animals for sacrifice but also had the precept of "abstaining killing", which was beneficial to the protection of cattle and the development of agriculture and animal husbandry, and also met the interests of farmers. Buddhism also expressed strong dissatisfaction with the caste system, and opposed Brahmans' opinion that the four castes were immutable and "Brahman was first". Sakyamuni advocated "equality of four castes". First of all, it was the equality of karma, that was, regardless of caste, class origin, and occupation level, metempsychosis was decided according to karma. Brahmanism advocated that only people of high-ranking castes contained Brahman elements to eventually combine and unite with Brahman, and acquire advanced "regeneration". Buddhism characterized people's religious dignity on the basis of their individuality and conduct, rather than as subordinate to the special status of a certain caste, and emphasized that every believer could expect to attain salvation by hard work. Buddhism broke the theory of racial superiority, emphasized the education of personality and self-improvement, and believed that people of low-ranking castes could also be born in wealthy families in the afterlife by doing good works and having good merits and virtues, while people of high-ranking castes may also be born in degrading families for doing evil and committing crimes. Next was the equality of practice of monks and the implementation of equality among sanghas. Buddhism disseminated that all people had the right to become monks, learn, and join sanghas, regardless of their class origin and caste. In the sangha of Sakya, the barber Upali was from a low-ranking caste. Inside the sangha, regardless of the original caste level, everyone was equal. Sakyamuni's concept of "equality of four castes" and equality of everyone in the field of religion embodied a certain democratic tendency, with the historical significance of progress. However, Sakyamuni's proposition of "equality of four castes" was not thorough, for he was not fundamentally opposed to the caste system of the whole society, but to Brahmanism, whose purpose was to improve the social status of Kshatriyas and wealthy businessmen, and especially to improve the political status of Kshatriyas. For the production of caste, Buddhism did not agree with Brahmanism's opinion that it was created by God, but put forward a new saying that it was produced by the social division of labor, and in the ranking of castes, it always put Kshatriya in the first place. It can be seen that it did not advocate the fundamental abolition of the caste system, but just wanted to belittle and deny the Brahman caste, and even accommodated the caste system and recognized social inequality. At the same time, it should be noted that Sakyamuni's theory of "equality of four castes" also objectively concealed the antagonism and struggle of classes, which in turn was conducive to the exploiting classes.

In addition, the Pratityasamutpada doctrine of Buddhism elaborated the theory of causality, and put forward the opinion that all things were composed of a variety of reasons and conditions and they were in the eternal change, which were all reasonable dialectic thoughts. Sakyamuni opposed sacrifice and did not worship idols, and he also attached importance to the self-cultivation of individual precepts and emphasized the self-improvement of the subjective personality, which was also the reasonable and positive side, although the religious life, way of practice, and target of relief that he designed were wrong and not desirable on the whole essentially. Sakyamuni also opposed theocracy and refused to recognize that God created the world. But he also recognized the existence of God; he did not recognize the immortality of soul, but advocated samsara and reincarnation, and therefore fell into a profound theoretical contradiction, which he was unable to solve.

Sectarian Buddhism, Mahayana Buddhism, and Esoteric Buddhism

The Buddhism founded by Sakyamuni experienced its early stage in India, and then successively experienced three stages of Buddhism: Sectarian Buddhism, Mahayana Buddhism, and Esoteric Buddhism, and descended in India at the beginning of the thirteenth century.

1 Sectarian Buddhism

During 400 years after 100 years from the death of Sakyamuni – namely, about the fourth century BC to the first century BC – it was the period of Sectarian Buddhism of Indian Buddhism. During this period, economically, slavery reached its peak and began to turn decadent. Politically and militarily, in 327 BC, Alexander's Greek troops invaded the northwest of the subcontinent, and occupied the area near the Indus Valley. Inferior officer Chandragupta of the Nanda Dynasty overthrew the dynasty, expelled the Greek invading army, merged the middle, western, and northern regions of India, and established the Maurya Dynasty. The grandson of Chandragupta, Asoka (ca. 273 BC–232 BC) further extended the territory to the southeastern region of India, and established an unprecedented large unified empire in Indian history. According to Buddhist records, Ashoka himself converted to Buddhism, and declared Buddhism as the national religion. Buddhism extended from the Indus and Ganges River Valleys to the subcontinent, and spread to a number of countries around it. About 180 BC, the Maurya Dynasty was destroyed, replaced by the Shaka Dynasty, which supported Brahmanism, and Buddhism was heavily hit. At this time, the northwest region had been invaded by the Greeks, Serbs, and Parthians, where they established new countries. The southeastern regions were also split into many small countries. India once again fell apart like before the Maurya Dynasty. With the growing spread of Buddhism, it had to adapt to these different regions, countries, ethnic cultures, religions, and ideological traditions, and accordingly it was necessary to make significant changes.

The early Buddhist doctrines were abstract, their myths were not developed, and their religious rituals were relatively monotonous and poor, which limited their spread and influence among the masses. In order to strive for its own survival and expand its own forces, Buddhism had to adapt to the masses' psychological need for rich mythological figures and passionate religious rituals, but this would cause its own changes. Early Buddhist doctrines and precepts were orally spread according to the custom at that time, passed on based on memory, and wrong memories were inevitable, incorrectly relaying erroneous information. In this way, later the monks' understanding of the original doctrine and precepts would be different. Because of these reasons, early Buddhism was gradually divided, and formed Sectarian Buddhism.

Sectarian Buddhism was the general term of the various factions divided from early Buddhism. At first, Buddhism was divided into two factions of Sthaviravada and Mahasanghika, known as the "fundamental split" of Buddhism in history. The original meaning of "faction" was "saying". Sthaviravada was the idea of some of the Venerable, belonging to the orthodox tradition. Mahasanghika was the idea of many monks, which was a faction that emphasized development. These two factions later continued to divide, and formed more factions. According to the record of *Samayabhedo paracanacakra sastra* of Northern Buddhism, written by Shi You and translated by Tang Xuanzang, firstly Mahasanghika divided into eight factions, and then Sthaviravada divided into ten factions, for a total of 18 factions. Mahasanghika successively differentiated into Ekavyavaharika, Lokottaravada, Kaukkutika, Bahusrutiya, Prajnaptivada, Caityavada, Aparasaila, and Uttarasaila. Sthaviravada differentiated into Sarvastivada and Haimavata (the former Sthaviravada). Sarvastivada differentiated into Vatsiputriya, which then differentiated into Dharmottariyah, Bhadrayaniyah, Sammatiya, and Sannagarikah. Sarvastivada also differentiated into Mahisasaka, which then differentiated into Dharmagnpta. Sarvastivada also differentiated into Kasyapiya and Sautrantika. There were 20 factions total, including the foregoing ones and Sthaviravada and Mahasanghika, and a simple list is shown in Figure 1.1. According to the records of *Mahavamsa* and *Dipavamsa* of Southern Buddhism, a missionary history or "island history", Sectarian Buddhism includes a total of 18 factions, excluding Aparasaila and Uttarasaila in the record of Northern Buddhism. In addition, the faction names and inheritance relations were different, and a simple list is shown in Figure 1.2.

The distinction between Sectarian Buddhism and early Buddhism and the differences within Buddhism were manifested in various aspects, such as religious practice, religious ideals, and philosophical theories.

In terms of religious practice, because of some believers' defiance of part of the precepts, Buddhism held several times of samgiti for this purpose, specifically discussing whether the orthodox disciplines shall be relaxed. For example, with the expansion of donation scope, people donated more and more items to the temple. It was originally stipulated that monks were not allowed to accept charity gold, silver, and property, but Mahasanghika thought that they could accept, while

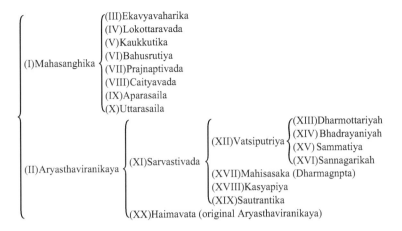

Figure 1.1 Sectarian Buddhism (Form 1)

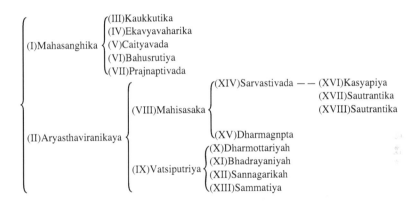

Figure 1.2 Sectarian Buddhism (Form 2)

Sthaviravada opposed the change, and Mahasanghika refused to obey and was then expelled and dismissed, thus forming a relatively independent faction.

In terms of religious ideals, Sthaviravada believed that Sakyamuni was a historical figure, and was great mainly for his noble ideals, correct thinking, superb wisdom, and pure spirit. The highest achievement for normal people who practice and learn Buddhism was not to become Buddha; they could only be Arahan close to Buddha, able to cut off all trouble, free from metempsychosis. Mahasanghika was different and tended to raise the image and personality of Sakyamuni, put forward the opinions of "superworld Buddha" or "supernatural Buddha", and regarded Sakyamuni as an extraordinary, supernatural existence, a real "god", free from feeling and desire with supernatural power. They absorbed and strengthened the creation of mythology to contrast the sacredness of Sakyamuni and created new rituals to worship Sakyamuni. They also belittled Arhat and stressed that they had many deficiencies. The claims of Mahasanghika were later inherited by Mahayana Buddhism and were further developed.

In terms of philosophical theory, Sectarian Buddhism had been extended from early Buddhism, which focused on life philosophy, to the field of cosmology. Because early Buddhism failed to expound Pratityasamutpada and the theory of the soul clearly and completely, a serious confrontation came into being inside Sectarian Buddhism on the subject matter of metempsychosis circulation and karma continuation, and the virtual or real existence of the universe.

Generally speaking, the factions of Sthaviravada were inclined to the "real" – namely, that spiritual and material phenomena were real. For example, "Sarvastivada" recognized the existence of the spirit and the material, and recognized all existence. From the concept of time, it was to admit that everything in the past, present, and future was ubiquitous. Abhidharmamahavibhasasastra of Sarvastivada insisted that since people had the notion that things existed in the past, present, and future, it proved that things actually existed, because if things did not exist, people did not have the object of thought. Moreover, according to Pratityasamutpada, past thought and behavior produced results. The cause led to the result, and results could be generated from emptiness. Since the cause could produce a result, it meant that the past cause was real and would always exist. Sarvastivada admitted that everything would always exist, which was contrary to the concept of "impermanence" of early Buddhism, thus making it a new philosophical theory.

Vatsiputriya, separating from Sarvastivada, divided every thing and phenomenon in the world into "past", "present", "future", "asamskrta", and "nirabhilapya", thinking that they all actually existed. It also emphasized that "Pudgala" (i.e., "I")[1] was "unsayable" and real. "Pudgala" and the human body were neither too familiar nor too distant. This was essentially a hazy, semi-real human, a physical soul, a carrier of metempsychosis. Vatsiputriya recognized "the existence of me", which was also a new saying contrary to the theory of "Anatman" of early Buddhism.

Sautrantika, separating from Sarvastivada, turned to confirm Sakyamuni's theory of impermanence, denied the argument of Sarvastivada that all things always existed, and stressed that everything existed only in the present. That is, it opposed the argument that everything would always exist, and advocated the theory of moment. Sautrantika believed that the so-called real existence or existence of things was in terms of playing a role of the thing, that things were real only if they played a role. Things could occupy only a specific time and space, and play their specific role. And the so-called playing a role meant producing a result. In other words, the real existence of things was true only when it produced a specific result. And the so-called specific result produced by things was to transform into the next mode of existence. In other words, anything was real only when it transformed into its next mode of existence, but did not exist forever. Sautrantika therefore drew this conclusion: the real existence or existence of things was momentary; things existed momentarily, but not forever. Sautrantika also denied the opinion that Nirvana was an eternal and happy realm, and believed that everything was impermanent and Nirvana was only the realm to stop suffering and metempsychosis. This is a tendency to say that things are empty. These were all arguments that tended to believe that things were empty. The argument of Sautrantika was opposed by Abhidharmamahavibhasasastra, reproved as a theory with nihilism.

Factions of Mahasanghika tended to talk about "dharma-sunyata", or recognize the real existence only at present, and believed that there was no entity in the past and the future. In connection with this, in terms of nature and its moksa, although both Mahasanghika and Sthaviravada claimed the "purity of nature", the meanings of the two factions' "purity of nature" were very different. Sthaviravada held that nature was originally clean, while Mahasanghika held that nature may be clean in the future, and the purity of nature was a realm that may be achieved in the future. In fact, it held that original nature was not clean, and had been stained, so it stressed that stained nature could be freed. It can be seen that the views of the two factions are antagonistic.

From the perspective of religious practice and religious ideals, Mahasanghika had a profound effect on the later Mahayana Buddhism. From the perspective of philosophical thought, the theory of Mahasanghika had more relations with Madhyamaka of Mahayana, and Sautrantika, separating from Sthaviravada, later further developed into Yogacara based on the impact of Madhyamaka of Mahayana.

2 *Mahayana Buddhism*

Mahayana Buddhism rose in around the first century AD, and it was the so-called Southern and Northern Dynasties Period in the history of the continent – namely, the time when the Kushan Dynasty and Andhra Dynasty separately existed. When the Kushan Dynasty was handed down to Kanishka (r. ca. AD 129–152), he united northern India, continued to expand it, and vigorously respected and spread Buddhism. The Andhra Dynasty was the most powerful country in southern India, which advocated Brahmanism, resisting Buddhism. The Kushan Dynasty began to split in the third century AD, and perished in the fifth century. The Andhra Dynasty perished in 225 AD, and then resumed a situation of local separatism. In about 320 AD, Chandragupta I established the Gupta Dynasty. When it was handed down to Chandragupta II (r. ca. AD 380–415), it occupied most territory of India. At this time, the economy was prosperous, and the culture was developed, which was called the golden age of India by historians. As slavery in India tended to disintegrate, the feudal system began to form in the Kushan Dynasty, which was completed when it came to the Gupta Dynasty. Accordingly, the caste system also developed into the surname class system – namely, the original castes were divided into thousands of surnames according to different occupations, which was hereditary. Intermarriage between different surname classes was not allowed. This surname class system was similar to the system of hereditary aristocracy in Chinese history. The Gupta Dynasty worshiped Brahmanism, but did not reject Buddhism. Later, with the decline of national power, it began to attach importance to Buddhism. Mahayana Buddhism was produced in the context in which slavery in India transformed into feudalism, class relations were recombined, and new class contradictions gradually arose and sharpened.

After the rise of Mahayana Buddhism, in order to compete for the orthodox status of Buddhism, it belittled early Buddhism and Sectarian Buddhism as Hinayana. Yana meant carrying (e.g., carriage and ship) and road. "Maha" meant big. "Hina" meant small. It seemed to Mahayana Buddhism that Hinayana was "small road", the doctrine of Sakyamuni for people with small *indriya* (root device). Mahayana Buddhism declared that it could carry the infinite beings from this shore of Life River to the *parimam tiram* (other shore) of Bodhi Nirvana, and achieve Buddha-fruit. During the formation and evolution of Mahayana, there were mainly two factions of Madhyamika and Yogacara.

(I) Madhyamika

Madhyamika advocated not missing any side when observing problems (e.g., sunyata and existence were on one side, law and anitya were on one side) – namely, integrating two sides, in line with *majjhima patipad* (the Middle Path), which was how it got its name. It was founded by Nagarjuna (ca. 150–250) and his student Deva (ca. 170–270). Nagarjuna was from southern India and belonged to the caste of Brahman. He had read Brahman books since childhood, and became a famous Brahman teacher in his youth; besides, he also mastered astronomy and geography, mapping and hoard (hidden treasure), and all kinds of Taoism. Later Nagarjuna converted to Buddhism, mastered Tripitaka, moved to the snow-capped mountains in northern India, and lived in a pagoda temple. He met an old monk who taught him classic Mahayana, and then he traveled around the country to spread the Mahayana doctrine. Later he returned to the southern India for indoctrination, causing Madhyamika of Mahayana to sweep the whole of India. Nagarjuna wrote many works, enjoying the title "Author of a Thousand Works". His disciple Deva was also from southern India and belonged to the caste of Brahman, and later followed Nagarjuna to become a monk, developing Nagarjuna's theory of Madhyamika. Later Nagarjuna committed suicide and died, and Deva was killed by a Brahman, which indicated that the ideological struggle at that time was very intense. The successor of Deva was Rahula, who handed his leadership down to Bhavaviveka and Buddhapalita, and then split into different factions. The important descendants of Bhavaviveka included Santaraksita, Kamalasila, and Haribhadra, and the important descendants of Buddhapalita included Candrakirti, who was succeeded by Dharmapala and Gayadeva. Santideva succeeded Gayadeva, who was then succeeded by Mitra.

Madhyamika regarded the *Pancavimsatisa-hasrika-prajnaparamita* as the main classic. *Madhyamika-sastra, Dvadashanikaya-Shastra,* and *Mahaprajna-paramita-sastra,* written by Nagarjuna, and *Sata-sastra,* written by Deva, were the basic theoretical works of this faction. Madhyamika opposed the opinion of some factions of Sectarian Buddhism that everything really existed, and believed the suffering of life lay in that people did not have a real understanding of everything in the world, and produced useless theory that confused right and wrong. To relieve suffering, the most fundamental task was to understand the "reality" of all things, and recognize that there was no entity of everything – namely, no "dharma-kaya", but "sunyata", "Atyanta-sunyata". This was the theory of sunyata, and this faction was also known as "Madhyama". The basis of the "sunyata theory" of Madhyamika was Pratityasamutpada, which held that since everything was produced based on other causes and conditions, but not from itself, it proved that it did not really exist. Generating based on conditions proved the inner untruthfulness of things. Anything, as long as it existed based on the existing things, must lose the right to claim that it had inner authenticity. The dependent existence was not the real existence. The original Pratityasamutpada of Buddhism held that there was a reason for anything; otherwise it was not a real thing – that is, because there was a reason for things, so it was real. Madhyamika believed that all things with a reason were not real – namely, it was not real for it had a reason. This was based on the original Pratityasamutpada, which further developed into the cosmology of "dependent origination and the emptiness of nature" and "everything is empty".

(II) Yogacara

During about the fourth century AD to the fifth century AD, Yogacara became the mainstream of Mahayana Buddhism in India after Madhyamika. "Yoga" meant correspondence, referring to a practice method to understand "truth". Before Sakyamuni created Buddhism, there was a Yoga faction in ancient Indian philosophy, advocating "self-mastery" and the practice methods that focused on researching breath adjustment and meditation. These methods were also absorbed by Buddhism. According to legend, Yogacara of Buddhism was named for Asaga once he was enlightened by Maitreya Buddha and recited *Yogacara-bhumi-sastra* as the basis of the doctrine. This faction worshiped Maitreya as the ancestor, whose actual founders were two brothers, Asaga and Vasubandhu. They were from Gandhara in northern India in about the fifth century, both starting from Sarvastivada of Hinayana. Asaga first learned and practiced the theory of sunyata of Hinayana, but was not satisfied. According to legend, later he turned to Mahayana with the instruction of Maitreya. Vasubandhu deeply studied Abhidharma[2] of Sarvastivada, and wrote *Abhidharmakosa-sastra*. He was very confident in theories of Hinayana, and opposed the Mahayana doctrine. But later he turned to Mahayana with the help of Asaga. The brothers together promoted Maitreya's theory, and founded Yogacara.

Yogacara took *Sandhinirmocanavyuhasutra* and *Yogacara-bhumi-sastra* as its main classics. Asaga's *Mahayanasa mparigrahasastra*, Vasubandhu's *Twenty Verses on Consciousness-Only*, *Thirty Verses on Consciousness-Only*, and *Lucid Introduction to the One Hundred Dharmas* play the most important roles in creation. Following Vasubandhu, there were two schools, Bandhusri and Citrabhana, and Gunamati, Sthiramati, and Paramartha continued to develop Vasubandhu's doctrines, which were early Yogacara. In addition, Dinnaga, who inherited Bandhusri and Citrabhana, paid particular attention to Hetuvidya – namely, logical argument and epistemological discussion. Asvabhava, Dharmapala, Silabhadra

(Xuanzang's master), and Dharmakirti, who inherited Dinnaga's ideas, were known as the late Yogacara.

Yogacara inherited the concept of observing emptiness from Madhyamika, but also thought that the argument "everything is empty" would lead to denial of the existence of Sambo (Buddha, dharma, monk), the main body of Buddha and the ideal realm, and form a theoretical crisis, endangering the existence of Buddhism itself. So this faction put forward the doctrine of Consciousness-Only. The consciousness of all beings was the source of all things; because all things changed from consciousness, they (realm) were all not existing (empty). The consciousness could realize all things, and therefore consciousness existed. Thus Yogacara advocated the existence of consciousness. Consciousness could realize all things, which was also the subject of metempsychosis. Thus Yogacara further proposed the purpose of "asraya-paravrtti" and replaced "relief" with it. In the "asraya-paravrtti", "asraya" meant change and transformation; "paravrtti" referred to the inherent and continuous state of consciousness ("Storehouse Consciousness"). Asraya-paravrtti was to solve the problem of consciousness – namely, to start from people's inherent and continuous state of consciousness, and think that people's change of consciousness would affect behavior, and could change the objective environment. With subjective and objective interaction, the whole understanding of behavior and environment would transform. All beings also became Buddha with this transformation. Although it was meaningful for Yogacara to pay attention to the research on the relationship between the subject and the object, it was a typical subjective idealist philosophy because it was produced by attributing the objective thing to subjective consciousness.

(III) Differences between Mahayana Buddhism and Hinayana Buddhism

The emergence of Mahayana Buddhism was the second major division inside Buddhism after Sectarian Buddhism, and also had the greatest impact on the early Buddhism and Sectarian Buddhism. From the whole history of Indian Buddhism, this was the largest division in history. Mahayana Buddhism denounced the early Buddhism as "Hinayana". Early Buddhist scholars did not admit that they were Hinayana, and regarded themselves as the orthodox followers of Buddhism. They accused Mahayana Buddhist doctrine of being fictitious, and emphasized that "Mahayana was not Buddhism", that Mahayana was not the correct transmission of Buddhism. There were great differences between Mahayana Buddhism and Hinayana Buddhism spiritually and essentially, which were mainly manifested in the following four aspects:

1   In the view of the Buddha, Hinayana generally thought that Sakyamuni was an enlightened one, leader, ancestor, and missionary, while Mahayana, because it emphasized relying on the Buddha's grace and his salvation, regarded the Buddha as Superman. Mahayana covered myths with Sakyamuni, worshiped him as the supreme god character with full wisdom, the ruler of parimam

tiram. Different from Hinayana, which disliked the human body and did not shape statues of God, gods of Mahayana were tangible, and its adherents sculpted gorgeous statues of Buddha, built magnificent halls, and worshiped the Buddha. Hinayana generally believed that there was only one Buddha – namely, Sakyamuni. Mahayana increasingly declared that the various local gods were the incarnations of Sakyamuni, and advocated that there were innumerable Buddhas in the whole world, such as Aksobhya, Amitabha, Maitreya Buddha, and Bhaiṣajyaguru. This further promoted that the Buddha was the embodiment of the power of the whole universe, the ruler of the whole world and the Land of Utmost Happiness.

2 In the pursuit of ideals, Mahayana promoted great compassion and delivering all living creatures from torment, emphasizing that becoming a Buddha and establishing the Pure Land were the highest goals. Hinayana promoted personal "extinction of body and mind – all defilements" and achievement of Arahan as the ultimate goals. Hinayana emphasized personal relief, while Mahayana was committed to rescuing all beings. The relief pursued by Hinayana emphasized cutting off trouble, extincting life and death; Mahayana, such as Madhyama, thought that Bodhi (consciousness, wisdom) shall be the goal, which was the Buddha body. Mahayana thought that as long as all beings removed avijja (ignorance), they could enter the ultimate realm – namely, Nirvana. The ideal of delivering all living creatures from torment lay not in perishing but in eternal life. Mahayana also began to engage in missionary activities to save the monks of others as Bodhisattva, and formally put forward the name of Bodhisattva, which was taken as preparation for enlightenment (Buddha) – namely, the so-called candidate Buddha. However, Hinayana did not recognize Bodhisattva at all.

3 In the practice method, Hinayana thought that the reason for suffering of life lay in the nature of life – namely, all kinds of behavior ("karma") and trouble ("confusion") produced suffering, so people should pay attention to "education" and respect "knowledge", pursue "karma" and cut off "confusion"; so it advocated the individual living apart from society and suppressing sensual passion. In other words, to achieve ideals, people had to become monks and suppress sensual passion. Mahayana believed that the reason why life needed relief was not because life was painful but because life was empty. At the same time, the problems of life should not be solved alone, but be fully solved; not only they themselves shall relieve suffering but also they shall make others free from suffering, to emphasize the common transformation of "collective karma" of all beings. They paid attention to behavior, stressed that people should not escape from the real world but face the real world, understand it, and strive to make their own religious practice, not divorce themselves from the reality of the world, so as to get relief in reality. Therefore, Mahayana, especially in the early stage, attached importance to staying at home, but did not advocate becoming a monk. In fact, according to some of the claims of Mahayana, it was difficult to become a monk. For example, only wealthy people who stayed at home could donate money. At

22   *Indian Buddhism*

the same time, the monks' way of life also changed, especially the senior monks, who accepted a lot of donations, ate exquisite food, and dressed in noble gorgeous robes. The former residences in caves and monasteries were replaced by solemn and magnificent monastery buildings, where they held religious ceremonies, studied classics, wrote scriptures, and lived a religious life with a distinct enjoyment.

4   Regarding theories, the main classic of Hinayana was *Agamasutra* and so on, and the ones of Mahayana included *Maha-prajna-paramita-sutra*, *Saddharmapundarikasutra*, *Avatamsaka Sutra*, *Vimalakirti-mivadesa-sutra*, and *Sandhinirmocanavyuhasutra*. Hinayana's style of study was to stick to the Buddha's doctrine, and believe that the Buddha was true. If the Buddha said there was a certain concept, then that certain type existed. They generally recognized only "anatman" – that is, humans did not have an independent eternal entity, but were empty, and the universe was not empty but real. Mahayana adherents interpreted the Buddha's doctrine freely with their own style, and they thought that not only the human being was empty but also Dharma[3] (thing) was empty – that is, there was no independent eternal entity in the universe, but also emptiness – "everything was empty". The subject and the object were empty, and everything was like a bubble, like a dream.

3   Esoteric Buddhism

Esoteric Buddhism began in the seventh century AD and became increasingly close to Brahmanism/Hinduism in the eighth century AD, and became dominant in Buddhism until its extinction in the early thirteenth century. As early as the sixth century, the Gupta Dynasty had collapsed, and Silaolitya (590–648) of Harsha's Empire (Kanyakubja) conquered some of the areas in middle, eastern, northern, and western India. At that time, the united situation would even compare to Gupta Dynasty. At that time, Xuanzang was studying in India, and witnessed the unification of India, just like the united Gupta Dynasty seen by Faxian. Silaolitya worshiped Hinduism, but also attached importance to Buddhism, and his support of Buddhist activities in the magnificent Nalanda Temple, which was a remarkable example. At this point, Mahayana Buddhism revived, but after the death of Silaolitya, India again fell into the separatist situation, lasting 500 years, and Mahayana Buddhism was also affected. At about the end of the eighth century, three larger kingdoms appeared in India – namely, the Pratihara Dynasty in middle India, the Rashtrakuta Dynasty in southern India, and the Pala Dynasty in eastern India. The Pala Dynasty became the overlord of the kingdoms in northern and southern India, and the rulers worshiped Buddhism. King Dharmapala (r. ca. AD 770–810) thought the scale of the magnificent Nalanda Temple was not yet large enough, and established the larger Vikramasilavihara on the hill on the south bank of the Ganges River. According to historical records, there were 108 small monasteries around the big Bodhi Buddha temple in the center, most of which belonged to Esoteric Buddhism, and a small number belonged to Exoteric Buddhism. Vikramasilavihara was the center of Esoteric Buddhism. From about the end of the tenth century to the first half of the eleventh century, the Islamic tribes built in Afghanistan dealt a heavy blow to India, and the Indian Buddhist Center was gradually transferred to the region of Eastern Pala Dynasty. The dynasty tried to use religion to resist foreign aggression. In this context, Esoteric Buddhism also needed to strengthen jointly with Hinduism to resist the enemy together, so it was more and more assimilated into Hinduism. At the end of the twelfth century, King Muhammad in Afghanistan was ambitious about political expansion, and after he unified Afghanistan, he invaded India extensively as far as the Ganges Valley, occupied Bengal, destroyed the dynasty, and replaced the Pala Dynasty. At the beginning of the thirteenth century, the only Buddhist temple in India was burned down, which was a historic sign that proclaimed the extinction of Buddhism in India.

The main characteristic of Esoteric Buddhism was to advocate the connections between the body, words, and meaning to obtain the fruit of *utpada*. In other words, the hands combined Mudra (gesture), the mouth recited a mantra, and the heart thought of Buddha; the three corresponded and became the Buddha. Thus, other kinds of factions that expressed Buddhist doctrine with language and texts were collectively referred to as "Exotic Buddhism". Esoteric Buddhism advocated magic, whose doctrine was popular and ritual was simple. Later, it advocated becoming a Buddha immediately, and the so-called Buddha was the "happy" realm for ordinary people. It promoted low-level fun to adapt to the demands of some of the ignorant people falling behind in society. Esoteric Buddhism did not exclude Mahayana Buddhism, and regarded it as a preliminary stage, while itself was a senior stage. It considered that there was also ranking in Mahayana, in which Madhyamika was higher than Yogacara. For Esoteric Buddhism that randomly separated Mahayana Buddhism, it was hard for factions of Mahayana Buddhism to independently develop. Esoteric Buddhism also advocated the "six" origins, said to promote the universe ontology and the phenomenon of two, both by the theory of "six" origins, and preached that the entity of universe and phenomenon were integrated, both constituted by "six" origins (land, water, fire, wind, air, consciousness), and all beings in the universe were the embodiment of the "six Dharmakaya", which was the real body of the Buddha – namely, all beings in the universe were the incarnation and product of the Buddha. This was an extremely mystical preaching.

4 The "revival movement" of Indian Buddhism

After 600 years of silence of Buddhism in India, a "revival movement" was set off in the late nineteenth century. In 1891, Sri Lankan aristocrat Dharmapala founded Maha Bodhi Samagama in Colombo, and the next year the headquarters moved to Calcutta in India. Sthaviravada was introduced to India from Sri Lanka. The Samagama carried out missionary activities actively in India, with great influence. In 1956, the former attorney general of the Congress Party government, Ambedkar, and others motivated 500,000 "untouchables" to convert to Buddhism in Nagpur. In 1957, the newly joined Buddhists organized a Buddhist party – the Republican

Party. Upper classes of Buddhists also strengthened Buddhist activities in border areas and ethnic minorities, and actively developed believers.

The outward spread of Indian Buddhism

Indian Buddhism spread from the South Asian subcontinent to other countries from the third century BC, during the reign of Ashoka in the Indian Maurya Dynasty. During his reign, Ashoku not only was keen on militarism and outward expansion but also vigorously fostered Buddhism, and encouraged and sent Buddhists to spread Buddhism. There were roughly two routes from north to south for Buddhism to spread outward. The northern route was divided into two routes, one of which was to spread to the mainland of China via Central Asian regions, and then spread to the Korean Peninsula, Japan, Vietnam, and other places via China; the other was to spread to Tibet, China, where Tibetan Buddhism was formed, and then spread north to Mongolia, the Soviet Union, and spread south of Nepal and northern India. Buddhism spread south to Sri Lanka, and then to other countries like Myanmar, Thailand, Cambodia, Laos, Malaysia, Indonesia, and so on via Sri Lanka, as well as ethnic minority areas of Dai, De'ang, and Bulang in Yunnan, China. Northern Buddhism was mainly Mahayana, whose classics were mostly translated from languages of various nations in Central Asia and India's Sanskrit into Chinese and Tibetan. Southern Buddhism was mainly Sthaviravada of Hinayana, whose classics were compiled in Pali.

1 *Profile of Indian Buddhism's introduction to the north*

Buddhism spread north to Bactria, Parthia, and IndoScyths, and crossed Cong Ridge (Pamir) into the northwest of China; later, with the opening of the western transport in the Han Dynasty, it spread to the mainland of China. After its spread and evolution in China, eight factions of Buddhism formed during the Sui and Tang Dynasties, which led to the unprecedented development of Buddhism. In the fourth century AD, Buddhism was introduced into the Korean Peninsula; after the middle of the seventh century AD and the eighth century AD, the "five factions and nine mountains" formed, in which "five factions" referred to Vinaya, Dharma character, Dharma nature, Nirvana Sutra, and Hwaom, which formed in the seventh century. "Nine mountains" referred to nine factions of Zen that formed after the eighth century: Kaji Mountain, Silsang Mountain, Tongni Mountain, Sagul Mountain, Songju Mountain, Saja Mountain, Huiyang Mountain, Pongnim Mountain, and Sumi Mountain. After the fourteenth century, the Ly Dynasty stressed promoting Confucianism and restraining Buddhism, which weakened Buddhism. At present, Buddhism is Korea's largest religion, whose believers account for about half of all religious believers. In the sixth century, after Buddhism was introduced to Japan from China via the Korean Peninsula, many factions were successively set up, becoming Japan's main religion. After the Meiji Restoration in the nineteenth century, the emperor of Japan, in order to strengthen autocratic rule and improve the authority of the royal family, launched the movement of "abolishing Buddhism", but soon it was fostered again and regained development. Now there are many Buddhist factions in Japan, with nearly 100,000 temples or missionary places, and 80 million believers. Among the traditional Buddhist factions, the important ones now include Jodo Shinshu, Zen, Nichiren Shu, and Shingon Shu. Sokagakkai, Komeito, and Risso Koseikai of Nichiren Shu had a great social impact in Japan. At about the end of the second century AD, Buddhism was introduced to Vietnam, and during the eleventh century to the thirteenth century, more than half of the people of the country were Buddhists, showing great power. Zen and the Pure Land School of Chinese Buddhism were mainly spread; the Linji School of Zen had the greatest impact.

In about the seventh century, after Buddhism was introduced into Tibet, China, it was integrated with the local religions, and formed a new type of Buddhism – Tibetan Buddhism. At the end of the thirteenth century, Kublai Khan made Tibetan Buddhism the national religion of the Yuan Dynasty. Later, Tibetan Buddhism was spread among the lower-class people in Mongolia, and became the main religion there, where nearly half of the men were lamas. After the founding of the People's Republic of Mongolia, the number of lamas greatly reduced, and Tibetan Buddhism also failed to play much role in the community. Tibetan Buddhism was also spread to the Siberia area in the Soviet Union, and had a certain impact on the people.

2 Profile of Indian Buddhism's introduction to the south

In the third century BC, Ashoka of the Indian Maurya Dynasty sent his son to promote Sthaviravada in Sri Lanka, and the king of Ceylon led the whole clan to convert to Buddhism. Since then, Buddhism was gradually spread on the island. In the twelfth century, Mahaviharanikaya of Sthaviravada was designated as the national religion. After the sixteenth century, Sri Lanka became a colony, and sanghas were destroyed. After the independence of Sri Lanka, Buddhism developed rapidly, and had a growing impact on the world. There are now about 10 million believers, accounting for 67 percent of the total population. Buddhism was introduced into Myanmar from Sri Lanka before the fifth century AD and gained great development. Now there are 25 million believers, accounting for four-fifths of the total population. There are more than 20,000 monasteries in the country and more than 100,000 pagodas, known as the "nation of pagodas". In the third century AD, Buddhism was introduced into Thailand, and Mahayana Buddhism was spread in northern and central Thailand. Since the seventh century, Mahayana Esoteric Buddhism was spread in southern Thailand. In the eleventh century, Sthaviravada was introduced to Thailand from Burma and Sri Lanka. In the thirteenth century, the third king of the kingdom of the Sukhothai Dynasty, Rama Kham Heng, declared that Sthaviravada was the national religion. Thailand is currently the only country in the world that takes Buddhism as its national religion. The white of the three-color Thai national flag represents Buddhism. Ninety-five percent of the country's citizens believe in Buddhism. From the king to the people, almost everyone engages in Buddhist rituals. Every man has to get tonsured and be a monk once in his lifetime to get the qualification of adult, including even the king. Now there are 260,000 monks wearing yellow robes in the country, temples are built all over the country's urban and rural areas, and there are Buddhist festivals all year round. Monks not only participate in the country's political activities and administration but also take charge of national basic education. As the "yellow-robe teachers" and "bald doctors" loved by the people, they are highly respected by the community. They do not engage in production, and make a living by mendicity. Because its Buddhism is particularly prosperous, Thailand is also known as "the nation of Buddhism" and the "yellow-robe Buddhist country". As early as the third century BC to the second century BC, Sthaviravada of Indian Buddhism and Brahmanism were introduced into Cambodia at the same time. In the third century AD, Mahayana Buddhism was introduced. In the sixth century, Cambodia had become the Buddhist center in Southeast Asia. In the ninth century AD to the thirteenth century AD, Buddhism and Hinduism (its predecessor was Brahmanism) were flourishing at the same time. The world-famous Angkor Temple, built in the twelfth century to the thirteenth century, is the artistic crystallization of these two religions. In the fourteenth century, Thailand invaded and promoted Sthaviravada, making it the national religion of Cambodia, which was canceled in 1976. Ninety percent of Cambodian residents believe in Buddhism, and there are now more than 60,000 monks. Buddhism was also introduced to Laos early, in the fourteenth century. Sthaviravada was introduced from Cambodia and worshiped as the national religion by the king. In the middle of the sixteenth century, Laos became one of the Buddhist centers in Southeast Asia. In the nineteenth century, due to foreign aggression, Buddhism weakened. Since the 1930s, it has been reviving. About half of the country's residents believe in Buddhism. In addition, in the fifth century AD, Sarvastivada of Buddhism was introduced into Indonesia and replaced the status of Brahmanism. In the seventh century, Indonesia became an important Buddhist center in Southeast Asia. In the eighth century, Mahayana Esoteric Buddhism was introduced into Indonesia and was regarded as the national religion. In the sixteenth century, the process of Islamization in Indonesia was completed and Buddhism tended to decline. Mahayana Esoteric Buddhism and Sthaviravada of Hinayana were also introduced to Malaysia, and were in their full flush after the eighth century AD. In the fifteenth century Islam was made the national religion, and Buddhism rapidly declined. In the nineteenth century, as Chinese Buddhists came to Malaysia, Buddhism was restored.

Notes

1 "Pudgala": Indian Jainism used it to refer to matters. There were two usages in Buddhism: one was another saying of "I", referring to the main body of metempsychosis; the other had the same meaning as "human". Here it refers to "I".
2 "Abhidharma" meant interpretation of the Buddhist scriptures. Buddhist scriptures were normative "law", and the interpretation of "law" was called "Abhidharma".
3 "Dharma" referred to all things, and existence, whether it was material, spiritual, ontological, or phenomenal, was called "Dharma". Buddhist doctrine was also one of the things, and therefore also called "Dharma". Here it refers to all things.

2 Buddhism's introduction into China and its change and development

Since Buddhism was introduced from India, after gradually adapting, it was slowly spread, and tended to flourish in the Sixteen Kingdoms and the Eastern Jin Dynasty. There were many factions in the Southern and Northern Dynasties, and eight sects formed during the Sui and Tang Dynasties, after Buddhism entered its peak stage. Extreme prosperity foreboded the beginning of its decline. Later, Buddhism gradually declined in the Han Dynasty, but Tibetan Buddhism, an important sect of Chinese Buddhism, emerged in Tibet, continuing to spread.

In the long-term spread, evolution, and development of Buddhism, with the support and constraint of feudal state power, Chinese Buddhist scholars and the broad masses of monks engaged in religious theoretical activities, such as classics translation, classics annotation, classics interpretation and creation of the theory system, and religious practice, such as building temples and statues and engaging in meditation and practice, which made Buddhism increasingly adapted to the characteristics of the Han nationality and other ethnic minorities; Buddhism gradually become Chinese-style Buddhism. Over 2,000 years, Buddhism has not only expanded the breadth and depth of Chinese intellectual circles but also enriched Chinese people's cultural life and religious life, and brought complex social impacts and multiple social consequences.

The beginning of the introduction of Buddhism into China

There were two routes for Indian Buddhism to be introduced into the mainland of China: one was the land route to the Xinjiang region in China via Central Asia, and then deep into the mainland; the other was the sea route to Guangzhou via Sri Lanka, Java, the Malay Peninsula, and Vietnam – namely, being introduced into Chinese mainland via the route of the South China Sea. Since Emperor Wu of Han operated the Western Regions, the land route had become the thoroughfare for east-west traffic, where commercial trade and envoy exchange were very frequent. This land route included northern and southern routes. The southern route was from Dunhuang, across the desert, to Khotan via Shanshan, south of the Taklamakan Desert and north of the Kunlun Mountains, and then to Da Shashi in the northwest. The northern route was from Dunhuang (now Hami) and then Kucha (now Kuqa) via Turpan, and then to Shule (now Kashi City). In the Eastern

Han Dynasty, An Shigao and Lokaksema came to the mainland of China via these two routes. Most of the Indian monks coming to China arrived in the mainland via these two routes, and seldom took the sea route, which may be because the sea route was developed later than the land route. According to historic record, in the Southern and Northern Dynasties, there were famous classics translation masters coming to China to spread Buddhism by sea.

As for the exact time when Buddhism was first introduced to China's mainland, there were different opinions in history, many of which were imagined assumptions, making it difficult to examine now. There were two most important arguments: the first believed it was introduced in the tenth year of Yongping during the reign of Emperor Ming in the Eastern Han Dynasty. It was said that when Emperor Ming was on the throne, he sent people to the Western Regions for Buddhism and Taoism, who met Sramana Kasyapamatanga and Dharmaraksa in IndoScyths, invited them to Han, and carried the figures of Buddha and classics to Luoyang with white horses. Emperor Ming built the White Horse Temple for the two monks to live in. This was the historical narrative of the first introduction of Buddhism spread most widely among ancient Buddhists. The second believed Buddhism was introduced during the reign of Emperor An in the Western Han Dynasty. The main basis for this argument was the record of *Dongyi Biography* in Volume 30 of *Records of the Three Kingdoms – History of Wei*, in which Pei Songzhi cited *Brief History of Wei-Xirong Biography* written by Yu Huan in Wei. The biography stated, "In 2 BC, Yicun, envoy of IndoScyths, dictated *Buddha Classics* to the disciple of learned scholar, Jing Lu". The foregoing two arguments were 70 years apart, which was still close. If these two arguments are integrated, the first introduction of Buddhism was during the two Han Dynasties, about the first century AD.

As a foreign religion introduced into China, at first, Buddhism needed to get the support of the ruling class and get popular among the people. In the Eastern Han Dynasty, the royal family believed in the Huang-Lao School and the fairy technique, and the doctrines of Buddhism were also regarded as "empty" and compared to the Huang-Lao School. Sakyamuni was considered to be a great god, and Buddhist rituals were also regarded as similar to sacrifice; thus Buddhism was advocated by emperors. For example, it was recorded in *History of the Later Han Dynasty – Biography of King of Chu*, "King of Chu (Liu Ying) recited texts of the Huang-Lao School, and worshiped Buddha". Emperor Huan also worshiped Buddhism, and cast a gold Buddha statue in the palace, beside the statue of Laozi, worshiping to pray for longevity and fortune.

In China, the spread of Buddhism was synchronized with the translation of Buddhist classics. Buddhist scriptures could not be read and accepted by the Han people unless they were translated into Chinese. At this time, the monks who came to China attached great importance to the work of translation, creating conditions and laying the foundation for the spread of Buddhism. According to historical records, translation of Buddhist scriptures in late Eastern Han Dynasty began with An Shigao. An Shigao was a scholar proficient in Abhidharma and Zen from Parthia (now the northeast of Iranian plateau), and he translated a lot of classics, such as *Anapanasmrti, The Sutra about the Five Skandhas, the Twelve Entrances and the Eighteen Dhatu of Elements*, *Dashiermengjing*, and *Xiaoershimenjing*, among which the most important were Zen classics. In addition, Lokaksema from IndoScyths translated *Vajracchedikaprajnaparamitasutra*, *Pratyutpanna Sutra*, *Surangamasamadhisutra*, and so on, among which the main ones were *Mahayana Mahaprajn-aparamitasutra* and Zen classics. An Shigao and Lokasema were known as two great translators of the Han Dynasty. In addition, Zhu Foshuo, An Xuan, Srsimha, and Kang Mengxiang came to China and had their own translations.

Indian Buddhism was introduced into China when India's Mahayana Buddhism flourished, so the introduction of Indian Buddhism into China was not synchronized with the development of Indian Buddhism. The previous Indian Hinayana Buddhism was introduced into China with Mahayana Buddhism at the same time. But Mahayana Buddhism was the earliest to be introduced into China, especially the classics of Prajna. Later, with the increase of translations of Mahayana Buddhism and Hinayana Buddhism, Chinese Buddhism was also faced with the problem of how to deal with their similarities and differences, and later finally a way of integrating them was opened up.

The initial spread of Buddhism in the Three Kingdoms and Western Jin

With the support of the feudal rulers, during the Three Kingdoms and the Western Jin Dynasty, Buddhism began to spread. According to historic record, Emperor Ming of Wei, Cao Rui, once built temples, and Prince Chensi, Cao Zhi, also liked to read Buddhist scriptures. Sun Quan of Kingdom Wu once built a temple and pagoda, named Jianchu Temple. Under the influence of the palace that worshiped Buddhism, Buddhist faith gradually spread to the people. According to the record of Volume 1 in *Shi Shi Ji Gu Lve*, in the Western Jin Dynasty, with the centers of Luoyang and Chang'an, 180 temples were built, and there were more than 3,700 monks and nuns. This shows that Buddhism kept a foothold in the cities of political centers, and had a certain force.

During the Three Kingdoms, the career of Buddhist translator was also further developed. At this time, there were a lot of translators, among whom the most famous was Zhi Qian. Zhi Qian was the disciple of Lokaksema, who worked on the cause of translation all his life. The important books translated by him included *Vimalakirti*, *Paramita*, and *TaiziRuiyingBenqiJing*. He also annotated *Life and Death Classic*, translated by himself, which was the earliest classic with notes. Secondly, monks also translated a lot of Buddhist scriptures, and annotated and prefaced them. A characteristic of translation in the Three Kingdoms is that translators were used to expressing Buddhist thought with Taoist terminologies, which shows Buddhism's trend of being combined with the inherent culture of China.

In the Western Jin Dynasty, classics translation was still the main activity of Buddhism. At this time, there were over ten domestic and foreign Sramanas and lay Buddhists engaged in the translation, among whom the most important was Dharmaraksa. According to historical record, Dharmaraksa was a national master of IndoScyths who lived in Dunhuang and traveled in the west with his master, familiar with 36 languages of the western countries. He collected a large number of Buddhist scriptures, and translated *Pancavimsatisahasrika-prajnaparamita*, *Saddharmapundarikasutra*, and *Vimalakirti*, about 150 books and 300 volumes. He also inherited the tradition of the Three Kingdoms, focused on the translation of Mahayana classics, and elucidated the theories of emptiness.

In AD 250, Dharmakala from middle India traveled to Luoyang, where he translated the *Monks' Precepts* and became initiated into monkhood. This was the beginning of being initiated into monkhood or nunhood in China. Since then, the situation in which monks only cut off their hair and did not abide by the Buddhist system changed. Because of this, Dharmakala was later worshiped as the first ancestor by Vinaya. At the same time, Parthian Sramana Dharmastya also translated one volume of *Dharmagnpta Karma*. This belonged to *Dharmaguptavinaya* of Dharmagnpta in Sthaviravada of Hinayana, which had a considerable impact on China's Vinaya School, which worshiped *Dharmaguptavinaya*. At that time, Zhu Shixing was initiated into monkhood according to *Dharmagnpta Karma*, which was the beginning of official monks in China. Zhu Shixing also went to Khotan (now south of Xinjiang) to look for classics, and was the pioneer for Chinese monks to travel to the west.

The prosperity of Buddhism in the Sixteen Kingdoms in the Eastern Jin Dynasty

During the Sixteen Kingdoms in the Eastern Jin Dynasty, the north and south separated, and the north was torn apart. There were 16 kingdoms, including Zhao, Qin, Yan, Liang, Xia, and Cheng founded by Xiongnu, Jie, Xianbei, Di, and Qiang. The South was ruled by the Eastern Jin Dynasty. Most of the rulers of the north and south, especially the rulers of the northern minorities, vigorously promoted Buddhism in order to maintain their own rule; due to the long years of war, people were destitute, which made the workers hope to relieve their suffering by worshiping gods and Buddha. The support and promotion of the upper rulers and the need and longing of the lower masses provided fertile soil for the development of Buddhism, so that Buddhism was vigorous. A large number of Buddhist scriptures were translated, Chinese Buddhist monks' academic papers emerged, different schools of Prajna were set up, and Buddhist believers rapidly increased among the people, all of which converged in the first climax of the development of Chinese Buddhism.

1 Buddhism in the Sixteen Kingdoms

Among the Sixteen Kingdoms, Later Zhao, Former and Later Qin, and Northern Liang promoted Buddhism most actively, especially the two Qin. Buddhism of the two Qin Dynasties was very important in the history of Chinese Buddhism. Its important representatives included Dao An and Kumarajiva. The activities of the two had a profound effect on the subsequent development of Buddhism.

Chang'an, the capital of the Former Qin Dynasty, was located in the traffic hub to the Western Regions, which was the Buddhist center in the north of China. Fu Jian, the highest ruler of the Former Qin Dynasty, believed in Buddhism, and once sent troops to attack Xiangyang to welcome Dao An to host Buddhist affairs in Chang'an. Dao An (312–385; there was also another argument that he lived from 314 to 385) was a disciple of Buddhacinga, a famous monk in the Later Zhao Dynasty, in his early years. According to historical record, Buddhacinga once influenced Shi Le, the ruler of the Later Zhao Dynasty with Taoism, and prevented his killing, which attracted many believers, and promoted the development of Buddhism. Dao An followed Buddhacinga for more than ten years, and laid a solid foundation for Buddhist theories. After the death of Buddhacinga, Dao An gradually became the Buddhist leader in the north, with a great impact. In his whole life, there were mainly two aspects of Buddhist activities of Dao An: the first was to organize the translation of, sort out, and elaborate classics, and create a school with the purpose of "Abhutva"; the second was to cultivate the north and the south and establish sanghas to preach religion and train disciples. For the first aspect, Dao An presided over translation in Chang'an, translated ten books and 187 volumes totally, and compiled content for Buddhist scriptures. According to historical record, there were about 60 kinds of his works, with 16 existing prefaces for classics and one volume of *Classical Note*. For the second aspect, Dao An attached great importance to preaching personally, and actively developed disciples and expanded impact. When he was in Hebei and Xiangyang, he had hundreds of disciples, which was the largest sangha from north to south of China at that time. He once led thousands of monks in Chang'an. Dao An had more than a dozen brilliant disciples, among whom Hui Yuan was the Buddhist leader in the Eastern Jin Dynasty after him. Dao An dispersed disciples and went out for missionary work twice, and further spread Buddhism in the Yellow River Valley and the Yangtze River Valley. In addition, Dao An decided that monks had no surname, and all Sramana were called Shizi; he developed monk precepts and made rituals for monks, nuns, and other Buddhist monks to follow, laying a preliminary foundation for the later temple system. Dao An called himself "Mitianshi Dao An", demonstrating elegance. In fact, from aspects of translation, cultivation, education, and developing precepts, he really deserved to be the first master to build Chinese Buddhism.

Buddhism was more prosperous in the Later Qin Dynasty than in the Former Qin Dynasty. Especially the ruler of the Later Qin Dynasty, Yao Xing, advanced classical translation and cultivation far beyond the previous generation, with the assistance of a translation master, Kumarajiva, which had an epoch-making significance in the history of Buddhism. Kumarajiva (344–413) was from Qiuci (now South Kuqa in Xinjiang). His father abandoned the post of prime minister and became a monk, and was the advisor for the king of Qiuci. Following his mother, Kumarajiva became a monk when he was 17 years old, and then they traveled to northern India together, learning Dharma and studying Mahayana. He was especially proficient in the Madhyamika doctrine of Mahayana, deeply mastering Samadhi. Later he preached in the Western Regions, with a great reputation. As

32 *Buddhism's introduction into China*

Dao An repeatedly persuaded Fu Jian to welcome Kumarajiva to China, Fu Jian really sent general Lu Guang to lead troops to attack Qiuci and welcome Kumarajiva. But unfortunately, when Lu Guang went back to Liangzhou, the kingdom had been subjugated. Later, Yao Xing, the king of the Later Qin Dynasty, sent the army to Liangzhou to welcome Kumarajiva to Chang'an. Yao Xing respected Kumarajiva very much and worshiped him as the national advisor, and asked him to host the translation of Buddhist scriptures. Kumarajiva had translated a total of 35 books and 294 volumes, such as *Amitabha Buddhist Scriptures*, *Pancavimsatisa-hasrika-prajnaparamita*, *Astasahasrika-prajnaparamita*, *Saddharmapundarikasutra*, *Vimalakirti*, *The Diamond Sutra*, *Mahaprajna-paramita-sastra*, *Sata-sastra*, *Madhyamika-sastra*, *Dvadashanikaya-Shastra*, and *Satyasiddhi-sastra*. Prior to this, there was only sporadic translation of Buddhist classics, and the large number of translations began with Kumarajiva. At that time, classics of Mahayana also preliminarily came into being. Not only was the number large, but also the quality was high. As for the literary form, the simple style in the past was changed, and turned to pursuing pragmatism and meaning expression, so the translation matured. The classics translated by Kumarajiva systematically introduced the theory of Madhyama for the first time, which played a very important role in the transplantation and spread of Mahayana Buddhist theory in China. Kumarajiva paid attention to interpreting "Abhidharmapitaka". For example, the translation of Buddhist scriptures such as *Madhyamika-sastra* had a great significance for the creation of Buddhist sects. In addition to his achievements in translation, a Buddhist achievement of Kumarajiva was to preach by combining Buddhist translation and cultivate a large number of Buddhist disciples. At that time, there were 3,000 Sramanas coming to Chang'an from other places, mostly studying after Kumarajiva. Among them, Seng Zhao, Dao Sheng, Dao Rong, Hui Guan, Seng Rui, Dao Heng, Hui Yan, and Tan Ying were very famous. Seng Zhao and Dao Sheng were important figures in the history of Chinese Buddhism and philosophy. Seng Zhao was famous for being good at Pratityasamutpada, and his works were compiled into *Theory of Zhao*. Dao Sheng deeply studied Nirvana based on Prajna, and created a new style.

2 Buddhism in the Eastern Jin Dynasty

There were two Buddhist centers in the south in the Eastern Jin Dynasty: the first was Donglin Temple in Mount Lu, presided over by Huiyuan, and the second was Daochang Temple in Jiankang. Huiyuan (334–416) once followed Dao An for about 25 years, and was the most satisfactory disciple and effective assistant of Dao An. Huiyuan lived in Donglin Temple in Mount Lu for over 30 years. He carried out a large number of activities there. He gathered masses and gave lectures, wrote articles, elucidated karma and the theory of immortality, reconciled contradictions between Confucianist and Buddhist doctrines, and promoted the "combination of Confucianism and Buddhism". All these had a profound impact on the subsequent development of Buddhism. Huiyuan had a deep concern that Buddhist scriptures were not complete in Jiangdong areas, and Zen laws and precepts were lacking, so he sent disciples Fa Zheng and Fa Ling on a pilgrimage for Buddhist scriptures to the Western Regions. When he learned that Kumarajiva came to Chang'an, he immediately wrote to him, to exchange academic teachings and ask and answer regarding classics argumentation; he also asked Buddhabhadra and Sanghadeva to translate classics, thus promoting the wide circulation of Buddhist Zen, Prajna, and Abhidharma in the south. In addition, Huiyuan trained a large number of disciples, laying a solid foundation for the spread of Buddhism in regions south of the Yangtze River. He also led his 123 disciples, including Liu Yimin and Zhou Xuzhi, to vow in front of the statue of Amitayus, longing for the Western Paradise. Huiyuan's activities played a very important role in the development of Buddhism in the south since the Eastern Jin Dynasty.

In Jiankang, the capital of the Eastern Jin Dynasty, Buddhism was also flourishing. At that time, the famous monks Buddhabhadra and Fa Xian adopted Daochang Temple as their base for translating Buddhist scriptures and spreading Buddhism. Buddhabhadra was proficient in Hinayana Zen and *vinayapitaka*. After he came from India to China, he first lived in Chang'an, and was excluded by disciples of Kumarajiva, for he disagreed with the arguments of Kumarajiva; so finally he led over 40 disciples, such as Hui Guan, to go south. Firstly he translated *Yoga-carya-bhum* in Mount Lu, and later translated 50 volumes (later generations thought it was 60 volumes) of *Avatamsaka Sutra*, and also cooperated with Fa Xian on the translation of *Mahasanghavinaya*. Buddhabhadra spread Zen; especially "Avatamsaka Sutra", translated by him, was a great contribution to Buddhism.

3 Characteristics of Buddhist activities in the Sixteen Kingdoms in the Eastern Jin Dynasty

The Sixteen Kingdoms in the Eastern Jin Dynasty were politically divided from north to south, but exchanges of Buddhist activities in the two regions were very frequent, showing the basic trends and common characteristics of Buddhism spreading in the same era. These are mainly as follows.

(1) Great achievements in the translation of Buddhist scriptures

As Fu Qin opened up the Western Regions, in addition to Kumarajiva and Buddhabhadra, monks of various sects of Mahayana and Hinayana kept coming to the mainland of China from the Western Regions, providing a very favorable condition for translation of all types of Buddhist scriptures. Throughout the translation activities over more than 100 years of the Eastern Jin Dynasty, translated Buddhist scriptures were mainly as follows:

1. Mahayana theory: Mahayana classics translated by the great translator Kumarajiva provided the most important classical argument and ideological basis for the creation of the Sanlun School and Tiantai School of Buddhism in the Sui and Tang Dynasties. *Avatamsaka Sutra* translated by Buddhabhadra became the basic proof of the Yanhua School in the Tang Dynasty.

2 Hinayana theory: Under the auspices of Dao An, Dharmanandi translated the most important classics in the early history of Buddhism, *Madhyamagama* and *Ekottarikagama*, and Fonian interpreted *Caturagama* and *Dirghagama*. *Abhidharmamahavibhasasastra*, translated by Sanghabhuti, and *Abhidharmahrdayasastra* and *Tri-dharmika-sastra*, translated by Sanghadeva upon the invitation of Hui Yuan, were all important Hinayana theories. Kumarajiva translated *Satyasiddhi-sastra*, which was a work of transmission from Hinayana to Mahayana. On this basis, later the Satyasiddhi-sastra School developed.
3 Mahayana and Hinayana Zen: Hinayana's *Yoga-carya-bhum*, translated by Buddhabhadra, and Mahayana's *Dhyana-nisthita-samadhi-dharmaparyaya-sutra*, compiled by Kumarajiva, played an important role in the subsequent popularity of Zen.
4 Esoteric classics: *Mahamayurividyarajni* and *Mahabhis! eka-mantra*, translated by Srimitra.
5 Precept: Five Hinayana precepts were spread in India, and 61 volumes of *Sarvastivadavinaya*, 60 volumes of *Dharmaguptavinaya*, and 40 volumes of *Ma-hasahghav-inaya* were translated in China successively, becoming the basis of Chinese Buddhist precepts.

(II) Rise of westing movement for Dharma

As Indian monks and monks from the west came to China, the Chinese monks' interest and will of westing for Dharma was aroused. Some monks traveled far abroad, and sought Buddhist scriptures. At this time, among the westing monks, Fa Xian had the greatest achievements. After he became a monk, Fa Xian (ca. 337–422) deeply felt that though the Buddhist scriptures had been translated, the disciplines were incomplete and precepts were not prepared. So in AD 399, about five people, including Hui Jing, started from Chang'an, crossed Liusha River and Cong Ridge, and went to India to seek discipline. After 15 years, they passed nearly 30 countries, and later they returned home by sea via Sri Lanka and Java Island in Indonesia. Fa Xian was all alone, and brought back the missing basic elements in Mahayana and Hinayana after great hardships. The introduction of "vinayapitaka" and *Agamasutra* depended on him. Later he translated six volumes of *Maha-parinirvana* together with Buddhabhadra in Daochang Temple in Jiankang, firstly advocating Buddhata and "Icchantika",[1] which had a huge impact on Buddhist thought at that time. He also wrote *Travels in Buddha Lands*, also known as *Fa Xian Biography*, to introduce conditions of India, Sri Lanka, and other countries, which not only played a great role in guiding westing for Dharma later but also provided extremely precious material for the study of ancient history and geography of the South Asian subcontinent, which was a permanent contribution of his to Asian culture. There was also another batch of monks who went to India for Dharma at the same time as Fa Xian – namely, five people, including Bao Yun and Chi Yan, who also succeeded in study. Four years after Fa Xian traveled to the west, 15 people, including Zhi Meng, went to India to seek Dharma, which also played a certain role in promoting academic exchanges between China and India.

*(III)   The rise of the ideological trend of praying for Maitreya
         Pure Land and Amitabha Pure Land*

Famous monks in the Eastern Jin Dynasty were all keen to go to "Pure Land" after death in faith and practice. Dao An once led his disciples to vow in front of the statue of Maitreya to pray for Maitreya Pure Land. Maitreya Pure Land was "Tusita". Buddhist scriptures said that there were inner and outer yards, of which the outer yard was the world of desire (the world with appetite and lust in which beings lived), and the inner yard was the pure land in which Maitreya lived. Buddhist scriptures advocated that if people were converted to Maitreya and upheld his name, they could go to the pure land after death. Later, Zhu Fakuang created Amitabha Pure Land (Western Paradise World), and Zhi Daolin was also fascinated by the Western Paradise World, where the so-called Amitabha was. He asked a painter to draw a figure of Amitabha, devoutly worshiped, and wrote *Praise to Figure of Amitabha* himself. He believed that as long as he recited *Amitabha* sincerely, he could go to Amitabha Pure Land after death. It was mentioned earlier that Huiyuan was enthusiastic about Amitabha Pure Land, and once led his disciples to vow to yearn for the Western Paradise World. Hui Yuan's faith in Amitabha had an influence on later generations, and he was respected as the ancestor of the Pure Land School in the Tang Dynasty. Dao An prayed for the pure land connecting the afterlife to the secular world, while Hui Yuan and others prayed for the Western Paradise in the future. They sincerely believed in the existence of heaven and Buddha land, and that people had an afterlife. Such desire that required transcending real suffering and yearned for pure land was a reflection that Indian Buddhism conquered intellectual ideology in the people after it was introduced into China.

*(IV)   Formation of the "six schools and seven sects" of Prajna and
         theestablishment of "Bu Zhen Kong Lun" of Seng Zhao*

Since Lokaksema translated *Vajracchedikaprajnaparamitasutra* in the end of the Eastern Han Dynasty, the main trend of Buddhism theory in the Jin Dynasties gradually formed. As the meaning of various *Prajnaparamita-sutra*, such as *Asahasrika Prajnaparamita Sutra, Pancavimsatisahasrika-prajnaparamita* was not expressed smoothly, and metaphysics focusing on the discrimination of existence and nothing prevailed in the Wei and Jin Dynasties, and even Buddhist scholars tended to understand and explain the thought of *Prajna* with the opinion of metaphysics, which led to the emergence of various contrary opinions on the understanding of "emptiness" and formation of the "six schools and seven sects". "Six schools" referred to: (1) the Benwu School – Dao An advocated that before all manifestations of nature, emptiness was the beginning of all beings; Zhu Fashen and Fa Tai said that things came from nothing; (2) the Jise School – Zhi Daolin said that Jise referred to emptiness of nature; (3) the Xinwu School – Zhi Mindu advocated that nonego did not affect existence and nothing; (4) the Shihan School – Yu Fakai said that all things in the world were the embodiment of the mind; (5) the Huanhua School – Daoyi said,

"The laws of the world were all like fantasy"; (6) the Yuanhui School – Yu Daosui thought that all things in the world were formed by karma, and there was no entity. The Benwu School differentiated into the Benwuyi School, so they were also known as "seven sects". Distinguished from the basic points of view, the Benwu School, Jise School, and Xinwu School were most representative. The formation of the "six schools and seven sects" of Prajna reflected the footprints of the independent development of Chinese Buddhism; it was not entirely in line with the intention of Indian Prajna, because Kumarajiva translated books like *Madhyamika-sastra* and *Sata-sastra*, which systematically introduced Prajna, based on fully understanding and grasping the meaning of Prajna. Seng Zhao wrote texts like *Bu Zhen Kong Lun*, which clearly expounded that the meaning of being not real was empty, and criticized the theories of "six schools and seven sects", so that the Prajna theory of Chinese Buddhism was pushed to its peak.

Emergence of the Buddhist schools in the Southern and Northern Dynasties

After the separatist state of the Sixteen Kingdoms of the Eastern Jin Dynasty, it continued to split for 160–170 years in the Southern and Northern Dynasties. This was the era in which Buddhism was further spread. Its main feature was that various schools centering on studying a certain part of Buddhist scriptures emerged, with one argument, contending with each other, showing an unprecedented prosperity.

1 Rulers flattering and exterminating Buddhism

Most of the emperors of the Southern Dynasties attached importance to the promotion of Buddhism, among whom the most prominent was Emperor Wu of Liang. He always occupied the throne of emperor, clung to the power and honor of the world, but also was blindly dedicated to the pursuit of relief and "happiness" of life. He used to worship Taoism, and became converted to Buddhism in the third year of his reign, promoting Buddhism almost to the status of national religion, and he also served as a servant in Tongtai Temple many times, after which the ministers spent large sums of money redeeming him back to the palace, so as to erect merits and virtues, and also enrich the monastery economy. He also strictly kept discipline, abstained from wine and meat, paid attention to classical translation, personally preached, wrote books, propounded ideas, and suppressed the theory of spiritual perishability. Buddhism, relying on the support and advocacy of the autocratic imperial power of Emperor Wu of Liang, reached an unprecedented level. However, in the late years of Emperor Wu of Liang, "Hou Jing chaos" broke out, and Buddhism was hit. Emperors of the Chen Dynasty also followed the rules of Emperor Wu of Liang, among whom Emperor Wu and Wen of Chen also promoted and used Buddhism by serving in temples. According to historical record, there were 2,846 Buddhist temples and over 82,700 monks and nuns in Liang in the Southern Dynasty at the peak of Buddhism.

Most of the rulers of the Northern Dynasty also attached importance to the use of Buddhism, but there were a few who adopted the policy of exterminating Buddhism. Emperor Daowu of the Northern Wei Dynasty believed in Buddhism, but later Emperor Taiwu repeatedly restricted and cracked down on Buddhism, and even ordered the killing of all the Sramana, which was the beginning of exterminating Dharma of "Sanwu Yizong" in the history of Chinese Buddhism. After Emperor Wencheng succeeded to the throne, he ordered the revival of Buddhism, cut Yungang Grottoes, and engraved Buddha statues. Emperor Xiaowen also widely organized Buddhist affairs and vigorously promoted Buddhism. He also ordered the households under monachal officials to sacrifice grains to them for the use of Buddhist affairs. He made some of those who were guilty of felonies and the official slaves Buddhist servants serve in miscellaneous affairs and farm in temples. After that, Emperor Xuanwu and Xiaoming of the Northern Wei Dynasty also actively worshiped Buddhism. Due to the strong advocacy of the rulers, the court and the commonalty all followed, and to the end of Wei Dynasty there were more than 2 million monks and nuns and more than 30,000 temples. All the monasteries had a lot of land wealth, and accumulated wealth by renting land or enslaving the dependent farmers, operating businesses, and practicing usury, and gradually formed a relatively independent monastery economy at this time. Buddhism could be described as in its full flourish. After the split of the Northern Wei Dynasty, the rulers of the Eastern and Western Wei also greatly promoted Buddhist Dharma, and Buddhism continued to move forward. The Northern Zhou Dynasty replaced the Western Wei Dynasty and rose, and Emperor Ming also strongly worshiped Buddhism, but Emperor Wu, who inherited his throne, attached importance to Confucianism, repeatedly gathered masses to discuss pros and cons, depth and shallowness, and similarities and differences among Confucianism, Taoism, and Buddhism, and asked more than 2 million monks and Taoists to resume secular life. He also destroyed the territory of Buddhism. Emperor Wu of the Northern Wei Dynasty and Emperor Wu of the Northern Zhou Dynasty destroyed Buddhism, and were both related to the struggle between Confucianism, Taoism, and Buddhism, the effect of a large number of monks on the source of troops, and also the personal belief of the highest ruler. When these contradictions temporarily eased, Buddhism would be able to recover. After Emperor Wu of the Northern Zhou Dynasty died, Emperor Xuan and Emperor Jing later restored Buddhism.

2 Further development of the translation of various Buddhist scriptures

The translation of Buddhist scriptures had never been interrupted in the Southern and Northern Dynasties. In the Southern Dynasties, translation affairs were the most prosperous in the early period of the Liu and Song Dynasties and Liang at the end of the Chen Dynasty; the translation master Paramartha brought 240 cases of Sanskrit scriptures to China from Funan (now Cambodia area) at the end of Liang and the beginning of Chen, when there were a lot of wars. With his strong perseverance, he translated a large number of Buddhist scriptures in his vagrant

38 Buddhism's introduction into China

life and advanced the translation course of the Southern Dynasties. In addition, Gunabhadra, who came to China from India, also translated a number of important books, making an important contribution to the dissemination of Yogacara. In the Northern Dynasties, Bodhiruci, known as the master of classical translation, carried a large number of Sanskrit books to Luoyang via the Western Regions from North Asia, and systematically translated books of Mahayana Yogacara, with a great impact. In addition, some other translators translated a large number of books. In the Southern and Northern Dynasties, a total of nearly 700 Buddhist scriptures and 1,450 volumes were translated. These Buddhist scriptures were different from some books of Mahayana Prajna in the Eastern Jin Dynasty, but widely involved various factions of Indian Buddhism, especially Mahayana Yogacara, which was rising in India. At that time, important and influential translated works included the following.

1   *Mahayanasa mparigrahas'astra* and *Paramartha's Translation* written by Asaga and Vasubandhu. They were translated by Paramartha in Chen. These two theories had a great influence on the Buddhist theories, and since then, masters of Shelun emerged, creating the school of Shelun.
2   *Dasabhumikasutrasastra*, written by Vasubandhu. It was translated by Bodhiruci and Ratnamati in the Northern Wei Dynasty in Luoyang. Later, some monks became masters of Dilun for following and carrying forward *Dasabhumikasutrasastra*.
3   *Mahaparinirvana-sutra* was translated by Dharmaksema in the Northern Liang Dynasty, containing 40 volumes. Later in early Liu Song, Hui Guan and Xie Lingyun added items, modified and polished texts, and condensed it to 26 volumes based on the translation of Dharmaksema mainly and *Mahaparinirvana* translated by Fa Xian.
4   *Lankavatarasutra* was translated by Gunabhadra in Liusong. According to legend, this classic had been advocated by Dharma, Hui Ke, and others, which had a great impact on the formation of Beizong of Zen. In the Northern Wei Dynasty, Bodhiruci thought the translation of Gunabhadra was obscure, so he re-translated it to make it accessible, and named it *Saddharmalaṅkāvatāra sūtram*. The difference between these two translations had become a source of some of the heterodoxies of Zen masters in the north.
5   *Mahisasakavinaya*, containing 30 volumes, was translated by Ying Daosheng and Hui Yan, who were asked by Buddhajiva after he came to Jiankang in Liu Song. Thus, the interpretation of the four precepts (*Sarvastivadavinaya, Dharmaguptavinaya, Mahasaghavinaya,* and *Mahisasakavinaya*) widely spread in Han was completed.

3   Various classics scholars, precept scholars, and Abhidharmacarya rose in swarms

Buddhist scholars in the Southern and Northern Dynasties attached much importance to reciting Buddhist scriptures, and thus formed a special trend of focusing on a certain theory, and number of well-known masters emerged. They mentioned chapters and competed on sentences, with no innovation; they paid attention to the teacher and inheriting relationship, but had no ancestral system. These were schools of different opinions based on sermons of different theories. In the Southern Dynasties, at the beginning, Nirvana scholars emerged instead of Prajna scholars; when Nirvana theory prevailed in the Liang Dynasty, at the same time, masters of Three Treatises established their own schools. Up to the Chen Dynasty, "Three Treatises" was more advocated, and took away the status of "Satyasiddhi-sastra" and collaborated with "Nirvana". In the Northern Dynasties, due to the introduction of Buddhist theory of the Southern Dynasties, there were more scholars, among whom the most important ones were Abhidharma Shi, Shicheng Shi, Nirvana Shi, Dilun Shi, and Shelun Shi.

(I) Common classics scholars and Abhidharmacarya in the Southern and Northern Dynasties

1   Shicheng Shi: Buddhist scholars who studied and carried forward *Satyasiddhi-sastra*. *Satyasiddhi-sastra* was written by Harivarman from India. "Shi" referred to "the Four Noble Truths" of Buddhism: Suffering, origination, cessation, and path. "Shicheng" was the principles to establish the Four Noble Truths. The central content was mainly about "atma-sunyata", such as no water in the bottle and no original nature of human beings. It also talked about "dharma-nairatmya", such as no entity of the bottle and no original nature of the objective world. It criticized various factions with this, and especially criticized Abhidharma of Sarvastivada, which was considered the work of transmission from Hinayana to Mahayana. After Kumarajiva translated this theory for the convenience of beginners, his disciples, Seng Dao in Liu Song and Seng Song in the Northern Wei, who further studied on this, annotated it, forming the northern and southern systems – Shouchun (now Shou County in Anhui) System and Pengcheng (now Xuzhou in Jiangsu) System – since lecture and study had been very popular, and widely spread. At first, Shicheng Shi also promoted the "Three Treatises" translated by Kumarajiva. To the end of Qi, they turned to *Satyasiddhi-sastra*, and collaborated with the ideas of *Saddharmapundarikasutra* and *Nirvana*, carried forward in the Yangtze River Valley, and prevailed. Shicheng Shi also had a wide impact on scholars of the "Three Treatises", *Nirvana, Mahayanasamparigrahasastra*, and Zen. To the Sui Dynasty, after Ji Zang created the Three-Treatise School and judged *Satyasiddhi-sastra* as Hinayana, Shicheng Lun tended to decline, and disappeared in the early Tang Dynasty.

2   Nirvana Shi: Buddhist scholars who studied and carried forward *Nirvana*. In the Eastern Jin Dynasty, Fa Xian and Buddhabhadra translated six volumes of *Maha-parinirvana*, which was the first objection to *Mahaparinirvana-sutra*. In the Northern Liang, Dharmaksema translated the fist, middle, and last parts of *North Nirvana*, a total of 40 volumes, which was called *Northern Nirvana*. In early Liu Song, Hui Guan and Xie Lingyun expanded

it into 36 volumes, which were known as the *Southern Nirvana*. This classic mainly promoted that "Nirvana was immortal, the Buddha had the true self; all beings had Buddhist nature", and confirmed that everyone could become a Buddha. But *Maha-parinirvana* also said that "Icchantika" had no Buddhist nature. At that time, Zhu Daosheng analyzed the purpose of classics, and pointed out that "Icchantika contains the living type, why did it have no Buddhist nature? It seems that this classic is not telling enough!" (*YiChengFoXingHuiRiChao*, written by Japanese Sramana, cited in *Famous Monk Biography*). He advocated the theory that "Icchantika can become a Buddha", which was regarded as deviant and was expelled from the monks. After *Mahaparinirvana-sutra* was introduced to the South, it was claimed that Icchantika could become a Buddha, which matched what Zhu Daosheng previously said. Later Daosheng preached in Mount Lu, who was the first Nirvana Shi in the Southern Dynasties. Daosheng also established the meaning of "sudden enlightenment into Buddha", and opposed the prevailing theory of "gradual enlightenment into Buddha". At that time, Hui Guan, who also learned after Kumarajiva with Daosheng, held the theory of "gradual enlightenment into Buddha". Thus, the two systems of Southern Nirvana Shi formed. In the north, Hui Song and Dao Lang had attended the translation site of Dharmaksema, and Dao Lang wrote *Nirvana Annotation*, and put forward that "majjhima patipad" was the theory of Buddhist nature, becoming the earliest Nirvana Shi in the north. After that, Nirvana Shi from the north to the south started a long-term debate around *Nirvana* on issues such as whether there was a Buddhist nature, what a Buddhist nature was, and whether Buddhist consciousness was sudden or gradual and so on. The interpretation of the "Nirvana Buddhist nature" was the central issue of Chinese Buddhist doctrine in the Southern and Northern Dynasties, forming the heterodoxy of 12 factions. This debate was still quite intense until the Sui Dynasty; in the Tang Dynasty, due to the rise of the forces of schools such as Tiantai and Three-Treatise, Nirvana Shi gradually declined.

3   Abhidharma Shi and Jushe Shi: Abhidharma Shi referred to Buddhist scholars who studied and carried forward *Abhidharma* of Sarvastivada of Hinayana. Since the Eastern Jin Dynasty, various types of *Abhidharma* of Sarvastivada had been translated, mainly including *Eight Skandha of Abhidharma* and *Abhidharmahrdaya'sastra* translated by Deva of the Former Qin Dynasty, and *Samyuktabhidharma-hrdaya-sastr* translated by Harivarman in Liu Song. The basic idea of these books was to prove that humans were empty, the world was real, and all things were composed of an eternal entity because of karma and co-generation by analyzing Buddhist concepts. They advocated that *Abhidharma* began from Dao An and Hui Yuan in the Eastern Jin Dynasty, and since *Samyuktabhidharma-hrdaya-sastr* was translated, the Abhidharma School began to flourish, and gained the title of "Abhidharma Shi". One of the best, Hui Ji in the south, explained *Abhidharma* in Zhaoti Temple, Jiankang in Liang, and there were thousands of audience members. Hui Song in the north often gave lectures in Pengcheng, with the title of "Abhidharm

Confucius". Since the "Shicheng" School in the south gradually flourished at the end of Liang, Paramartha translated *Paramartha's Translation* in Chen, and some Abhidharm scholars transferred to the Jushe School and became Jushe Shi. The southern Abhidharm declined since then. But the northern Abhidharm scholars still prevailed until the beginning of the Sui Dynasty. To the Tang Dynasty when Xuanzang re-translated *Abhidharmakosa-sastra*, the scholars set off the climax of study, the old translation of Abhidharm began to decline, and some writings were gradually lost because nobody cared.

4   Shelun Shi: Buddhist scholars who studied and carried forward *Mahayanasamparigrahas'astra* translated by Paramartha. *Mahayanasamparigrahas'astra* was an important work of Indian Mahayana Yogacara, written by Asaga. In the Northern Wei, Buddhasanta translated it, but it was not widely circulated. Later, Paramartha re-translated it when he was in Chen, and he also translated *Annotation to Mahayanasamparigrahas'astra* of Vasubandhu, which was vigorously carried forward by Hui Kai, Dao Ni, and Fa Tai, who were disciples of Paramartha. After Jing Song learned *Mahayanasamparigrahas'astra* from Fa Tai, he returned to Pengcheng in the north and started preaching, and he had a lot of disciples. In early Sui, Tan Qian moved from Pengcheng to Chang'an to carry forward *Mahayanasamparigrahas'astra*. The theories of Shelun Shi were not exactly the same, but the main theory was that the eighth "Layavijāna"[2] was sorcery, which was the basis for all phenomena; but there was a pure consciousness in this sorcery. In this way, in addition to Astavijnana, the pure consciousness in "ayavijāna" was the ninth "Amala-vijnana" (i.e., true Buddhist nature), which thought that as long as all beings strove to develop pure consciousness in "ayavijāna" to rule sorcery, they could enter Amala-vijnana and become a Buddha. Thus it was confirmed that all beings had a Buddhist nature, and could become a Buddha. After Xuanzang returned home from India, he re-translated *Mahayanasamparigrahas'astra*, and took it as one of the many ordinances of Yogacara; thus the old texts of Shelun Shi lost their significance, and those who especially carried forward *Mahayanasamparigrahas'astra* tended to decline.

(II)   Unique precept scholars and Abhidharmacarya in the Southern Dynasties

1   Three-Treatise Shi: Buddhist scholars who studied and carried forward the "Three-Treatise". The "Three-Treatise" referred to *Madhyamika-sastra, Satasastra*, and *Dvadashanikaya-Shastra*, which were the important sastras of Mahayana, and elucidated the theories of Madhyamika. Ever since Yao Qin, when Kumarajiva translated the "Three-Treatise", his disciples like Seng Zhao and others all deeply studied. However, the rise of the Three-Treatise began from Seng Lang in the Liang Dynasty; later, with the promotion of Seng Quan and Fa Lang, it formed a sect until Ji Zang in the Sui Dynasty.

2   Sarvastivadavinaya Abhidharmacarya: Buddhist scholars who studied and carried forward *Abhidharmacarya*. *Abhidharmacarya* was the basic precept book of Hinayana. Vimalaksa started to preach it in Jiangling after supplementing and correcting it, after which the school of "Sarvastivadavinaya" arose. In the Southern Dynasty, Seng Ye, Zhi Cheng, and Seng Yao carried forward his school. It prevailed in Qi and Liang.

(III)   Unique precept scholars and Abhidharmacarya in the Northern Dynasties

1   Dilun Shi: Buddhist scholars who studied and carried forward *Dasabhumikasutrasastra*. This was the most influential school of Buddhism in the Northern Dynasties, which was different from the theory of emptiness of nature of Prajna spread for a long time based on the theory of *citta-matra*. *Dasabhumikasutrasastr* was written by Vasubandhu. This book discussed and explained *Avatamsaka Sutra-Shidipin*, and gave play to the ten levels (Di) and doctrine of practice of Bodhisattva. In the Northern Wei Dynasty, Bodhiruci and Ratnamati translated this theory; because their practice of them was not the same, there were different explanations among their disciples who inherited *Dilun* from them, forming two schools from the north to the south, called the Xiangzhou (now north of Anyang City, Henan) Southern faction and the Xiangzhou Northern faction. The Southern School was represented by Huiguang, disciple of Ratnamati, and subsequent important scholars included Fashang and Huiyuan in Jingying Temple. The Northern School was represented by Dao Chong, disciple of Bodhiruci, and subsequent scholars included Zhinian. The focus of the debate between the Northern and Southern Schools was the problem of "future constant" and "present constant". "Constant" was a synonym of Buddhist nature or Nirvana – that is, whether Buddhist nature was a congenital ("present constant") or acquired ("future constant"). The Southern School thought that "ayavijāna" was the "pure original nature", "Tathagatagarbha", and "bhuta-tathata". Tathagatagarbha possessed all merits, which was the basis of all phenomena, and thus advocated that the Buddhist nature of all beings was inherent – namely, congenital. However, because this consciousness "changed with wild fancy", and gave birth to the secular world, all beings should strive to practice, keep away from pollution, and keep clean, so as to became a Buddha. This was the theory of "present constant" of the Southern School. The Northern School was different, and believed that "ayavijāna" was the basis of all phenomena; all merits were acquired, and so was the Buddhist nature. To become a Buddha, one had to practice – namely, "present constant". The claim of the Northern School system was similar to that of Shelun Shi Alayavijnana, but not as deliberate or popular as Shelun Shi, so it was united in Shelun Shi. Thus, the confrontation between the Northern and Southern Schools evolved into the argument of Dilun Shi and Shelun Shi. Until the early Tang Dynasty, the Buddhist community was still talking

about it. Xuan Zang was determined to go to India to seek Dharma because these difficult problems could not be resolved. The theory of the Southern School also changed later, and its basic point of view was adopted later by Huayan School scholars, with a great impact on the formation of the Huayan School. But once it was adopted by Huayan School scholars, there was no room for independent publicity, so the Southern School disappeared.

2   Silun Shi: Buddhist scholars who studied and carried forward *Mahaprajna-paramita-sastra*, *Madhyamika-sastra*, *Sata-sastra*, and *Dvadashanikaya-Shastra*. This school attached equal importance to *Mahaprajna-paramita-sastra* and "Three-Treatise". Its famous scholars included Dao Chang in Northern Qi and Tan Luan in Eastern Wei. Both Dao Chang and Tan Luan later returned to the pure land.

3   Dharmaguptavinaya Shi: Buddhist scholars who studied and carried forward *Dharmaguptavinaya*. In the Northern Wei Dynasty, Fa Cong and Dao Fu especially carried it forward. Later, Huiguang wrote *Note to Dharmagupta-vinaya*, which made this school prevail, and there were many disciples.

4   Lankavatarasutra Shi: Zen masters who took *Lankavatarasutra* as verification. The full name of *Lankavatarasutra* was *Lankavatara-sutra*. There are now three types of Chinese translations of *Lankavatarasutra*, and the popular version was translated by Gunabhadra in the Southern Song, a total of four volumes. "Lankavatarasutra" was the name of mountain; "Abaduoluo" meant "entering", the sutra for Buddha to enter the mountain. The text advocated that all beings in the world were the "embodiment of self-heart", and insisted on "forgetting words and thoughts, no hamper to correct meditation" in practice – namely, emphasizing intelligent consciousness but not words. According to legend, Zen Master Bodhidharma taught Hui Ke four volumes of *Lankavatarasutra*, after whom there were disciples, such as Zen Master Seng Na and Seng Can, and later it directly developed into Zen in the north.

4   *Different characteristics of Buddhism in the north and south*

During the period of Wei, Jin, and the Southern and Northern Dynasties, especially in the northern regions, due to long-term wars, frequent fighting, and changes of political power, some scholars and monks traveled to the south between the Han and Wei Dynasties, two Jin Dynasties, and around the establishment of Liu Song, which led Buddhist talents to transfer to the south, and the academic center also transferred to the south. The confrontation between the northern and the southern regimes in the Southern and Northern Dynasties and the regional hindrance promoted the formation of different Buddhist styles. The significant manifestation of such difference was that the Southern Dynasty focused on theories and metaphysical thought, while the Northern Dynasty advocated practice, where Zen especially prevailed.

Buddhism in the Southern Dynasties inherited the tradition of Buddhism in the Eastern Jin Dynasty, which preferred to talk about argumentation. It was called "Buddhist dharma advocated the virtuous" (Volume 17, *Hui Si Biography*, of

Continued Eminent Monk Biography) and "Buddhism prevailed" (Volume 20, *Fifth Chapter of Learning Zen*, of the same book), which reflected this feature. In the Southern Dynasties, doctrines like "Nirvana", "Shicheng", and "Three-Treatise" were very popular, and debates on issues like Nirvana Buddhism, sudden enlightenment, and gradual enlightenment were very intense. At this time, although the mainstream status of Prajna study was replaced by Nirvana study, it was still popular. To the Chen Dynasty, Emperors Wu, Wen, and Xuan promoted the highly thoughtful "Three-Treatise", which later led Ji Zang to create the Three-Treatise School in the Sui Dynasty. At the same time, the Buddhist field and atheists also debated on theoretical issues, such as karma and spiritual perishability or immortality, whose large-scale and fierce debate were rare in the ancient Chinese history of thought.

Rulers of the Northern Dynasty were mostly uneducated and few were literate and famous Buddhist monks did not advocate empty talk of theories. Compared with Buddhism in the Southern Dynasty, Zen, law, and faith of Pure Land were developed; especially Zen was the most prosperous. It was recorded in Volume 2, *Chongzhen Temple*, of *A Record of Buddhist Temples in Luoyang* that since the monk Hui Yi of Chongzhen Temple went to Bailu Mountain to live in seclusion and cultivate himself, "monks in the capital were all engaged in Zen chanting, and no longer preached". In addition to Lanka Shi, famous Zen masters emerged one after another – for example, there were hundreds of scholars of Xuangao Zen in Northern Wei. In addition, Tanwupi, Ratnamati, and Buddhasanta, who came to China, also carried forward Zen. In Northern Qi, Seng Chou gave lectures in many places, teaching Zen with great reputation. Later, Dao Xuan treated him as equal to Dharma. For another example, the pioneers of the Tiantai School, Hui Wen and Hui Si, also advocated Dinghui, which was taken seriously by Zen schools in the north to the south. Emperor TaiZu of Zhou respected Zen master Seng Shi in Northern Zhou very much, and converted to him. As for ordinary monks who practiced Zen, there were more. The power of Northern Buddhism also surpassed that of the South, and Huiguang of Northern Qi was regarded as the ancestor of Dharmaguptavinaya. Tan Luan, who promoted the faith of the Pure Land, also had activities in the Northern Wei Dynasty. The academic atmosphere of famous monks in the Northern Dynasties had a great influence on ordinary Buddhist monks and folk believers, so that everyone emphasized the industry. One of the outstanding manifestations of such atmosphere was to attach importance to carving statues. For example, Yungang and Longmen Grottoes were carved in the Northern Wei Dynasty on a large scale and with great skill. Because they needed to invest a lot of manpower and financial and material resources to carve statues, the northern monks and believers at home also set up a Buddhism organization, "Yi Yi", for each clan and village, and some dignitaries and monks also set up a Buddhist organization, called "Fa She", to be engaged in Buddhist activities together. In terms of Buddhist organization, the north also surpassed the south.

It should be noted that the differences between Buddhism in the Southern and Northern Dynasties were relative and they also had something in common. Southern Buddhism also advocated practice, but only Zen prevailed in the beginning of the LiuSong Dynasty, and tended to decline to the end of LiuSong. However, Zen was enduring in the north. Buddhism in the Northern Dynasties also attached importance to argumentation, but only the Abhidharm and Chengshi Schools of Hinayana prevailed, while the Mahayana doctrine prevailed in the south. In addition, also because of the inveteracy of Prajna emptiness, and the unprecedented popularity of Nirvana Buddhism, even the ideal thinking of the *Lankavatarasutra* and *Sandhinirmocanavyuhasutra* was not popular.

The creation and prosperity of Buddhism in the Sui and Tang Dynasties

After four to five centuries of spreading, Chinese Buddhism entered the formation and development periods of the sectarians. In the Sui and Tang Dynasties, the north and south were politically reunified, the national economy was prosperous, and international cultural exchanges were active; Buddhism also followed the tendency of seeking common points and combined northern and southern ideological systems, and schools evolved into several new sects. Sects were different from schools, which had their own unique doctrines and different rules, and they were related to the right of inheritance and therefore more emphasized lineage. Buddhist sects with local flavors were created in the Sui and Tang Dynasties, forming an epoch-making significant feature in the history of Chinese Buddhism.

1 The rulers' use, advocacy, and restriction of Buddhism

After Emperor Wen of Sui reunified the north and south, he immediately changed the policy of Emperor Wu of the Northern Zhou Dynasty that exterminated Buddhism, and vigorously restored and supported Buddhism. According to historical record, he encouraged monks, and there were up to over half a million new monks (see Volume 10, *Shi Jing Song Biography*, of *Continued Eminent Monk Biography*) at that time. He also set up monk officials at all levels to manage the affairs of monks and nuns. Emperor Yang of Sui also believed in Buddhism. When he was still Prince Jin, he invited Zhi Kai to organize Bodhisattva vows. He worshiped Zhi Kai as a wise man, and provided favorable conditions for him to create the Tiantai School. After he ascended the throne, he also claimed to be a Bodhisattva disciple, made people become monks, built temples and statues, organized translations, and tried to protect and promote Buddhism. However, Emperor Yang of Sui also ordered Sramanato respect for kings, and ordered the monks and nuns with no deity to resume secular life, demolished excessive temples, and limited the development of Buddhism.

The rulers of the Tang Dynasty also attached great importance to the reorganization and use of Buddhism. Due to repeated proposals of the imperial astronomer Fu Yi, Emperor Gaozu of Tang ordered the eradication of Buddhism, which was not implemented, for a palace revolt happened later. Emperor Taizong of Tang attached importance to the translation of Buddhist classics, and organized a large-scale translation site for Xuanzang, who returned from India. He also issued an imperial edict to establish Buddhist temples in "places in war" in the country, mourning the dead soldiers to appease the people. Later, Empress Wu Zetian made use of *Dayun Classic* of Buddhism to deify her usurpation of power as consistent with the authorization of Maitreya. She ordered that "Buddhism shall be superior to Taoism, and monks shall be superior to Taoists" (Volume 113 of *Collection of Tang Dynasty Imperial Edicts and Orders*), and she also directly supported Fa Zang in creating the Huayan School. Later, Emperor Xuanzong of Tang eradicated monks and nuns for a time, but believed in the newly introduced Esoteric Buddhism, and promoted the formation of Esoteric Buddhism. Later, the An-Shi Disturbances occurred, Hui Neng's disciple Shen Hui went north to Luoyang, to help the government collect monks and tax, and subsidize military fees, which the spread of Buddhism more convenient. He took the opportunity to promote his master's doctrine, so that Southern Zen founded by Hui Neng obtained a stable position in the north. However, since the middle of the Tang Dynasty, corvée was heavier day by day: "rich families and strong men get tonsured to avoid corvée". (Volume 211, *Tang-Second Year of Kaiyuan Period of Emperor Xuanzong* of *History as a Mirror*), and people used monasteries as shelter. The monastery took advantage of the occasion in which the system of land equalization was destroyed and occupied private farms and expanded manors; they also managed to avoid taxes, and made profits by operating businesses, opening pawnshops, and practicing usury. When Xin Tifou described the serious situation in which the Buddhist monasteries occupied social properties during the reign of Emperor Ruizong of Tang, he said, "Buddhism occupied 70 percent or 80 percent of the wealth in the world" (Volume 101, *Xin Tifou Biography*, of *Old History of Tang Dynasty*). At that time, Buddhist monasteries nearly monopolized the social wealth. In this way, although Buddhism had the effect of keeping people on the rails, the contradictions between the monastery economy and national interests were deepening and sharpening, leading to the intention of the imperial court to destroy Buddhism since the reign of Emperor Jingzong and Wenzong of Tang; after Emperor Wenzong, Emperor Wuzong finally put it into practice, and ordered the demolition of monasteries around the country, and ordered monks and nuns to resume secular life. From the second to the fifth year of Huichang's reign (AD 842–84), a total of about 4,600 monasteries were demolished, more than 260,000 monks and nuns resumed secular life, 150,000 slaves were liberated, and a lot of monastery land was confiscated. This was an unprecedented heavy blow to Buddhism, and was greatly related to the future fate of Buddhism. The vast majority of Buddhist sects recovered after this setback. In terms of the history of Chinese Buddhism, the An-Shi Disturbances and the destruction of Buddhism in Huichang in Tang Dynasty were two major turns for changes in Buddhism. After the An-Shi Disturbances, Hui Neng Zen destroyed the sect of Shenxiu Zen. Since the An-Shi Disturbances, the Li Tang regime gradually declined, which also led to the intensification of the contradictions between the economy and Buddhism, and the resulting destruction of Buddhism in Huichang declared a basic end of the heyday of Buddhism.

2 Great achievements in the translation of Buddhist scriptures

The translation of Buddhist scriptures in the Sui and Tang Dynasties was basically dominated by the country, which set up translation pavilions or designated temples, or organized translation sites, and invited translators to translate. In the Sui Dynasty, translators like Jnanagupta and Dhamagupta translated 59 books and 262 volumes with Chinese Sramana Yan Cong and others. The translation of Buddhist scriptures in the Tang Dynasty was the most impressive. For example, Chinese monk Xuanzang made a lot of accurate translations with his deep learning and cultivation, and he translated 75 books and 1,335 volumes, involving various aspects, like the Consciousness-Only, Prajna, and Pandan, with brilliant achievements. For another example, Yijing translated 61 books and 260 volumes, Bukong translated 104 books and 134 volumes. The number and quality of classical translation in the Tang Dynasty surpassed its predecessors, and a total of 372 Buddhist scriptures and 2,159 volumes were translated. At this point, the important scriptures of Indian Mahayana Buddhism had basically been translated.

With the increase in classical translations, they needed to reorganize the catalog to make it convenient to read, copy, and collect translations in monasteries. In the Sui Dynasty, Yan Cong and others recompiled *Catalog of Scriptures* into *Catalog of Renshou Classics*. Based on this, the Tang Dynasty also compiled several catalogs, including 20 volumes of *Buddhism Catalog in Kaiyuan* compiled by Sengzhi in the eighteenth year (AD 730) of Kaiyuan. It collected 1,076 books and 5,048 volumes; later, it became the authoritative evidence for writing and engraving all classics.

3 The Zhiyi and Tiantai Schools

The Tiantai School was formed in the Sui Dynasty, which was the Buddhist sect founded earliest in our country. It was called the Tiantai School by later generations, for the founder Zhiyi lived in Tiantai Mountain (now Tiantai County, Zhejiang Province). And it was also known as the Fahua School, for its religious meaning was based on *Saddharmapundarikasutra*. According to the genealogy of this religious sect, its first ancestor dated back to Nagarjuna in India, the second ancestor was Zen monk Hui Wen in Northern Qi, the third ancestor was Huisi, and the fourth ancestor was Zhiyi, after whom were five ancestors, Guanding, Zhiwei, Huiwei, Xuanlang, and Zhanran. And the actual founder was the fourth ancestor, Zhiyi.

The secular surname of Zhiyi (538–597) was Chen, and he was from Yingchuan (now Xuchang, Henan). He was the second son of Chen Qizu, Meng Yang Gong, during the reign of Emperor Yuan of Liang, born in an aristocratic family with noble pedigree. He witnessed the frequent changes of dynasties in the Southern and Northern Dynasties, during which period relatives separated and people were displaced, so he lamented the uncertainty of life and became a monk. He became a monk at the age of 18, and learned after Huisi at the age of 23. Huisi attached importance to both Zen (Ding) and Buddhist argumentations (Hui). Zhiyi learned Zen and practiced Fahua Samadhi. He succeeded in study when he was about 30 years old. Later, he went to Jinling to give lectures on classics like *Saddharmapundarikasutra*, spread Zen law, and won the admiration of courtiers. Eight years later, he went to Tiantai Mountain and built a thatched hut, in which he lived for ten years. Emperor Xuan of Chen gave taxes of Tiantai County to him to provide financial support for the temple he was in. Later, Zhiyi, at the invitation of Junior King Chen, returned to Jinling. At this time, he had had a set of his own teaching of doctrines and views of Buddhism, and set a new standard for righteousness. After Chen was destroyed, he roamed in Jing and Xiang. He stayed in Mount Lu. Later, at the invitation of Prince Jin, Yang Guang, he went to Yangzhou to ordain Bodhisattva precepts, and obtained the title of "wise man" from the emperor, so he was also known as "wise master". Emperors Wen and Yang of Sui paid great attention to and respected Zhiyi. He got many farms with the agreement of Emperor Yang of Sui; at the same time, Zhiyi also repeatedly said, "I support the territory of Sui". Zhiyi built 36 temples in his whole life, and personally made many people monks. After he died, Yang Guang, according to his wish, built a temple in Tiantai Mountain, and gave the tablet of "Guoqing Temple".

Zhiyi took *Saddharmapundarikasutra* as the last argument of Sakyamuni Buddha, which was the classic with the highest authority, and worshiped it as essential. He took *Mahaprajnaparamita Upadesha* as a guideline, absorbed the thoughts of Three-Treatise Shi and Nirvana Shi in the Southern Dynasties, and inherited and developed the view and practice methods of "one mind and three views" of Huiwen and Huisi to organize his own doctrine system. The thought of Zhiyi was mainly reflected in the "three major books of Tiantai" – namely, *Fa Hua Xuan Yi*, *Fa Hua Wen Ju*, and *The Great Samdhi and Vipa'Syana*, recorded by his disciples based on his lectures during the Chen and Sui Dynasties. In addition, the "five small books of Tiantai" – namely, *Avalokitesvara Xuan Yi*, *Avalokitesvara Yi Shu*, *Golden Light by Xuanyi*, *The Deep Meaning of Suvarnaprabh Asottamasutra*, *Diction of Suvarnaprabh Asottamasutra*, and *Annotation to Amitayurdhyanasutra* – reflected his thoughts. His theory was characterized by the establishment of the double practice principle of Ding (Zhi) and Hui (Guan), and emphasis on the dual operation of doctrine and view. It developed from "one mind and three view" to connection of three truths of Kong, Jia, and Zhong, and the theory of "integrate harmony of three truths", as well as the theory of "one thought and three thousand" that short mental activities contained all the phenomena in the world. Zhiyi's disciple Guanding wrote a large number of Sutra commentaries to widely carry forward the idea of this sect. Later, because of the blockbuster of the Consciousness-Only School and Huayan School, the Tiantai School fell into disgrace. To the ninth ancestor Zhanran, he took the resurgence of this sect as his own mission, and further put forward the theory of "the Buddha nature remaining in all wheat", that grass, wood, and masonry had Buddhist nature. Zhanran then passed down to his disciples Dao Sui, Xing Man, and Guang Xiu. In the later years of Guang Xiu, he was confronted with the destruction of Buddhism in Huichang during the reign of Emperor Wuzong, and the Tiantai School declined.

4 Sanjie Jiao

Sanjie Jiao was named because it advocated that Buddhism was divided into three ranks. It was also known as the "Pufa School" because it advocated general belief in all the Buddhist Dharma, which was founded by Xinxing in the Sui Dynasty. Xinxing (540–594), whose secular surname was Wang, was from Wei County (now Anyang City, Henan). He became a monk when he was young, got widely involved in classics and theories, and paid attention to practice. He was called in to the capital in the early Sui Dynasty (ca. AD 581), where he established a third-rank ashram to promote Sanjie Jiao. He took "Sanjie Dharma" written by himself as the main basis, and divided all Buddhism into three categories according to "Shi", "Chu" (the world), and "Ji" (human), and each category was divided into three ranks: the first rank was the Dharma Perfect Age, and "Chu" was the Pure Land of Buddhism, where only Buddha and Bodhisattva practiced Mahayana; the second rank was the Dharma Semblance Age, "Chu" was soil, humans were mixed up, and Mahayana and Hinayana prevailed; the third rank was the Dharma Ending Age, 1,000 years after the death of Sakyamuni, "Chu" was also soil, and humans were "evil". Xinxing believed that it was the Dharma Ending Age then, and all beings should not be satisfied with only chanting the name of one Buddha, chanting one sutra, but should be converted to all the Buddhas ("universal Buddha"), and believe in all Buddhist Dharma ("universal dharma"). He advocated that being converted to Pufo and Pufa was the only method for all beings to be saved in the Dharma Ending Age.

In terms of practice, Sanjie Jiao advocated adopting ascetic practices, begging for food, and eating one meal one day. It opposed idolatry, and did not advocate chanting the name of Amitabha Buddha. It believed that all beings were the true Buddha, so all men and women shall worship Buddha, which was known as "universal worship". It implemented "forest burial" after death – namely, putting the body in the forest for birds and animals to eat, which was called alms giving with food. It also operated an "inexhaustible treasury" (saved and donated money), persuaded believers to donate money to the monastery to save, and then donate or loan to poor believers, and also provided for the repair of the temple. This also established the independent economic base of the sect.

Xinxing's disciples included Benji, Jing Ming, and many others, who built five temples in Chang'an: Huadu, Huiri, Guangming, Cimen, and Hongshan. It prevailed for a while. But after the creation of Sanjie Jiao, it was repeated prohibited by the court and attacked by other Buddhist sects, especially the Pure Land School. In AD 600 in the Sui Dynasty, the court banned it. In AD 695 in the Tang Dynasty, Empress Wu Zetian also clearly sentenced it as heresy. In the first year of Kaiyuan during the reign of Emperor Xuanzong of Tang (AD 713), the inexhaustible treasury was abolished, which cut off its economic sources. But the potential force of Sanjie Jiao still existed, and it was popular for more than 300 years with the people, and was annihilated at the end of Tang.

5 *Ji Zang and the Three-Treatise School*

The Three-Treatise School was a sect formed in the Sui Dynasty. It was so named because it took *Madhyamika-sastra*, *Sata-sastra*, and *Dvadashanikaya-Shastra* of the Indian Madhyamika as its main basis. It was also known as the "Faxing School" because it advocated that "all dharma was empty". Because the Tiantai

School and Huayan School also claimed to be the "Faxing School", it was also known as the "Kong School". The Three-Treatise School was in fact a sect of Indian Madhyamika, the direct successor of the teachings of Nagarjuna and Deva.

"Three-Treatise" was handed down between masters and disciples after it was translated by Kumarajiva, and researchers emerged in large numbers. Sengzhao "ranked No. 1 in Jiekong among the disciples of Kumarajiva" (Jizang, *Bai Lun Shu Xu*), so he was worshiped as the "beginning of Xuanzong" by Jizang, the founder of Three-Treatise, and was often mentioned together with Shi Zhao. Shi Zhao's theory was originally spread in the north, and Seng Lang, who used to study "Three-Treatise" in Liu Song, came to the regions south of the Yangtze River during the Jiang Dynasty, and lived in places like Sheshan in the suburb of Jiankang to promote the righteousness of "Three-Treatise". Later, Seng Quan and Fa Lang passed on, so the sect of "Three-Treatise" came into being. Since then, Jizang carried forward the theory and created sects.

The secular surname of Jizang (549–623) was An, whose ancestors were from Parthia in the Western Regions, so he was also known as "Hu Jizang". His ancestors moved to Nanhai (now Guangzhou) to avoid revenge, and then moved to Jinling (now Nanjing). Jizang was born in Jinling, and then followed Fa Land to become a monk and learn "Three-Treatise", and succeeded in study at the age of 19. At the end of Chen and beginning of Sui, regions south of the Yangtze River were in havoc, and Jizang collected books in waste temples and widely read, which led to a great increase in his knowledge. After the Sui Dynasty obtained Baiyue (now Zhejiang, Fujian area), he went to Jiaxiang Temple in Kuaiji Mountain (now Shaoxing, Zhejiang) to preach, and there were more than 1,000 learners, so he was known as "Jiaxiang master". Later, at the invitation of Emperor Yang of Sui, he went to Chang'an and lived in Riyan Temple, where he completed the annotation to "Three-Treatise", and wrote his representative work *Deep Meaning of Three-Treatise*, establishing his own main idea of the sect and creating the Three-Treatise School. The central theory of this sect was based on Paramartha and Samvrti-Satya, which revealed all the falsehoods from the empty entity, and advocated that all beings in and outside the world were generated by karma and had no original nature – namely, nothing to gain; but to guide all beings to use pseudonyms, it was "majjhima patipad" – namely, the theory of majjhima patipad of nothing to gain. Jizang's disciples included Hui Yuan, Zhiyi, and Shuofashi. Yuan Kang, disciple of Shuofashi, was called in by Emperor Taizong of Tang to Chang'an to give lectures on "Three-Treatise". He wrote a lot, and only three volumes of *Zhao Lun Shu* exist now. At this time, the Tiantai School and Consciousness-Only School prevailed; the Three-Treatise School declined soon after it got popular.

6 Xuan Zang and the Consciousness-Only School

The Consciousness-Only School was founded by Xuanzang and his disciple Kuiji in the Tang Dynasty. It was so named because it analyzed and interpreted the concepts of all the phenomena of the world with many Buddhist scopes, and promoted the idealism that "everything was consciousness only". Because they both lived in

Cien Temple, Kuiji was also known as Master Cien, so it was also called the Cien School. It was called the Yoga School because it took *Yogacara-bhumi-sastra* as the fundamental teaching. *Sandhinirmocanavyuhasutra*, *Vijnaptimatratasiddhi-sastra*, and *Yogacara-bhumi-sastra* were the most basic books of this school.

Xuanzang (about 600–664) was proficient in scriptures, precepts, and theories, and known as "Sanzang Master", which was unprecedented in China at that time. He was commonly known as Tang Sanzang, Tang Monk, which was the highest praise and greatest respect to him. The secular surname of Xuan Zang was Chen, and he was from Goushi County in Luozhou, Henan (now south Yanshi County in Henan Province). When he was a kid, due to poverty, he lived in Pure Land Temple in Luoyang with his second elder brother. When he was 13 years old, he became a monk in Luoyang, and was exceptionally selected. Later at the end of Sui, peasant armies rose, so he went to Chang'an, Chengdu, Jingzhou, Zhaozhou, and Yangzhou with his brother, and then returned to Chang'an. Because he visited famous masters in various places, and learned all their doctrines, he was elected as one of the ten moral people of Zhuangyan Temple. Xuan Zang deeply felt that Buddhist doctrines in various places were different at that time, and he was especially keen to resolve the failure to unify the argument on Buddhist natures between Shelun Shi and Dilun Shi, which prevailed in the early Tang Dynasty. At this time, Prabhakaramitra came to China from India, promoted the grand lecture scale of Nalanda Temple at that time, and introduced that *Yogacara-bhumi-sastra* taught by Master Silabhadra was the highest system of theory at that time. So Xuan Zang made the great aspiration of going on a pilgrimage for Buddhist scriptures in the west, and officially applied to go to India, which was not allowed. In the third year of Zhenguan (AD 629), due to the serious famine in the north, the court allowed Taoists to go out to seek food. Xuanzang took the opportunity to go westward, passed Yumen, crossed Liusha River, Cong Ridge, and snow-capped mountains, and experienced difficulties and obstacles before entering the territory of northern India. Xuanzang started from Chang'an and learned along the journey. It took him about four years to arrive in Nalanda Temple in Rajagraha of Indian Magadha, which was the highest institution of Indian Buddhism at that time. More than 4,000 monks in the temple welcomed his arrival, and he was worshiped as one of the ten moral people with extremely preferential treatment. Xuan Zang learned Buddhist scriptures like *Yogacara-bhumi-sastra* from Silabhadra in Nalanda Temple very well. In order to participate in study more extensively, five years later, he left Nalanda Temple and traveled all over India. Four years later, he returned to Nalanda Temple; later, at entrustment of Silabhadra, he gave lectures on *Consciousness-Only Selection Theory* to the public in the temple, and communicated on the controversy between Madhyamika of Mahayana and Yogacara. He wrote 3,000 eulogies of *Hui Zong Lun* in Sanskrit, which were highly praised by Indian monks. At the invitation of Siladitya, to subdue the doctrine of *Breaking Mahayana* of Hinayana in South India, he wrote 1,600 eulogies of *Zhi E Jian Lun* in Sanskrit. Later, Siladitya also set up a General Assembly for Xuanzang in Kangakubja, and ordered Indian Sramana, Brahman, and scholars of other schools to attend. Eighteen kings, more than 3,000 monks from various countries, more than

1,000 monks in Nalanda Temple, and more than 2,000 people of Brahmanism and other schools attended. The General Assembly set the arguments of *Hui Zong Lun* and *Zhi E Jian Lun*, and let anyone contradict them. After 18 days, the assembly ended, and no one could make changes to even one word. Since then, Xuan Zang was unanimously respected by Mahayana and Hinayana, and worshiped as "Mahayana Master" and "Relief Master". He was the only one to have such a reputation. At this time, Xuanzang had succeeded in study. In fact, his knowledge was so broad that he had surpassed his teacher Silabhadra, and became the supreme authority of Indian Mahayana. He played an important role in Indian Mahayana Buddhism and its continuous advancement.

Xuan Zang was in a foreign country, but his heart was in the motherland. Although the Indian king and scholars entreated him to stay repeatedly, he still resolutely returned to the east, and returned to Chang'an in the first month of the nineteenth year of Zhenguan (AD 645). According to historical record, it took Xuanzang 17 years to fetch the scriptures from the west, and he passed 110 countries and regions, traveled 50,000 li, and brought back 520 suitcases of Mahayana and Hinayana scriptures and 657 nooks. When Xuanzang met with Emperor Taizong of Tang after he returned home, he declined Taizong's suggestion of resuming secular life and entering politics, but was willing to write *Records on the Western Regions of the Great Tang Empire*[3] at the request of Taizong. Xuanzang put his interest and energy mainly into translation of Buddhist classics after he returned home. With the strong support of the court, Xuanzang systematically conducted translation, and after 19 years of hard work, a large number of scriptures and treatises on Yogacara, Abhidhamma, and Prajna were translated, such as 200 volumes of *Abhidharmamahavibhasasastra* of Hinayana, 100 volumes of *Yogacara-bhumi-sastra*, which epitomized Yogacara, and 600 volumes of *Mahaprajnaparamitasutra*, the fundamental classic of Madhyamika. Because Xuanzang translated the Buddhist theories inherited by Nalanda Temple in its most popular period, and the translation was of high quality, it was called a "new translation" by future generations, and it actually opened up a new era in the history of Chinese classical translation.

There was a galaxy of talents among Xuanzang's disciples. The most famous ones included Shen Fang, Jia Shang, Puguang, and Kuiji, known as "four magical disciples of Xuanzang". But only Kuiji, who was talented, really inherited *dharmalaksana*, directly mastered Xuanzang's teaching, and could carry it forward. Kuiji was the nephew of Yuchi Jingde, the founding general of Tang, and he became Xuanzang's disciple at the age of 17. He wrote a lot, with the title of "author to a hundred notes and commentaries". *The Commentaries on Vijnanamatrasiddhi Sastra* written by Kuiji was worshiped as a criterion by later scholars of Vijnaptimatrata. Because Kuiji wrote a lot of elucidation of scriptures and treatises, and strongly promoted the establishment of the Consciousness-Only School, it could also be said, in fact, that the scale of the Consciousness-Only School was established and strengthened by him.

The Consciousness-Only School inherited Mahayana of India – namely, inheriting from Asaga and Vasubandhu to the doctrine of Yogacara of Dharmapala, Silabhadra, and Bandhuprabha. The basic theory of it was to argue that there was no outside world and there was eternal knowledge in logical ways – namely, the doctrine of "vijnapti-matrata an-artha"; it attached great importance to "transformation of the basis" – namely, changing the idea, transforming from confusion in consciousness to the purpose of practice; it advocated five castes, and believed that sentient beings with no self-nature could never become a Buddha, which changed the view that "all beings had Buddhist nature" in the past. This sect was the direct successor of the doctrine of Indian Asaga and Vasubandhu. But the theory of this sect was too cumbersome and did not meet the trend, so it was inherited by two generations after Kuiji, Hui Zhao and Zhi Zhou, and declined after only three generations.

7 The Vinaya School

The Vinaya School was a sect based on *Dharmaguptavinaya* of Hinayana Dharmagupta with the interpretation of Mahayana doctrine. Because it especially preached *Dharmaguptavinaya* in Buddhist precepts, it was also known as the "Dharmaguptavinaya School". It was also called the "Nanshan School" and "Nanshan Vinaya School" for the founder Dao Xuan lived in Zhongnanshan, Shaanxi, founded the precept platform, and developed the Chinese Buddhist system.

Since the Eastern Jin Dynasty, the four precepts of Indian Hinayana were widely circulated in our country. In the Southern and Northern Dynasties, as the state's management of the Buddhist monks was increasingly strict, masters teaching precepts in Buddhism appeared. There were Sarvastivadavinaya masters in the Southern Dynasties and *Dharmaguptavinaya* masters in the Northern Dynasty. To the Tang Dynasty when the country was reunified, unified disciplines were also needed inside Buddhism to strengthen its own organization; in this case, Dao Xuan created the Vinaya School.

Dao Xuan (596–667) was called the "Nanshan precept master". His original surname was Qian, from Wuxing (now Huzhou, Zhejiang), and it was also said that he was from Dantu (now in Jiangsu). He became a monk at the age of 10, and he followed Zhishou to take complete precepts at the age of 20. Dao Xuan studied widely, and focused on studying precepts. He undertook the system of the Northern Dynasties from Huiguang to Zhi Shou, and specialized in carrying forward *Dharmaguptavinaya*. At the same time, for he participated in the translation site of Xuanzang and was deeply affected by the Consciousness-Only School, he also explained *Dharmaguptavinaya* with Mahayana doctrine. He wrote books on precepts, such as *Dharmaguptavinaya Exegesis*, *Dharmaguptavinaya Deletion and Supplement*, and *Dharmaguptavinaya Deletion and Supplement Collection*. His doctrine was mainly the theory of consciousness and precept substance. The so-called precept substance referred to the substance received by the disciple in the heart when being initiated into monkhood from the master – namely, an evil-proof function psychologically composed in the way of granting and receiving. Dao Xuan declared that *Dharmaguptavinaya* was connected to Mahayana, and took the seed hidden in "Alayavijnana" as the precept substance. He divided precepts into Varitta and Caritta, and provided 250 precepts of Buddhist monks and 384 precepts of Buddhist nuns; "Varitta" meant "not doing evil", and "Caritta" meant "doing good", including being initiated into monkhood or nunhood and teaching precepts and provisions of life. He said that *Dharmaguptavinaya* belonged to Hinayana in form, but belonged to Mahayana in content. Dao Xuan had thousands of disciples, and his disciple's disciple Dao An obtained the handwriting of Emperor Zhongzong of Tang, so as to make the area between Changjiang and Huaihe which believed in *Sarvastivadavinaya* change to believing in Nanshan *Dharmaguptavinaya*, so that the national Buddhist precepts tended to be unified.

However, due to different understandings and uses of *Dharmaguptavinaya*, contemporaries of Dao Xuan included the Xiangbu School of Fa Li (569–635) in Riguang Temple in Yangzhou, and the Dongta School of Dongta Huaisu (625–689) in West Taiyuan Temple in Chang'an. They formed their own factions, debated for a long time, and could not be unified. In the thirteenth year of Dali in the Tang Dynasty (AD 778) Emperor Daizong ordered the scholar representatives of the three factions to assemble to discuss the unity of the popular precepts. Although the country came forward to reconcile the contrary opinions, it was not effective. However, due to the prevalence of the Nanshan School, the other two factions could not recover. In China's Buddhism, as a result of the prevalence of Dao Xuan's faction, the monks still paid attention to following Varitta and Caritta of Sthaviravada when studying Mahayana doctrines.

8 Fa Zang and the Huayan School

The Huayan School was named because it worshiped *Avatamsaka Sutra* as the highest Buddhist code of Buddha, and unified all doctrines with it – that is, it set up the faction according to *Avatamsaka Sutra*. Besides, it was also known as the "Xianshou School" for Empress Wu Zetian granted the title "Xianshou" to its founder, Fa Zang, who was called "Master Xianshou" by descendants. It was also known as the "Dharmadhatu School" for it gave play to the purpose of "Dharmadhatu causation".

The heritage system of the Huayan School's theories was generally regarded as Du Shun (Fa Shun) – Zhi Yan – Fa Zang – Chengguan – Zong Mi. Zhiyan (602–668) wrote *Avatamsaka Sutra Sou Xuan Ji*, *Hua Yan Yi Cheng Shi Xuan Men*, and *Hua Yan Kong Mu Zhang* to elucidate the scriptures of "Hua Yan". The ancestral home of Fa Zang (643–712) was Kangju in the Western Regions, and he was born in Chang'an. He first learned *Avatamsaka Sutra* from Zhiyan, and won his deep appreciation. Later, he took part in the new translation of 80 volumes of *Avatamsaka Sutra*, and had a more thorough understanding of the scriptures. Then he explained the new *Avatamsaka Sutra* to Empress Wu Zetian; it was said when he explained "Hua Zang Shi Jie Pin", "the ground shook", and Empress Wu Zetian especially awarded him. Later he was invited to preach in the Palace of Eternal Life, where he took the golden lions in front of the palace as a metaphor, and made Empress Wu Zetian suddenly understand, which was later sorted out in *Hua Yan-Golden Lion Chapter*. To teach those who did not know that "endless Dharmadhatu had layers of net" and integrate those who did not hamper argumentation, he took ten mirrors, and arranged them in all locations against each other, and in the middle he placed a Buddha statue, and lit a light to enlighten each other. Fa Zang also ordained Bodhisattva precepts for Emperor Ruizong of Tang and became his teacher. Emperor Zhongzong awarded him with the third official rank and five grand Huayan Temples. He wrote hundreds of volumes of books, the main among which were books about "Avatamsaka Sutra", such as *Avatamsaka Sutra Tan Xuan Ji* and *Avatamsaka Sutra Yi Cheng Jiao Yi Fen Qi Zhang*, with his own new understanding.

Based on *Avatamsaka Sutra*, Fa Zang also absorbed some of the theories in Xuanzang's new translation, completed reconciliation, enriched the views, and established the sect. He preached the theory of "dharmadhātu causation", and believed that the ontology was the basis and origin of the phenomenon, and all the phenomena came from the ontology. This shows that it was harmonious between all phenomena and the ontology, between phenomenon and phenomenon. The doctrines of the various Buddhist sects were also harmonious. "Harmony" was the method to observe the universe and life, and also the highest level of understanding.

The theory of Fa Zang was once later modified by his chief disciple Hui Yuan, so it was not widely disseminated. But soon Chengguan (737–838/738–838) took the restoration of Huayan orthodoxy as his own responsibility, criticized Hui Yuan's theory of reconciling and Pratityasamutpada, and gave play to the teachings of Fa Zang again. Later, Zong Mi (780–841) blended the thoughts of Zen and the Huayan School, promoted the theory of consensus of Zen and Buddhism, and established the new development track of the Huayan School. After the death of Mizong, destruction of Buddhism in Huichang during the reign of Emperor Wuzong occurred, which was a heavy blow to the Huayan School, and the monasteries were destroyed, the scriptures and treatises were lost, and the sect declined.

9 Esoteric Buddhism

Esoteric Buddhism was also known as "Mi Jiao", "Mi Mi Jiao", "Mantrayana", "Vajrayana", and so on. It was named because it claimed that it was taught the secret doctrine by Vairocana, and was the real word and teaching, with no abhiseca or imparting, and arbitrary learning and display of others were not allowed. Esoteric Buddhism was a sect characterized by using spells (Dharani) as a convenience. Esoteric Buddhism was originally a product combining part of factions of Mahayana Buddhism, Brahmanism, and Hinduism in India since the seventh century; because of the developed Sino-Indian traffic at that time, it was soon introduced into our country. In the fourth year of Kaiyuan during the reign of Emperor Xuanzong of Tang (AD 716), Subhakarasimha brought *Mahavairocanasutra* of Indian Esoteric Buddhism, and translated with his disciple Yi Xing; in the eighth year of Kaiyuan (AD 720), Vajrabodhi and his disciple Amognarajra introduced *Vajrasekharasutra*, which was translated by Amognarajra, and they started to spread and study Indian Esoteric Buddhism. Later, Subhakarasimha and Vajrabodhi, who studied these two doctrines, taught each other to enrich and combine, and founded Esoteric Buddhism in China.

Esoteric Buddhism believed that all things in the world, Buddha, and all beings were created by ground, water, fire, wind, air (gap), and knowledge (consciousness). The former "five elements" were "Rupadharma", belonging to "Garbhadhatu". Consciousness was citta-dharma, belonging to Vajradhatu, which was different from Garbhadhatu, and in terms of performance of "rational virtue", any dharma could not destroy it, but it could destroy all troubles, which was how it was named. Rupadharma was integrated with citta-dharma, and Vajradhatu was integrated with Garbhadhatu. The two radiated all things in the universe, but were also in the hearts of all beings, so there was no fundamental difference between the Buddha and all living beings. If all beings could reach correspondence among the body, mouth, and meaning, they could make their own body, mouth, and meaning clean, and correspond to the Buddha's body, mouth, and meaning, so that they could "become a Buddha". Esoteric Buddhism was also known as "Yogacara Esoteric Buddhism" for it practiced correspondence of three tantras (Yogacara). The *sadhana drubtab* of this sect was extremely complex, which required secret teaching of the mentor ("Acarya"). Because it had the most intense mysterious color, and was particularly liked by the rulers of the Tang Dynasty at that time, it was the fashion for the nobility to believe in Esoteric Buddhism. However, after Amognarajra, it declined.

10 The Pure Land School

The Pure Land School was so named for it especially practiced the method to Amitabha Pure Land in the afterlife. It was created by Shan Dao in the Tang Dynasty. Buddhist scholars since the Song Dynasty, according to unreliable information and legend, found that Huiyuan in Mount Lu in the Eastern Jin Dynasty once invited 18 people and set up "White Lotus Society", wishing for the West Pure Land in afterlife, and worshiping Hui Yuan as the ancestor of the Pure Land School. Therefore, this sect was also known as the "Louts School". The establishment of the Pure Land School was the result of development of the faith in Amitabha, and its establishing clue should be traced back to Tanluan (477–543) in the Northern Wei Dynasty. Tan Luan promoted *dharma-paryaya* of Pure Land in Xuanzhong Temple, Shanxi. He wrote books like *Wang Sheng Lun Zhu*, and created two doctrines of "duskara-carya" and "Sahaji-yana" in accordance with *Dasabhumika-vibhasa-sastra* of Nagarjuna. He claimed that the world was feculent, and it was difficult to rely on "self-power" to get relief without the help of Buddha. The doctrine that got relief with "self-power" was "duskara-carya", and the doctrine that wished for pure land in the afterlife by virtue of the Buddha's desire (others' power) was "Sahaji-yana". Tan Luan believed that people could go to the pure land in afterlife after they died if they devotionally chanted "Nama Amitabha". In the early Tang Dynasty, Dao Chuo (562–645) was inspired after seeing the tablet inscription that recorded the deeds of Tan Luan in Xuanzhong Temple, and then he devotionally studied dharma-paryaya of Pure Land, chanted "Nama Amitabha" every day, and vigorously promoted that dharma-paryaya of Pure Land that went to the Western Paradise by virtue of Amitabha Buddha was the only way out. His disciple Shan Dao (613–681) later preached in Guangming Temple in Chang'an, wrote *The Commentaries on The Amitayurdhyana Sutra* and

Wang Sheng Zan and so on, elaborated the theoretical basis of the sect, composed complete rites and rules of the Pure Land School, and formally established the Pure Land School. According to historical record, at that time, there were innumerable people that followed Shan Dao; some chanted *Amitabha* for 100,000–500,000 times, and chanted the name of Buddha 10,000 times to 100,000 times every day, and the faith in Pure Land was greatly developed.

The basis of the Pure Land School was three scriptures and one treatise – namely, *Aparimitayur-sutra, Amitayurdhyanasutra, Amitabha,* and *Wang Sheng Lun* of Vasubandhu. The theory of this sect took practitioners' chanting of the name of Buddha as the internal cause, and Amitabha's desire as the external cause; both internal and external corresponded to each other, to the Western Paradise. This sect stressed that people did not necessarily have to understand Buddhist scriptures or sit quietly and study; as long as their faith was strong and they chanted the name of Buddha, they could enter the Buddha field. There were originally three kinds of dharma-paryaya to chant the name of Buddha: the first was to chant the name of Buddha; the second was to view and think – namely, to view 32 kinds of laksana of Buddha and 80 kinds of good; the third was Dharmmadhatu. Master Huiyuan in Mount Lu promoted the latter two kinds of dharma-paryaya to chant the name of Buddha, Tan Luan integrated the three kinds of dharma-paryaya to chant the name of Buddha, and later to Dao Chuo and Shan Dao, it turned to focusing only on chanting the name of Buddha.

Before the creation of the Pure Land School, Buddhist sects in the Sui and Tang Dynasties, because the idealism theory was esoteric, or because the rituals were extremely complicated, were more popular among the court and the upper intellectuals, and the theories of the Pure Land School were simple; the dharma-paryaya was easy, which was more suitable to be spread among people, so it was generally popular with the support of the ruling class.

11 Hui Neng and Zen

Zen was so named because it advocated generalizing all practice of Buddhism with meditation. It was also known as the "Buddha heart School" for it claimed that it "passed on Buddha heart", and took the enlightenment of the original Buddhist nature of the so-called all-being as the main purpose. In the Tang Dynasty, Sehnxiu in the north advocated gradual enlightenment, and Hui Neng in the south advocated sudden enlightenment, so different factions formed, with the names of "northern and southern sects", "Northern and Southern Zen". Later, the southern sect created by Hui Neng replaced the northern sect created by Shenxiu and became the mainstream of China's Zen. The southern sect did not pass on Cidi Zen, practiced since ancient times, but Zushi Zen, which was directed at the sudden practice and enlightenment of nature. Later, Southern Zen was divided into two factions, Nanyue Huaijiang, and Qingyuan Xingsi. In the late Tang Dynasty and the Five Dynasties, Weiyang and Linji separated from the faction of Nanyue, and Caodong, Yunmen, and Fayan separated from the faction of Qingyuan, which were collectively known as the five schools of Zen, or the five sects.

According to legend, during the reign of Emperor Wu of Liang in the Southern Dynasties, Bodhidharma came to Jinling from southern India to see Emperor Wu. Because the views of the two were different, they crossed the river to go north, and taught Zen in the Northern Wei Dynasty, with the idea that all things in the world were created by heart and promoted in *Lankavatarasutra* as proof. Dharma disseminated the dharma (and Kasaya) to Huike, and Huike passed on to Seng Can. The three were later worshiped as the first ancestor, second ancestor, and third ancestor by Zen, known as the faction of "Lanka Shi". In the early Tang Dynasty, Daxin inherited the legacy of Seng Can, but he also referred to dharma-paryaya of Prajna in addition to Lanka Zen, and was known as the fourth ancestor. Daoxin had a disciple called Farong, who turned to the faction of Niutou Zen because of living in Niutou Mountain in Jinling, and the inheritance ended after several generations. Daoxin's direct disciple was the fifth ancestor Hongren (601–674). He disseminated dharma in Fengmao Mountain for more than 40 years, often persuaded monks to study *The Diamond Sutra*, and promoted that all things in the world were unreal, that people should not stick to the real world. His argument was known as "Dongshan dharma-paryaya". Hongren had up to 700 disciples, among whom the famous ones included Shenxiu and Hui Neng, who respectively created factions of "North Gradual" and "South Sudden" later. Shenxiu (about 606–706) was originally *sthavira* under Hongren, with the titles of master in two cities, and national master of three emperors. His disciples Puji and Yifu imparted Zen in Chang'an. The northern sect stressed "cleanness", advocated gradual practice, and required meditation and a restrained heart. It prevailed once.

Hui Neng (638–713) was known as the sixth ancestor of Zen. His original surname was Lu, from Fanyang, Hebei (now south Beijing), and his father was relegated to Xinzhou, Lingnan (now Xinxing County, Guangdong). A few years after Hui Neng was born in Xinzhou, his father died. His family was poor, and he had to sell firewood to support his old mother. According to legend, one day he heard someone chanting *The Diamond Sutra* in the market, and got enlightened, so he went to Fengmao Mountain to see Hongren. Hongren ordered him to pound rice. Eight months later, Hongren gathered his disciples and asked each of them to write a verse in order to pass on his legacy according to their understanding of Zen. Sthavira Shenxiu wrote in his verse, "The body is a bodhi tree, the heart is like the mirror stand, always wipe to prevent dust". It was regarded as a masterpiece, and spread over the whole temple. Hui Neng also asked others to write a verse after he heard it: "Bodhi was no tree, mirror had no stand, the Buddhist nature was clean originally,[4] and where is dust!" Hongren thought his insight was thorough, secretly passed on his legacy to him at night, and told him to quickly go south and live in seclusion, and come out when the time was right. So Hui Neng went to Caoxi, Guangdong (now southeast of Qujiang County), and lived in seclusion in the areas in Huaiji for 15 years before he went south to Faxing Temple in Guangzhou (now Guangxiao Temple). According to legend, at that time, there were two monks debating wind and flag. One said that the wind was moving, while the other said that the flag was moving, and they kept debating. Hui Neng cut in: it was not the wind that moved, nor was it the flag, but the heart. The monks were very surprised.

The abbot of the monastery, Master Zongyin, invited him to the top seat and asked Dharma, to which Hui Neng answered fluently. Hui Neng took the opportunity to show the mantle and alms bowl, and then taught Zen to the monks at his invitation. Soon, Hui Neng returned to Baolin Temple (now Nanhua Temple) in Caoxi. He was also invited to preach to the public in Dafan Temple in Shaozhou, and then his disciple Fahai recorded it as *Altar Sutra*. The main idea of this sutra was to pay attention to the clean nature, and emphasize self-realization. It believed that people were all born with the nature (Buddhist nature), and they could become a Buddha if they thoroughly saw this nature. That was to promote making a direct attack on a subject, seeking enlightenment, suddenly seeing the nature, and becoming a Buddha. Hui Neng promoted the dharma-paryaya of sudden enlightenment, and also combined with secular beliefs and worshiped *The Diamond Sutra* to get rid of the tedious ideological restraints. But he did not specialize in Zen meditation, and believed that people could experience the realm of Zen while walking, living, sitting, and lying in all the time. This was contrary to the gradual enlightenment advocated by *Lankavatarasutra* in which Shenxiu believed, thus forming a confrontation between the northern and southern sects. Zen of Hui Neng's faction advocated not writing text, not spreading doctrine outside the sect, not focusing on Zen meditation, and emphasizing sudden enlightenment, not only different from the previous Zen including Shenxiu but also different from Indian Buddhism and other schools in China, which was an unprecedented great change in the world history of Buddhism, especially in the Chinese history of Buddhism.

Hui Neng had many disciples, among whom the most famous ones included Huairang, Xingsi, and Shenhui. Later Shenhui went north to Henan to promote Hui Neng's Zen, and held a meeting in Dayun Temple in Huatai (now Huaxian, Henan) to discuss the inheritance of Dharma's sect, assess the north to the south, strive for orthodoxy, assert that Shenxiu and his disciple Puji had not get Hongren's legacy and were not orthodox, and criticize Northern Zen as "declining", which resulted in the impression that Hui Neng was the direct successor of Dharma, a great increase in the power of Southern Zen, and the gradual decline of Northern Zen. But Shenhui's sect (later the Heze School) did not flourish. Huairang's Nanyue School and Xingsi's Qingyuan School were widely spread in the late Tang Dynasty.

Huairang (677–744) learned after Hui Neng for 15 years after he became a monk in childhood, and later he went to Nanyue to disseminate the dharma. His most famous disciple was Daoyi (709–788). The original surname of Daoyi was Ma, and he was later known as Master Ma. He became a monk at a young age, and later built a temple in Nanyue and lived there, where he sat in meditation always. It was recorded in Volume 5 of *Transmission of the Lamp* that Huairang asked, "What does Dade[5] sit in meditation for?" Daoyi answered, "to become a Buddha". Huairang picked up a brick and ground on the stone in front of Daoyi Temple. Daoyi asked, "Why are you grinding the brick?" Huairang answered, "to grind into a mirror". Daoyi asked in surprise, "How can you grind a brick into a mirror?" Huairang asked in reply, "If a brick cannot be ground into a mirror, how can one sit in meditation to become a Buddha?" Daoyi was rather amazed and asked Huairang for advice, and he learned the essential later. Later he went to areas in Fujian and Jiangxi to establish temples and gather disciples to preach; with many disciples, Zen greatly flourished at that time. Master Ma's famous disciple Huaihai (720–814) later created a Zen temple in Baizhang Mountain in Hongzhou (now west of Fengxin County, Jiangxi), developed a "Zen school rules", and provided a priesthood, systems, and rituals in a Zen monastery, which became the model of "temple rules" later. Master Ma and many disciples, among whom was Lingyou (771–851), lived in Weishan, Tanzhou (now Ningxiang County, Hunan Province), long after inheriting Dharma, where he carried forward the doctrine for many years. Lingyou's disciple Huiji (814–890) later inherited from his teacher in Yangshan, Yuanzhou (now Yichun, Jiangxi Province), setting up a new faction. They advocated that all beings and all things had a Buddhist nature, and if people had a clear heart to see the nature, they could become a Buddha. "Not touch a dust, not abandon a dharma. Handle things with one principle, like a Buddha" (Volume 9 of *Transmission of the Lamp*); this was known as the "Weiyang School". Another disciple of Huaihai, Xi Yun (?–855) lived in Huangboshan in Gaoan (now Yifeng County, Jiangxi Province), whose disciple Yi Xuan (?–867) later built Linji Temple by the Hutuo River in Zhenzhou (now Zhengding County, Hebei Province), setting up a new large sect, known as the "Linji School". This sect paid attention to face-to-face questions and answers, preached according to different objects, especially used sticks and shouting, and did not give a direct answer to questions, but hinted and inspired the questioner with a stick or a shout, to make learners "realize" with rapid means or aphorisms, and the keen words[6] were very sharp. Its "School style" was characterized by "going out of the original style" (Volume 2 of *Ren Tian Yan Mu*). It was the most popular since the Middle Tang Dynasty.

Xingsi (?–740) was from Luling, Jizhou (now Ji'an County, Jiangxi Province). He learned Dharma from Hui Neng, then went back to Ji'an, and lived in Jingju Temple in Qingyuan Mountain to carry forward Dharma. Another disciple of Hui Neng, Xiqian (700–790), after the death of Hui Neng, came to Qingyuan to follow Xingsi, and went to the South Temple in Nanyue after learning Dharma, where he built a temple on the big stone in the east of the temple, called "stone monk" by people then. At that time, Xiqian and Daoyi were respectively the central figure of Zen in Jiangxi and Hu'nan, collectively known as two masters. Xi Qian handed down to Weiyan, Weiyan handed down to Tansheng, and Tansheng handed down to Liangjia (807–869), who lived in Dongshan, Junzhou (now Yifeng, Jiangxi), to spread Dharma. His disciple Benji (840–901) lived in Caoshan (now Yihuang, Jiangxi) to carry forward Dharma after learning it. Liangjia and Benji advocated new doctrines and promoted the ideas that the true meaning of Dharma was not opposed to things in the world; "family tradition was fine, words and deeds corresponded, benefit things" (Volume 3 of *Ren Tian Yan Mu*), known as the "Caodong School". Xiqian also preached, and then handed down to Chongxin, Xuanjian, and Yicun. Yicun's disciple Wenyan (?–949) lived in Guangtai Temple in Yunmenshan, Shaozhou (now north of Ruyuan County, Guangdong), to carry forward Dharma, and believed that the Buddhist nature existed in everything generally, the truth could not be said, and students should be randomly taught. The sect style was "lonely and pagodaing, difficult to integrate" (Volume 2 of *Ren Tian Yan Mu*), known as the

"Yunmen School". Another sect of Yicun was handed down to Guichen by Shibei, and Guichen handed down to Wenyi. Wenyi (885–958) expounded and propagated Zen style that "applies medicine to diseases, tailor according to stature" (Volume 4 of *Ren Tian Yan Mu*) in Qingliang Temple in Jinling (now Nanjing), gathering a lot of learners. After the death of Wenyi, Li Jing, emperor of the Southern Tang Dynasty, granted him the title of "Great Dharma-Eye Zen Master", and since then the sect created by him was called the "Dharma-Eye School".

Combined with the traditional argument, the genealogy of Zen Buddhism can be summarized as shown in Figure 2.1.[7]

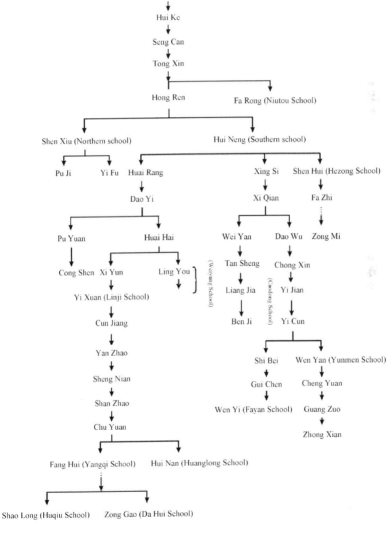

Figure 2.1 Genealogy

In the Tang Dynasty, Zen had a spirit of innovation, which advocated that no confusion led to no understanding, little confusion led to little understanding, and great confusion led to great understanding. Zen also guided in the mountainous areas, promoting cutting firewood and drawing water, developing according to environment. Mountain people were plain, and thus easy to be conquered by Zen, which was able to widely circulate among the people, and gradually became the mainstream of Buddhism since the Middle Tang Dynasty.

Buddhism continued to decline since the Five Dynasties

Since the Five Dynasties, Buddhism was on the decline, and began to fall from its peak. At the same time, because of the different Buddhist policies in various dynasties, the rise and fall of Buddhism in various regions were not the same, and the changes of various sects were also not balanced, which led to different characteristics of different Buddhist sects in different times.

1 The basic trend of Buddhism's development since the Five Dynasties

During more than 50 years in the Five Dynasties, the north and the south split. There were a lot of wars in the north, and the society had unrest. In general, the state adopted a policy of strict restrictions on Buddhism. In the second year of Xiande (AD 955), Emperor Shizong of the Later Zhou Dynasty strictly reorganized Buddhism, and implemented elimination. More than half of the Buddhist temples were abandoned and copper Buddha statues were all confiscated to cast money to fill the national treasury, and thus northern Buddhism declined. The situation in the south was different; the states were at peace, the society was stable, and the court enthusiastically protected Buddhism, which led to different degrees of development of Zen, the Pure Land School, and the Tiantai School based in the south.

The Song Dynasty, including the Northern Song Dynasty and the Southern Song Dynasty, lasted 320 years. After Emperor Taizu of Song, Zhao Kuangyin ascended the throne, reversed the policy of Later Zhou, and took measures to protect Buddhism. He once dispatched 157 people including Sramana Xingqin, to India to seek Dharma, broadened the number of monks, and allowed monasteries to hold profitable business like *Changshengku*, mills, and shops, and thus the monastery economy developed. At the same time, its conflict with the government's fiscal revenue grew, leading Emperor Huizong in the late Song Dynasty to forcibly combine Buddhism and Taoism, change Buddhist temples into Taoist temples, and make the names of Buddha, monks, and nuns Taoist, which was a heavy blow to Buddhism. But soon after Buddhism was restored. After the Song Dynasty moved southward, the court adopted the policy of using and restricting Buddhism, so that Buddhism was able to maintain itself; especially Zen and the Pure Land School were popular. The Tiantai School also had certain development, and the Huayan School also revived for a while.

The Liao and Jin Dynasties, which corresponded to the Northern and Southern Song Dynasties, ruled the north of China for about 330 years. Emperors in the Liao Dynasty adopted the policy of protecting Buddhism, and Buddhism reached its peak during the reigns of Shengzong, Xingzong, and Daozong. Engraving scriptures (e.g., the engraved scriptures on rocks in Yunju Temple in Fangshan, Beijing), building pagodas, and cutting grottoes came into fashion for a while. In the Liao Dynasty, the Huayan School, centered on Wutai Mountain, was the most developed. The royal family in the Jin Dynasty also worshiped and supported Buddhism, so Buddhism was also quite developed, among which the most popular was Zen. However, after Zhangzong, the court over-issued empty identification cards of monks[8] in order to raise military fees, which promoted the proliferation, corruption, and increasing decline of Buddhism.

During the 100 years of the Yuan Dynasty, Kublai Khan believed in Lamaism at the beginning, worshiped famous Tibetan monks as the emperor teacher, and provided that each emperor had to be firstly initiated into monkhood before ascending the throne. As a result of strong support for Buddhism of the dynasty, the monastic economy developed abnormally, owning a large amount of land and operating industrial and commercial businesses. At that time, quite a lot pawnshops, restaurants, mills, fisheries, warehouses, hotels, and shops were run by the monasteries. In addition to Lamaism in the Yuan Dynasty, Zen was also circulating. Besides, in addition to the traditional sects, there were the Baiyun School and White Lotus School in regions south of the Yangtze River. The Baiyun School was named for the founder, Qingjue (1043–1121), who at the end of the Northern Song Dynasty lived in Baiyun Temple in Hangzhou. This sect worshiped *Avatamsaka Sutra* as the highest doctrine, excluded Zen, advocated conformity among Confucianism, Buddhism, and Taoism, and paid attention to loyalty, filial piety, and beneficence. Believers were vegetarian, known as Taoists "eating vegetables", and commonly known as the "Baiyun Diet". The "White Lotus School" was founded by Sramana Mao Ziyuan in the early Southern Song Dynasty, who built "Lotus School's Confession Platform" in the west of Qingpu County, Shanghai, calling himself "White Lotus Mentor", persuading people to believe in the Pure Land School's doctrine, and advocating *buddhanusmrti* and vegetarianism, and the believers were known as "White Lotus Cai Ren". The founders of these two sects were banished to remote areas for they were believed to "spread wizardry" and "spread fallacies to deceive people". In the Yuan Dynasty, the White Lotus School also absorbed other religious ideas, mixed with the Maitreya faith, evolved into the White Lotus Society, and become a secret religion among the people. The peasant uprising at the end of the Yuan Dynasty once used it. Until the Ming and Qing Dynasties, both sects were prohibited.

The Ming Dynasty lasted 276 years. The founding emperor, Ming Taizu, was once a monk; in view of the historical fact that farmers used secret religions to rise up, he especially reorganized Buddhism, and limited the development of it. At this time, there was a fashion for lay Buddhists at home to study Buddhism, and Song Lian, Li Zhi, Yuan Hongdao, Qu Ruji, Jiaohong, Tu Long, and so forth had all written Buddhist works, which had a certain impact on the revival of Buddhism.

Qing Dynasty lasted 268 years. The Qing Dynasty inherited the Buddhist policy of the Ming Dynasty; differently it also attached importance to Lamaism. There were a lot of Ming loyalists who became monks, such as Fang Yizhi and Zhu Da. The official and private business of engraving scripture was quite prosperous in the Qing Dynasty. For example, lay Buddhist Yang Wenhui (1837–1911) founded the Jinling scripture engraving site in Nanjing, which played an important role in the revival of Buddhist culture in the late Qing Dynasty. In the thirty-third year of Guangxu's reign (1907), he also founded a Buddhist school – Qi Huan Vihara, in which Ouyang Jian and Taixu were disciples. Yang Wenhui believed in the Pure Land School and Huayan School, and in his later years, he deeply explored dharma-laksana, which was later expounded and propagated by his disciple Ouyang Jian, having a certain impact on the emergence of Buddhism in the Republic of China.

2 The historical evolution of Buddhist sects since the Five Dynasties

Since the Five Dynasties, among the Buddhist sects, it was mainly Zen that was popular, followed by the Pure Land School, and then the Tiantai School and Huayan School. In the long period thereafter, there was a trend of integration of the sects; especially Zen and the Pure Land School were combined, and Zen and the Pure Land School were combined with other sects respectively, such as "Tiantai Zen", "Huayan Zen", and "Nianfo Zen".

(I) Zen

It has already been mentioned that the base of Hui Neng Zen was the southern mountainous area with superior geographical conditions, so it still greatly developed in the Five Dynasties. The Yunmen School and Fayan School separated from Qingyuan, popular in the areas of Jiangsu, Zhejiang, Fujian, and Guangdong. Together with the Weiyang School, Linji School, and Caodong School, five sects of Zen were completely established. In the Song Dynasty, Zen was still the most popular sect of Buddhism. But in the early Song Dynasty, the Weiyang School was not spread any more, and the Caodong School and Fayan School were also flagging; what prevailed all over were the Linji School and Yunmen School. During the Northern Song Dynasty, Huinan (1002–1069) and Fanghui (992–1049), disciples of Chuyuan of the Linji School, respectively founded the Huanglong School and Yangqi School, collectively known as seven sects with the Linji School and others. The Huanglong School was named because Huinan lived in Huanglongshan, Longxing Prefecture (now Nanchang, Jiangxi). The Yangqi School was named because Fanghui lived in Puming Temple in Yangqishan, Yuanzhou (now Yichun, Jiangxi). The two sects prevailed in the south. Until the Southern Song Dynasty, the Huanglong School tended to decline, while the Yangqi School became the orthodox of Linji. Dahui Zonggao of the Yangqi School advocated Kanhua Zen, which meant taking some of the words in the statements ("public record") of ancestors to judge the right and wrong as "head phrase" (i.e., topic) to study, which had a very far-reaching impact. Chongxian of the Yunmen School wrote *A Hundred Classic Extolments*, which greatly boosted the sect. Besides, Qisong of the Yunmen School reversed the common idea of consistency between Zen and Buddhism at that time, and re-stressed that Zen was outside Buddhism. At the same time, he also wrote *Fu Jiao Pian*, trying to reconcile the contradictions between Confucianism and Buddhism. The Yunmen School tended to decline until the Southern Song Dynasty. In addition, although Zhengjue of the Caodong School had a deep friendship with Zonggao, he promoted Mozhao Zen, advocating sitting quietly and thinking of the mind, and opposed Kanhua Zen, which caused mutual blame with Zonggao. Since then, although the Linji School was popular and the Caodong School was also popular, in general, Zen became increasingly stagnant in doctrine and thinking.

(II)   The Pure Land School

Since the Song Dynasty, the Tiantai School and other Buddhist sects had been linked to faith in the Pure Land School and advocated the practice of buddha-nusmrti, and all sects had the doctrine of pure land, while the pure faith in Pure Land was rare. In this way, on the one hand, the popularity of Pure Land belief was promoted; on the other hand, the typical Pure Land School also lost its independent features for it was related to other sects. This was also the basic characteristic of the Pure Land School after the Song Dynasty.

(III)   The Tiantai School

After the destruction of Buddhism in Huichang in the Tang Dynasty, classics of the Tiantai School were all lost. During the Five Dynasties, King WuYue, Qian Hongchu, sent envoys to visit Korea for religious scripts of the Tiantai School, and got most of the books of Zhiyi and some of the other commentaries. Thus, with abundant books of the sect, it was revived in the Jiangsu and Zhejiang areas. In the Song Dynasty, Zhili, Qingzhao, and Zhiyuan debated the authenticity of the detailed version of Zhiyi's *Jin Guang Ming Xuan Yi*, and divided into two factions of Shanjia and Shanwai. Zhili believed that the detailed version of *Xuan Yi* was true, and held the "fake-mind theory" in terms of dharma-paryaya of thinking of mind – that is, to take fake mind as the object of thinking of mind. Qingzhao and Zhiyuan believed that the concise version of *Xuan Yi* was true, and by Fahua, the only knowledge of, advocated "true-mind theory" with the impact of the theories of the Fahua School and Consciousness-Only School – that is, to take the nature as the observing object. The two sides debated for seven years and failed to be unified. The disciples of Zhili, Fanzhen, Shangxian, and Benru were known as the three masters of Siming, carrying forward the doctrine of Zhili, calling themselves "Shanjia", and depreciated Qing Zhao, Zhiyuan, and others as "Shanwai". Later, the influence of Shanjia surpassed Shanwai, and prevailed in the Southern Song Dynasty on behalf of the Tiantai School. In the Ming Dynasty, Zhixu was the last master of the Tiantai School.

(IV) The Huayan School

After the destruction of Buddhism in Huichang in the late Tang Dynasty, the Huayan School had been relatively quiet. To the beginning of the Song Dynasty, Changshuizi inherited the idea of consistency between Buddhism and Zen of Zongmi's sect in the Tang Dynasty and revived Huayan School. His disciples included Jingyuan and others. Later, the Korean prince Uich'on came to China and learned after Jingyuan, and he greatly helped the revival of the Huayan School for he brought a large number of commentaries of people of the Huayan School in the Tang Dynasty on *Avatamsaka Sutra*. In the Southern Song Dynasty, the Huayan School was also active. After the Song Dynasty, some Buddhist scholars still paid attention to some of the books of the Huayan School, but the spread of this sect was getting weaker.

(V) The Vinaya School

Since the Five Dynasties, the Nanshan Vinaya School had been popular in areas of Jiangsu and Zhejiang, whose center moved to Hangzhou. In the Northern Song Dynasty, Yunkan once wrote *Hui Zheng Ji*, which explained Daoxuan's *Xing Shi Chao*, and later the school that inherited this one was known as the "Huizheng School". The disciple of Yunkan's disciple, Yuanzhao preached with the doctrines of the Tiantai School, and also annotated *Xing Shi Chao*, which was called *Zi Chi Ji*, but he had different interpretations of some of the rules and *Hui Zheng Ji*, so he set up the "Zichi School", which prevailed later, and was inherited for a long time.

The formation and development of Tibetan Buddhism

Tibetan Buddhism is an important branch of Chinese Buddhism. It was named because it was mainly formed, spread, and developed in Tibetan areas, which was a Tibetan-language Buddhism. Tibetan Buddhism is commonly known as Lamaism. "Lama" is a transliteration of Tibetan, meaning "guru", which is an honorific title of the monks. Lamaism was the product of the long-term interaction and fight between Buddhism and the original Bon-Religion in Tibet. Mahayana was spread from India to Tibet and widely circulated, including Exoteric Buddhism and Esoteric Buddhism; Esoteric Buddhism was especially prosperous. Lamaism absorbed some of the deities and ceremonies of Bon-Religion based on the teachings of Buddhism, and formed unique Lamaism, practicing both Exoteric Buddhism and Esoteric Buddhism, with Exoteric Buddhism first and then Esoteric Buddhism. The main sects included Nyingma (Mongolian Lamaism), Sakya (floral religion), Kagyu (white religion), and Gelug (Shamanism).

1 The first and second propagation of Tibetan Buddhism

The historical development of Lamaism in Tibet was usually divided into two periods, of which the first propagation was from the seventh century AD when Buddhism rose in Tibet to the time when Darma (r. AD 836–841) devastated Buddhism.

Since then, Buddhism broke off for more than 100 years. In AD 978, Buddhism began to revive in Tibet, which was the beginning of the second propagation.

The "first propagation" began in the period of Srongtsen Gampo, with the promotion of Trisong Detsen; it reached its peak during the period of Ralpacan, lasting about 200 years. In the sixth century, the Tibetan area had become a slave society. In the seventh century, the leader of Ya'nan Tribe, Srongtsen Gampo, unified the tribes on Qinghai-Tibet Plateau, and established the unified Tubo Dynasty, centered on Lhasa. Srongtsen Gampo's slavery regime implemented the policy of opening up in political, economic, cultural, and other aspects, which created favorable conditions for the introduction of Buddhism. Srongtsen Gampo married Bhrikuti Devi of Nepal and Princess Wencheng of the Tang Dynasty, and took Buddhist icons and classics into Tibet for the first time. Srongtsen Gampo built Moggam Temple and Jokhang Temple for the two princesses, and worshiped Buddha. He also organized the translation of Buddhist scriptures in Tibet. As the royal family worshiped Buddhism, idolatry and theocratic concepts of Buddhism were initially spread in Tibet.

The spread of Buddhism was strongly resisted and opposed by the nobility of Bon-Religion. Bon-Religion was a primitive religion originally practiced by the ancient Tibetans, who believed in animism, worshiped heaven, earth, sun, moon, stars, stone, water, grass, vegetation, animals, and so forth, and paid attention to rites of sacrifice, god dance, and divination; it dominated in the early Tubo Dynasty. After the death of Srongtsen Gampo (AD 650), the development of Buddhism was slow, and later during the reign of Tride Tsuktsen (r. AD 704–755), imperial princes and court ministers who believed in Bon-Religion expelled monks using the excuse of natural disasters, and the development of Buddhism was greatly damaged. After the death of Tride Tsuktsen, his son, Trisong Detsen (r. AD 755–797) succeeded to the throne at a young age. A group of forces that worshiped Bon-Religion and opposed Buddhism took the opportunity to carry out the large-scale extermination of Buddhism. After Trisong Detsen grew up, he eradicated the representatives of anti-Buddhism forces and vigorously promoted Buddhism. He ordered that except for a few prayer methods, all the books of Bon-Religion shall be destroyed and all subjects shall believe in Buddhism. He sent people to Nepal to invite Shantarakshita, the representative of Buddhism at that time, to come to Tibetan to preach. He also sent people to the cradle of Indian Esoteric Buddhism to invite Padma Sambhava and fought against wizards of Bon-Religion with Esoteric Buddhism. Every time Padma Sambhava defeated some wizards of Bon-Religion, it was proclaimed that a certain god of Bon-Religion had surrendered and conferred the title of Dharmapala of Buddhism. The basic rituals of Bon-Religion, such as witchcraft and sacrifice, were also absorbed to promote the content of Buddhism in the form of Bon-Religion. Trisong Detsen also established the first standard monastery in Tibet – Samye Monastery in AD 766 – and began to tonsure the Tibetan monks and establish the sangha system; at the same time, Buddhist books were widely translated, including scriptures and treatises of Exoteric Buddhism and Esoteric Buddhism. At this point, Buddhism had taken shape in Tibet, which overwhelmed Bon-Religion and took the dominant position.

After the death of Trisong Detsen, mu-ne-btsan-po and Sadnalegs succeeded to the throne in succession, and Buddhism continued to develop. To Ralpacan (r. AD 815–836), the royal family's support of Buddhism reached its peak. Monks participated in Tibetan politics, and affairs of state were decided by the top people of Buddhism. The administrative system was also based on Buddhist scriptures. It was also decreed that seven households shall support a monk, and those who treated Buddha, Dharma, and monks disrespectfully shall be heavily punished. Ralpacan's extreme worship of Buddhism caused the dissatisfaction of the forces of Bon-Religion. In AD 836, the aristocracy of Bon-Religion killed Ralpacan while he was drunk, and enthroned Darma. Darma reigned for five years, and greatly devastated Buddhism. Buddhism, especially Exoteric Buddhism, was extremely heavily damaged, and only Esoteric Buddhism continued to be handed down for it was secretly handed down. Darma's destruction of Buddhism marked the end of the "first propagation" of Buddhism.

During Darma's reign, frost, flood, drought, plague, and other natural disasters took place for years. Under the impact of the slave uprising, the Tubo Dynasty fell apart. Later, Darma's descendants each ruled their own regimes in their own territories respectively, and established feudal serfdom. Later, all the feudal lords gradually re-fostered Buddhism to serve their own rule, so that at the end of the tenth century, Buddhism was introduced back to the Tibetan area from the upper route (Ali) and down route (Dokham), and Tibetan Buddhism revived again, entering the stage of "second propagation". Since then, Buddhist forces under the control of different feudal lords gradually formed different sects, whose practice and heritage lineage were different from each other. What formed the earliest was Nyingma, followed by Kadam, Sakya, Kagyu, Zhi byed pa, Spyod-yul-pa, Jonang, and Gelug, with the most profound impact. Some of the most important sects are briefly introduced ahead.

2 Nyingma, Sakya, and Kagyu

(I) Nyingma (Mongolian Lamaism)

During the "first propagation", the Indian monk Padma Sambhava was invited to Tibet to teach mantra, which later formed the sect of Esoteric Buddhism. At that time, there was no sect name. After the formation of other sects of Buddhism in the "second propagation", it was called "Nyingma". "Nyingma" had two meanings, "ancient" and "old". "Ancient" meant that the teachings of this sect were handed down from Padma Sambhava in the eighth century AD, 300 years earlier than the other sects; "old" meant that this sect focused on promoting the old mantra translated in the Tubo period. Nyingma worshiped Padma Sambhava as the founder, and believed in the old mantra, which was different from other sects advocating "new Dharma" at that time. Thus, the monks of this sect wore a red hat, and they were commonly known as "Mongolian Lamaism". Nyingma was characterized by not focusing on precepts and being dedicated to mantra. It saw carrying forward Shastras of the Anuttarayoga Tantra as the way to "relieve" and "become a

Buddha". The development of this sect was dispersive, not very close to powerful local groups. But later in the early Qing Dynasty, with the fifth Dalai Lama's support, it reached its heyday.

(II) Sakya (floral religion)

"Sakya" was a place name – now Sakya County, Shigatse, rear Tibet, and also the name of Lama Temple. "Sakya" means "white soil" in Tibetan, and the temple was named Sakya Temple for it was built on white land. The founder, Kontchok Gyalpo (1034–1102), learned the new mantra from Vbro-mi, and built a temple in Sakya in rear Tibet, calling it "Sakya". It was commonly known as the "floral religion" because red, white, and black stripes symbolizing Manjusri, Avalokitesvara, and Vajra-dhara were painted on the temple walls of this sect. Sakya Temple had been handed over from generation to generation by the family of Kontchok Gyalpo. This sect did not prohibit taking a wife, but forbade contact with women after childbirth. Its teaching emphasized abandoning all "evil acts", penancing, and understanding that neither human body nor the universe was real, so as to get rid of all troubles, really comprehend Dharma, obtain Buddhist wisdom, and achieve the Nirvana realm. This sect reached its heyday in the Yuan Dynasty, when the fifth generation of founder Phagspa (1235–1280) once enlightened Kublai Khan, and was honored as an "imperial teacher". He also created Mongolian, called "Gyalwa Karmapa", and later he was appointed the Dharma King of Tibet and Tibetan king, governing the political and religious powers of Tibet, and officially created the system of "unifying politics and religion" in Tibet. At the end of the Yuan Dynasty, the status of Sakya was replaced by Kagyu, and only the political and religious powers in the Sakya region remained.

(III) Kagyu (white religion)

"Ka" meant oral instruction in Tibetan – namely, the verbal directions of teachers. "Gyu" meant the inheritance of Shastras in Tibetan. It was called "Kagyu" because it paid the most attention to teachers' verbal directions and heritage. Besides, it was also commonly known as the "white religion" because the monks of this sect dressed in white skirts and shirts. It was founded by Marpa (1012–1097) in the eleventh century. He went to India to study Shastras three times, and claimed that he had achieved the realm of "Wan You Yi Wei". Later, his disciple Milarepa inherited from him and then handed down to *dwags-po-lha-rje*. It was integrated with the doctrine of Kadam,[9] and became a very powerful, important sect. The doctrine of this sect was mainly to inherit the doctrine of Mahayana in Indian Buddhism and focus on proving the emptiness of nature with *tsunenori* – namely, to focus "heart" on a realm in practice, and then observe whether the "heart" focused on one realm was inside or outside the body. If one could find that there was nowhere to be found, then he/she could understand the "heart" was not real, but empty, which meant achieving the realm of "unity of emptiness, wisdom and relief". This sect had a large number of branches, and the upper class of Phagmodrupa and Karmapa had been imperially conferred by the Yuan and Ming Dynasties, following Sakya to take charge of the Tibetan regime. Numerous factions led to long-term fighting among them, and resulted in chaos in the Tibetan area. In the thirteenth year of Chongzhen in the Ming Dynasty (AD 1640), Gushri Khan entered Tibet, and took the regimes of front and rear Tibet, so Kagyu lost political power. In the Qing Dynasty, Gelug was in power, while only four branches of Kagyu, Drigung, Zhuba, Karma, *vbrug-pa-bkav-brgyud*, and Dalong still had a certain religious power.

3 Gelug (Shamanism)

"Gelug" meant good rules in Tibetan. It was named because this sect's doctrine was the most perfect. It was also called "new Kadam" because it was established based on Kadam. It was also known as "Gadeng" because the founder, Tsongkhapa, built and lived in Gadeng Temple to carry forward Dharma and preach. Besides, it was also known as the "Ganden sect" for it took Ganden Monastery as its main monastery. The lama of this sect wore a yellow hat, so it was commonly known as "Shamanism". Gelug was one of the largest and most powerful and influential sects in Tibetan Lamaism.

At the beginning of the fifteenth century, Tsongkhapa (1357–1419) founded Gelug after reforming the other sects based on the teachings of Kadam. Tsongkhapa was formerly known as "Luosangzaba", born in Huangzhong, Qinghai. Huangzhong was called "Tsongkha" in Tibetan; "pa" was one of the ending lexemes in Tibetan. Tsongkhapa originally meant "person" in Tsongkha. Tsongkhapa's father, Darughachi, believed in Buddhism. At the age of 7, Tsongkhapa followed the famous Lama Dudjom Rinpoche to become a monk, and learned a variety of teachings for ten years. When he was 16 years old, he went to Tibet for further study. He studied Dharma with teachers in areas over front and rear Tibet, studying the scriptures and treatises of Exoteric Buddhism and Esoteric Buddhism, with deep attainments. On account of corrupt situations in which Lamaism's precepts were destroyed, and monks lived dissolutely, he carried out reforms. He included Buddhist scriptures and collected various sects to confirm that Candrakirti of Madhyamika in Buddhism Mahayana was authentic. He advocated centering on "the view of Mahayana" and advocated that because the original nature was empty, there could be an origin; because there was an origin, the original nature was empty. Thus life, death, Nirvana, and all things were false. He wrote books such as *Lam Rim* and *Great Exposition of the Path of Secret Mantra*, clarifying the practice order of Exoteric Buddhism and Esoteric Buddhism, and promoting attaching equal importance to study and practice, Exoteric Buddhism and Esoteric Buddhism, and that monks shall strictly abide by the precepts, and not marry, drink alcohol, or kill. He stipulated a strict organizational system of temples, study processes and examinations of monks, and the promotion system,[10] forming different grades of lama. He and disciples cut clothes, held bowls and sticks, and kept calm while reducing desires. Because monks in the past all wore a yellow hat, Tsongkhapa also wore a yellow hat, forming the sect style. The representative of the Phagmodrupa ruling group, which governed most areas of Tibet, Drakpa Gyaltsen, and others funded Tsongkhapa to found and preside over the Great Prayer (i.e., The General Assembly) in Lhasa in the seventh year of Yongle's reign in the Ming Dynasty (AD 1409), and built Ganden Temple for him, promoting the formation of Gelug.

Tsongkhapa had a lot of disciples. After his death, the force of Gelugu continued to expand, and Drepung Monastery, Sera Monastery, and Tashilhunpo Monastery were constructed. Because it prohibited lamas from marrying, in order to solve the problem of the inheritance of religious leaders, Gelug adopted the inheritance of reincarnation of the living Buddha based on the combination of the reincarnation and the economic interests of the temple. In 1546, Kundang Gyatso, the chief abbot of Drepung Monastery, the base Camp of Gelug, died, and the upper lama in power found 3-year-old Sonam Gyatso, born in the old noble family in Tubo from Duilong in front Tibet, and welcomed him to Drepung Monastery as the reincarnated soul boy of Kundang Gyatso, to inherit the position of monastery abbot, as the leader of the Gelug temple group. In order to resist the exclusion of hostile sects, the sect also contacted the Mongolian military forces moving to the south of Qinghai, and preached to Qinghai and Mongolia areas. In 1578, Sonam Gyatso met with Altan Khan, the famous leader of the Mongolian Tomoto clan in Qinghai, and later generations called him "Vajradhara Dala Lama Knowing Everything". "Knowing Everything" was Chinese, meaning "knowledgeable and omniscient"; "Vajradhara" was Sanskrit, referring to Vajradhara, meaning "strong and immortal"; "Dalai" was Mongolian, meaning "the sea"; "lama" was Tibetan, meaning "guru". It meant great eminent monk who was omniscient and strong like the sea. Later, the Gelug temple group, according to this title, confirmed that the last disciple of Tsongkhapa, Gendun Drup, was the first Dalai Lama, Kundang Gyatso was the second Dalai Lama, and Sonam Gyatso was the third Dalai Lama. In 1642, the fifth Dalai Lobsang Gyatso destroyed Tsangpa of Kagyu with the help of his teacher, Lobsang Chökyi Gyaltsen, and the forces of Gushri Khan of Mongolia, and established the local feudal regime of Gelug, which "unified politics and religion". In the ninth year of Shunzhi's reign in the Qing Dynasty (AD 1652), the Dalai Lama went to Beijing on pilgrimage, and the following year, he was conferred by the Qing court, received the title of the chief leader of Tibetan Buddhist sects, and confirmed the political and religious status of the Dalai Lama system in Tibet. Since then, reincarnation of all generations of Dalai Lamas must be conferred by the central government, which became a custom. In 1645, Gushri Khan presented the title of "Panchen Bogoto" to the fifth Dalai's teacher, Lobsang Choekyi Gyalsten, to disperse the Dalai Lama's political and religious power. "Pan" was Sanskrit, meaning "proficient scholar"; "chen" was Tibetan, meaning "big"; "Bogoto" was Mongolian, meaning "wise and courageous person". The title meant "great man with profound knowledge, wisdom and courage, settling in Tashilhunpo Monastery permanently". After Lobsang Choekyi Gyalsten died, the fifth Dalai Lama also selected a "reincarnated soul boy", Lobsang Yeshe, for him and established another reincarnation system of Gelug. Lobsang Choekyi Gyalsten was known as the fourth Panchen; the first three Panchen were subsequently confirmed, and Lobsang Yeshe was the fifth Panchen. In the fifty-second year of Kangxi's reign

(AD 1713), the central government of the Qing Dynasty confirmed the fifth Panchen Lobsang Yeshe as Panchen Erdene. The status of Panchen Erdene was officially confirmed. "Erdene" was Manchu, meaning "the treasure". "Panchen Erdene" meant "the wise and brave precious scholar". Since then, Dalai and Panchen became the two reunification systems of the living Buddha of Gelug, which was handed down from generation to generation, belonging to Gelug. With the strong support of the Qing Dynasty, Gelug became the orthodoxy of Lamaism and the sect in power in Tibetan areas, and was also widely popular in Mongolian and Tibetan areas.

In the sixteenth year of Qianlong's reign in the Qing Dynasty (AD 1751), the Qing Dynasty reformed the Tibetan political system, abolished the original princes, set up the grand minister resident of Tibet, and empowered the seventh Dalai Lama to establish Kashag,[11] which was presided over by four Kalon[12] (one monk and three seculars). It upheld the intention of the grand minister resident of Tibet and the Dalai Lama to jointly manage the local administrative affairs in Tibet, which became a custom. Since then, the typical system of "unified politics and religion" in which the Gelugian temple monk ruling group and secular aristocracy jointly ruled Tibet was more complete, and continued until 1959.

Notes

1 This referred to people who had great greed and did all kinds of evil with no goodness.
2 Layavijāna referred to the inner basis and potential function that contained and produced all the phenomena.
3 Also known as "Records on the Western Regions", "Travel Notes to Western Regions", "Xuanzang Travel Notes", and "Supplementary Biography". The book covered the conditions of 138 countries and regions he experienced and heard, and retained valuable information, such as the historical relics, customs, scenic spots, and folklores of the Western Regions, Afghanistan, Pakistan, and India, with high academic value.
4 This is according to the Dunhuang version of *Altar Sutra*; usually this sentence is "there was nothing originally".
5 "Dade": The honorific title of monk.
6 "Keen words" refer to rapid Q&A – words deeply implicit yet with no trace.
7 The genealogy shown in Figure 2.1 is from the Tang Dynasty to the Five Dynasties and the Song Dynasty. "→" in the figure means direct inheritance relationship, and "... →" means there is an omission.
8 "Dudie": The identification cards issued to monks by the feudal government. Monks had to pay money, and those who held this card could be exempt from taxes and corvée.
9 Kadam: "Ka" meant Buddha's language in Tibetan. "Dam" meant teaching in Tibetan. It was named because it believed that all the Buddha's languages guided the believers to practice. In the beginning of the "second propagation" in Tibet, those who learned Shastras looked down upon Exoteric Buddhism, those who paid attention to precepts opposed Shastras, and the practice order of doctrine was very chaotic, with great difference among Exoteric Buddhism, Shastras, and precepts. King Ali invited the Indian monk Attisha to Tibet to carry forward Dharma. Attisha wrote "Bodhi Dao Deng Lun", clarifying the unity of doctrines of Exoteric Buddhism and Esoteric Buddhism and the order of practice, and he also spread Dharma throughout Tibet. Attisha's disciple Dromtönpa (1005–1064) built Rav-sgreng Temple as fundamental Taoist Bodhimanda, promoting Attisha's preaching, and formed a faction later. It spread widely in the twelfth and thirteenth centuries. Later it was integrated into Gelug.

10 Gelug advocated practicing both Exoteric Buddhism and Esoteric Buddhism – Exoteric Buddhism first and then Esoteric Buddhism. To complete the whole process of Exoteric Buddhism and Esoteric Buddhism, monks had to enter the "Dratsang" (Buddhist Institute) of Exoteric Buddhism first, and joined in the preparatory class, known as "dpe-cha-ba", meaning "students". Dpe-cha-ba students firstly learned some of the most basic Buddhist knowledge under the guidance of the mentor, and then were promoted to the formal class by recommendation of the mentor. The monks are upgraded year by year. There were 15 grades in Drepung Monastery, and 13 grades in Sera Monastery and Ganden Temple. When monks upgraded to the highest grade, with the mentor's recommendation and approval of their application, they were eligible to participate in the examination for the Geshe degree. After they received the Geshe degree, the study of Exoteric Buddhism was completed, and then they upgraded to Gyuto and Gyudmed to study Esoteric Buddhism, the main content of which was Guhyasamāja tantra, Cakrasaṃvara Tantra, Yamantaka, and other minor Tantra and Dhammapala. This was also a long and difficult process.
11 Kashag: Tibetan, meaning "organs that issue orders" – namely, the original Tibetan local government.
12 Kalon: Tibetan, the original Tibetan local government officials. According to the official system of the Qing Dynasty, it was the third grade, with important power.

3 Various Buddhist classics

Buddhist classics were often referred to as Buddhist scriptures and Tripitaka. The origin meaning of "Tripitaka" in Sanskrit was the bamboo suitcase holding all kinds of things. Buddhist scholars used this title to sum up all the classics of Buddhism, with the meaning of almost "all books". "Classics" in Chinese referred to vertical lines, meaning that they could pass through a variety of Buddhist argumentation. It imitated Confucianism, which named its works "Five Classics" or "Six Classics" to show respect. Tripitaka, broadly speaking, included "Sutra Pitaka" – namely, books narrating in the tone of Buddha Sakyamuni; "Vinaya Pitaka" referred to precepts constraining words and deeds; "Abhidhamma Pitaka" referred to works interpreting scriptures theoretically and giving play to them. Buddhist scriptures were divided into Sutra, Vinaya, and Abhidhamma, so they were called "Tripitaka". In a narrow sense of the word, Tripitaka specially referred to the "Sutra Pitaka" part of it, including the classics told by Sakyamuni and collected by later disciples, and the classics created in the form of "Evam Maya Srutam"[1] in all dynasties. Buddhist scriptures were also known as "Sutra" to show that they fit the truth and the requirements of all beings. Tripitaka contained vast and numerous volumes, and to describe the large and full amount of it, it was also known as "Zhong Jing", "Collected Classics", "Yiqie Jing", and "Dazang Jing". Since the Sui and Tang Dynasties, Buddhist scriptures were more often called Tripitaka. Buddhism also called its own classics "internal code", and called books outside Buddhism – namely, the so-called secular books and books of "outside schools" – "external code".

Tripitaka originally referred to Chinese Buddhist scriptures, and now it generally refers to Buddhist scriptures in all languages. In addition to Chinese Tripitaka, there was also Pali Southern Tripitaka, as well as Tibetan, Mongolian, Manchu, Tangut, and Japanese Tripitaka. Among them, the most important ones were Chinese, Tibetan, and Pali Tripitaka; Chinese Tripitaka was the most abundant and complete. Buddhism originated in ancient India, but only Chinese versions of Buddhist classics were preserved most in the world, and are now the giants among various versions of Tripitaka, with an important position.

Among Buddhist books, the most important were the works of Indian Buddhist scholars, followed by works of Chinese Buddhist scholars; in addition, there were works of North Korean, Japanese, and other countries' Buddhist scholars. Classics were collected in Tripitaka several times in India, added with the writings of monks in China and other places, and were added to, supplemented, edited, and revised all the time. From pattra leaves to translation, copying, stone inscription, it was engraved into books, with more than 20,000 volumes and tens of millions of words, becoming the most extensive book in human history. The content of Buddhist classics was very rich, and contained a wide range of discussions related to Buddhism and culture – political ideas, ethics, philosophy, literature, art, and customs. Therefore, it was not only an important code for studying Buddhism but also important information for studying ancient oriental culture.

Collection of Buddhist scriptures

When Sakyamuni promoted Buddhism, he passed it on only through oral instruction and his deeds rather than the text record, and his disciples also followed the Dharma according to their teacher's instruction. After the death of Sakyamuni, his disciples, in order to avoid the loss of Buddhist doctrines over the course of time, and also to keep the Dharma from other "outside schools", and let future Buddhist disciples always have something to follow, collected Buddhist scriptures. The so-called collection, according to our usual explanation, meant editing. But the original meaning of collection in Sanskrit was monks' assembly to chant classics together. The ritual was to convene the monks to organize the assembly according to the precepts and elect the most prestigious monk as sthavira, who boarded the high seat to narrate what the Buddha said, and if all the monks had no objection, that meant it was all passed and recognized to conform to what Sakyamuni said when he was alive. Indian nations were accustomed to memory and oral tradition. The earliest collection of the Buddhist scriptures merely edited the teachings of Sakyamuni into brief statements through the form of question and answer, so as to make it convenient for Buddhist disciples to chant together. Later, the practice of writing was introduced, and commonly recognized Buddhist Dharma was written on pattra leaves to be handed down to future generations. It can be seen that the Buddhist scriptures were not only the writings of Sakyamuni but also a collective creation. According to legend, during the 400 years after the death of Sakyamuni, a total of four assemblies were held, forming Hinayana Buddhist classics.

The first assembly was held by his chief disciple Mahakasyapa three or four months after the death of Buddha Sakyamuni. Five hundred monks (also known as Arhats) were elected to collect classics in *Pipphalaguha* near Rajagraha. Ananda, who was the most learned, recited the Dharma (Sutra Pitaka) told by Sakyamuni while he was alive; Upali, who was the most disciplined, recited the sangha precepts formulated by Sakyamuni (Vinaya Pitaka). He recited them a total of 80 times, so it was called *Eighty Vinaya Recitation*. This was the first assembly in the history of Buddhism. It was also known as the "500 assembly" because it gathered 500 monks to participate. This assembly was only an oral recitation, with no text, but later the classic script took this as its basis.

The second assembly was held about 100 years after the death of Buddha, hosted by Yasa. Seven hundred monks were gathered in Parikara Park in Vaisali to solve the doubt of precepts. Based on the different understandings of precepts, two factions were generated: one faction consisted mostly of elders, which was named "Sthaviravada"; the other had more people, which was named "Mahasamghika". In the next century, Mahasamghika was divided into eight factions.

The third assembly took place about 200 years after the Buddha was destroyed, when Ashoka of the Indian Maurya Dynasty designated Buddhism as the state religion, which made Buddhism increasingly flourish; however, at the same time, people outside the religion sneaked into the Buddhists to distort the doctrine of Buddhism. At that time, Moggaliputta Tissa gathered 1,000 monks for Sthaviravada in Pataliputta to remove the non-Buddhist doctrines mixed in. Tissa elucidated Buddhist doctrine at the assembly and attacked heterodoxy, since there had been Sutra, Vinaya, and Abhidhamma. After this assembly, there were notes in Pali and Sanskrit. After about 100 years, Sthaviravada was divided into ten.

The fourth assembly was held in Kasmira (Kophen) 400 years after the Buddha destroyed. There were two kinds of statements about this assembly: the first was recorded in Northern Buddhism. Parsva gathered 500 Arhats during the reign of Kanishka in the Kushan Dynasty, which made Vasumitta chief, collected Buddha's words, and edited and annotated Tripitaka. The second was that 500 Arhats and 500 Bodhisattva were gathered, Katyayana was made chief, and Bodhisattva Asvaghosa was appointed the writer to carry forward Buddha's words.

The foregoing is a brief introduction of the history of Buddhist Hinayana classics. As for the formation of Buddhist Mahayana classics, although there were legends of collection and secret assembly, there was no definite instruction of historical data. Mahayana classics formed gradually over a long time. Although they contained the doctrine of Sakyamuni, they were more fabricated by descendants. Many books were created in the form of "Evam Maya Srutam". Although the authors advertised that they had personally listened to the Buddha, in fact, they were created by descendants. In ancient India, the individual was not taken seriously, and some of the Buddhist books were even anonymous, and faked as written by Sakyamuni. A considerable amount of Buddhist literature was actually handed down and revised from generation to generation, with gradual accumulation.

Translation of Buddhist codes

There were three systems of China's translation of Indian Buddhist books generally: Chinese translation, Tibetan translation, and Dai translation.

1 Chinese translation of scriptures

The translation method of Buddhist scriptures of China had roughly undergone a process from "oral instruction" – that is, oral recitation – to translation of scriptures. The initial translation was basically based on contents of scriptures orally recited by translators, such as An Shigao and Lokaksema in the Eastern Han Dynasty. Even Samghabhuti, Samghadeva, Dharmayasa, Punyatara, and Dharmaruci in the

Eastern Jin Dynasty still recited based on memory and then wrote in Chinese. The Buddhist scriptures were widely spread to China later, especially since the Southern and Northern Dynasties. The original texts of Buddhist scriptures were written in various languages. The Indian Buddhist scriptures were mainly Sanskrit classics; then it was Kharosthi commonly used in the northwest of India and Central Asia, which was later eliminated because of the revival of Sanskrit, and Kharosthi scriptures were also lost. The third was Pali, evolving from local spoken languages in southern India. As Indian Buddhism was introduced into the Chinese mainland via the Western Regions, the local Parthian, Sogdian, Khotanese, and Kuchean Buddhist scriptures also became the originals for Chinese translation of Buddhist scriptures. Buddhist codes in the languages of the Western Regions were also known as "Hu Ben". Since the Six Dynasties, there had been a distinction between the Hu Ben and Sanskrit versions of original Buddhist scriptures, and the Sanskrit version was put above Hu Ben. Chinese translation of Buddhist scriptures could be roughly divided into five periods:

> The first period was from the Eastern Han Dynasty to the Western Jin Dynasty. In this period, translation of Buddhist scriptures was not planned, and whatever was encountered was translated. Most of the translators were Western monks, most of whom did not understand Chinese, and had to ask the Hans to assist with Chinese translation; however, the Hans who assisted translation did not understand foreign languages. This brought great difficulties to translation. At this time, a lot of scriptures were translated, but mostly they were sporadic but not systematic, and the literary form of translation had not been established, so the translation failed to express the correct meaning and achieve a high quality. This period was an exploratory stage.
>
> The second period was the Eastern Jin Dynasty and two Qin Dynasties. The translation of this period had made some progress. It began to develop from one or two people's translation to cooperative translation among many people – namely, collective translation – and the division of labor was also more detailed and specific. The translators were mainly monks in India and the Western Regions, most of whom did not understand Chinese, but a few people, such as the translation master Kumarajiva, who was not proficient in Chinese but could understand the meaning of text, helped to improve the quality of translation. Kumarajiva's main translation of Buddhist scriptures marked the beginning of classical translation's maturity. At that time, due to the rise of the fashion of going west to seek Dharma, Chinese monks, such as Faxian, Zhimeng and Zhiyan, all understood Sanskrit, and each had his own translation, marking the beginning of independent translation of the Hans. Various types of Buddhist scriptures translated during this period were comprehensive, with impressive achievements, laying a foundation for the establishment of Buddhist barriers. Buddhist scholars at that time also paid attention to summing up the lessons of translation – for example, Dao An pointed

out the problems existing in translation – namely, "five biases and three difficult problems to translate". "Five biases" referred to: (1) inverted sentences; (2) preference for classical Chinese; (3) deletion of sentences chanted repeatedly; (4) deletion of explanatory sentences in a paragraph; (5) deletion of sentences that repeated the former paragraph. "Three difficult problems to translate" referred to: (1) the requirement of being both true and easy to understand; (2) Buddha's wisdom being far apart, which was difficult to understand;(3) the past being far away, so there was no evidence to prove it. (See Volume 8, *Preface of Pancavimsati-sahasrika-prajnaparamita*, of *Compilation of Notes on the Translation of the Tripitaka*.) It stressed that translation should not lose its basis, and should strive to conform to the original meaning. Dao An advocated literal translation, while later Kumarajiva advocated free translation. It was said in *Kumarajiva's Biography*, Volume 2 of *Memoirs of Eminent Monks*, "Monks discussed the Western literature and its similarities and differences, and said, 'India paid much attention to rhetoric, and its gatha (poetry) was suitable for singing with chord. People who met the king must be moral; people who saw the Buddha shall sing for it. However, when Sanskrit was translated to Chinese, the main points remained, but the rhetoric was not similar, and the temperament of gatha was also different. It was like chewing rice to feed people – not only the taste was lost, but also disgusted people'". The saying that translation was like "chewing rice to feed people" was a wonderful metaphor, also described the difficulties and hard experience that Kumarajiva encountered in the translation process.

The third period was the Southern and Northern Dynasties. Key Buddhist scriptures had been initially translated up to the Eastern Jin Dynasty, after which the Buddhist scholars' interest and energy turned to study, mastery, and creation of schools. Relatively less importance was attached to translation of Buddhist scriptures than in the Eastern Jin Dynasty and two Qin Dynasties. The focus of translation also changed from the classics to codes – for example, the translation of truth reflected such features.

The fourth period was the Sui and Tang Dynasties. Translation of Buddhism codes truly matured until the Sui and Tang Dynasties, whose outstanding characteristic and basic symbol were that Chinese monks who were proficient in doctrines and Sanskrit served as the main translators. At the same time, the translation system was also improved, and the purpose of classical translation was clear and more systematic. During the Zhenguan period in the Tang Dynasty, Tang Xuanzang presided over translation, which was in its heyday in the history of Chinese Buddhist classical translation. Xuanzang not only had a high degree of Buddhist attainments but also was proficient in Sanskrit, translating a lot of high-level Buddhist scriptures, and his translation was called "new translation". According to historical record, Xuanzang "translated quite smoothly"

(Volume 4 of *Continued Memoirs of Eminent Monks*; page 455, Volume 50 of *Taisho-pitaka*).

During Fuqin's reign, Dao'an once organized the translation field in Guanzhong, and after the Yao Qin Dynasty set up a national translation field, inviting Kumarajiva to preside over translation. Since then, translation fields kept increasing. To the Tang Dynasty, Xuan Zang set up a huge translation field, and the court sent a minister to monitor and guard the translation field. The procedure and division of labor in Buddhist scriptural classical translation field in the Tang Dynasty were as follows: (1) translation master – namely, the host of the translation field, the person in charge of the translation. He was also known as the translator, responsible for solving problems in the translation process. (2) Zhengyi, also known as "Zhengfanyi". Their status was lower than the translation master. They assessed Sanskrit with the translation master to correctly understand the original meaning of Sanskrit scriptures, and judge whether there was a difference between the meaning of the translation and the Sanskrit, so as to amend. (3) Zhengwen, also known as "Zhengfanben". They listened to the translation master reciting Sanskrit aloud to check whether the recitation was wrong. (4) Shuzi, also known as "Duyu", as well as "Yiyu" and "Chuanyu". They translated the corresponding Sanskrit into Chinese according to the original meaning of the Sanskrit – namely, transliteration. (5) Bishou, also known as "Zhibi". They translated Sanskrit into Chinese. For example, Shuzi wrote the Sanskrit "sutra", and Bishou then translated it into "sutra" in Chinese. (6) Zhuiwen, also known as "Ciwen". Because of the different language customs and sentence structure between Sanskrit and Chinese, someone was needed to adjust the sentence structure according to the situation and straighten up the words. (7) Canyi, also known as "Zhengyi". They re-translated the translated Chinese back into Sanskrit, and compared the two to judge right and wrong. (8) Kanding, also known as "Jiaokan", "Quanding", and "Zongkan". They cut lengthy and repetitive sentences, and made sentences more concise and accurate. (9) Runwen, also known as "Runse". They were responsible for polishing diction. (10) Fanbei. The scripture chanter chanted aloud in accordance with the rhyme of the newly translated scriptures to test whether it was pleasant. It can be seen from the foregoing process of translation that the Chinese translation of scriptures at that time was the product of very serious processes, the crystallization of collective wisdom, and the labor of all. Xuan Zang also stipulated the principle of "five not translating" for the work of translation: "(I) Mimigu, such as Dharani; (II) Handuoyigu, such as the six doctrines of Bhagavat; (III) Ciwugu, such as jambu; (IV) Shugugu, such as Anuttarasamyaksambodhi, which was not uninterpretable, but it was because the Sanskrit was often used since Molten; (V) Shengshangu, such as Prajna, respect, wisdom and lightness" (Zhou Dunyi: *Original Preface of Translation Collection*, see *New Translation Collection*). Such provision of Xuanzang emphasized loyalty and prudence, which did not reluctantly translate, full of difficulties and experiences of translators.

The fifth period was the Song Dynasty. This was the end of the Chinese translation of Buddhist scriptures. In the Tang, Song, and Five Dynasties, wars were still frequent, and translation was on the verge of desuetude. In the Song Dynasty, it once rose, when Taizong set up a classical translation academy and organized classical translation, and the translated books mostly belonged to Esoteric Buddhism. The rulers of the early Song Dynasty, believing that some content of Esoteric codes was too lustful, also limited classical translation, so the condition was not as prosperous as the Sui and Tang Dynasties. Since then the cause of the Chinese translation of Buddhist codes also ended.

Seen from the history of Chinese translation of Buddhist scriptures, most of the Chinese translation of Buddhist scriptures was completed in the Wei, Jin, Southern and Northern Dynasties, and Sui and Tang Dynasties. During this period, Kumarajiva, Gunarata, Xuan Zang, and Amognarajra were called the "four great translators". There were more than 200 Buddhist translators whose names were recorded, and more than 2,100 types of Buddhist scriptures and more than 6,000 volumes were translated. Indian Buddhist scriptures were systematically introduced to China, which greatly promoted the spread and development of Buddhism in our country.

2 Tibetan translation of scriptures

From the seventh century, when Buddhism was introduced to Tibet to the twelfth century, a large number of Buddhist books were translated in Tibet. Tibetan translation is mainly based on the Sanskrit original, and what was missed in Sanskrit was supplemented according to Chinese; Khotan translation of scriptures was mainly according to the original Sanskrit copies, and they were translated according to Chinese and Khotanese if the Sanskrit was lacking to make up for the deficiency. In the second half of the fourteenth century, Tshal-Pa Kun-dga rdo-rje revised "Kangyur" and Bu-ston Rin-chen-grub revised "Tengyur", which constituted the two components of Tibetan Tripitaka. Between them, "Zhengzang" was called "Kangyur", meaning "the verbal directions of Buddhism", collecting writings of Sutra, Vinaya, and Mantra, equivalent to the contents of Sutra and Vinaya in Chinese Tripitaka, totaling 107 suitcases and 1,055 books. "Fuzang" was called "Tengyur", meaning "Abhidhamma". It included elaboration and annotation of Sutra and Vinaya, and sadhana drubtab of Esoteric Buddhism – namely, the three parts of praise, interpretation of scriptures, and interpretation of mantra – totaling 224 suitcases and 3,522 books. In addition, there was "Songbeng", the writing of a Tibetan monk. About four-fifths of the content of Tibetan Tripitaka were not available in Chinese Tripitaka, especially the part of Esoteric Buddhism. In the Qing Dynasty, the Tibetan Buddhism codes were translated into Mongolian and Manchu, and carved into Mongolian and Tibetan Tripitaka.

3 Dai translation of scriptures

Indian Pali Buddhism was introduced into our country in the early thirteenth century via Myanmar, and spread in Dai areas in Xishuangbanna and Dehong in Yunnan. Because of the different dialects, there were three kinds of languages used for translation: Xishuangbanna Dai, Dehong Dai, and Daibeng. The content of Buddhist scriptures was divided into four parts: Sutra, Vinaya, and Abhidhamma, and codes outside Tripitaka, in which Sutta Pitaka took up the most, having 5,372 books, while Abhidhamma Pitaka had only seven books, which belonged to Sthaviravada of Hinayana Buddhism.

The translation of Buddhist scriptures was a major event in the history of Chinese cultural thought. Buddhist books, with the ideological system of religious belief and completely different language and cultural system, came from distant India, bringing new elements and stimulation to Chinese culture. There were numerous Buddhist codes, whose development, like raging waves, fully impacted the traditional Chinese culture, and brought unprecedented changes to it. Buddhist books, with their unique roles, were branded in the long history of China since the Han Dynasty, waiting for people to sum up and comment on them.

Writings of Chinese monks

With the increase in the translation and introduction of Buddhist scriptures, Chinese monks gradually deepened their understanding of Buddhist argumentation. Since the Jin Dynasty and the Southern and Northern Dynasties, Chinese Buddhist scholars had been more diligent in writing, constantly enriching and developing the content of "Tripitaka" with their own writing. The writing of Chinese monks became an extremely important part of Buddhist scriptures, which included works different from Indian Buddhism, reflected the characteristics of Chinese Buddhism, and had a very prominent position throughout the Buddhist scriptures.

Chinese monks' writing of Buddhist scriptures, according to the catalog edited by the contemporary famous Buddhist research expert Mr. Lv Cheng, contained 582 books and 4,172 volumes,[2] including the majority of the existing writings before the Tang Dynasty and important writings after the Tang Dynasty, as well as a small amount of writing of scholars of Korean and Silla popular in our country. From the forms of writings, they could be divided into chapter, treatise, quotation, historical biography, pronunciation and meaning, catalog, miscellaneous essays, collection, and so on. From the number of writings, the chapters took up the most, reflecting the Buddhists' worship of classics and enthusiasm for explaining classics. The next was the treatise, reflecting the creative enthusiasm and unique insights of Buddhist sectarians in the Sui and Tang Dynasties, embodying the sinicization of Buddhism. The number of historical biography was also considerable, reflecting the Chinese monks' attention to the strength of historical records. Among all the writings, *Altar Sutra* of Hui Neng, the actual founder of Zen in the Tang Dynasty, was the only one to be known as "sutra" and handed down to future generations. This was a manifestation of Zen scholars' resistance to Indian

82 Various Buddhist classics

Buddhism and highlighting of Chinese ancestors' doctrines. The Buddhist books written by Chinese Buddhist scholars were very important historical materials for studying the history of Chinese Buddhism, history, history of philosophy, history of literature, and history of art. To understand Chinese Buddhism, of course, we should first understand Indian Buddhism, but the key lies in the study of Chinese Buddhism. Only by deeply studying the works of Chinese monks can we truly grasp the thought of Chinese Buddhism. Therefore, we should pay high attention to the treatises, quotations, and part of the chapters. For example, Hui Yuan's *Shamen Bujingwangzhelun*, *Sanbaolun*, and *Mingbaoyinglun*, Sengzhao's *Zhaolun*, Jizang's *Profound Meaning of the Three Treatises*, Zhiyi's *Exposition of the Deeper Meaning of the Lotus Sutra* and *Great Samadhiand Vipa'syana*, Kuiji's *Chengweishilun Shuji*, *Commentaries on Nyyapravea* and *Dachengfayuanyilinzhang*, Zhiyan's *Huayanjing Souxuanji*, Fa Zang's *Huayanjing Tanxuanji*, *Huyan-Chengjiaoyifenqizhang*, and *Huyanjinshizizhang*, Zhanran's *Jin Gang Pi*, Hui Neng's *Altar Sutra*, Zongmi's *Essay on the Origin of Man* and *Preface of the History of Zen's Idea in Tang Dynasty*, *The Five History Books on Zen Quotation* edited by Puji, *The Quotation of Ancient Buddhist Saints* edited by Zang, Yanshou's "Record of the Mirror of Orthodoxy", Qi Song's "Fu Jiao Pian", and Zongg Gao's *Zheng Fa Yan* are all important Buddhist scriptures, which need our in-depth study, analysis, criticism, and summary.

In addition, *Compilation of Notes on the Translation of the Tripitaka* written by Liang Sengyou, and *The Anthology of Hong Ming* compiled by him, and *Detailed Anthology of Hong Ming* and *Fayuan Zhulin* collected by Dao Xuan are extremely important data on Buddhist thought. *Memoirs of Eminent Monks* in the Three Dynasties, Hui Jiao's *Memoirs of Eminent Monks* in Liang, Daoxuan's *Continued Memoirs of Eminent Monks* in Tang, and Zaning's *Memoirs of Eminent Monks in Song* are not only important for the study of Chinese Buddhism history but also important historical material for studying Chinese history.

Transcribing, engraving, and printing of Tripitaka

The spread of Buddhist scriptures, along with the progress of printing history, generally went through the evolution process from transcribing scriptures to engraving scriptures, and then to printing scriptures.

1 Transcribing scriptures

Before the invention of the new printing technology, the circulation of Buddhist scriptures had to rely on transcribing on paper – that is, to be spread among monasteries and people in the form of transcripts. As transcribing was not easy, since the Six Dynasties, the fashion of constructing Sutra Pitaka to collect the volumes of scriptures prevailed among large monasteries. According to the rough statistics of the existing records, merely during the century from Emperor Wu of Chen who ordered the transcription of Tripitaka to Ximing Temple, which transcribed Tripitaka during the reign of Emperor Gaozong of Tang, the royal family and common people transcribed up to 800 pitaka, which was a striking number. The cause of transcribing scriptures extended until the Baoda period (943–957) in the Southern Tang Dynasty, and the number was more impressive. But unfortunately, the vast majority of this batch of Sutra Pitaka transcribed with hardship by ancient people was not handed down. Now the transcribed scriptures of the Six Dynasties and the Sui and Tang Dynasties found in Dunhuang Grottoes, although fragmentary, can still be called the world's treasures. These transcribed scriptures have a high historical value for the study of religion, philosophy, language, cultural relics, and archaeology.

2 Engraving scriptures

In the ancient Central Plains, there were two forms of engraving scriptures, which went through two stages. The first was stone engraving, and the second was wood engraving. Buddhist scriptures engraved on stone were also known as stone scriptures. Stone engraving first appeared in the middle of the sixth century AD during the Northern Qi Dynasty, whose representative included *The Diamond Sutra* in Sutra Rock Valley in Mount Tai, Shandong, *Avatamsaka Sutra* in Wind Valley in Taiyuan, Shanxi, *Vimalakirti Sutra* in Xiangtangshan in the north of Wu'an, Hebei, and so on. To the Sui Dynasty, stone carving still continued to develop. The most famous was the Buddhist scripture engraved on the stone in Dafangshan, Youzhou – that is, in Yunju Temple in Fangshan District (Beijing now). During more than 1,000 years from the Daye Period during the reign of Emperor Yang of Sui to the Tianqi Period in the Ming Dynasty, over 15,000 pieces of stones were engraved with 1,122 books and 3,572 volumes of Buddhism scriptures. Jing Wan, the founder of stone engraving of Yunju Temple, said in the inscription in the eighth year of Zhen'guan in Tang (634), "Buddha of the Future intended to take this scripture as master copy when he was in a difficult time, if possible, it's wished not to open it". The monument of engraving scripture was sealed in the cave and crypt. Buddhists learned the historical lesson that the Northern Wei Dynasty and the Northern Zhou Dynasty had burned statues and eradicated Buddhism by virtue of political power, cleverly took use of the natural conditions of the north, engraved on the stones, and buried them underground, so as to enable the Buddhist scriptures to be spread for a long time and make Buddhist Dharma eternal. The Buddhist scripture engraved on the stone in Yunju Temple became China's precious cultural heritage with its rareness, unique form, and rich content.

With the invention and progress of woodcut printing, in the Tang Dynasty there had been a small amount of Buddhist scriptures engraved on wood. The only entity that exists now is *The Diamond Sutra*, engraved in the Xiantong period during the reign of Emperor Yi of Tang (AD 860–84). There was the printing of "Jetavana Anathapindada-arama" on the title page and inscription of "on the fifteenth day of the fourth month in the ninth year of Xiantong". Unfortunately, this extremely valuable cultural relic has long been lost abroad. According to the existing information, the construction of wood engraving of Tripitaka began from the fifth year (AD 972) of Kaibao during the reign of Song Taizu, Zhao Kuangyin, until the Qing

Dynasty. During about 1,000 years, there had been more than ten times the official and private wood engraving of the Tripitaka, and the general situation of these versions is as follows:

1. *Kaibaozang*: It was named because it was engraved during the Kaibao period in the reign of Song Taizu. It was also known as the "Shu version" for it was engraved in Yizhou (Chengdu). Its printed copies had become the common criterion for later printing of all the official and private engraving in our country, well as Korea and Japan. Now only a few volumes of aberrant copies remain.
2. *Qidanzang*: It was firstly engraved in the first year of Jingfu during Liaoxingzong's reign (AD 1031), and it took over 30 years to complete. In recent years, 12 volumes have been found in a wooden pagoda in Yingxian, Shanxi; there are also remnant volumes of *Kaibaozang*, and both of these texts are rare treasures of China.
3. *Chongningzang* (version of Dongchan Temple, Fuzhou): It was engraved in the late Northern Song Dynasty, and its layout was imitated by many later versions. Now only around 20 volumes remain.
4. *Piluzang* (version of Kaiyuan Temple, Fuzhou): It was engraved between the two Song Dynasties, and now only one volume remains in Shanxi.
5. *Yuanjuezang*: The engraving was completed in the early Southern Song Dynasty, which was named because it was engraved in Yuanjue Temple, Sixi, Huzhou (now Wuxing, Zhejiang). Now there are only scattered versions in China.
6. *Zifuzang* (Sixi version): The engraving was completed in the middle Southern Song Dynasty in Zifu Zen Temple in Sixi. A total of 1,459 books and 5,940 volumes were contained. Now more than 5,300 volumes are collected in the Beijing Library.
7. *Zhaochengzang*: It was engraved in the Jin Dynasty, and supplemented in the Yuan Dynasty; there was no previous record, and it was found in Guangsheng Temple in Zhaocheng County, Shanxi, in 1933. More than 6,900 volumes of Tripitaka were contained, and 5,600 volumes remain now. This Tripitaka not only preserved the original version of the officially engraved Tripitaka but also added a lot of important works, and thus it had a very high value.
8. *Qishazang*: It was firstly engraved in the late Southern Song Dynasty, and completed in the Yuan Dynasty, lasting nearly 100 years. It was so named because it was engraved in Qisha Yansheng Temple (later renamed Qisha Zen Temple) in Chenhu, Pingjiang Prefecture (now Chenhu, Wu County, Jiangsu). It was preserved in Shaanxi and Shanxi, but slightly incomplete. In 1931–1933, 500 books were printed according to Shaanxi Tripitaka, and what was missed was supplemented with a version of *Zifuzang*.
9. *Puningzang*: It was engraved in the early Yuan Dynasty, and was preserved in Yunnan, Shanxi, Shaanxi, and other provinces.
10. *HongFa Zang*: According to legend, it was the official version of the Tripitaka in the Yuan Dynasty; however, so far no printed copies have been found.

11 *Hongwunanzang* (initially engraved *Nanzang*): Zhu Yuanzhang, Taizu of Ming ordered its engraving. The only existing copy is now in Sichuan Provincial Library, slightly incomplete.
12 *Yonglenanzang*: It was generally known as *Nanzang*. It was the Hongwu version of Tripitaka re-engraved in the Yongle Period during the reign of Zhu Di, but slightly changed. Now it is preserved in many libraries around China.
13 *Yonglebeizang*: After *Yonglenanzang* was completed in the seventeenth year of his reign (AD 1419), Emperor Yongle ordered the engraving of scriptures in the nineteenth year of his reign (AD 1421) in Beijing, which was completed in the fifth year (AD 1440) of Zhengtong during Ming Yingzong's reign. The northern and southern versions of Yongle Tripitaka, due to a large number of print runs and distribution to temples in the country, were the versions preserved most among all the Tripitaka.
14 *Jiaxingzang*: It was engraved in the late Ming and early Qing Dynasties. It was firstly engraved in Wutai Mountain in Shanxi, where inscription was inconvenient due to cold weather, so later it was moved to places like Jingshan in Yuhang County, Zhejiang, to continue the engraving, and finally it was collectively inscribed in Lengyan Temple in Jiaxing and began to circulate. So the pitaka was named *Jiaxingzang*, also known as *Jingshanzang*. This pitaka was characterized by abandoning the folded version and turning to wire-bound versions; in addition, the whole pitaka was divided into *Zhengzang*, *Xuzang*, and *Youxuzang*. *Zhengzang* was the copy of *Yonglebeizang*, while *Xuzang* and *Youxuzang* collected foreign books. The improvement of version format and absorption of Buddhist codes outside the pitaka of *Jiaxingzang* had a great impact on the later engraving and compilation of Tripitaka.
15 *Qingzang*: It was also known as *Longzang*, which was the official version of Tripitaka in the early Qing Dynasty. Among Tripitaka engraved on wood, it was the only version that was basically preserved.

In foreign countries, versions of engraved Chinese Tripitaka included *Gaolizang* of Korea and *Hong'anzang*, *Tianhaizang*, and *Huangbozang* of Japan. Among them, *Gaolizang* used the "Shu version", "Qidan version", and the original engraved version of *Gaolizang* more (*Gaolizang* was engraved three times for it had been burned) for collation, which had a high value as historical material.

3 Printing scriptures

With the continuous progress in printing, circulation of modern Chinese Tripitaka relied more on printed versions, and now there are six types: (1) *Pinjiazang*, printed in 1909–1913 by Shanghai Pinjia Vihara based on *Hongjiaozang*, edited and printed by Hongjiao Academy in Japan, slightly changed and compiled. (2) *Puhuizang*, the pitaka (not yet finished) edited and printed in 1943, part of which was the Buddhist books not collected by other pitaka and part of the books in the Southern Tripitaka translated in Japanese. The foregoing two were printed at home. The following four were printed in Japan. (3) *Hongjiaozang*. (4) 卍*Xizang*. (5) 卍*Xuzang*. These were completed based on widely collecting the Buddhist books preserved in China and Japan but not listed in Tripitaka over the past dynasties. (6) *Taisho-pitaka* (its whole name was *Taisho Tripitaka*), edited and printed in 1924–1934. The whole pitaka contained 55 volumes of main chapters, 30 volumes of continuation, and 15 volumes of supplements (12 volumes of figures, 3 volumes of the total catalog). The main chapters contained 2,236 books and 9,006 volumes. Volume 56–84 of the continuation was the writing of Japanese Buddhist scholars on annotation, commentary, and elucidation of the sects, and Volume 85 collected 189 types of ancient lost books, doubtful and bogus Sutra, and annotation in the Southern and Northern Dynasties and Tang Dynasty. It is now a relatively complete Tripitaka, although there are many wrong words and sentences. It collects a total of 3,053 Buddhist scriptures and 11,970 volumes, and is commonly used by international scholars.

In the late 1980s, under the leadership of the State Council's Ancient Books Publishing and Publication Planning Group, Professor Ren Jiyu presided over the compilation of *Chinese Tripitaka (Chinese part)*, collecting all the Buddhist books in various versions of Chinese Tripitaka at home and abroad according to the content system, up to more than 4,200 types and 23,000 volumes. It was divided into the main chapter and continuation, in 220 volumes. It was based on the only remaining complete copy in the world – *Zhaochengzang*, collated according to eight representative versions, including *Fangshan Stone Sutra, Zifuzang, Qishazang, Puningzang, Yonglenanzang, Jiaxingzang*, and *Gaolizang*, photocopied and published, providing complete and rich research materials for the Buddhist community and academic community, with important historical value.

The catalog and structure of Buddhist scriptures

The catalog of Buddhist scriptures records the title, author, content, and so forth of Buddhist scriptures, and is an important tool to guide reading and retrieval of Buddhist scripture. The organization of the catalog of Buddhist scriptures has a certain order, reflecting the content's structure.

1 The catalog of Buddhist scriptures

The catalog of Buddhist scriptures is also known as the "Sutra Catalog". It was so named because Buddhist scholars before the Eastern Jin Dynasty also called Vinaya and Abhidhamma Sutra. Later, due to the clearer understanding of Sutra, Vinaya, and Abhidhamma, it was not called the "Sutra Catalog" anymore after the Tang Dynasty, but was changed to the "Catalog of Holy Code", "Talisman Catalog", "Shijiaolu", and "Internal Code Catalog".

With the increasing number of Buddhist books translated into Chinese, some Buddhist scholars began to compile the catalog of Buddhist scriptures to facilitate searching on the one hand, and to avoid mixing them up on the other hand so as to facilitate the uniform organization of Buddhist scriptures. In the long process of transcribing and spreading the translation, there were various differences of non-recorded translation (no translator or translating date is known), recorded translation (translator and translating date were recorded), single translation, re-translation (the second or multiple translation of the same Buddhist scripture), different translation (several translations of the same Buddhist scripture were different from each other), full translation, transcribing translation, and Dajing and Bieshengjing (drawn from the whole), and also the emergence of doubtful and bogus Sutra, which all needed to be edited for authenticity, compiled, and tested. Therefore, since the Eastern Jin Dynasty, there were catalog works of Chinese Buddhist scriptures in almost all the dynasties. According to incomplete estimates, until the late Qing Dynasty, there had been more than 50 kinds, and more than 30 kinds are currently handed down.

The earliest production of the catalog of Buddhist scriptures was begun by the famous monk Dao An in the Eastern Jin Dynasty. The catalog compiled by him was later known as the *Comprehensive Catalog of Scriptures*, referred to as *An Catalog* for short. The original copy had been lost, but it could be evidenced by the *Compilation of Notes on the Translation of the Tripitaka*, which was written by Sengyou in the Liang Dynasty, referred to as *Youlu* for short. This compilation recorded the catalog, preface, and translators' biographies for the Sutra, Vinaya, and Abhidhamma translated from the Eastern Han Dynasty to the Liang Dynasty. This is the only Sutra Catalog that currently exists in China, containing a total of 15 volumes, divided into four parts: collection record, catalog, preface, and biography, all having a very important historical value.

While compiling *Compilation of Notes on the Translation of the Tripitaka* with Sengyou, the Buddhist believer Emperor Wu of Liang ordered translation scholars to revise the catalog of Buddhist scriptures and distribute it after approval. In this way, the transmission of bogus Sutra and production of private versions were limited. Since then, the power of compiling Buddhist scriptures was vested in the emperor, and there were official catalogs. From Emperor Wu of Liang to Emperor Qianlong in the Qing Dynasty, there were 17 official compilations of catalogs, of which the following three were the most important:

1 *The scripture catalog* compiled in the fourteenth year (AD 594) of Emperor Wen of Sui was also known as *Fajinglu* for it was compiled by Fajing and others. This catalog was divided into nine categories, and 2,257 books and 5,310 volumes of Buddhist scriptures were incorporated.
2 *Kaiyuansijiaolu*, compiled in the eighteenth year (AD 730) of Emperor Xuanzong of Tang, was also known as *Kaiyuanlu*. It was compiled by Zhisheng and contained a total of 20 volumes, divided into the total catalog and supplementary catalog with ten volumes. It was famous for rigorous compilation, informative records, and exquisite checking. It recorded the translated catalogs and biographies handed down from the Han Dynasty to the Tang Dynasty, and incorporated 1,076 books, 5,048 volumes, and 480 sets of Tripitaka. Later Zhisheng also created a method to number the Tripitaka catalog with *Thousand Character Classic* and compiled four volumes of *Kaiyuansijiaolulvechu* to facilitate retrieval. *Kaiyuanlu* not only later

88 *Various Buddhist classics*

became a blueprint for the catalogs of various schools but also provided the basis for later printed Tripitaka, had a great impact on the later spread of Buddhist scriptures, and was the most important ancient Buddhist catalog.

3   *Zhiyuanfabaokantongzonglu,* compiled in the fourteenth year (AD 1287) of Kublai Khan's reign, was compared to the Tibetan version and Chinese Tripitaka by Tibetan monk Phagspa, who noted the similarities and differences between the two, and annotated the Sanskrit transliteration of the catalog of Buddhist scriptures. It had a certain academic value.

The ancient Chinese Buddhist catalog continued to improve, and had an important historical value. But there were also a number of shortcomings. Later, Japan's *Taisho Tripitaka* broke through the original format of Chinese Tripitaka, and made progress, but there were still shortcomings. In view of the shortcomings of the previous compilation of Chinese Tripitaka, for example, the distinction of classes was not very appropriate, Shiyi (translation lost) and Youyi (with translation) of scriptures were mistaken, and the translation was confused, so doubtful and bogus books were miscollected. In the *New Chinese Tripitaka Catalog* compiled by Lv Cheng in the 1960s, the catalog was divided into five categories: Sutra Pitaka, Vinaya Pitaka, Abhidhamma Pitaka, Esoteric Pitaka, and writing. This catalog was briefly classified and numbered, and the translated terms, different translations, and translators were checked and the evidence was indicated. This was an important advance in the scientific compilation of the new Tripitaka catalog.

2   *The structure of Buddhist scriptures*

Chinese Buddhist scriptures' catalog organized a large number of Buddhist literature in different categories, reflecting the system and content of Buddhist scriptures. The Sutra Catalog usually divided Buddhist scriptures into five categories of form: Sutra Pitaka, Vinaya Pitaka, Abhidhamma Pitaka, Esoteric Pitaka, and miscellaneous pitaka.

> Sutra Pitaka: The "sutra" here did not refer to all Buddhist scriptures, but specifically referred to "Sutra Pitaka" of "Tripitaka". Sutra Pitaka was divided into two sub-items – namely, Mahayana and Hinayana sutra – and the sub-item was also divided into several parts – for example, Mahayana sutra was usually divided into Shes-phyin, Dkon-brtsegs, Dajibu, Phal-chen, and Nirvana, and the rest was divided into re-translation and single translation; Hinayana sutra was usually divided into Agama and the single translation. These scriptures clarified the doctrine of the basis, ways, methods, and realm of Mahayana and Hinayana, and showed the characteristics of them.
> Vinaya Pitaka: It was divided into Mahayana and Hinayana Vinaya, which made detailed provisions for precepts and ordaining rites.
> Abhidhamma Pitaka: It was divided into Mahayana and Hinayana Abhidhamma, and also in two parts, Shijing and Zongjing, in terms of content. Shijing was the sastra that interpreted Buddhist sutra, and Zongjing was the book that elucidated the doctrines of various factions.

Esoteric Pitaka: It was generally divided into Vajrasekhara, Garbha, Susiddhi, and Mantra.

Miscellaneous pitaka: It was divided into Indian writing, Chinese writing, and other sub-items.

The foregoing is the classification of the structure of Buddhist scriptures made by the Buddhist community from the perspective of concept of faith. In terms of general cultural knowledge, the vast number of Buddhist scriptures can be divided into six aspects:

1. The story of the life and mission of Sakyamuni, and the biography of Bodhisattva and eminent monks. Such Buddhist scriptures were used to set an example for believers to follow and to expand promotion and influence.
2. The provisions of sanghas' organization and precepts. These were the norms to guide the monks' lives and constrain their behavior, so as to maintain order in sanghas.
3. The narration of the history of sects – namely, the history of factional differentiation and evolution.
4. The reference books and introductory books for learning basic Buddhist knowledge – namely, books that introduced Buddhist scriptures, interpreted the concept of terms, and Buddhist catalogs.
5. Writings on Buddhist theory, which elucidated the fundamental opinions of Buddhism on life and the universe, criticized anti-Buddhist thought, and mutually criticized sects within Buddhism.
6. Practice, practice forms, and cultivation methods of monks, including works on the aspects of Esoteric rites.

In terms of their purpose, the foregoing six categories of Buddhist scriptures can also be summed up in two major categories: the first was to promote, and the second was for the monks to read. For example, "Sutra" in "Tripitaka" was mostly for promotion, such as the famous *Amitabha*, *Lotus Sutra*, *Manavaipulyamahasannipatasutra*, *Ratnakuta*, *Avatamsaka Sutra*, and *Prajnaparamita*, as well as biographies of Buddha and "metaphor" stories, including *Buddhist Parables*. As for "Vinaya", it was for Buddhist believers to learn and practice, and mantra was also internal, but it was often external in application for publicity's sake. "Abhidhamma" was also mostly for publicity, and a part of it was for internal debate, for only the monks' internal reference.

Notes

1 "Evam Maya Srutam": "Evam", Buddhism language in scriptures; "Maya Srutam" – namely, "what I hear".
2 See details in Lv Cheng: "New Chinese Tripitaka Catalog", pp. 124–154, Jinan, Qilu Publishing House, 1980.

4 The basic doctrines of Buddhism

The basic doctrines of Buddhism referred to the most important and core ideas, theories, doctrines, and beliefs in the vast religious thought of Buddhism. They generally contained two aspects closely related to each other: the first was the aspects of life, which elaborated the nature of phenomena in life, pointed out the way to escape the suffering of life and the ideal state that should be pursued in life, which was the doctrine on the ethical religious ideal, the basis of the whole Buddhist doctrine, and the most important; the second started from the exploration of life, followed by the exploration of negotiation between man and the universe, thus starting to seek the "reality" of universe, and forming the world views of "origin", "impermanence", and "anatman" ("emptiness"), and is the most philosophical religious theory, as well as the philosophical basis of ethical religious ideals.

The ethical religious ideal of Buddhism

The ethical religious ideal of Buddhism was based on the "Four Noble Truths" put forward by Sakyamuni and developed by later generations. The "Four Noble Truths" referred to KuDi, JiDi, MieDi, and Daodi. "Di" meant "truth"; "Ku" was suffering; "Ji" was cause; "Mie" was Nirvana; and "Dao" was approach, method. The four noble truths expounded the four truths: the painful phenomena of life, the causes of the suffering of life, the ideal realm guiding one to get rid of the suffering of life and liberate oneself from suffering, and the way to liberate oneself from suffering and realize the ideal realm. This was the basic view of the Buddhist philosophy of life.

1 The nature and value of life

(I) The position of man in the universe

Buddhism put forward the argument that sentient and enlightened life in the universe could be divided into ten categories, called "Four Saints and Six Mortals". "Four Saints" referred to Sravaka, Pratyekabuddha, Bodhisattva, and Buddha. Sravaka refers to the enlightened sage who hears Sakyamuni's teachings, Pratyekabuddha refers to the spiritual leader who understands Buddha's truth alone,

Bodhisattva is the candidate of Buddha, and Buddha is the greatly awakened who has achieved the highest achievements. Although there were differences in achievement of practice and levels of consciousness among the four, they were all enlightened sages beyond metempsychosis, and were thus called "saints". The "Six Mortals" were different from the "Four Saints". The "Six Mortals", also known as the "Six Approaches", "Liuqu", "All beings", and "Sattva", were the mortals who had not detached from metempsychosis with no liberation. Specifically, the "Six Mortals" referred to the following:

1. Heaven: It was so named because it was natural, clean, and bright, unmatched by the human world. It referred to the general gods, also known as "heavenly gods". Heaven is divided into several levels, among which the four Heavenly Kings are closest to the human world, and Tavatinsa was a high-level heaven. All these gods protected Dharma. Heaven was the most superior among the "Six Mortals", but there were still ups and downs, and it had not detached from metempsychosis.
2. Human: Human beings.
3. Asura: Sanskrit transliteration, abbreviated as "Sura". The paraphrasing was "non-heaven" and the devil. Buddhism said that Asura's ability was like heaven, but it was driven out of heaven because of being angry and aggressive, losing the virtue of heaven.
4. Beast: Also known as "Bangsheng". It referred to the birds and animals, as well as all the animals flying, creeping, swimming in water, and hiding underground.
5. Ghost: It was so named because it was greatly feared. It relied on the sacrifices of the descendants, or made a living by picking up abandoned things in the human world. There were many types of ghosts, such as Dacai Ghost, Xiaocai Ghost, Duocai Ghost, and Shaocai Ghost. Among ghosts, Yaksha and Rakshasa had great authority, while the hungry ghosts were in the worst condition, often suffering from hunger and thirst, and might not get any food for thousands of years; even if they got food, they would be immediately burned to ash. The hungry ghosts took up the most among all the ghosts, so usually when we mention ghosts, we refer to hungry ghosts.
6. Hell: This was the place with the lowest status and was the most painful in which to endure hardships. Those who had done all kinds of evil and committed numerous crimes suffered here. Buddhism usually depicted a fire in hell, covered with hot copper beds and iron columns, and those who had fallen into hell would be burned here. There are three categories of hell: the first is the fundamental hell, which is divided into eight hot hells and eight cold hells. For example, the eighth Avichi hell among the eight hot hells, also known as the relentless hell, in which the sinners' suffering never stopped, was the most painful. The second was the close hell, and the third was the lonely hell, in the intermontane wilderness, under trees or in the air.

Buddhism advocated that humankind was one of the "Six Mortals", in a low position in the universe, which shows Buddhism's basic position of scorning life. But man

92   The basic doctrines of Buddhism

was in the second level among the "Six Mortals", which was a relatively high level, close to the gods. If you believe in Buddhism and practice hard, you will be able to rise into the circle of "four saints" via "heaven", and get relief. This was the promise of Buddhism to humans with greater possibility of becoming a Buddha than beasts, showing its attention and expectations to humans. In general, contempt for life was an important feature of Buddhism.

(II)   The essence of humanity

What was human? Buddhism believed that the human body was a combination of *panca-skandha*. "Skandha" meant accumulation. Panca-skandha referred to the five elements to constitute what was human: rupa, *vedana, samjna, samskara*, and vijnana. "Rupa" meant material, referring to the flesh. Specifically, it included Caturmahabhuta: *prthivi-dhatu* (ground), *ab-dhatu* (water), *agni-dhatu* (fire), and *vayu-dhatu* (wind). Flesh and bones belonged to prthivi-dhatu, essence and blood belonged to ab-dhatu, body temperature and heat belonged to agni-dhatu, and breath and movement belonged to vayu-dhatu. Caturmahabhuta constitutes the body of a human. "Vedana" referred to emotions and feelings, such as suffering, happiness, pleasure, and worry. "Samjna" referred to rational activities and concept functions. "Samskara" specifically referred to bulesis. "Vijnana" unified the consciousness of the foregoing activities. Rupa was the material phenomenon, and vedana, samjna, samskara, and vijnana belonged to spiritual phenomena. Humans had bodily and also spiritual activities. Humans were the combination of material phenomena and spiritual phenomena. Buddhism advocated that humans were constituted by panca-skandha, which scattered and died out, and was uncertain and illusory. Humans were like flowing water and independent flame, with no fixed entity: panca-skandha would eventually separate and dissipate, and humans simply did not have a real ontology. Therefore, the essence of humans was "empty". The "empty" here not only meant that the dissipation of panca-skandha after the death of humans was empty but also the concordance of panca-skandha before death was empty. The latter also stressed the true meaning of emptiness most in Buddhism. It should be admitted that the human in Buddhism was the unity of material phenomena and spiritual phenomena, which was reasonable, but it was not correct to deduce that the essence of man was "empty".

(III)   The value of life

The basic starting point of Buddhist theory was to conclude that life was "painful", and the human life and survival were "painful". "Suffering" did not specifically refer to the feelings of suffering, but spiritual persecution – namely, the meaning of persecution. Buddhism believed that everything was changing and volatile, and the vast universe was nothing more than the field gathering suffering. Because people could not dominate their own life, and were often forced to face the consequences caused by uncertainty, they had no peace, but only suffering. The suffering usually spoken of in Buddhism included various kinds of suffering, such as the two kinds of suffering, the three kinds suffering, the four kinds of suffering, the five kinds of suffering, the eight kinds of suffering, even the 110 kinds of suffering, and so on. The so-called two kinds of suffering referred to internal suffering and external suffering. There were two aspects of internal suffering – namely, the suffering of physical illness and contradictory psychological activities of feelings, will, and thinking. External suffering referred to disasters in the outside world. As for the so-called three kinds of suffering, the first was the suffering of pain or the suffering of painful things, such as hunger, thirst, cold, and heat; the second was the suffering of change or the suffering of changes to happy events, such as turning from wealthy to poor; the third was pervasive suffering, or the suffering of elapse of things. The four kinds of suffering referred to birth, death, illness, and old age. The five kinds of suffering integrated birth, death, illness, and old age into one suffering, and added suffering of *apriya-samprayoga-duhkha*, the suffering of love and farewell, and the suffering of not-getting and *pancaupadana-skandhah*. The eight kinds of suffering divided birth, death, illness, and old age in the five kinds of suffering into the four kinds of suffering again, and added the four latter kinds of suffering. The eight kinds of suffering were the most common argument, whose specific content contained the following:

1. The suffering of birth: When people had not been born, they stayed in womb for ten months; as if in the dark hell, whenever their mother drank hot soup, they would suffer from boiling. When they were born, the cold wind touched them like a knife cutting them. They suffer when staying in the womb or getting out of the womb. After they were born, the suffering of old age, illness, and death came one after another.
2. The suffering of old age: When people got old, their hair turned white, their teeth fell out, their muscles slackened, their sensory organs failed, their mind became unconscious, and their life was going to end, gradually dying.
3. The suffering of illness: One was the physical illness, from head to toe, from inside to outside; various diseases attacked, which was very painful; the other was emotional illness, or feeling sad and distressed.
4. The suffering of death: One was impermanence of life, which ended when humans died; the other was death in accidents or disasters.
5. The suffering of hate: People might not love either the subjective or the objective aspects, because of their hatred of things or people from whom they would like to keep away, but unfortunately, they could not avoid enemies. When enemies met, the hated things came one after another.
6. The suffering of love and farewell: People may love both the subjective and objective aspects, but farewell was inevitable, and love was difficult. For example, father and son, brothers, couples, friends loved each other and got along well, but they could not avoid separation, and even a great disaster, resulting in death and great suffering.
7. The suffering of not-getting: People's demands, desires, and love could often not be satisfied, and they failed to get what they sought; the more they failed to get, the greater the suffering.

8   Pancaupadana-skandhah: Also known as "Wuyunchengku" or "wuchengyunku". This was the convergence point of all suffering – namely, all sufferings were attributed to the suffering of panca-skandha. When panca-skandha combined with "Qu" (referring to a stubborn desire, persistent love), there were all kinds of greed, known as "pancaupadana-skandhah". Here, "Qu", referring to persistence, was the key. With pancaupadana-skandhah, there would be suffering. The seven sufferings of birth, death, illness, old age, duhkha, love and farewell, and not-getting came to panca-skandha, and people's bodies and hearts were full of various sufferings, known as "pancaupadana-skandhah". Buddhism advocated that the suffering of not-getting was the total reason for the previous six kinds of suffering, which was suffering due to pancaupadana-skandhah. Among the eight kinds of suffering, pancaupadana-skandhah was the root of other sufferings, and also the convergence of all the sufferings. Chinese monks echoed that people's faces were in the shape of the character "suffering".

The eight kinds of suffering were divided into two categories, among which the former four sufferings were natural physiological phenomena – namely, the process of life was a continuous process of different suffering. The fifth suffering to the seventh suffering referred to the boredom of being connected to hated things, the sadness of parting from favorite things, and suffering of failing to satisfy a demand, which focused on social phenomena, social life, and relationships between people. Buddhism attributes the former seven kinds of suffering finally to pancaupadana-skandhah, explaining that panca-skandha was suffering, and persistence and greed are suffering – in other words, human life is suffering, and survival is suffering.

Buddhism also exaggerated and absolutized the suffering of life in time and space, promoting that past, present, and future lives were all suffering. The world that life faced was also suffering: "there was no peace, the world was like a fire house" (Lotus Sutra); the world was the fire house, the boundless sea of suffering. All beings were caught in the raging fire house, suffering and sinking in the vast sea of suffering.

Life was the proposition of suffering, a theoretical foundation of the Buddhist outlook on life. Life and people's feelings were painful and happy. Buddhism believed that life was suffering, and all feelings were suffering; happiness was a special performance of suffering. It was precisely because the founder of Buddhism described life as the course of suffering that the basic position of going beyond mundane affairs was laid.

Buddhism regarded life as a painful process, and promoted the opinion that everything was suffering and the suffering sea was boundless, which firstly reflected the cruel reality that the slavery society in the northeast of ancient India at that time was still a living hell, where slave owners were vulgar, greedy, brutal, and lecherous, and the serious inequality caused by the caste system brought infinite suffering to the broad masses of people. Secondly, it also reflected the low level of life and medicine in ancient India at that time, which was a tropical area with high mortality, and people's health was not guaranteed. Buddhism's opinion that life was suffering, in essence, was a tortuous reflection of the suffering caused by slavery, the people's groans under the double oppression of society and nature. At the same time, it should also be emphasized that the judgment of Buddhism on the value of life was negative and one-sided. It not only obliterated the joy of life but also mentioned physical suffering and social suffering in the same breath, and put physical suffering in the first place, which one-sidedly exaggerated physical suffering and covered up the seriousness of social suffering and class oppression. It described laborers and exploiters as having the same suffering, which obscured the grim facts of the class contradictions in slave society. It distorted the substance of social suffering, and obliterated the important fact that class oppression and exploitation were the basic cause of the suffering of people.

2 The root of suffering of life

(1) 12 karmas

Where did the suffering of humans come from? Where did the life of humans come from? What decided the fate of humans? Sakyamuni disagreed with the argument of the Indian thought community at that time, which was that everything in life was dominated by the will of God; neither did he agree with the opinion that everything was decided in the past life and could not be changed later, and he also opposed the opinion that everything in life had no karma. Sakyamuni believed that these were irresponsible arguments about their actions, and he argued that everything was made up of karma and causality; similarly, the suffering, life, and fate of humans were also caused by themselves and they shall suffer.

As mentioned earlier, Buddhism attributed the root of suffering of life to "pan-caupadana-skandhah" – that is, the direct cause of the suffering of life was "birth", which was the beginning of suffering, and life was a suffering entity. Thus, Buddhism, again from the perspective of the life process, divided life into many parts, which were combined into an endless suffering chain, and thus further elucidated the suffering of life and its roots. In this regard, the arguments of five karmas, nine karmas, ten karmas, and 12 karmas were recorded in Buddhist scriptures. Among them, the 12 karmas spread in the north were more discussed and later identified by Mahayana Buddhism. The 12 karmas referred to avijja, samskara, vijnana, *namarupa, sad-ayatana, sparsa*, vedana, priya, *upadana, bhava, jata*, and jara-marana. The specific contents and interrelationships of the 12 karmas were as follows:

> Avijja led to samskara: "Avijja" referred to ignorance, and ignorance of Buddhism. For example, life was impermanent, and it ended finally, but people often pursued its "permanence". Life was constituted by "panca-skandha" with no entity, but people often believed there was "ego" – the eternal immortality (entity) was real. These were all performances of ignorance. "Samskara" meant bulesis. "Avijja led to samskara" meant that different types of bulesis were caused by ignorance.

Samskara led to vijnana: "Vijnana" referred to citta and spiritual activities. It was driven by bulesis, and drove citta to the corresponding place.

Vijnana led to namarupa: "Vijn" referred to the heart and spirit; "ana" referred to the body. "Namarupa" referred to the spirit and shape. "Vijnana led to namarupa" meant physical and mental development in the womb.

Namarupa led to sad-ayatana: "Sad-ayatana" was also known as "liuru", referring to eyes, ears, nose, tongue, body, and heart[1] – namely, the five senses and heart (collectively referred to as the "six organs"). Here it meant that the fetus, due to chaos of mind and body, developed different organs for cognition – namely, the stage in which the fetus is being born.

Sad-ayatana led to sparsa: "Sparsa" referred to touch. Here it meant that after the birth of fetus, the six kinds of organs for cognition had contact with the outside world and produced touch, equivalent to the stage of young children.

Sparsa led to vedana: "Vedana" meant feelings. With age, the mind gradually developed, and the organs for cognition could receive external reactions when contacting the outside world, and produced three feelings: suffering, happy, or not suffering or happy. It was equivalent to the boy stage.

Vedana led to priya: "Priya" meant desire, love, and greed. When people went into the youth stage, they had priya for the outside world.

Priya led to upadana: "Upadana" referred to the pursuit. After adulthood, greed turned stronger, and people pursued every enjoyable thing in the outside world, and persisted in it.

Upadana led to bhava: "Bhava" referred to thinking and behavior, various types of thinking and behavior due to persistent pursuit. These thoughts and behaviors could produce goodness and badness in the future, and was thus named "bhava".

Bhava led to jata: "Jata" referred to the afterlife. The confusion, goodness, and badness caused by priya, upadana, and bhava would definitely produce retribution, which led to the reincarnation of the afterlife.

Jata led to jara-marana: Jata must lead to jara-marana.

The aforementioned 12 links led to one after another, so they were called the 12 karmas. The 12 karmas explained the causal links between the life and death of creatures. It emphasized that the 12 links consisted of the causal cycle in order, and anyone was, before liberation, in the endless cycle according to it. The 12 karmas were a summary of the phenomena in life, and also the cause of the suffering of life. Hinayana Buddhism believed that in the 12 karmas, the first two karmas – namely, avijja and samskara – existed as the reasons for present existence, belonging to the result caused by the past; the eight karmas in the middle, from "vijnana" to "bhava", were based on present existence, among which vijnana, namarupa, sad-ayatana, sparsa, and vedana were the present five results caused by avijja and samskara in the past, while priya, upadana, and bhava were the present three reasons that would lead to results in the future; and the last two karmas – namely, jata and jara-marana – belonged to the future, meaning the result in the afterlife caused by priya, upadana, and bhava in this life. In this way, the 12 karmas included the past, present, and future lives, with causes and results. Later, Mahayana Buddhism developed it into the theory of two lives and one cause for one result.

According to the history of Buddhism, when Sakyamuni was about to become a Buddha, he observed the 12 karmas reversely – that is, from jara-marana to avijja – and drew this conclusion: the true driving force of phenomena in life, and the ultimate cause of the suffering of life, was "avijja" – namely, blind ignorance of the reality of life. If people could correctly understand the reality of life and know the truth of the 12 karmas, they could destroy avijja. Without avijja there would not be samskara, until there was no jata and jara-marana, and all suffering was gone. So they reached the realm of Nirvana.

It should be certain that the causal relationship between the life and death of creatures revealed by the 12 karmas was not objective and practical. Although some of the parts of the 12 karmas also reflected the cause of generation of human feelings, desires, and behavior, it was an idealist fiction in general. Why? First of all, the analysis of the causal relationship of the 12 karmas would inevitably lead to the immortality of the soul. Early Buddhism did not think that vijnana was the soul, which was different from the soul indeed, but as a spiritual activity, vijnana formed human life when it was combined with namarupa. As the reason for namarupa, it was difficult for vijnana to be sharply demarcated from the soul. Vinjnan and bhava manifested mutually. Bhava referred to ideological behavior, whose role was to cause the result in the afterlife, to turn to another form of life. Here bhava was taken as the reason and condition for reincarnation, containing the physical content of reincarnation, so it was also interlinked to the soul. Secondly, in the 12 karmas, in addition to emphasizing that vijnana was the initial reason, the evil nature and role of priya were also one-sidedly emphasized. Early Buddhism opposed people's nature and pleasure of pursuing survival and reproducing life, and opposed the greed of wealth, power, and fame. This argument mixed up the greed of exploiters and the normal life demands of workers, regarded both of them as greed and a kind of mental state of people, and took them as the cause for reincarnation of life, which was wrong. Finally, life and death were interdependent, and life was bound to go into death, but it could not be generally said that life was the direct cause of death. The interdependent relationship was not equal to the causal relationship. The direct cause of death was disease and aging.

(II)   Retribution and reimbursement

Sakyamuni also linked and unified the 12 karmas, karma, and reincarnation, and illustrated the different fates of all beings with retribution and reimbursement.

In the age of Sakyamuni, there were two sharply opposed theories in the Indian intellectual circle: reincarnation and anti-reincarnation theories. The so-called reincarnation, "Lun", was the wheel of vehicles, and "Hui" referred to the rotation of vehicles. Reincarnation was the metaphor of the circle of life and death of all beings, which never ended, like the wheel that keeps rotating. At that time, there were three main opinions that advocated reincarnation: the first was Brahmanism, which promoted that the Brahmanist god was the Creator, endowing humans with their souls, and Brahman was the "parmatman", while the human soul was the "small self". The soul belonged to the heart. If humans could practice keeping still and in deep meditation, purify the soul, abolish all kinds of material desires with ascetic practices, and sacrifice to the Brahman for atonement, then their souls would be able to go with Brahman after death; otherwise they would fall to a lower realm than this life in their afterlife. The second was Yogacara, which opposed the argument that the soul turned from Brahman, and believed that the human soul was independent, not attached to God, known as "purusa". If a person indulged in sensual pleasures in this life, purusa would fall into a more painful place in the afterlife; on the contrary, if they practiced the meditation of Yogacara, and restrained the lust rising from purusa, they could go beyond reincarnation after death and get relief. The third was the mechanical predestination holders, who believed that not only the suffering and happiness, good and bad fortune of this life were decided by actions in the past but also actions in this life were prescribed by the past. People should obey the arrangement until the past purva-karma was eliminated, and the soul would be freed. Anti-reincarnation was the argument of Lokayat of ancient materialism, which believed that the human body was constituted by "Caturmahabhuta" (four gross elements) – ground, water, fire, and wind – and the human body produced feeling and thinking. When humans died, their body turned back into the "four gross elements", and also stopped feeling and thinking. There was no soul after death, let alone reincarnation. Sakyamuni's point of view was different from the foregoing ones. He called the argument that the soul was immortal and reincarnation was continuous the "nityadrsti tirthaka", a wrong theory that regarded the soul and reincarnation as real and constant; he also called the argument that denied the soul and reincarnation "uccheda-drsti tirthaka", saying it was a wrong theory that annihilated the mind and body. He started from the angle of the behavior and moral responsibility of the subject, absorbed and transformed the ideas of other schools, combined karma with reincarnation, and expounded the argument of retribution and reorganization.

Sakyamuni promoted that karma was the cause of the retribution of all beings, and the motive of reincarnation. The action of all beings, and their will dominating actions, was essentially karma. "Ye" referred to action or deed. To do a thing with prior mental activity was *manas-karman*; when it was said, it was *vak-karman*; actions performed physically were *kaya-karman*. Sakyamuni believed that manas-karman, vak-karman, and kaya-karman of all beings were often determined by avijja – namely, ignorance. Sentient beings had no self and were impermanent, and will die after all, but they asked it to be itself and constant. The behavior of all beings was often the performance of such ignorance. The behavior of all beings caused by such ignorance was the total source of suffering. Karma embodied the power and role, merit and fault. Sakyamuni believed that the influence of karma would not be eliminated, and the good and evil karma of sentient beings would cause corresponding retribution. For example, when the life of a person ended, the sum of his/her actions over the whole life (which in many respects was equal to the individual's character) would produce an overall result and determine the character of the survivor in the afterlife. Different natures of karma led to different retribution and different realms in the afterlife. Buddhism promoted that all beings were in the causal relationship of good and evil. Those who did good rose, while those who did evil fell with their sin. In such rising and falling, death and life, they continued rising or falling in all their lives, constantly going up and down in the sea of suffering, in the "six reincarnations". Only when they were converted to Buddhism, abandoned evil, did good, and devotedly practiced could they jump out of the six reincarnations and get relief beyond life and death.

The theory of retribution and reincarnation emphasized the role of the individual in "karma", and that everything was self-inflicted, which was different from the claim that God dominated people's fate from the outside, and objectively played a certain role in exhorting and restraining the behavior of people; it advocated that the activities of people would certainly bring some consequences and retribution, which, under certain conditions, within a certain range, in a certain sense, also had its reasonable side. For example, people would be affirmed by history for being engaged in good and just causes, but get punished by history for doing evil. But it should be said that this is conditional, not unconditional. In class society, the fate of the individual was mainly determined by the class and status. In a society where the exploiting class dominated, wealth was the privilege of the exploiting class, while inferiority was the fate of the exploited class, and it was difficult to change this pattern under the condition that the class status did not change. In the class society, it was common that good people had accidents while bad ones got lucky. Buddhism generally promoted that good karma led to good retribution and evil karma led to bad retribution in ethics, which was only the comfort of personal conscience at most. Buddhism attributed the weal and woe of this life to the karma of the past life, and promoted that the karma of this life would be judged by God after death, and such theological fiction was actually equal to recognizing that good and evil in reality were inconsistent with weal and woe.

3 The ideal realm of life

Buddhism put the trend of life in two opposite ways: the first was that the lack of harmony between the needs of life and the environment produced all kinds of suffering, whose reason was unknown to people and the solution could not be found, so people had to follow the crowd, and obey the arrangement of fate, falling into continuous reincarnation, known as "pravrtti"; the second was to the take the opposite approach to "pravrtti", destroy it, change it, and reverse it, known as "vyupasama". This was the so-called two opposite series of life. The latter was to pursue the highest ideal realm of life.

Early Buddhism borrowed the Brahman's concept of Nirvana to mark the highest ideal realm of Buddhism. Nirvana was Sanskrit transliteration. As for the paraphrasing, Kumarajo translated it into "Mie" or "Miedu", and Tang Xuanzang translated it into "Parinirvana (Yuanji)". The so-called extinction referred to destroying trouble, and the cause and effect of life and death. As for the so-called Yuanji, Yuan meant "completeness", which could not increase or decrease;

Ji meant "silence", which could not go bad. Yuanji meant that everything around Nirvana had true nature. Before Xuanzang, "Mie" or "Miedu" was more used China, and after Xuanzang, Yuanji was more used. There were many classifications of Nirvana, usually divided into Nirvana with remainder and Nirvana without remainder. Nirvana with remainder referred to the removal of greed and trouble – namely, the elimination of the cause of life and death – but as retribution of karma in the past life, the body still existed in the world, which also thought and acted, and was not complete Nirvana. Nirvana without remainder was relative to Nirvana with remainder, which is in a higher realm. In this realm, not only the cause of life and death was eliminated but also the retribution of life and death was eliminated, which was the highest ideal realm. There are differences and links between the two kinds of Nirvana, and Nirvana without remainder was the continuation and development of Nirvana with remainder.

There was great difference between the interpretations of Nirvana of Mahayana and Hinayana Buddhism. In other words, the Buddhist ideal of life had a historical evolution.

Hinayana Buddhism's Nirvana doctrine was negative. It regarded life as great suffering, starting from which it believed that when the human body died, the suffering of life also ended. So it took the state of elimination after practice, in which troubles were eliminated and no trace was left after death, as the goal, just like the light's flame was blown out. As for people who became Arhat after practice and entered Nirvana after death, what was the situation after that? Existence or inexistence? Hinayana Buddhism believed that this was a problem difficult for the human mind and language to discuss and describe, which was like a forest only for travelers to roam in, a puppet show only for secular entertainment, which could produce only controversy, entanglement, and suffering, but did not help to obtain consciousness and enter Nirvana.

Nagarjuna, one of the founders of Madhyamika of Mahayana Buddhism, opposed Hinayana Buddhism, which took Nirvana without remainder as the supreme realm of pursuit, broke through the thinking pattern of Hinayana Buddhism, and put forward new ideas from a new perspective. He believed that Nirvana was consistent with the nature in the world, which were both "empty" with unspeakable "marvelous existence", completely unified. He alleged that Hinayana Buddhism did not understand this truth, disgusted and abandoned the world, and pursued the ultra-world Nirvana, which would never really achieve Nirvana. Nagarjuna believed that the goal of sentient beings should be a correct understanding of "dharmata" (the original face) of all things and application of it – namely, to remove all *prapanca* and "show dharmata". Dharmata was the content of Nirvana, and the Nirvana realm was the understanding and application of it. This kind of Nirvana was also called "Dharmata Nirvana".

There were two main points of the content of Dharmata Nirvana: firstly, according to dharmata, things in the world moved, lived, and died, while Nirvana was beyond that. But all the phenomena in world were empty, taking emptiness as dharmata. The original nature of Nirvana was also empty. Both were empty, so it could be said that the dharmata of things in the world was the content of Nirvana, and also that the world was the same as Nirvana – namely, to combine them with dharmata. This was what Nagarjuna said: "There was no difference between Nirvana and the world. There was no difference between the reality of Nirvana and world" (*Madhyamika-sastra-On Nirvana*).

Nagarjuna believed that if people did not have real wisdom, they would reverse things, resulting in the endless suffering of life; on the contrary, if they could really understand all things had nothing to do with people's subjective dedication, that there was no entity known and described by general people – that is, to experience emptiness (no original nature), and turn things to the original pure appearance – they reached the Nirvana realm. The second was to emphasize that in order to achieve real Nirvana, they could must never stop. Because everything was interrelated, so were people. The human was a whole, not just an individual, and could not act alone but act together, benefiting themselves and others and integrating themselves in the vast ocean of beings in order to obtain real relief. In this way, on the way to Nirvana, they would realize that there were many things to do, and the work of delivering all living creatures from torment could never be finished, so they could never stop in the middle. As they desired to deliver all living creatures from torment, even if their own consciousness had reached the Buddha's situation, and could enter Nirvana without remainder, they would never enter. This was the so-called wisdom, not living in life and death; not living in Nirvana. This is also called "Nirvana with no abode".

The sect of Nagarjuna, according to the theory that dharmata of the world was the content of Nirvana, believed that acting in accordance with the reality of the world was in response to Nirvana, and such practice tended to believe that Nirvana was a process, a process gradually turning from pollution to cleanness, from heterogeneity to purity. This truth was later expounded and propagated by Yogacara of Asaga and Vasubandhu. Asaga and Vasubandhu proclaimed the category of "asraya-parivrtt" to replace relief. That was to influence the behavior by changing understanding, and then change the objective environment. In the process of cultivation, if people gradually replaced the concept and understanding of pollution with the concept and understanding of cleanness, then changed the whole understanding, and brought about changes in behavior, the changes in behavior would bring about environmental changes. So life also turned from pollution to cleanness, and gradually changed, and finally pollution was gone with full cleanness, and the whole physical and mental appearance completely changed, achieving the Nirvana realm. This was another important theory of Nirvana after Madhyamika.

Some sects of Mahayana Buddhism also opposed Hinayana Buddhism's opinion that denied permanence, happiness, self, and cleanness as being the basic requirements of life, emphasized that the Nirvana realm had four good properties of permanence, happiness, self, and cleanness, even eight features of permanence, constancy, peace, coolness, agelessness, athanasy, cleanness, and happiness, and advocated pursuing and finding real permanence, happiness, self, and cleanness of life, which opened up another new religious way for the ideal of life.

Hinayana Buddhism took "nothingness" as the content of Nirvana, which ignored the status and meaning of life in the universe, denied the spirit of active struggle that life should have, and reflected the pessimistic estimation and negative attitude to life. Madhyamika of Mahayana Buddhism took dharmata of all things as the content of Nirvana, and dharmata was believed to be empty, which indirectly denied the authenticity of the objective world. Followers of Hinayana Buddhism took the understanding of the inauthenticity of objective world as the highest spiritual realm, which was a mystical idealism. But Madhyamika integrated the world and Nirvana, canceled the gap between the reality of the world and the other world, and shortened the distance between humans and the Buddha, which in fact increased the practical content of the Nirvana doctrine. Mahayana Buddhism scholars advocated the study of knowledge serving the world, such as astronomy, geography, medicine, and technology, which affected not only the direction of Buddhism but also cultural development.

4 The way of life relief

Buddhism had a lot of discussion on the liberation of life and ways to achieve the highest ideal realm, and its factions, especially Mahayana and Hinayana, had inconsistent arguments. The following is a brief introduction to the content of typical Noble Eightfold Paths, Three Practices, and Six Perfections.

(I) Noble Eightfold Paths

As mentioned earlier, in the time of Sakyamuni, it had become common practice for believers of various Indian sects to become monks and cultivate themselves. Sakyamuni did not believe in the self-abuse of asceticism, and believed that pure abstinence was worthless and futile; he also opposed lustism, believing that this could not get rid of painful entanglement. He put forward the argument of no suffering and no happiness, a total of eight paths, known as the "Noble Eightfold Paths". The Noble Eightfold Paths referred to eight kinds of proper ways to become a Buddha, also known as "eight holy paths". The specific content was as follows:

1. Samyag-drsti: The correct view to leave evil – namely, the four truths of the Buddha's speech – away from claims only focusing on gods, self, or material things. Simply, it was Buddhist wisdom.
2. Samyak-samkalpa: It referred to the subjective departure from the secular, leaving absurdity and evil for the pure wisdom of Buddhism thinking.
3. Samyak-vac: Pure and good language, an argument in line with Dharma – that is, not talking nonsense or engaging in abusive expressions, slander, or violent language, away from all the prapanca.
4. Samyak-karmanta: Proper activities, behavior, and work in accordance with Buddhist requirements – that is, not killing, stealing, prostituting oneself, or doing evil.
5. Samyag-ajiva: The proper life – namely, the necessities of life according to the standards of Buddhism, away from all improper occupations, such as fraud, pride, or star divination, which should all be opposed.

6 Samyag-vyayama: It referred to correct efforts to prevent evil to do good, and proceed to liberation. That is, to try to prevent evil thoughts and cut off those already produced; strive to have a good heart, and make it perfect; distinguish good and evil according to the standards of Buddhism; stress self-awareness and effort, and oppose being slack and lazy.
7 Samyak-smrti: The correct idea – that is, to hold correct Dharma and remember the four truths.
8 Samyak-samadhi: Correct meditation – that is, to keep the body upright and maintain concentration and silence. Focus on one realm, away from the chaotic heart, concentrate the mind, do deep meditation, observe the whole world with the wisdom of Buddhism, like a pool of clear water, in which fish and gravel were clearly visible, have insight into real life, and comprehend the meaning of the Four Noble Truths to get relief.

The Noble Eightfold Paths could be divided into two categories: one was the spiritual life, dominated by Samyag-drsti, supplemented by Samyak-samkalpam, Samyak-smrti, and Samyak-samadhi; the other was material life, dominated by Samyag-ajiva, supplemented by Samyak-karmanta. Samyak-vac and Samyag-vyayama belonged to both. Samyag-drsti and Samyag-ajiva was respectively the main point of spiritual life and material life of Buddhist believers, and had great significance in the Noble Eightfold Paths, which established principles and laid a foundation for the practice of Buddhists.

(II) Three Practices

The Noble Eightfold Paths could be attributed to Three Practices: precept, meditation, and wisdom. Samyag-drsti, Samyak-vac, and Samyak-karmanta belonged to "precept", Samyak-smrt and Samyak-samadhi belonged to "meditation", and Samyag-drsti and Samyak-samkalpa belonged to "wisdom". Samyag-vyayama was the attitude toward studying Buddhism, which was full, but it was also an embodiment of wisdom, and could be attributed to "wisdom". Precept, meditation, and wisdom were interrelated, and were generally considered to be the full content of the practice of Buddhist learners. Mahayana's and Hinayana's attitude to the Three Practices was not consistent. Hinayana Buddhism strictly distinguished them, while Mahayana Buddhism attributed precept and meditation to wisdom and integrated the Three Practices. Hinayana Buddhism claimed precept and meditation as mechanical norms, while Mahayana Buddhism flexibly used precept and meditation for convenience.

1 PRECEPT

As one of the Three Practices, precept referred to the rules made by Buddhism for monks and believers at home in order to prevent evil. According to its content, it was divided into Zhichiie and Zuochijie. As for the so-called Zhichiie, "Zhi" meant preventing and stopping, referred to all kinds of precepts to prevent evil, such as the five precepts, eight precepts, ten precepts, and complete precepts. As for the so-called Zuochijie, "Zuo" meant good practice, referring to precepts to keep all good practice, such as 20 Skandha.[2] Zhichijie and Zuochijie respectively prevented evil, and complemented each other. Precept and Vinaya were often used in conjunction, known as the precepts. The precepts also referred to all Buddhist precepts made for the monks and the believers at home. But there was also a difference between Vinaya and precept; if Vinaya was spoken of alone, it referred to abstinence for monks and nuns, and was said to be able to subdue evil, and lay Buddhists could not know.

The five precepts, as it has been mentioned, referred to no killing, no theft, no prostitution, no nonsense, and no drinking. Later, considering that general believers at home were occupied by trifles, and it was difficult for them to adhere to the five precepts every day, for this purpose, six fast days per month were set, in which people had to stay away from all secular things and comply with the five precepts; in addition, three precepts were added to the eight ones. The added three precepts were: (1) to not engage in any pleasing entertainment or arbitrarily dress up – in other words, not to listen to music or dance, not to watch dramas, perfume, rub ointment on, or modify themselves; (2) to not sit or sleep in a magnificent bed; and (3) to not eat food at the improper time – that is, no meal after noon. Among the three precepts, the first and second were precepts, while the third was a fast. Together with the former five precepts, they were collectively known as "eight fasts". The eight precepts were more stringent than the five precepts, but they were temporarily implemented, such as six days in one month, or even one day, which could be flexibly implemented. During the period when believers at home were initiated into priesthood, they lived a religious life similar to monks. The ten precepts referred to the ten rules for monks older than 7 and younger than 20 and nuns. Among them, the provisions of the first, second, fourth, and fifth precepts were exactly the same as the corresponding precepts in the five precepts. The third precept was no physical pleasure – namely, no sex or even marriage. The latter five precepts divided the sixth precept of the eight precepts into two: no perfume and no song and dance, and the others were exactly the same, and then added one precept of no accumulation of treasure, for a total of ten precepts. The complete precept was for monks and nuns. The number of precepts was different; usually, according to *Dharmaguptavinaya*, there were 250 precepts for monks and 348 precepts for nuns. It was so named because compared to the ten precepts for monks and nuns, the precepts were complete. The complete precepts made various detailed and strict rules for the religious and daily lives of monks.

Mahayana precepts made further developments based on Hinayana precepts. Hinayana Buddhism focused on the liberation of life and death, and inferring that the root of life and death was greed, so it made withdrawal of personal greed the basic content of the rules. Later, Mahayana Buddhism emphasized that selfish greed was the root of all evil, such as obstructing, infringing, and destroying others to seek personal gain, and that the precepts must be rooted in withdrawing selfishness and greed; it accordingly put forward "Sattvartha-kriya-sila" to educate all beings. The key of Mahayana was the "10 heavy precepts" and "48 light precepts". The ten heavy precepts were: (1) precept of killing; (2) precept of burglary; (3) precept of prostitution; (4) precept of nonsense; (5) precept of selling wine; (6) precept of talking about the four beings (monks, nuns, and male and female lay Buddhists); (7) precept of praising oneself and slandering others; (8) precept of parsimony and slander; (9) precept of hatred and destruction of others and refusing their confession; (10) precept of slander Sambo (Buddha-dharma-sangha). Among the ten heavy precepts, the precept of praising oneself and slandering others was very important, which was the center of the latter six newly added precepts, and the others just expanded it. Mahayana Buddhism also stressed that this precept was connected to wisdom, paying attention to the perfection of the spiritual structure. Those who violated the ten heavy precepts committed the crime of damaging the school, and would be expelled from the sangha, so they were heavy precepts. In contrast to them were the 48 light precepts, which were for light crimes. The contents included the precept of not respecting teachers and friends, the precept of alcohol, and the precept of eating meat. Those who violated these precepts should repent according to the precepts, but not be punished. Mahayana precepts considered drinking a light precept, indicating that the restraint of the material life of Buddhists relaxed, and its disposition was also more flexible.

2 MEDITATION

"Meditation" was the free translation of Samādhi in Sanskrit, whose transliteration was "Samadhi". It meant that the heart was focused on a spiritual state and not scattered, which was taken by Buddhism as the psychological condition to get definite understanding and determine judgment. There were two kinds of meditation: the one was "born meditation", referring to an inherent spiritual function of people; the second was "cultivated meditation", referring to the effort to acquire Buddhist wisdom, merit, and supernatural powers. There were differences between Zen and meditation; "Zen" was the transliteration of Dhyānan in Sanskrit, whose paraphrasing was "silent thinking", "practice of thinking", "abandoning evil", "merit monastery", and so on, meaning that the heart was tranquil and deep in thought. Chinese Buddhist scholars usually combined Zen and meditation, whose meaning was wider. Chinese Zen was named "Zen", which further expanded the concept of meditation, focusing on a "cultivating heart" and "seeing nature", no longer confined to the form of sitting silently and concentrating on observation.

Buddhism had always attached great importance to meditation. Early Buddhism and Sectarian Buddhism believed that the religious practice of the believers was "darsana-marga" first – that is, to understand the four truths before "bhavana-marga". Bhavana-marga was practice, whose main method was meditation. Later, Mahayana Buddhism further took meditation as the way to enlighten Prajna theories. There were many arguments on meditation among various Buddhist factions, among which the most basic included "four meditations", "Zen of chanting Buddha's name", and "dharmata Zen".

"Four meditations", also known as "four silent thinking", were the basic meditations of Buddhism to treat delusion and produce merit; their content was as follows:

> First meditation: The realm of disgusting and leaving the residence of all beings full of appetite and lust by observing, so as to be happy.
> Second meditation: The function of further annihilating the celebrated dictum, so as to form a firm belief in Buddhism in the heart, and generate new joy.
> Third meditation: Abandoned the joy acquired from the second meditation, lived in the realm with no suffering or happiness, and used Samyak-smrt to study hard, thus producing "wonderful joy".
> Fourth meditation: Abandoned the wonderful joy acquired from the third meditation, and focused only on cultivation and merit, thus producing the feeling of "no suffering or happiness".

The four meditations were special psychological feelings with "no suffering and no happiness" formed by guiding all beings to break away from desires, and concentrating on the cultivation of Buddhist merit through four levels of meditation.

"Zen of chanting Buddha's name" was to concentrate on thinking of the 32 appearances and 80 characteristics[3] of Buddha, with the help of Buddhist wisdom, so as to make the Buddhas appear, increase a special power, and faster reach Buddha's realm.

As for "Dharmata Zen", Madhyamika of Mahayana Buddhism thought it (the truth of things) was "empty", and advocated connecting Zen and the view of emptiness, and seeing the emptiness of all things as well as the role of all things in the Zen view, with neither neglected. Dharmata Zen was to take Zen as the method of the Prajna theories of Mahayana.

3 WISDOM

Wisdom was the paraphrasing of Mati in Sanskrit, referring to the spiritual role to thoroughly understand the matters, decide, and obtain a decisive understanding. Here it meant the Buddhist wisdom that could make the practitioners get rid of troubles and get relief. Practice for training and increasing the wisdom of Buddhism was known as wisdom. Buddhism usually divided wisdom into three kinds: (1) hearing wisdom, referring to listening to the Dharma and learning Pancavidy[4] – namely, the wisdom heard from others; (2) thinking wisdom, to think according to wisdom heard from the former and understand – namely, the wisdom obtained from their own thinking; (3) cultivating wisdom, to practice meditation according to the wisdom obtained from hearing and thinking, and understand the truth of life and universe – namely, the wisdom from enlightenment. Thus they became wise and cut off all the trouble of ignorance, entered the realm of Nirvana, and became a Buddha. Wisdom mainly elucidated the Buddhist outlook on life and cosmology, whose content was extremely rich and vast, omitted here.

(III) Six Perfections

Mahayana Buddhism believed that if there was no relief for all beings, there would be no real relief for individuals, so it put forward the slogans of "helping people in distress" and "delivering all living creatures from torment", and correspondingly it expanded the Three Practices centered on individual practice to "Six Perfections" with a wide range of social content. "Perfections" was the paraphrasing of paramita in Sanskrit. Six Perfections meant the six ways and methods to take people from this shore of life and death to the other shore of Nirvana. This was the main content of Mahayana Buddhism. The specific content of Six Perfections was as follows:

1. Dāna: Dāna meant helping the poor and satisfying the seekers with their own wealth, energy and intelligence, which was a practice method that benefited others while helping seekers accumulate merit and get relief. Hinayana also talked about Dāna, whose purpose was to get rid of personal parsimony and greed, so as to avoid poverty in the afterlife – namely, to start from personal interests and relief. Mahayana was associated with the doctrine of great compassion to release the souls of all beings from suffering, so the objects of Dāna also far exceeded the scope of human beings, and extended to birds and beasts, insects and fish. Mahayana Buddhism attached great importance to Dāna, and ranked it as the first among Six Perfections. In Mahayana scriptures, there were a large number of fables, such as donating all one's wealth, saving lives, and sacrificing himself to feed a tiger, and even the prince not only gave his own country, field, and wife but also committed suicide to sacrifice his own limbs and internal organs to others. Such self-sacrificial moral behavior reflected a lofty, brave, and great spirit on the one hand, but was also blind, stupid, and absurd on the other hand. Buddhism also promoted that people who donated to the monasteries and monks could be blessed, accumulate merit, and even achieve results, so as to absorb social wealth and expand the monastery economy. At the same time, it was also engaged in some social relief activities for better propaganda and education. These all show the complex character of Mahayana Buddhism and the multiple natures of Dāna.
2. Sila-Paramita: The foregoing five precepts, ten heavy precepts, and 48 light precepts were important content of Sila-Paramita. The rules of Mahayana Buddhism emphasized the "precept of killing" – that is, protecting sentient beings – and then it relaxed the constraints on religious life and the daily life of believers, and enforcement of rules was also more flexible and tolerant.
3. Kshanti-Paramita: It means being loyal to the faith and be content with suffering and humiliation. Mahayana Buddhism proclaimed that enduring intolerable things was the source of happiness. It required believers to prefer to endure "hot fire chopping" than do things harmful to all beings. Kshanti of Mahayana Buddhism was a virtue under certain conditions, but a non-virtue

in some conditions. In fact, Kshanti did not work as a universal code of moral behavior.

4   Viraya-Paramita: It means keeping striving to do good, stop evil, turn from pollution to cleanness, relieve others' suffering, deliver all living creatures from torment, and never retreat.
5   Dhyna-Paramita: As mentioned earlier, Mahayana Buddhism's meditation did not focus on sitting silently in meditation, but emphasized understanding the reality of things, and connecting meditation activities throughout the education of delivering all living creatures from torment.
6   Wisdom: On the one hand, it attached importance to observing reality of all phenomena with the theory of dependent origination and the emptiness of nature and understanding the "truth" that the nature of all beings was empty; on the other hand, it put more and more emphasis on the "convenience" of "delivering all living creatures from torment ", advocated adapting to changing circumstances, and took facilitating the education of all living as the highest purpose.

Mahayana Buddhism, in addition to the traditional methods of cultivation, added the two items of Dāna and Kshanti-Paramita, and placed them in prominent positions, which a manifestation of its concept of compassion. Mahayana Buddhism also emphasized the individual's efforts, going forward, never retreating – that is, emphasizing the subject's self-consciousness and role. As for Sila-Paramita, Dhyna-Paramita, and wisdom, its specific content and focus also changed and transferred. "Six Perfections" embodied the ethical concepts of Mahayana Buddhism, which took infinite mercy as its starting point, saw restraint of selfishness and salvation of others as the criteria for behaviors, and saw "egoism and altruism" and "conscience" – namely, unity between individual interests and the interests of all beings, between relief for one person and relief for humankind – as the basic principles of social and ethical relations, and also as the highest ideals of relief of life. This remarkable change in Mahayana Buddhism was a result of the increasing secularization of Buddhism, and the need to adapt to the conditions and needs of different times, different nations, and different regions to expand the power and influence of Buddhism. Because the ethical concepts embodied in these methods of practice, such as compassion, egoism, and altruism, apply to sentient beings universally, Kshanti and Viraya-Paramita were similar and connected to the idealized moral norms of ancient society, and thus led to motives of goodness, benefiting the country and people, and inspired people's enthusiasm about heroic struggle and self-sacrifice.

The theory of Buddhism on the "authenticity" of the universe

Buddhism explored the "authenticity" of life to get rid of the suffering of life. Because the human being lived in the real world, and had all kinds of direct and close relationships with the objective world all the time, Buddhism then explored the "authenticity" of universe, and offered various interpretations of how everything in the world came into being and the true nature of all things, forming a cosmology theory. The basic argument of this doctrine was Pratitya-samutpada, the theory of impermanence, and the theory of anatman.

1 *Pratitya-samutpada*

Pratitya-samutpada was the theoretical foundation of the whole Buddhist doctrine, and various theories were tributaries of this source. In the "Pratitya-samutpada", "Pratitya" was the conditions on which the result relied, and "samutpada" meant coming into being. Pratitya-samutpada focused on "Pratitya", while "samutpada" was just a function of Pratitya. Pratitya-samutpada referred to the beginning of all things and phenomena, which were all determined by each other; without relationship and conditions, there would not be any thing or phenomenon.

The meaning and content of Pratitya-samutpada were very rich, and its core was the succession of cause and effect. The basic arguments of "impermanence" and "anatman" derived from this theory. Pratitya-samutpada believed that "whenever there is A, there is B; whenever A rises, B rises" (Volume 47 of *Madhyamagama-sutra*). Things were born for a reason. One cause could not produce an effect, and any fruit must have at least two causes. Any separate cause, without an appropriate outer edge, could not produce an effect. All things and phenomena in the world came from karma; all things in the world were interrelated, interdependent, and mutually conditioned. In other words, all things were mutually causal, in continued causal relationships. Vertically, cause and effect were over the past, present, and future, continuing like an endless ring with no interruption. Any cause could be produced by the former, and any origin had its origin, causes had causes, origins had origins, going forward like water, with no birth or end, continuing with no beginning and no end; horizontally, cause and effect were connected, interdependent, mutually conditioned, intricate, and boundless. All things in the world were in an endless network of cause and effect with no beginning and no end. All things in the world were created and made by karma, not by a Creator in the world. There was no humanized Creator in the world or humanized origin of the universe, and there was no master of all things. All things in the world were created by karma, and there was no independent eternal reality – namely, anatman. All things in the world were in the causal link, subject to time and space constraints, and changing – namely, "impermanence".

The essence of Pratitya-samutpada was the causal relationship between things. Pratitya-samutpada advocated that all things in the world were created by karma, any cause had an effect, and any effect came from a cause. The so-called cause was the reason, and the so-called effect was the result. There was a difference between cause and pratitya. For the result produced, the cause was close while Pratitya was far. Cause and Pratitya were also universal; sometimes Pratitya was known as the cause, and sometimes the cause was also known as Pratitya, while sometimes they were collectively known as karma, generally referring to relationships and conditions. Buddhism's causal theory discussed the general causal relationship among material phenomena in the world, and confirmed that the four elements of ground, water, fire, and wind could produce each other, with the function of producing new material phenomena; material phenomena caused by the four elements had an impact and effect on the subsequent occurrence of material phenomena. Buddhism's causal theory also affirmed the role of the human being in the creation of things, and paid attention to the entity's moral practice and behavioral responsibility. This all had reasonable ideological content. However, Buddhism's causal theory mainly focused on the classification of human mental activities, on human psychology and behavior, with particular attention to action (cause) and retribution (effect). The central issue of causal theory was to clarify the two opposite trends in life: one was to do evil actions and caused constant circulation – namely, metempsychosis; the other was to do good and led to Nirvana. These were the two so-called laws of causality: pravrtti and Nirvana. It should be noted that Buddhism's causal theory rose in the form of expounding the general principles of the causal phenomena in the universe, but in the final analysis, it provided the philosophical basis for religious belief.

Pratitya-samutpada was the original theory of Sakyamuni, which was fundamentally opposed to the theories of no cause, contingency, and one cause (God-ego transformation) in India at that time. Mahayana and Hinayana factions took Pratitya-samutpada as their own theoretical basis for a world outlook and religious practice, and the ideological differentiation and theoretical differences of all factions arose from different views of origin.

2 The theory of impermanence

The theory of impermanence is an important theory derived from Pratitya-samutpada. "Permanence" means constancy. "Impermanence" means not constant. Buddhism believes that all things in the world were created by karma, are subject to conditions and constraints, and therefore are in the process of birth, mutation, and elimination, with no permanent nature.

The meaning of the theory of impermanence had a process of development and expansion. The idea of impermanence put forward by early Buddhism focused on providing arguments for the thesis of the suffering of life. Followers of the theory believed that life was impermanent, so everything was suffering. The theory of 12 karmas was to systematically clarify the process of life's impermanence and metempsychosis, in which there were neither invariable things nor pleasant things, indicating that life was an infinitely painful process. In the view of early Buddhism, human desires were infinite. Once a demand was met, a new demand arose. But such indefinite demand was bound to not be fully satisfied, and catch humans in suffering a failure to realize demands. Moreover, it was common to have requirements of life, for everyone wanted their nice life to remain constant, but there was a contradiction between the wish to keep constant and the reality of change; once the contradiction could not be resolved, it would lead to suffering. Therefore, early Buddhism also opposed two views of other schools of India at that time: The first is nityadrsti. Brahmanism believed that the self was permanent, and early Buddhism also called it mithya-drsti. The second is uccheda-drsti. Some Sramana believed that everything would be destroyed, and everything was gone after human death; "Atman" may not bear retribution, and early Buddhism also called it mithya-drsti.

Later, when Buddhist factions elaborated the theory of impermanence, they not only focused on proving that life was suffering but also widely became involved in all phenomena, and became the theory that discussed the existence and changes of all things in the world. They emphasized that everything did not have a single, isolated, absolute existence, but was dependent on other things. In this way, as long as there was a little change in things, it would cause the changes of other associated things, and things associated with other things also changed, so all things created by karma were always changing. It was utterly impossible to make things created by karma not change.

Buddhism believed that there are two kinds of impermanence: period impermanence and moment impermanence. Period impermanence meant that all things kept changing in a period, and finally went to their end. Birth, aging, illness, and death of human beings, arising, abiding, and changing, and the extinction of all existences, vivarta-kalpa, vivarta-sthayin-kalpa, samvarta-kalpa, and samvarta-sthayin-kalpa of the world, though long or short, were the embodiment of periodical impermanence. Moment impermanence, "moment" was the paraphrasing of "ksana"[5] in Sanskrit. Everything had not only period impermanence but also impermanence of arising, abiding, changing, and dying in a certain moment. In other words, before destruction, in every moment, it kept changing. Some Buddhist scriptures said that impermanence was quick, a moment of changes; stone, fire, wind, and light were not enough to describe moment impermanence of all things. Buddhism also advocated that although there were two kinds of impermanence, it had no beginning or end. People had birth, aging, illness, and death, but there was life before life, which transformed into other life after death, continuing without a break. Things were created by karma, and turned into other things after destruction due to karma. The world also continued cycling in the order of vivarta-kalpa, vivarta-sthayin-kalpa, samvarta-kalpa, and samvarta-sthayin-kalpa, again and again. In short, all things in the world kept changing forever, with no beginning or end.

Buddhism believed that everything in the world, including humankind, was flow, and everything was only in the eternal flow, like water and flame, in the process of constantly changing. This was undoubtedly an excellent dialectical concept, the most meaningful contribution of Buddhism in theory. However, it was clearly not correct for Sakyamuni to illustrate the suffering of life with the change of things; it was also not dialectic for him to take the pursuit of the immortal Nirvana realm as fate. Buddhism advocated that everything kept changing, opposed "permanence" with "impermanence", which became an important theory of Buddhism against Brahmanism, which indirectly reflected the struggle of the Indian thought community to deny and affirm the social structure. However, all the relativist tendency of Buddhism regarding impermanence finally developed into believing in "Tathagata", which means "unspeakable" and "incredible", and turned breaking other people's "permanence" into standing as their own mysterious symbol, thus falling into mysticism.

The theory of anatman

The theory of anatman was another important theory derived from Pratitya-samutpada. "Atman" in Buddhism meant the master and entity. "Atman" was a constant entity that had a self-dominating function. In other words, "Atman" was an entity with no collection, dissociation, or change, an independent eternal master. The "anatman" meant that all beings did not have an independent invariable entity or master, and nothing had atman or a soul playing the role of dominating. In other words, there was no single independent, self-existing, self-determined eternal thing in the world, and all things were composed of karma, and were relative and temporary.

The concept of "anatman" of early Buddhism was aimed at the theory of "anatman" of the Indian factions at that time, especially the theory of the Brahman that brahma-atma-aikyam was purusa. According to *Madh yamagama-sutra*, there were three kinds of arguments that advocated the existence of purusa: the first was to think that the feeling was purusa; the second was to believe that purusa was a sensible master; the third was that purusa had no feeling, but its tool could feel. Early Buddhism refuted these one by one, and pointed out that there were a variety of feelings – happy, painful, unhappy, and not painful – which could not all be purusa, and any kind of feeling was varying and impermanent, and could not be purusa. Feeling was not purusa, neither was purusa the master that could feel, and thus could not have feeling. Since purusa could not feel, its tool could not have feeling, either. Early Buddhism also opposed Brahmanism's belief that Mahesvara created the world, and believed that there was change and destruction, trouble and disaster, hatred and ugliness in the world, which proved that the world was not created by Mahesvara, or that Mahesvara also had trouble and ugliness. Early Buddhism did not deny the existence of Mahesvara, but believed that he was only a high being dominated by his own karma.

Buddhism promoted that there were two kinds of "atman": one was the belief in the inherent existence of a subjective self, and the other was the belief in the inherent existence of objective dharmas. The dedication to atman was called "atma-graha", also called "atma-drsti". Atma-graha was divided into two kinds: the attachment to the belief in the existence of an inherently existent self and the attachment to external objects, which were both the most important ideas that Buddhism would get rid of. Corresponding to two kinds of atman and atma-graha, there were also two kinds of "anatman": one was "pudgala-nairatmya", and the other was "dharma-nairatmya". Impermanence must lead to anatman. "Impermanence led to suffering", life was distress, not comfortable, and humans could not dominate themselves, which was anatman – namely, pudgala-nairatmya. Moreover, everything else was anatman. Because everything was changing at all times, it could not be said that there is a certain self, called "dharma-nairatmya". Such a theory of pudgala-nairatmya and dharma-nairatmya was the basic doctrine of early Buddhism, and also the fundamental difference from the other schools of India at that time.

There was also an evolutionary process of the meaning of anatman. Hinayana Buddhist scholars believed that human beings were most likely to be dedicated to themselves, so they highlighted pudgala-nairatmya. They promoted that the human being is the aggregation of body and the spirit, composed by panca-skandha, called human, yet unreal. Like a house composed of rafters and tiles, without which there was no house, humans were composed physically and mentally, and without leaving panca-skandha they could not be human. Humans were also like water and light flame, continuing infinitely. People's physical and psychological states of existence were impermanent, and death was the dissolution of human life factors, the performance of impermanence. However, secular people did not understand this truth, believed that the human being was a real entity, produced the concept of atman, got keen on differences from each other, developed greed, ignorance and silliness, formed various troubles, and then made various karmas. Where there was karma, there was metempsychosis. So atma-graha was the source of all evil and suffering, which must be completely broken. Generally speaking, Hinayana Buddhism did not deny the physical existence of the material world, such as mountains and rivers, but emphasized that it had no eternal entity. However, such a contradictory theory confronting things and entities provided the basis for Mahayana Buddhism to negate the authenticity of the objective world later. Mahayana Buddhist scholars believed that all things other than humans were the same as humans, which were the aggregation of various factors, with no independent entities either – namely, dharma-nairatmya. But beings did not understand this truth, and believed that things were real entities, which hindered the understanding of Buddhist "truth". While they broke pudgala-nairatmya, they also paid special attention to breaking dharma-nairatmya, and promoted the theory that everything was empty.

Early Buddhism propagated the theory of anatman, and denied the existence of the self-entity, but it affirmed the role of all karma, and promoted the reincarnation of karma, which left a huge theoretical contradiction. Later, some scholars of Sectarian Buddhism advocated the belief in the inherent existence of a subjective self, and also put forward "antara-bhava" as the contact and transition of reincarnation. Yogacara of Mahayana Buddhism established "alaya" and its seed as the basis and foothold of metempsychosis and Nirvana, which were various idealist solutions proposed to overcome the foregoing contradictory theories.

In accordance with the theory of anatman, all things had no self-nature; then how did humans carry out thought and consciousness? How to distinguish and identify complex and different things? For the needs of consciousness, Yogacara put forward the idea that "dharma had self-nature", and believed that things had a variety of "self-natures" in order to delineate the boundaries and scope of different things, to facilitate the development of thinking activities – that is, to enable things to be identified, and consciousness to be carried out. At the same time, Yogacara attributed all things to turning from consciousness, constituting a unique idealist doctrine.

Notes

1 Here it referred to the organ that uniformly considered impressions of the five sensory organs – namely, "heart".
2 "Skandha" means "gathering" – namely, precepts complied according to category. "20 Skandha" was mainly about the provisions for sangha rituals and monks' living ritual system.

3 "Thirty-two appearances" and "80 characteristics": They meant that Buddha was born divine, different from common people, who had 32 distinctive features, known as "32 appearances", and he had 88 secret hidden characteristics, known as "80 characteristics", collectively known as "excellent characteristics". "Thirty-two appearances" include long fingers, standing with the hand touching the knee, a golden appearance, thin skin, 40 teeth, a big tongue, green eyes, and so on. "Eighty characteristics" mainly referred to the Buddha's head, face, nose, mouth, eyes, ears, hands, feet, and other features that looked strange, such as the first characteristic of thin, long, bright, and clean nails, like red copper; the twenty-eighth characteristic of red and shiny lips; the thirty-third characteristic of a slender nose with invisible nostrils; the eightieth characteristic of hands, feet, and chest with auspicious signs.
4 "Pancavidy": "Vidya" meant "knowledge". "Pancavidy" meant "five categories of knowledge". The first was sabda-vidya – namely, phonology and language science; the second was silpakarma-vidya – namely, technology and the calendar; the third was cikitsa-vidya – namely, medicine; the fourth was hetu-vidya – namely, logic and epistemology; the fifth was adhyatma-vidya – namely, Buddhism.
5 "Ksana", the ancient Indian time unit, meaning "a very short period of time"; it was estimated that it was about 1/56 of a second.

5 Buddhist system and ritual

This chapter includes two parts: Buddhist system and Buddhist ritual. The Buddhist system is the law and regulation of sanghas, involving a series of provisions on life and the methods of doing things for Buddhist monks and sanghas. Buddhist rituals refer to the rituals and procedures practiced by monks – namely, the way to practice.

Buddhism had sanghas, and thus required a system. Indian monks and nuns made discipline the standard of life, and Chinese sanghas developed a number of other regulations to constrain the words and deeds of monks and nuns in addition to disciplines. In the Eastern Jin Dynasty, as the number monks and nuns increased gradually, Dao'an began to advocate serious discipline, and rules governed the following areas: the first was the method of offering incense, arranging seats, and giving lectures and speeches, the second was the method of daily practice at six times (three times in the daytime and three times at night), eating, and singing, and the third was the method of posadha, commission, and confession. This was the beginning of the various ritual systems later, and the impact was extremely far-reaching. Since then, the Buddhist community and the official circle also repeatedly developed regulations for the monks and nuns. China's monk system mainly evolved two aspects: the first was the state's jurisdiction. Because there were many monks and nuns, the state strengthened management through the upper layers of Buddhism, and ruled monks with monks. King Yaoxing of Qin designated Sengqi as Sengzheng, the first grade in the Buddhist hierarchy, which was the beginning of such a system. Sengtong and Senglusi in later dynasties were also designated for the management of Buddhists. The second was the temple system of the Zen monks, which was designed for Zen monks living in the mountains and countryside. In the later Tang Dynasty, Huaihai wrote *Baizhang Regulations*, and the Yuan Dynasty re-revised it; it became the basic rules of the later monasteries.

Believers and the monk register

1 Appellation of believers

Buddhists worshiped the Buddhist founder Sakyamuni as their teacher, and claimed themselves to be his disciples. There were four categories of Buddhists, known as the four kinds of disciples – namely, monks and nuns, and male and female lay Buddhists at home. There were also four categories of monks and nuns – namely, monks, nuns, acolytes, and novice nuns. "Monk" was translated as "bhiksui"[1] in Sanskrit. It meant begging for food, but also had the meaning of frightening demons, destroying evil, and purifying life. Bhiksu were monks who had received complete precepts. "Bhiksuni" meant "nun". "Ni" meant "women" in Sanskrit, referring to nuns who had received complete precepts. The monks were also known as "shaman". The Sanskrit word "sangha" meant the public, and three or more monks were collectively called a sangha. Ancient Indian sects advocated that people shall become monks and practice to a certain age, and monks were called "Sramana", meaning to stop all evil. As the other sects of India were not introduced to China, Sramana also became the special appellation of Buddhist monks. Monks were also known as "upadhyaya" among the people, which was the transliteration from Sanskrit, and the paraphrasing was "teacher". In China, it was generally the honorific name of the Buddhist teacher; later it became monks' general appellation. Among the aforementioned appellations, monk and Sramana were more used in writing, while sangha and upadhyaya were more used in spoken language. In the upper echelons of Buddhism, those who were Buddhist literati and were good at explaining texts were called "Masters". Sometimes, in order to show respect to general monks, they were also called "Master". In China's Mongolian and Tibetan areas, people call monks "lamas". Lama was the transliteration from Tibetan, meaning "guru", which was an honorific name of scholarly eminent monks in Tibetan Buddhism, equivalent to upadhyaya in the Han region, and also meant "master". Han people often called Mongolian and Tibetan monks collectively "Lama".

Male lay Buddhists at home were known as "upasaka"; female lay Buddhists at home were known as "upasika". "Upasaka" was Sanskrit, meaning "men who practiced Sambo closely". "Upasika" was also Sanskrit, meaning "women who practiced Sambo closely". Buddhists at home were commonly known as "grha-pati". "Lay Buddhists at home" was the paraphrasing of "grha-pati" in Sanskrit, originally referring to people who accumulated wealth, and later it became the special appellation of Buddhists at home.

2 The process of joining Buddhism

Buddhist believers had to go through certain procedures to leave the family and practice on their own, which was conditional. The general procedure, in accordance with the provisions of Buddhist precepts, was first to find a monk in monastery and ask him to be one's "master". This monk then explained the situation to the monks of the whole monastery, and widely collected opinions; after getting a consensus, this man could be accepted as a disciple. Then he would be tonsured, accept Sramanera precepts, and become a Sramanera. Sramanera was Sanskrit, meaning abiding the rules of monks, preventing evil, and showing mercy. The monks could not accept Sramanera precepts until they reached 7 years old. To the age of 20, the abbot and master, with the approval of monks, convened ten elders to ordain Bhiksu precepts, and then the Sramanera became a monk. Monks could not leave their master until five years after they accepted Bhiksu precepts, and then they practiced alone, wandered around, and lived in monasteries. As for women, they also had to find a nun as master first and accept Sramanerika precepts. At the age of 18, they accepted Siksamana precepts to become *Sikkhamana*, meaning women who learned dharma. At the age of 20, they accepted Bhiksuni precepts from bhiksuni and then bhiksu. So after accepting precepts twice, they became bhiksuni. When Mahayana Buddhism prevailed in India, bhiksu who practiced Mahayana Buddhism could also accept Bodhisattva precepts on a voluntary basis. Emperor Wu of Liang and Emperors Wen and Yang of Sui in ancient China all accepted Bodhisattva precepts, and were thus called "Bodhisattva precept disciples". It was convenient for monks to resume secular life; as long as they stated to anyone, they could give up the identity of monks.

This set of procedures to become monks in Buddhism had different specific practices in different regions and different times. In the Han region in China, it was stringent in the Tang and Song Dynasties, and more relaxed after the Yuan Dynasty. Starting with the Yuan Dynasty, the ordained ones had to burn incense above their heads (3, 9, or 12 incenses) as the sign of their life-long pledge. In the 1980s, the Buddhist community abolished such outmoded conventions in the Han region.

Buddhism unified strict requirements about the clothing of Buddhist monks, but had no special provisions for lay Buddhists at home. Buddhism first provided that monks wear only three types of clothes: the first was called five-clothing – namely, underwear made of five strips of cloth, for daily work and bedtime; the second was called seven-clothing – namely, tops made of seven strips of cloth, for chanting and listening to lectures; the third was a coat, made of from 9 strips to 25 strips of cloth, for rituals or going out. Each strip of the cloth of monks' clothing was made of a long and a short (five-clothing) piece, two long and one short (seven-clothing) pieces, or three long and one short (coat) pieces. Such style was called "Tian Xiang", like field and ridge, criss-crossing, meaning that the monks could serve as the blessing field for all beings; thus it was also known as "Futian clothing" – that is, robes. In the cold areas of China, it was difficult to keep out the cold when wearing these three types of clothes, so a type of secular clothes with a round neck and square robe was added. Later, common people abandoned this style, while a square robe with a round neck became monks' special clothing.

Buddhist believers at home also had to go through certain procedures and needed approval of the master to become formal Buddhists at home – upasaka and upasika. The basic condition of lay Buddhists at home was to be converted to three refuges: converted to Buddha, converted to dharma, and converted to monks. Conversion was the meaning of trust, to seek refuge for their own physical and mental life with Buddhism Sambo, and practice in accordance with the teachings of Buddhism Sambo. The ceremony was to ask a master to describe the meaning of the three refuges for them in accordance with the *Rituals of Three Refuges*, and they claimed to be converted to Sambo evermore; in this way, they became a lay Buddhist at home. If they then accepted the five precepts from the master, they could become five-precept upasaka and upasika. Later, if they further accepted Bodhisattva precepts from the master, they could also become Bodhisattva precepts upasaka and upasika. If lay Buddhists at home wanted to give up their identity, they only had to state it to anyone.

3 Dudie and the monk and temple registers

In order to control and manage the monks and civilians, ancient Chinese feudal dynasties also set up systems of Dudie and the monk and temple register. "Du" meant access, and "Die" meant the certificate. Dudie was the certificate issued to legal monks. Monks and nuns were protected and exempted from rent and corvée with this credential. Dudie could also play the role of travel passport. The monk register was a book that recorded the monks' name, age, place of origin, and so forth, which was equivalent to the current household registration book, managed by the state. Temple register referred to a book that recorded the temple's building date, name, circumstances, and so on. Since the Tang and Song Dynasties, the construction of temples had to be approved by the government, and the name of the temple was also issued by the government.

Officials began to issue Dudie from the tenth year of Dazhong in the Tang Dynasty (AD 856), and provided that monks receive Dudie when they became monks and receive Jiedie (certificate of initiation into priesthood, with legal status) when they accepted precepts. Those who wanted to become a monk had to first serve as a "walker" in monasteries, doing all kinds of labor, but they were not tonsured, and could accept Sramanera precepts from their master. To the time of becoming monks set by the government, those who passed the government's screening or the test of scriptures could receive Dudie, and their monk register was designated as belonging to a certain monastery; at this time they obtained the qualification of monk and were allowed to be tonsured. Then they went to the monastery and were allowed by the government to accept Bhiksu precepts and receive Jiedie. The mentor who ordained precepts was also designated by the government. Those who were tonsured without the permission of the government – that is, were tonsured privately – would be punished. The Qing Dynasty later abolished Dudie, and Jiedie was also changed to being issued by the temple. That is, only Jiedie was retained while Dudie was abolished. There was no limit on becoming monks or on monks initiating others into priesthood. Some of the imperial courts and local officials and bullies also made money from selling Dudie, or ran a business for profit. Dudie in the Song Dynasty was once used as a currency.

Temple and regulation

1 Temple

Buddhism said that when many monks gathered, it was like a large cluster of trees, so that the place where monks gathered was called a temple. The temple was also used to show that there were strict rules and laws for monks by comparing them to vegetation growing in order. The term temple in Chinese Buddhism usually referred to Zen monasteries, which were also known as Buddhist temples. But other sects later also followed the Buddhist temple system and called them temples. Since the Song Dynasty, Buddhist temples had been differentiated, forming a variety of different types. Initially there were three types: A-B disciple temple, Shifang abbot temple, and imperial abbot temple. Temples in which disciples of their own served as abbot in turn were called A-B disciple temples, or A-B temples for short. Temples that invited famous monks from all places to serve as abbot were called Shifang abbot temples, or Shifang temples for short. Temples whose abbot was appointed by the court were called imperial abbot temples, or imperial temples for short. Later, the court canceled the system of appointing abbots, so there were only two types of Buddhist temples. The A-B disciple temple implemented the master-disciple hereditary system, and was known as the tonsure temple or descendant temple. The descendant temple was also called the "little temple". Each temple was subordinate to a certain sect, inherited and rarely changed. The abbot temple was elected and supervised by officials, and was known as the Shifang temple. It was divided into two kinds: one handed down according to genealogy of law, and was known as the initiation temple; the other implemented the Shifang election system, and was called the selection temple.

2 Regulation

China's temple regulation formed in the Tang Dynasty. Before that, the management system in which "the three cardinal guides" took charge of monks formed in the Qin Dynasty. The three cardinal guides included the sthavira, temple abbot, and Karmadāna. The sthavira was the master of the whole temple; the temple abbot was in charge of the affairs of the whole temple; the Karmadāna managed monk affairs. To the Tang Dynasty, due to political unity and great national strength, sects stood in great numbers, requiring a set of unified temple systems suitable for Chinese national conditions. After Emperor Wuzong of Tang wiped out Buddhism, the majority of sects fell and never rose, and only simple and easy Zen, the Pure Land School, was popular. Since Hui Neng founded Zen, the quantity of Zen monks surged during more than 100 years, but they passed on Taoism, and mostly lived in caves, or lodged in temples of the Vinaya School. In some monasteries, more than 1,000 and even more than 2,000 people lived there. A famous monk of Zen, Huaihai, believed that it was to ignore superiority and inferiority for Zen monks to live in the temples of the Vinaya School, and not standardized for the abbot's sermon and collective practice life, so he, according to China's national conditions and Zen characteristics, split the difference between precepts of Mahayana and Hinayana, and firstly creatively set the temple regulations. Because Huaihai lived in Baizhang Mountain in Fengxi, Jiangxi Province, the descendants called him "Baizhang Zen Master", and the regulations were formulated by him as *Baizhang Regulations*. Huaihai's regulations were generally popular among Zen monks, and also praised by the court; thus they were popular all over the country, and their impact was extremely wide.

Baizhang Regulations had the meaning of peaceful and quiet rule, and was the temple system of Zen system – namely, procedures of Zen monastery organization and rules for the daily conduct of the temple public. *Baizhang Regulations* made clear provisions for the abbot, Dhammasala, monk hall, and dorms. The general provisions were that the abbot of the temple was the master of the Zen public, with the highest status, living in Fangzhang.[2] There was no Buddha hall in the monastery, but only Dhammasala (later a Buddha hall was also built). The Zen public lived in the monk hall according to the order of accepting precepts. Huaihai advocated the rural Zen life of "no labor, no food", implemented "Puqingfa" – namely, the system of generally inviting the Zen public to labor – and provided for all classes to participate in collective production labor to achieve self-sufficiency. Indian Buddhist precepts prohibited monks from "digging land", for it was believed that digging land would sever earthworms, destroy formicaries, and chop mussels, which was killing and violated the primary discipline; thus it was strictly prohibited. Huaihai advocated the combination of cultivation and labor production, which was a major breakthrough and reform of Indian Buddhist precepts, and had progressive significance. *Baizhang Regulations* also provided for ten dorms, and a leader appointed for each dorm to manage various affairs. Later, as the temple organization increasingly grew, all kinds of positions emerged endlessly, which was too chaotic, so *Baizhang Regulations* was revised and enlarged in the second year of Chongning in the Northern Song Dynasty (AD 1103), called *Chongning Regulations*. *Baizhang Regulations* was called *Ancient Regulations* or *Ancient Rules*.[3] Later there was *Xian Chun Regulations* in the tenth year of Xianchun in the Southern Song Dynasty (AD 1274), and *Zhida Regulations* in the fourth year of Zhida in the Yuan Dynasty (AD 1311). In the third year of Yuantong in the Yuan Dynasty (AD 1335), the court asked the Jiangxi Baizhang abbot, Zen Master Dehuito, to re-revise the book, which was rectified by Dadeng, the abbot of Jinling Dalongxiang Jiqing Temple, and named the *Imperial Revised Baizhang Regulations*, issued nationwide for common compliance. In fact, the content and spirit of this book of regulations were quite different from *Ancient Rules*, which was a brand new book of regulations.

Imperial Revised Baizhang Regulations was divided into nine chapters, and the first four chapters were not set in the precept book or *Ancient Rules*. It mainly provided rituals of consecration, national death day, prayer, the Buddha's birthday, Nirvana Day, Dharma's death day, Baizhang's death day, and the ancestors' death day of temples, which further reflected that the feudal dynasty strengthened the control of temples to make Buddhism more effectively serve the feudal rule. Chapter 5 to Chapter 9 contained the rules and regulations of the temple, mainly regarding monastic activities, such as admission, withdrawal, classes, and evening meditation; the positions of the temple according to the court's civil and military official system; the personal etiquette of the Zen public and instruments, such as bells and drums. These provisions were widely popular in the monastery in the Ming and Qing Dynasties.

Rituals and standards

1 Daily recitation

Generally there were two methods of Buddhist practice: the first was learning doctrine, and the second was practicing meditation. As for the method of learning doctrine in early Indian Buddhism, firstly it was to listen to Sakyamuni's sermon and discuss it. Practicing meditation was to sit or Jingxing (wander in the forest while thinking). Later, there were Buddha statues and Buddhist scriptures in temples, so there were rituals of worshiping Buddha statues and chanting Buddhist scriptures. Monks chanted regularly, worshiped Sambo, and chanted Buddhist chants, which were known as recitation. In ancient India, Buddhist scriptures were read with intonation and expression and "three" rituals were implemented: firstly reciting poems praising Buddha collected by Asvaghosa, then reciting Buddhist scriptures, and stating a wish. This chanting method became the basic ritual of Buddhist recitation in Han areas in China.

In the early days when Buddhism was introduced into China, it consisted only of disciples learning from a master. To the Eastern Jin Dynasty, Dao An's disciples numbered up to hundreds, which made it difficult for disciples to learn from a master alone, so practice norms for monks and nuns were developed in which the methods of offering incense, arranging seats, and giving lectures were sermon rituals; daily practice was carried out six times, and eating and chanting were the rituals of recitation. These provisions were generally followed among the monasteries. Since the Song and Ming Dynasties, recitation at dawn and dusk was generally implemented in monasteries based on this; especially between the Ming and Qing Dynasties, recitation at dawn and dusk gradually fell into a pattern and became unified, and the implementing scope spread to monasteries and believers at home from various factions, becoming a fixed class that the entire temple must practice, and offenders were fined.

According to regulations since the end of the Ming Dynasty, Buddhists had "five classes" and went to the hall twice every day. There were two classes in the early hall, also known as early class, usually mainly chanting *Shurangama Mantra*. Shurangama meant that all things were solid. And then they recited *Sutra Hrdaya Prajna Paramita* (*Heart Sutra*). This sutra was the center of *Prajna Sutra*. There were three classes in the evening hall, also known as evening classes. They mainly recited *Bussetsu Amidakyo* to pray for their own life to the West Pure Land and chanted *Confession Text*; "confession" meant the elimination of karma in the past and not making new faults in the future; they also chanted *Mengshan Shi Shi*, and the monks took out a little rice from the vegetarian food at noon every day and recited *Mengshan Shi Shi* at night while giving the rice to hungry ghosts. *Mengshan* is now in Ya'an, Sichuan. According to legend, Master Amrta collected this text in this place.

2 The confession method and Daqi

(1) The confession method

Confession method was an important way of Buddhism's self-practice. It was a religious ritual to confess sins, chanting scriptures and worshiping Buddha, and vow to practice actively and never recede in the future. There were two types of confession methods: one was to collect all the rituals of doctrines of Buddhist scriptures and confessions; the other was to practice Śamath according to five repentances.[4] The confession method of Chinese Buddhism originated from the Jin Dynasty, gradually prevailed in the Southern and Northern Dynasties, and became greatly popular until the Sui and Tang Dynasties.

1 THE RITUAL OF CONFESSION

Since DaoAn and Hui Yuan implemented the confession method from the Jin Dynasty, Xiao Ziliang of the Southern Qi Dynasty wrote 30 volumes of *Jing Zhu Zi Jing Xing Fa Men* (one volume was collected in *Detailed Anthology of Hong Ming*). Emperor Wu of Liang ordered two books of confession to be made: one was *Liu Gen Da Chan*, which is lost now, and the other was *Liu Dao Ci Chan* – or *A Confessing Ritual on the Mercy Site*, now also referred to as *Liang Huang Chan* for short. This confession method was spread in China for the longest time. Emperor Wu of Liang wrote these two confessions to oppose the monks who ate meat at that time; he thought that eating meat did not conform to the decree of scriptures, so he prohibited eating meat, and ordered monks to confess for seven days. Later generations also often asked monks to practice this confession method to eliminate sin and avoid disaster. As all kinds of confessional methods began to get popular in the Southern and Northern Dynasties, Emperor Wu of Liang and Emperors Xuan and Wen of Chen also wrote articles to illuminate confession methods. Between the Sui and Tang Dynasties, Buddhist factions formed, and all factions wrote all kinds of confession methods according to the classics of their factions – for example, Shan Dao of the Pure Land School wrote *Pure Land Fa Shi Zan*, and Zongmi of the Huayan School wrote 18 volumes of *Yuan Jue Jing Dao Chang Xiu Zheng Yi*. In addition, Zhixuan at the end of the Tang Dynasty partly collected excerpts of *Yuan Jue Jing Dao Chang Xiu Zheng Yi* by Zongmi to describe three volumes of *Ci Bei Shui Chan Fa*, referred to as *Shui Chan* for short, which is still popular now.

2 CONFESSION METHOD TO PRACTICE ŚAMATH

This was founded by Zhiyi of the Tiantai School. Zhiyi referred to the previous dharma-paryaya of five repentances and a variety of praise and confession texts to form his own original confession method. This was the four kinds of Samadhi mentioned in Volume 2 of *Great Samadhiand Vipa'syana*: "Samadhi of semi-walking and semi-sitting" and "Samadhi of non-walking and non-sitting" – namely, "Fahua Samadhi", "Fangdeng Samadhi", "Qing Avalokitesvara Samadhi", and "Jinguangming Samadhi Act". Among them, "Samadhi of semi-walking and semi-sitting" was "Fahua Samadhi", which was an important way to practice Śamath. It focused on embodying Samadhi in confession methods. Its content and organization procedure were cleaning the field, cleaning the body, consecrating three karmas, worshiping Sambo, praising Sambo, paying respect to Buddha, confessing, wandering in the temple, chanting *Saddharmapundarikasutra*, and thinking of the only real realm, a total of ten methods. These ten methods were both practice methods and rituals of confession. Later scholars of the Tiantai School inherited from Zhiyi, and believed that confession was the important method for practicing

Śamath. They also made up a lot of confession methods in accordance with this form of organization. For example, Zunshi of the Song Dynasty lived in Ciyun Temple in Hangzhou, where he widely practiced confession methods, known as "Ciyun Chanzhu". He wrote *Confession Ritual for Pure Land in Afterlife*. Because of the popularity of the Pure Land School, this method was very popular. Zhili wrote *Great Confession Method*, whose full name was *Thousand-Hand Thousand-Eye Mahakaruna Mantra*. As the universal popularity of belief in Avalokitesvara, this method was gradually introduced to the people, and it's still the most popular confession method in China. Zhuxu of the Ming Dynasty wrote *Ksitigarbha Confession Method*, which was used by religious rites returning parents' grace, praying mostly for parents. To the Qing Dynasty, all kinds of confession methods appeared, such as *Yao Shi Chan* published in the Qing Dynasty, which was used mostly by religious rites avoiding disaster and extending life. So the content of confession methods also gradually changed. Originally Zhiyi developed confession methods to ease the mind by respecting, praising, and confessing, and then to observe dharmata through chanting scriptures and Zen meditation, to practice again and again to achieve enlightenment. But later these confessions rituals paid attention only to worshiping and confession, but abolished chanting and meditation, putting form above content, attending to trifles and neglecting the essentials, which completely lost the purpose of Śamath of the Tiantai School.

The foregoing two types of confession methods were the way for Buddhists to practice themselves, but not means to engage in Buddhist affairs for others to seek profit. But later it gradually became the custom for donors to give property to designate monks to practice confession methods and recite Buddhist scriptures. In this way, the confession method naturally became a Buddhist activity for monks to seek profit, with no essential difference from commercial transactions.

(II) Daqi

Daqi is an important Buddhist ritual of Zen and the Pure Land School. Zen focuses on direct reference to the origin of nature, and the whole Pure Land School was dedicated to pursuing Western Pure Land by chanting Buddhist scriptures, so their practice ceremony was not to worship or confess but to concentrate on study for seven days, called "Daqi". Daqi of Zen was called "Da Chan Qi", or "Chan Qi", and was a Zen activity in the winter. The activity of Daqi varied from 7 days to 70 days – usually from the fifteenth day of the tenth lunar month to the eighth day of the twelfth lunar month, a total of 49 days. Daqi of the Pure Land School was called "Da Nian Fo Qi", "Da Jing Qi", or "Fo Qi", and consisted mainly of chanting Buddhist scriptures, chanting only Amitabha, accompanied by beating wooden fish and chiming stones. It could be held at any time, and also lasted 49 days.

3 The bathing of the Buddha and the Buddhist Ghost Festival

There were many Buddhism festivals, and the largest was the Buddha's birthday and Pravarana Day. The bathing of the Buddha should be held on Buddha's birthday, and the Buddhist Ghost Festival should be held on Buddha's Pravarana Day.

(I) The bathing of the Buddha

Buddha's birthday was also known as the "Festival to Bathe the Buddha", and was a major festival to commemorate the birth of Sakyamuni. According to Buddhist legend, when Prince Siddhartha was born in Lumbini, there were nine dragons (another legend said two dragons) spitting perfume to bathe Buddha's body. Later Buddhists, according to this legend, held the "bathing of the Buddha" on each Buddha's birthday. The ritual was to set a basin in the main hall or in the open air to consecrate the statue of the birth of Sakyamuni. The statue was several *cun* high, in the shape of a standing boy, with his right hand pointing to heaven and left hand pointing to the ground. According to Buddhist legend, when Prince Siddhartha was born, his right hand pointed to heaven and left hand pointed to the ground, and he said, "I am the noblest in the world". In Indian style, the right was honored, so his right hand pointed to heaven; China honored the left, so the statues of Prince Siddhartha in Han areas in China mostly pointed his left hand to heaven. Buddhists bathed the statue of the prince with a variety of perfume to express devout celebration and support. The "bathing of Buddha" began to prevail in monasteries from about the late Han Dynasty, and later it gradually was spread to the court and officials; to the Southern and Northern Dynasties, it was more popular with the common people.

Buddhists in the Southeast Asian countries recognized the fifteenth day of the fourth lunar month as Buddha's birthday, and also the enlightening day and Nirvana Day of Buddha; so did China's Mongolian and Tibetan areas. There were three kinds of records of Buddha's birthday in Chinese Buddhist scriptures: the eighth day of the second lunar month, the eighth day of the fourth lunar month, and the eighth day of the twelfth lunar month. In the Northern Dynasties, the eighth day of the fourth lunar month was mostly recognized as the day for bathing of the Buddha; from the Southern Dynasties to the Tang Dynasty and early Liao Dynasty, Buddhists mostly bathed the Buddha on the eighth day of the second lunar month. In the Song Dynasty, it was changed to the eighth day of the twelfth lunar month in the north, while the south set it on the eighth day of the fourth lunar month. In the Yuan Dynasty *Imperial Revised Baizhang Regulations* set the eighth day of the fourth lunar month as the birthday of Buddha; since the north to the south took the eighth day of the fourth lunar month as the day for the bathing of the Buddha, when the Buddha bathing ceremony was held, and it has been handed down to this day.

(II) The Buddhist Ghost Festival

Buddha's Pravarana Day was on the fifteenth day of the seventh lunar month. As mentioned earlier, Buddhism stipulated that the monks shall settle in the temple to concentrate on practice from the fifteenth day of the fourth lunar month to the fifteenth day of the seventh lunar month, called "settlement", also known as "Jie

Xia" and "Zuo La". When the period of settlement expired on the fifteenth day of the seventh lunar month, a report and confession rally would be held, known as "Pravarana Day". On the fifteenth day of the seventh lunar month, the Buddhist Ghost Festival would also be held, which was a ritual of Buddhism to expiate the sins of dead ancestors. *Ullambanasutra* said that Sakyamuni's disciple Maudgalyayana saw his mother in the hungry ghost road, suffering a lot but not to be saved, so he asked Sakyamuni to rescue her. Sakyamuni told him to collect various food in Ullambana to support Pravarana monks in ten directions on the fifteenth day of the seventh lunar month, and to keep the parents in the past seven lives and present away from the hungry ghost road with such merit. Buddhists held the Buddhist Ghost Festival based on this section of the record. There were two kinds of explanations of the title of *Ullambanasutra*; one said "Ullam", which was a Sanskrit transliteration, meaning hanging up (hardship), and "bana" was Chinese, meaning vessel. It was said that such vessel could relieve the suffering of lingering dead ancestors. The second argument was that "Ullambana" was a Sanskrit transliteration, meaning saving hanging up. In fact the first explanation was misunderstood, and the second explanation was correct.

The Buddhist Ghost Festival held according *Ullambanasutra* started from Emperor Wu of Liang, after which it became a custom for emperors and common people.

4 *Shui Lu Rites and feeding Yankou*

Chinese Buddhist monasteries held a series of Buddhist activities every year, of which Shui Lu Rites was the largest, and also the most solemn; Feeding Yankou was the most frequent and popular.

(1) Shui Lu Rites

The full name of Shui Lu Rites was "Holy and Laical Shui Lu Serving and Fast Rally"; they were also known as "Shui Lu Bodhimanda", "Shui Lu Rally", "Shui Lu Gathering", "Shui Lu Fast", "Shui Lu Fast Rites", and "Beiji Gathering", and were very solemn rites in Chinese Buddhism. The rites took a long time – 7 days at least, 49 days at most. There were tens and even hundreds of monks participating in the rites, on a large scale. An inner altar and outer altar were used, and a variety of food was offered to support Buddha, Bodhisattva, gods, the Five Mountains, river and sea, the earth, the dragon god, death, and even beasts, hungry ghosts, and hell beings. Monks chanted and fasted, paid respect to Buddha, worshiped, and confessed. According to *Shishizhengming* of Song Zunshi, the rites were named "Shui Lu" because "it took the food of immortals from flowing water, and the food of devil from clean ground" (middle volume of *Jinyuan Collection*). Shui Lu Rites developed based on a combination of *Ci Bei Dao Chang Chan Fa* of Emperor Wu of Liang and Esoteric Buddhism in the Tang Dynasty. According to historical record,

> The so-called Shui Lu, . . . for Emperor Wu (of Liang) dreamed of a sacred monk telling, "in the six worlds and for four beings, the bitter was infinite,

why not hold Shui Lu (great fast) to generally help the being" . . . the emperor asked Zhigong to seek sutra and argument, for there must be a reason. So they sought pattra leaves, . . . they read books in the early evening, in which Ananda faced the devil king and set up the meaning equal eating, with system and rites, it was achieved in three years, and it was built in Jinshan Temple in Run (Runzhou, now Zhenjiang, Jiangsu). The emperor went there personally and convened monks.

(Song, Zongjian – *Shi Men Zheng Jing*, Volume 4)

To the Song Dynasty, Yang E wrote *Shui Lu Rites* (now lost), based on rites of Esoteric Buddhism, which played a great role in promoting the popularity of Shui Lu Rites. At this point, Shui Lu Rites prevailed in the world, especially after wars; it was often held by the court to expiate the sins of the dead. Su Shi once held Shui Lu Rites for his late wife, and wrote 16 texts of *Shui Lu Rites Praise*, called "Meishan Shui Lu". Shui Lu Rites continued until the Ming and Qing Dynasties.

(II)   Feeding Yankou

Feeding Yankou was a Buddhist ceremony held based on *Fo Shuo Jiu Ba Yan Kou E Gui Tuo Luo Ni Jing* translated by Amoghavajra. Yankou, also known as "Mianran", was the name of a hungry ghost king. According to the text described earlier, its shape was thin, the throat was as thin as a needle, and its mouth could spit flame. It was also said in sutra that once when the chief disciple of Sakyamuni, Ananda, lived alone and studied at night, a ghost king called Yankou told him: you will die in three days, reborn among the hungry ghosts. If you want to avoid this suffering, you must feed the ghosts tomorrow. To prevent himself from falling into the hungry ghosts, and also to the relieve the hungry ghosts, Ananda turned to Sakyamuni for help. Sakyamuni chanted a mantra for him, and taught him the method of feeding. Such method later became an act that must be practiced by people who cultivated Esoteric Buddhism. Esoteric Buddhism had special mantras for feeding the hungry ghosts and chanting rituals. The ceremony was usually held at dusk, and involved taking a clean vessel, pouring in clean water and a little rice cake, pushing the vessel with the right hand, chanting the mantra, later calling the name of Tathagata, then taking the food vessel, and sprinkling the contents on the ground, to release the souls of hungry ghosts. In the habit of modern times, feeding Yankou was also performed when great Buddhist rites completed, or in the middle of the funeral period.

Notes

1 "Bhiksu": Asian tropical herb. Bhikus in Buddhism referred to the vanilla produced in snow-capped mountains, which had a soft body, expanding in all directions. Its fragrance went far, and it could cure pain. Buddhism believed that the characteristics of monks were similar to the foregoing advantages of bhiksu, so it borrowed its name.

2 "Fangzhang": According to "Vimalakirti-mivade'sa-sutra", the bedroom of Vimalakirti was 1 square *zhang*, but the capacity was unlimited. Zen named the living room of the abbot for it, and thus abbot was also called "Fangzhang".
3 *Baizhang Regulations* was lost in the early Southern Song Dynasty. Currently, "Preface to Ancient Regulations", written by Yang Yi in Song, remains. (Refer to Volume 8 of "Imperial Revised Baizhang Regulations" edited by Dehui in Yuan.)
4 "Five repentances" refer to confession, persuasion, anumodana, parinama, and wish.

6   The Buddhist temple hall

The Buddhist temple hall was the place to worship Buddha and Bodhisattva, their "residence", and also the place where the monks lived and practiced, which had always been the center of Buddhist activities, the base of idolatry and religious propaganda. From the perspective of culture and landscape, as a comprehensive art museum gathering architecture, sculpture, painting, and calligraphy, the Buddhist temple hall was one of the centers of ancient cultural activities, and also an important place for people to rest and tour. It brought people the enjoyment of beauty, the influence of art, and magical association, and also provided creative passion, impulse, and inspiration for poets and painters. Buddhist monasteries were associated not only with religion, culture, art, and education but also with agricultural production, the business economy, and social welfare, with a variety of social functions.

The evolution of monastery construction

There were a number of yards in Buddhist temples, collectively known as the monastery. "Temple" was the original term for an ancient government office, such as Dali Temple, Taichang Temple, and Honglu Temple. Later it became the name of places where monks worshiped the Buddha According to legend, when Buddhism was first introduced to China, the Buddha statue was carried by a white horse to Luoyang. It was firstly placed in Honglu Temple, in charge of foreign affairs, and the next year, the White Horse Temple was built. Buddhist temples were also known as "Lanruo", a shortened transliteration of "Amacronrandotblwya" in Sanskrit. It originally referred to a place for quiet practice by monks, and later referred to Buddhist temples. For example, in Du Fu's poem "Lanruo on High Mountain, Layers of Smoky Glow" (*Visiting Zen Master in Zhendi Temple*), Lanruo referred to Buddhist temples. The temples were places to worship ancestors and the previous sages, and to worship Buddha. The huts in which ancient hermits lived were called "nunneries". Later this was also the term for Buddhist temples in which Bhikkhuni lived.

India's Buddhist temples were called "samgharama", or "sangha" for short. "Sangha" meant monks, and "rama" meant "yard", collectively known as the yard where monks lived. A sangha was divided into the vihara and caitya. The vihara was the preaching site at first, and later became the monks' residence. There were Buddha statues in the vihara, and in the middle was the hall, surrounded by the monks' rooms. The ruins of famous viharas Jetavana and Nalanda still survive. The caitya was also known as "Sarira Hall" because there was a dagoba. Caityas were generally cut by mountains – for example, Chinese grottoes such as Dunhuang, Yungang, and Longmen were affected by it. In addition, there was another type of "Amacronrandotblwya", the cabin built outside the village as a place for monks' quiet cultivation.

Buddhist Temples in Han areas in China experienced a long evolution process, which began in the Han Dynasty; they became popular in the Six Dynasties, prevailed in the Sui and Tang Dynasties, and declined in the Ming and Qing Dynasties. According to legend, from the early Eastern Han Dynasty when the White Horse Temple was built in the west of Yongguan, Luoyang, to the end of the Eastern Han Dynasty, large-scale Buddhist temples appeared – for example, Zerong built Futu Temple in Xuzhou; "the statue was made of copper, coated with gold. The temple could accommodate more than three thousand people, where they learned classes and chanted Buddhist scriptures. More than five thousand households were attracted" (Volume 49 of *Records of the Three Kingdoms, Biography of Liu Yao*). Since the Three Kingdoms, more and more temples were built in Chang'an, Luoyang, and the middle and lower reaches of the Yangtze River. To the Southern and Northern Dynasties, Buddhism flourished gradually, and even more temples were built. For example, in the Northern Wei Dynasty, there were 1,367 temples inside and outside Luoyang City, and more than 30,000 Buddhist temples in all the prefectures. The Northern Dynasties also focused on building grotto temples, which spread over mountains and crossed valleys, and were very magnificent. There were fewer grotto temples in the Southern Dynasties; Buddhist temples flourished everywhere. Du Mu, a poet in the late Tang Dynasty, described the prosperity of Buddhist temples at the time: "480 temples in the Southern Dynasties, so many in the misty rain" (*Jiangnan Chun Quatrains*). In fact, there were more than 500 Buddhist temples in the reign of Emperor Wu of Liang. In the Sui and Tang Dynasties, Buddhism was unprecedentedly developed, and Buddhist temples stood in great numbers. When Emperor Wuzong of Tang wiped out Buddhism, more than 4,600 imperial temples and more than 40,000 small temples were destroyed. Nanchan Temple and Foguang Temple in Wutai Mountain built in the Tang Dynasty are the oldest surviving Chinese temples. Buddhist monasteries since the Song Dynasty were generally divided into Zen and schools (Tiantai, Huayan, etc.) and the school of Vinaya; in the third year of Hongwu in Ming (AD 1370), the temples were divided into Zen, sermon (preach classics of all sects), and teaching (including practice and Buddhist affairs, etc.) temples, and monks of different professions dressed in robes of different colors. Since the Yuan Dynasty, China's Lamaism became increasingly prosperous, and Lamaist temples, especially the temples of Shamanism, reached their peak in the Ming and Qing Dynasties.

China's monastery buildings were generally divided into two types: those in the mountains and those on the plains; accordingly, the temple layout was also divided into two kinds: grotto temples and pagoda temples. Grotto temples were mostly cut by imitating caitya halls in Indian Buddhism, such as Dunhuang, Yungang, and Longmen Grottoes. There was a square pagoda or shrine in the middle of some holes to represent the status of caitya. In many grottoes, the big statue of Buddha was carved behind the middle, before the wall, on whose left and right were Bodhisattva and Heavenly Kings. Some of the grottoes had excess space in front, which was used to build more monasteries. The construction of grotto temples flourished from the North Dynasties to the Tang Dynasty, and went downhill beginning with the Song Dynasty. Pagoda temples were first known as "Futu Temples" for the earliest pagoda was called "Futu", which referred to the hall for worshiping Buddha. All pagoda temples had a pagoda built in the center of the temple. The temple's courtyard was surrounded; in front and behind the central yard were halls, and monks' rooms were on the sides. In the Northern Dynasties, it became the fashion for imperial princes and court ministers to donate their houses to be temples, and these temples were rarely rebuilt for they were originally private houses, and the main hall was used to worship in the pagoda. Around the Eastern Jin Dynasty and the Southern and Northern Dynasties, the layout of Han-style Buddhist temples was shaped, and basically used the courtyard style of traditional Chinese secular architecture. There were bent corridors, with beautiful wall paintings in the corridor. To the Sui and Tang Dynasties, the Buddhist temple building gradually changed the previous layout centered on the pagoda, and centered on Buddhist halls instead. Many temples had no pagoda, so the pagoda and temple were no longer used together. Even if a pagoda was built, another yard was built to place it in front of the temple, behind the temple, or on the sides. According to Chinese construction law, the main building was on the northern and southern axes, and the ancillary facilities were on both sides in the east and west, in a symmetrical layout. Chinese Buddhist temple buildings made the pagoda as the main body on the axis at first, and later made the hall the main body, so the pagoda was built in the vicinity.

China's Tibetan-style lamaseries were different from the symmetrical pattern of Han-style temples, in which the main hall was in the center, surrounded by scripture halls and Buddha halls. The lamasery was the place where lamas learned scriptures, and "Dratsang" (i.e., the college) was the main building of the temple. A big lamasery had five or six "Dratsang", while small ones had only one "Dratsang". Lamaseries also had "Lakang" (Buddha halls) to worship Buddha statues, lamas' residences, and a pagoda for the corpses of lamas. These colleges, Buddha halls, and residences constituted a group of buildings, whose layout made "Dratsang" the main buildings, which were tall and stood in the center of the lamasery, surrounded by thousands of low lama residences, with a clear three-dimensional outline. Large lamaseries often covered an area of more than 100 hectares, where thousands or even tens of thousands of lamas lived, like a religious city.

Configuration of the temple and naming explanation of statues[1]

1 Configuration of the temple

The hall was the main building of the Buddhist monastery, generally speaking, and places to worship the Buddha statue and implement religious services were called "temples". In the Song Dynasty, Confucius Temple was called "Dacheng Hall". Buddhism also referred to the main body besides houses (called "halls" or "huts") in the monastery as the hall. The place for monks to preach, practice, and live was called a "room". Since the Song Dynasty, the Zen monastery dominated, among which the system of the "seven-room temple" prevailed. Seven rooms referred to the Buddha room, Dhammasala, monk room, storeroom, gate, toilet, and bathroom. Larger monasteries also had an auditorium, scripture room, meditation room, pagoda, bell pagoda, and other buildings. Since the Ming Dynasty, the temple system had been established, and the statue setting in halls was also consistent generally. The configuration of the temple halls, taking the north to the south as the axis, from south to north, was roughly as follows: first was the gate, on the left and right of the gate was the bell pagoda, to the front of the gate was Heavenly King Hall, followed by Mahavira Hall, Dhammasala, followed by the depositary of Buddhist sutra (monastery library), and on the both sides were corridors, with solemn temperament. The side chambers on the left and right sides of the middle road included Samgharama Hall, ancestral hall, the Hall of Avalokitesvara Buddhisatva, and the hall of Medicine Buddha. Some temples had the hall of 500 Arhats. On the eastern side of the monastery (left side) was the monks' living area, with monk rooms, the storehouse, kitchen, dining hall, and reception room, and the western side (right side) was mainly a meditation hall to accommodate monks from all places. The whole temple consisted of multi-story courtyards, forming a unique area for the monks' religious life.

2 The three-door hall

The outer door of monasteries generally contained three doors; in the middle was a gate, and on both sides was a small door. The hall stood for "three relief doors", so it was called "three-door hall". Some monasteries, although they had only one door, were also called three-door. Three-door was also known as "mountain-door", because temples were mostly built in mountains. On the two sides in the three-door hall were two statues of heavenly guardians, holding *vajry* pestles. Vajry meant solid and sharp, able to destroy everything. Pestle was an ancient Indian weapon. A vajry pestle was the most solid weapon in ancient India. The heavenly guardians guarded the Buddha and Dharma. China's *Fengshen Romance* also called the heavenly guardians the two ferocious gigantic guardians, saying they were turning from Zheng Lun and Chen Qi after they died, but there was no such name in the Buddhist classics. According to *Guhyapada vajrah*, Volume 8 of *Maha-ratnakutasutra*, the heavenly guardians were originally the prince. Later after he believed in

Buddhism he swore to get close to Buddha, and be a guard to serve beside Buddha, hearing the Buddha's secrets. He later became the leader of the 500-attendant guard. There was only one "heavenly guardian" originally and only one statue at first. Because it did not meet the Chinese people's aesthetic concept of symmetry, one more was added. The duty of the heavenly guardians was to protect Dharma, so they were placed on the left and right sides of the three-door hall. The statues were tall and majestic, with angry expressions, wearing crowns, baring their upper bodies and holding vajry pestles, their feet separated. The left statue looked angry, with its mouth open, and the vajry pestle was like beating something; the right statue looked angry, with its mouth closed and eyes wide open, holding a vajry pestle horizontally. The two heavenly guardians guarded the gate together, showing the mighty and strict natures of Buddhism, garnering people's respect.

3 The Hall of Heavenly Kings

In the Hall of Heavenly Kings worshiped the statue of Maitreya Buddha, at whose left and right were the statues of four Heavenly Kings, and behind the statue of Maitreya Buddha was the statue of Skanda holding a pestle.

(I) Four Heavenly Kings

In ancient Indian mythology, there were four Heavenly Kings in Sumeru Mountain, and Buddhism learned this legend and transformed it. Buddhism usually divided the world into three realms of samsara: the desire realm, the form realm, and the formless realm. The lowest was the desire realm; the so-called all beings, including the human beings, belonged to this realm. There were six heavens of the desire realm, where the gods lived. The six heavens were divided into six layers. The first layer was the residence for the four Heavenly Kings and their dependents (close attendants, followers, and believers). The location of the four Heavenly Kings was on the mountainside of Sumeru Mountain. Gandhara stood on the mountainside, which had four peaks, and the four Heavenly Kings and their dependents lived respectively in these four peaks. The duty of the four Heavenly Kings was to "guard the world" – namely, to take charge of the territory of the Four Continents. The four Heavenly Kings each had 91 sons, helping them to guard the ten directions. The four Heavenly Kings also had eight famous generals each, managing mountains, rivers, and small gods of various places on behalf of them.

The statues of the four Heavenly Kings went through a process of gradual sinicization in China. The images of the four Heavenly Kings before the Tang Dynasty were as follows:

> Dritarashtra: He was named because he could protect the land. His body was white, dressed in armor and a helmet; he held a knife in his left hand and a spear in his right hand. There were also some images holding a bow. He guarded the continent of Purva-videhah.

Virudhaka: He was named because he could make others grow good roots. His body was blue; he also dressed in armor, holding a sword. He guarded the continent of Jambudvipa.

Virupaksha: He was named because he could observe and guard the people with his naked eye. His body was red; he also dressed in armor, and held a spear in his left hand and a red cable in his right hand. There were also some images holding only a sword. He guarded the continent of Avaragodaniya.

Vaishravana: He was the most famous among the four, with the most prominent status, and the closest relationship with Chinese religious culture. According to legend, he was the heavenly god Kumbira in ancient Hinduism, who gifted wealth. He undertook two duties, and was both the patron saint and the god of wealth, protecting people's wealth. Because of his unique identity, he was deeply admired by Chinese monks and loved by artists. There were a lot of Dunhuang frescoes about Vaishravana throwing treasures. According to legend, the family of Vaishravana was also very extraordinary; the Auspicious Fairy was his wife or sister. In some statues, the left retinue of Sakyamuni Buddha was the Auspicious Fairy, and the right retinue was Vaishravana, who had extremely high status. Vaishravana had five princes, among whom the second prince "Dujian" and the third prince "Nezha" were the most famous.

In Tang portraits of Vaishravana, his body was gold and dressed in armor; he wore a golden bird (or phoenix) crown, carried a long knife, held the pagoda of Sakyamuni Buddha in his left hand, and an Indian-style trident in his right (also with a stick or long spear). He stepped on three *yaksa*: the middle was called Prthivi, in the shape of a heavenly maid, the left was Nimacronlavajra, and the right was Vilamba, in the shape of ghosts. On the right of the heavenly king were the five princes and Yaksha, Rakshasa, and other subordinates; on his left side were five heavenly maids and his wife.

After the Song Dynasty, Buddhism was further integrated with the legend of Chinese superstition, so the role and images of the four Heavenly Kings, especially Vaishravana, were also greatly changed. Vaishravana gradually lost his special identity, and his position of the "god of wealth" was removed, putting him on an equal level with the other three Heavenly Kings. Interestingly, the character of Heaven Marshal Li holding a pagoda gradually evolved from him. Heaven Marshal Li holding a pagoda refers to Li Jing, a general guarding the border in the Tang Dynasty. Li Jing was used to turn Vaishravana into a Han Chinese. He held "Flayer" in one hand, and a pagoda in the other hand. He had a wife, three sons, and a daughter, among whom the most famous was Nezha. Nezha evolved from Nezha in Buddhism, turning a foreign person into a Chinese one, and then into an immortal. Heaven Marshal Li was also made the commander in chief of the Jade Emperor; Nezha acted as the front official, and his other two sons, Jinzha and Muzha, devoted themselves to practicing under the two Bodhisattva. This could be described as a talent exchange between Buddhism and Taoism!

As a result of the foregoing evolution, the four Heavenly Kings became the four guardians of Buddhism. The corresponding statues also changed. In the Yuan Dynasty, Dritarashtra was changed to holding Pipa, because he was the main music god of Shakra; Virudhaka held a sword; in the Ming Dynasty, Vaishravana was changed to holding an umbrella, to show a blessing; in the Qing Dynasty, Virupaksha was changed to holding an animal similar to a snake. The images of these four Heavenly Kings mainly show the function of bringing good weather for crops to meet Chinese people's psychology. This was consistent with the depiction of the novel *Fengshen Romance*, which also said that the four Heavenly Kings were originally four brothers in Jiamengguan in China: Mo Liqing, Mo Lihong, Mo Lihai, and Mo Lishou. Later, after Jiang Ziya opened Fengshenbang, they were sent to the west to be the four Heavenly Kings, which was a special performance of the national subjective consciousness.

(II) Maitreya Buddha

In the front of the Hall of Heavenly Kings the image of Maitreya was worshiped. According to legend, Maitreya was a monk during the Five Dynasties, from the Fenghua area in Zhejiang, formerly known as "Qici". He was fat and smiling, and often carried a stick with a bag on it. He begged and preached to the public in the downtown, known as the "Monk with a Cloth Bag"; later in the second year of Zhenming in the Liang Dynasty (AD 916), he died in Yuelin Temple in Fenghua, Zhejiang. While he was dying, he claimed to be the incarnation of Maitreya, and his descendants then build a statue of him in the Hall of Heavenly Kings in the temple. This could be described as the Chinese Maitreya Buddha. And according to *The Sutra of Maitreya's Ascension*, the *Sutra on the Descent of Maitreya* and *Ekottara Agama* in Indian Buddhism, Maitreya was from southern India. Maitreya was a disciple of Sakyamuni, and later lived in the inner yard of Tusita.[2] The sutra also said that after Sakyamuni Buddha's teachings were spread for 10,000 years, the morality of all beings in the world gradually improved, and they no longer needed Buddhism, so Buddhism died out. More than 800 years after that, Maitreya Buddha descended to the world from Tusita to become Buddha, so Maitreya was also called the future Buddha. In the Tang Dynasty, the images of Maitreya were all typical images of Buddha or Bodhisattva. Today, the sitting statue of Maitreya in Beijing Guangji Temple still remains an ancient legacy.

(III) Skanda

Skanda was a Buddhist heavenly god. According to legend, his surname was Wei and his name was Kun; he was one of the eight generals of Virudhaka. Dao Xuan once talked with the heavenly god, saying that Virudhaka had a general named Wei Kun, who often traveled around the eastern, southern, and western continents (there was no monk on the northern continent), and protected the monks. There was a legend about Skanda guarding the temple in Chinese Buddhist stories, and thus he was particularly respected by the Chinese monks; especially the temple built in modern times must serve him as a patron saint. In addition, there was the name of Skanda in the scriptures translated by Dharmaksema in the Northern Liang Dynasty – for example, *Suvarnaprabhasa* said, "All the gods of Feng Shui gods and heavenly god Skanda". Skanda was one of the gods worshiped in India, and Yiqie Jing YinYi was the wrong translation of "Skanda" in Sanskrit. In the eyes of Chinese monks, Skanda was a god integrating General Wei Kun and Skanda. Generally, the statues of Skanda wore ancient generals' uniforms, held a vajry pestle, and were placed behind the statue of Maitreya in the hall of the Heavenly Kings, facing the statue of Sakyamuni. Usually Skanda had two kinds of postures: the one was to put his palms together devoutly, with the horizontal pestle between his wrists; the other was to grip the pestle with his left hand, with his right hand on his hip; the left was slightly forward, facing Mahavira Hall, as if watching the movement of pedestrians. The latter had the same posture as Wei Hu in *Fengshen Romance*, who held a magic pestle in the hand.

4 *Mahavira Hall*

The main hall of the temple was also called Mahavira Hall. "Mahavira" was the title of Buddhist leader Sakyamuni, in honor of his morality and power. Buddhist scriptures said that he could subdue various demons like the five Skandha-demon, Klesha, and Yama. *Saddharmapundarika Sutra* praised him: "Mahavira was good indeed". It was called "Mahavira Hall" because the main statue worshiped in the hall was Sakyamuni. The main Buddha statue worshiped in the hall was called Yidam. Because of the different sects within Buddhism and the changes of advocacy in different times, there were great differences in Yidam worshiped in the main hall, including configurations of one statue, three statues, five statues, and seven statues.

The configuration of Mahavira Hall included one statue, three statues, or five statues of Sakyamuni or Vairocana or the Ambassad or Buddha. On both sides of the Buddha statues were usually statues of Kasyapa and Ánanda. On two sides of some halls and behind the hall were also placed statues of the 18 Arhats, three Hercules, and Island Avalokitesvara.

(1) One statue

The statue of Sakyamuni Buddha had three kinds of postures: sitting, standing, and lying down, and the majority were sitting. Sakyamuni's sitting method was called "lotus posture". Lotus posture was the sitting method of Buddha, which could be divided into two kinds: the first was "full-lotus posture" – namely, putting the left and right insteps under the left and right buttocks – commonly known as "double-leg sitting tailor-fashion", which could also be divided into two kinds: press the left buttock with the right foot first, then press the right buttock with the left foot; this was known as "anti-Devil sitting", and Zen monks mostly used this sitting method. First press the right buttock with the left foot, then press the left buttock with the right foot; this was known as "auspicious sitting", and Esoteric

Buddhism also called it "Lotus sitting". The second was "semi-lotus posture" – that is, pressing a foot under the other buttock – commonly known as "single-leg sitting tailor-fashion", and Esoteric Buddhism also called it "auspicious sitting". There were two kinds of lotus postures of Sakyamuni Buddha in Mahavira Hall. The one was called "meditation posture" – that is, putting the left hand on the left foot, meaning meditation; the right hand hangs straight down, called "ground-touching posture", and shows all the sacrifices of Sakyamuni before enlightenment. It could only be proved by the ground, for they were all done on the ground. This shape was called "enlightening statue". In another type of lotus posture, the left hand was put on the right foot, and the fingers bent upward into a ring; this was known as "preaching posture".

In the standing statue of Sakyamuni, the left hand sagged, and right arm bent and stretched upward. Sagging was called "Mudra of supreme generosity", meaning he could meet the aspirations of all beings. Stretching upward was called "Abhaya mudra", meaning that he could relieve the suffering of all beings. This standing statue was also known as the "Candana Buddha statue". According to legend, it was made by the Indian king Udayana with Candana in accordance with the image of Buddha while Sakyamuni was alive. Later, statues made according to this image were also called the Candana Buddha statue.

In the lying statue, the body lay sideways as if sleeping, with two legs stretched straight, the left arm on the leg, and the right arm bent and holding the head. It was said that this was the scene in which Sakyamuni said his last words to disciples when he was dying.

On two sides of the main statue in Mahavira Hall, there were often "attendants", usually two bhiksu statues. They were the two disciples of Sakyamuni; the older one was named "Kasyapa", and the middle-aged one was called "Ananda". Buddhism said that Ananda accepted and maintained faith in all Dharma, with a good memory. According to legend, after the Nirvana of Buddha, Kasyapa continued to lead the disciples, and was later known as the first ancestor. After the Nirvana of Kasyapa, Ananda continued to lead the disciples, and was later known as the second ancestor. There was also another type of close attendant of Sakyamuni: the two Bodhisattvas, named Manjusri and Samantabhadra. Sakyamuni and the two Bodhisattvas were collectively known as "Three Saints of Huayan". In some statues, two disciples and the two Bodhisattvas attended together. As for statues other than Sakyamuni Buddha, there were mostly two Bodhisattvas.

> Vairocana: Vairocana was worshiped in some Mahavira Halls. Vairocana's lotus throne was made of Chiba lotus, representing the World of the Lotus Sanctuary (the pure land of Vairocana of the Huayan School). Each lotus petal represented 1 billion worlds; each small statue of Buddha on the petals was Sakyamuni Buddha.
>
> Ambassador Buddha: In the main hall of temples of the Pure Land School, Amitabha or Ambassador Buddha was often worshiped. Ambassador Buddha was the standing statue of Amitabha, with the posture of welcoming all beings. The right hand sagged, in "Mudra of supreme generosity",

meaning he could meet the aspirations of all beings; the left hand was in front of the chest, and there was a golden lotus throne in the palm. The golden lotus throne was the seat of all beings in the Western Paradise. The Pure Land School said that the merits of all living beings were divided into nine levels, and thus it was named the "Nine-Level Lotus Throne". The golden lotus throne in the palm was to express the meaning of welcoming all beings. The Pure Land School taught that Amitabha was the leader of the Western Paradise, and all living beings willing to go there, as long as they called his name, could be welcomed by Amitabha after death to the Western Paradise. Amitabha also had attendants on both sides, Avalokitesvara and Maha-sthama-prapta, collectively known as the "Three Western Saints".

(II) Three statues

Since the Song Dynasty, three statues were often worshiped in larger Buddhist halls – namely, so-called three Buddhas in one hall. There are two categories of the three statues: three-body Buddha and Buddhas of Three Periods.

1   Three-body Buddha: Hinayana described the solemn specificity of Sakyamuni Buddha with 32 appearances and 80 characteristics. Mahayana Buddhism further pointed out that there were numerous "Buddhas", and the "body" had a variety of meanings, like "body" and "accumulation", which meant that the Buddha's body was achieved by consciousness and accumulation of merits. Thus there were arguments that Buddha had three bodies, or multiple bodies. Among them, the most common was the argument of three-body Buddha. Different scriptures and one treatise had quite different specific statements about the three bodies. There was the argument of dharma-kaya, sambhoga-kaya, and nirmana-kaya, among which the Tiantai School's argument of dharma-kaya, sambhoga-kaya, and nirvana-kaya was the most popular. The three-body Buddha in the main halls was shaped based on this argument. One of them was dharma-kaya Buddha, named "Vairocana", meaning all over the place, and that Buddha had inherent Dharma and could reflect it – the so-called absolute truth, embodying the Dharma itself, which was to personalize the Dharma. The one on the left side was sambhoga-kaya Buddha, which meant obtaining the body of Buddhahood via practice based on dharma-kaya, named "Vairochana Buddha", meaning the light shining all over, enlightening the absolute truth, and enjoying the so-called Buddha wisdom – namely, the so-called perfect virtue, which could show the wisdom of the Buddha body. The one on the right was nirmana-kaya Buddha, named "Sakyamuni Buddha" or "Sakya Buddha". Nirmana-kaya was the body being shown to educate and release souls from purgatory, and Sakyamuni's body was nirmana-kaya. Some Buddhist sects and books combined the two Buddhas.
2   Buddhas of Three Periods: There were two kinds of Buddhas of Three Worlds: Vertical and horizontal. Vertical Buddhas of Three Periods was

based on time, and the "world" here referred to the time of and individual life in metempsychosis. It was named because Buddha continued in the past, present, and the afterlife. Buddha of the Past referred to Dipamkara Buddha, who was so named because the Buddhist scriptures said everything was as bright as a lamp around him. He once predicted that Sakyamuni would become Buddha in the future, and he was the teacher of Sakyamuni, so he was Buddha of the Past. Buddha of the Present was Sakyamuni, in the middle. The right was Buddha of the Future – namely, Maitreya Buddha. He was also called Buddha of the Future because he was originally a Bodhisattva; later he descended to the world from Tusita and inherited the position of Buddha from Sakyamuni to become Buddha.

As for the Horizontal Buddhas of Three Worlds, the world here was relative to space – that is, Buddhas of three different worlds: the middle, the east, and the west, based on space. Bhaisajyaguru, leader of the Eastern world, sat on the left, held a bowl of sweet dew in his left hand, and held pills in his right hand. The Buddhist scriptures said that he had made 12 vows to meet all the wishes of all beings, and remove the suffering of all beings. The middle was the leader of our world, Sakyamuni Buddha; in the West was the leader of Western Paradise, Amitabha Buddha, sitting with his hands on his foot, with a lotus platform in his palm, meaning welcoming all beings.

On both sides of Buddhas of Three Worlds, there were also two standing or sitting Bodhisattva statues, who were attendants. Next to Bhaisajyaguru were Surya-prabha and Candra-prabha; next to Sakyamuni were Manjusri Bodhisattva and Samantabhadra; next to Amitabha Buddha was Avalokitesvara and Maha-sthama-prapta. Some Buddhist scriptures said that these six Bodhisattvas were the chief disciples of the three Buddhas. Buddhism said Manjusri was "wise", ranking first in wisdom and eloquence among the Bodhisattvas, winning the reputation of "great wisdom". He had surrendered 500 poisonous dragons in Qingliang Mountain. In his statue, he had five buns, sat on the lotus throne, drove a lion, which meant mighty wisdom, and held a sword, which meant sharp eloquence. Samantabhadra meant owning common virtue, representing "virtue" and "practice". "Virtue" was said to be the virtue prolonging life; as for "practice", it was said that he had made vows to carry forward Buddhist Dharma. In his statues, he drove a white elephant. Buddhism thought that the prudence of practice was like a white elephant, which was the symbol of Samantabhadra's great virtue.

(III) The Five Dhyani Buddhas

The term "Five Dhyani Buddhas" was the generic term for Buddhas in the east, west, south, north, and middle. Ancient temples of Song and Liao were mostly seen to worship the Five Dhyani Buddhas, such as the famous Huayan Temple in Datong, Shanxi, Kaiyuan Temple in Quanzhou, Fujian, and so on. Generally speaking, the statues of the Five Dhyani Buddhas were built in most Esoteric Buddhist monasteries. The position was as follows: in the middle was dharma-kaya Buddha, named Vairocana; the first on the left was Ratnasambhava, embodying blessings; the second was Akshobhya, embodying awareness; the first on the right was Amitabha, embodying wisdom; the second was Amoghasiddhi, embodying business. Esoteric Buddhism believed that these five Buddhas came from five kinds of wisdom, and could comprehensively describe the meaning of Buddha.

(IV) The seven Buddhas of the past

According to Volume 1 of *Dirghagama-sutra*, there were six Buddhas in front of Sakyamuni: Vipassi Buddha, Sikhin Buddha, Visvabhu Buddha, Krakucchanda Buddha, Konagamana Buddha, and Kassapa Buddha; together with Sakyamuni, they were called "the seven Buddhas of the past". They were seldom worshiped in Chinese monasteries, except in the main hall of Fengguo Temple in Yixian, Liaoning.

(V) 16 Arhats and 18 Arhats

The statues of the 16 Arhats and 18 Arhats were generally worshiped on the two sides of monasteries. Arhat came from Sanskrit transliteration, which was the highest level of the Hinayana Buddhist practice: destroy all troubles, accept the supply of heaven, and no longer be in metempsychosis but forever in Nirvana. Hinayana Buddhism believed that if all beings entered Nirvana, who was to carry forward Dharma? So later it advocated that, although the level of Arhat was achieved, they did not enter Nirvana, but continued to live in the world to promote Buddhist Dharma. There were usually 16 Arhats or 18 Arhats in Chinese Buddhist temples.

1   The 16 Arhats: According to Mahayana Buddhist scriptures, the 16 Arhats were the disciples of Sakyamuni. They followed Sakyamuni's entrustment not to enter Nirvana, lived in the world to promote Buddhist Dharma, were supported by common people, and blessed people. For example, Daotai and others of the Northern Liang Dynasty translated *Ru Da Cheng Lun*, which said, "The sixteen Arhats were all famous, scattered in various places ... Guarding Dharma". But the names of the other 14 Arhats were not listed. Zhanran of the Tang Dynasty wrote *Fa Hua Wen Ju Ji*, which said in Volume 2, "It was recorded in *Ratnamegha* that Buddha asked the sixteen Arhats to practice Dharma. The residence, the name and the number, etc. was recorded. Therefore, the saints vowed in front of the Buddha: 'We shall carry forward and protect the scriptures, not enter Nirvana'". But there is no scripture about the 16 Arhats in the existing *Ratnamegha*. In addition, the *Sutra on the Descent of Maitreya* and *Sariputra-pariprccha* said only the four major Arhats.[3] The current stories of the 16 Arhats were based on *Nandimitravadana* translated by Tang Xuanzang (referred to as *Fazhuji* for short). Nandimitra was said to be a famous monk in Simhala (now Sri

Lanka) 800 years after the Buddha died. According to *Nandimitravadana*, the 16 Arhats were Piolabharadvaja, Kanakavatsa, Kanakabharadvaja, Supia, Nakula, Bhadra, Karika, Vajraputra, Supaka, Panthaka, Rāhula, Nagasena, Ingata, Vanavasin, Ajita, and Cūdapanthaka. The first, Piolabharadvaja, had silver hair and long white eyebrows, was commonly known as "long-eyebrow Arhat", and was often worshiped in meditation halls and canteens. The sixth, Bhadra, was said to be a waiter for Buddha, in charge of bathing. He was often worshiped in Zen bathrooms. The tenth, Panthaka, and the sixteenth, Cūdapanthaka, were said to be brothers, of whom the elder was smart while the younger was dull. The eleventh, Rahula, was the son of Sakyamuni. Buddhism declared that on the night when Sakyamuni became a monk, his wife got pregnant, and gave birth to their son six years later, when Sakyamuni became enlightened. He became a monk at the age of 15, and was one of the ten chief disciples of Sakyamuni. The twelfth, Nagasena, once served the king Menander, and elucidated the basic principles of Buddhism.

After *Nandimitravadana* was translated, it had a great influence, and the image of the Arhats was commonly worshiped by the majority of the monks. The lack of information about the Arhats allowed Buddhist artists to imagine freely, thus providing and enriching subjects and contents of sculpture, paintings, and novels. According to historical records, in the Tang Dynasty, Wang Wei liked painting images of Arhats. After the Five Dynasties, the fashion of painting Arhats became even more popular. At present, what we see in Yanxia Cave in Hangzhou is the earliest statues of 16 Arhats, built by the brother-in-law of Qian Yuanguan.

2   The 18 Arhats: Partly because the images of Arhats were widely painted in the Five Dynasties, the 16 Arhats developed into 18 Arhats. According to the existing historical data, the earliest portrait of the 18 Arhats was painted by Zhang Xuan and Guanxiu in the tenth century. Later, when Su Shi saw the two paintings, he respectively wrote 18 praises for them, and also marked the names of the Arhats under the 18 praises of Guanxiu's painting. In addition to the former 16 Arhats listed in *Nandimitravadana*, Nandimitra was the seventeenth Arhat, and Pindolabharadvaja was the eighteenth Arhat (Volume 20, *Praises to Eighteen Arhat*, of *Dongpo's Complete Works*). Nandimitra was the author of *Nandimitravadana*, and Pindolabharadvaja was the disciple of Piolabhāradvāja. So this caused objection among later generations, who said that it was inconsistent. *Fo Zu Tong Ji* believed that the seventeenth and eighteenth Arhats were Kasyapa and Kundapadhaniyaka. Some said they were Matara-jin and the Monk with a Cloth Bag. Some people also thought they were Xianglong and Fuhu. Emperor Qianlong of the Qing Dynasty thought that the seventeenth should be Xianglong Arhat (Kasyapa), and the eighteenth should be Fuhu Arhat (Maitreya). After this imperial decision, this argument was resolved. The legend of the 18 Arhats was quite extensive, and later gradually replaced the legend of the 16 Arhats. Since the Yuan Dynasty, most monastery halls sculpted and worshiped the statues of 18 Arhats.

(VI)   Three sages

In some monasteries, three Bodhisattva statues were set behind the Buddha statue in the main hall: Manjusri, Samantabhadra, and Avalokitesvara. Because Avalokitesvara was also translated as "sage", they were commonly known as the "three sages". The statues of the three bodhisattvas showed them riding a lion, a white elephant with six teeth, and a Hou (a mythical creature), respectively. This was also related to folklore. *Fengshen Romance* turned the three sages of Buddhism into Superiorman Broad Altruist, Manjusri Immortal, and Cihang Taoist, who respectively rode a green lion, white elephant, and golden Hou, and thus the three sages were more and more sinicized.

(VII)   Island Avalokitesvara

In some monasteries, an island was built in the back of the main hall, on which Avalokitesvara stood. Next to the statue of Avalokitesvara were Sudhana and Dragon Lady, surrounded by statues of Avalokitesvara saving the eight difficulties, which were influenced by the description of *Journey to the West*.

5   Bodhisattva hall

Bodhisattva is a Sanskrit word, commonly interpreted as "sage". The statue of Bodhisattva in the world of Buddhism was second only to Buddha. According to legend, before Sakyamuni became Buddha, he took Bodhisattva as his title.

According to Buddhist scriptures, Bodhisattva could wear monks' clothes, and also casual dress. Chinese Bodhisattva images seldom wore monks' clothes. From the Tang Dynasty, the image and dress of Bodhisattva tended to fall into a pattern. Bodhisattvas in Buddhist scriptures were generally "good men", and Bodhisattva's appearance was also said to be "non-male non-female". Chinese Bodhisattvas mostly looked like women,[4] with a tadpole-shaped small mustache, which was removed starting in the Northern Song Dynasty. They had a round face, which got longer after the Song Dynasty. Their eyebrows were long and curved, and their eyes opened slightly, and they had a small mouth. They had a high bun or hanging bun, their long hair scattered down their shoulders, and they wore a fragrant crown. Their upper body was naked or obliquely wore clothes; after the Northern Song Dynasty, they wore clothes with sleeves, but still bared their breasts with shawls. They also wore ornaments. They wore an overskirt, and their feet were full and round. Bodhisattva's face and body were like female artists and aristocratic women in the Tang Dynasty; Bodhisattva's gorgeous clothes and ornaments integrated the fashions of aristocratic women in the Tang Dynasty and ancient Indian aristocratic decoration.

In the eyes of general Chinese Buddhists, as a leader, the image of Buddha was extremely noble, far from the secular world, giving people a sense of solemnity and isolation, but Bodhisattva saw delivering all living creatures from torment as the purpose, and came outside the lotus throne to the world to guide all beings,

142 *The Buddhist temple hall*

giving people a sense of kindness and intimacy. In this way, they gradually acquired a special belief in Bodhisattva. After the Sui and Tang Dynasties, through various interpretations, Buddhists promoted that some famous Bodhisattvas came to the east to settle down, and set up Bodhimanda. Famous Bodhisattvas in Chinese translations of Buddhist scriptures included Maitreya, Manjusri, Samantabhadra, Avalokitesvara, Maha-sthama-prapta, and Ksitigarbharaja. Maitreya later upgraded to the Buddha, and Maha-sthama-prapta failed to become independent and was obscure. Avalokitesvara, Manjusri, and Samantabhadra became the sinicized Bodhisattva, collectively known as the "three sages". The three sages and Ksitigarbharaja were also known as the Four Sage Bodhisattvas. Manjusri and Samantabhadra respectively took great wisdom and great deeds as reputation, Avalokitesvara Bodhisattva had the title of great mercy, and Ksitigarbharaja had the title of Great Wish. Manjusri Bodhisattva and Samantabhadra often appeared beside Sakyamuni Buddha as attendants, while Avalokitesvara and Ksitigarbharaja had their own homes, which could also reflect Chinese monks' intimacy with and worship of these two Bodhisattvas.

(1)   Avalokitesvara hall (Hall of Great Mercy)

Avalokitesvara was named because he (she) could "observe" all the sounds of the world. Avalokitesvara is a transcript of Sanskrit. Buddhism said that he (she) was the chief Avalokitesvara and left attendant of Amitabha, the leader of the Western Paradise, and one of the "Three Western Saints". He (she) showed the great mercy of all the Buddhas, and was the most urgent for salvation. According to *Lotus Sutra-Avalokitesvara*, he (she) had 33 incarnations, and could intervene in 72 kinds of disasters. As long as all beings recited his (her) name in disasters. "Avalokitesvara immediately heard the sound" and went to save them. Avalokitesvara also advocated relieving the suffering of all people, irrespective of high or low birth, became known for "infinite compassion and mercy . . . helping people in distress", and was referred to as "great mercy". In the Sui and Tang Dynasties, he (she) had gained universal belief in society. Worship of Avalokitesvara reflected people's worship of the god, with feminine beauty standing for the love of the mother and the great mercy. The suffering people who had experienced hardships of deep suffering hoped for a beautiful and kind shelter in the world of Buddha, and looked for a happiness giver.

Buddhist scriptures said that Avalokitesvara could turn into a variety of incarnations to relieve the suffering of all beings, so he (she) had a particularly large number of incarnation images, such as the "Six Avalokitesvara", "Seven Avalokitesvara" and "33-body" and "48-arm Avalokitesvara", mostly spread by Esoteric Buddhism. Usually, Avalokitesvara was relative to the overall representative of various Avalokitesvaras. The standard image was one head and two arms, wearing a crown that contained a statue of Amitabha Buddha, sitting and holding a lotus or statue. In addition there was the statue of "free Avalokitesvara", with one leg crossed and one leg sagging, looking very comfortable. Beside the statue was a bottle with nectar and a willow branch, and the figure sprinkled the nectar all over the world. There was a boy and a girl beside the statue of Avalokitesvara. The girl was the Dragon Lady. There was a story about the Dragon Lady becoming Buddha in *Lotus Sutra*, and Avalokitesvara lived in Putuo Luojia Mountain in the South China Sea, so there was a legend about the Dragon Lady worshiping Avalokitesvara. The boy was Sudhana, because *Avatamsaka Sutra* said Sudhana visited 53 Kalyana-mitra[5] to seek Buddhist Dharma, among whom he learned a lot from Avalokitesvara. In China, from about the Southern and Northern Dynasties to the Tang Dynasty, there was a clear turning point: Avalokitesvara's image changed from that of men to that of loving, elegant, beautiful, graceful women.

The full name of Thousand-Hand Avalokitesvara was "thousand-hand and thousand-eye Avalokitesvara", or "thousand-eyes and thousand-arm Avalokitesvara". Buddhist scriptures said that he (she) vowed to seek benefits for all sentient beings and so grew 1,000 hands and eyes. A thousand hands meant protecting all beings, and 1,000 eyes meant watching the world, which were performances of great mercy. Statues of Thousand-Hand Avalokitesvara generally had two hands and eyes, below which were the 20 hands, and each hand had one eye, a total of 40 hands and 40 eyes, and they each were in 25 kinds of living environments of all beings, for a total of 1,000 hands and 1,000 eyes. The most important feature of Thousand-Hand Avalokitesvara was the 42 arms. If the hands stretched down, the palms faced up, all turning into fearless hands to remove the fear of all beings; they held a tin cane, protecting all sentient beings; and they joined palms (two hands), making all people and ghosts love. In general, Thousand-Hand Avalokitesvara had standing statues, and 48-Arm Avalokitesvara had sitting statues. A thousand hands, 1,000 eyes, and 48 arms materialized and visualized Avalokitesvara. In fact, this was the method of romantic exaggeration to show magical power. In the Hall of Great Mercy of Longxing Temple in Zhengding, Hebei, a copper statue of Thousand-Hand Avalokitesvara was cast, 22 meters high. This giant statue, the Cangzhou lions, Dingzhou pagoda, and Zhaozhou Dashiqiao were called "four treasures of Hebei".

(II) Ksitgarbha hall

Ksitgarbha was a paraphrasing of Sanskrit. He was so named because he "was tolerant and still like the earth". The stories in Buddhist scriptures said that he was a Bodhisattva. Sakyamuni asked him to treat sentient beings universally during the period when Sakyamuni died and Maitreya Buddha was not born. He made a great vow to treat all sentient beings universally in reincarnation, and save them from all kinds of suffering before upgrading to Buddha, so his reputation was a "Great Wish". He made great wishes: to be filial to parents; to bear all hardship for all beings; to meet the life needs of all beings, to make grains, fruits, and trees grow; to eliminate disease; to deliver all living creatures from torment in hell. These great wishes were compatible with traditional Chinese Confucian ethical concepts, were also suitable for the agrarian national conditions of China, which were especially welcomed by the peasants, in conformity with the demands of the people to get rid of all kinds of suffering, and were easily accepted by the people. In this way, in addition to Avalokitesvara, Ksitgarbha was the Bodhisattva with the most believers among lower classes of people in ancient China.

Ksitgarbha had a different image from Manjusri, Samantabhadra, and Avalokitesvara, looking like a monk, in bhiksu dress. His statue was seated, holding a tin stick in his right hand, meaning caring for sentient beings, and also meaning strict precepts; he held wishful beads in his left hand, meaning satisfying the wishes of all beings. Some statues had one bhiksu statue and one elderly statue on the sides. It was said the elderly statue was of Min Gong, who donated to Ksitgarbha in Jiuhua Mountain, and the bhiksu statue was of was Min Gong's son, who later followed Ksitgarbha to become a monk.

6 Eastern and western side halls – Sangharama Hall and the ancestral hall

There were often eastern and western side halls on both sides of Mahavira Hall, and the eastern hall was generally Sangharama Hall, while the western hall was generally the ancestral hall.

(1) Sangharama Hall

Sangharama was a Sanskrit transliteration. The paraphrasing was "public garden", or "monk garden". It originally referred to the base to construct monks' rooms, and then transformed into the generic term for temples including land and buildings. Here Sangharama referred to "Jetavana Anathapindada-arama". Statues of gods guarding the land of Sangharama were worshiped in Sangharama Hall, which was also called the land hall in ancient times. Generally, the statues of Anathapindika, Prince Jeta, and his father, King Prasenajit, who built Jetavana Anathapindada-arama, were mostly worshiped, and the 18 gods who guarded Sangharama were also worshiped. The origin of Sangharama Hall was mentioned earlier: Anathapindika bought the garden of Prince Jeta to invite Sakyamuni to preach in Sravasti. Sangharama Hall was built to commemorate Anathapindika, Jeta, and King Prasenajit. In the middle of the hall worshiped King Prasenajit, who was later also converted to Buddhism, making a lot of contributions to the creation of Buddhism of Sakyamuni. On the left was Prince Jeta, and Anathapindika was on the right. On the two sides of the hall, 18 Sangharama gods were often worshiped as patron saints. Their names were recorded in *Shi Shi Yao Lan*, and some were small gods in myths and legends in the ancient Indian subcontinent, absorbed by Buddhism and transformed into patron saints. It is noteworthy that, according to the legend of Zhiyi, the founder of the Tiantai School, Chinese Buddhism also considered Guangong a Sangharama god, and worshiped him in a small niche because he was the Han "God". This showed that the Chinese people were very good at shaping ancient sages into gods, and also showed their great ability for absorbing and involving Buddhism.

(II) The ancestral hall

The ancestral hall mostly belonged to the Zen system in memory of the founder of the sect. In the middle of the hall was the first ancestor of Zen, Dharma, on the left was the sixth ancestor and actual founder of Zen, Hui Neng, and on the right side was Zen master Baizhang Huaihai, the third-generation disciple of Hui Neng who developed *Baizhang Regulations*. Later, other sects were also modeled on Zen to worship the statues of ancestors of their own sect in the ancestral hall in temples.

7 Arhat Hall

Five hundred Arhats were worshiped in Arhat Hall. Regarding the stories about the 500 Arhats, arguments in Buddhist scriptures were very inconsistent. For example, *Saddharmapundarika Sutra* had *Vyakarana of 500 Disciples*, saying that Buddha was Vyakarana of 500 Arhats. This referred to the 500 disciples who followed the teachings of Sakyamuni. It was also said that they were the 500 bhiksu gathered in the first assembly after Buddha died. Zhu Fahu of the Western Jin Dynasty translated *Sutra of Buddha's 500 Disciples Telling Their Origins*, recording the first assembly of 500 Arhats hosted by Kasyapa after Buddha. There was also an argument in Southern Buddhism that the 500 Arhats participated in the fourth assembly in current Sri Lanka. These statements not only were contradictory but also did not specify the names and deeds. The 500 Arhats were popularly worshiped in China in the Five Dynasties, and monasteries in various places established 500 Arhats Hall. Famous ones included Beijing Biyun Temple, Chengdu Baoguang Temple, Suzhou Xiyuan Park, Shanghai Longhua Temple, Hanyang Guiyuan Temple, and Kunming Qiongzhu Temple. The names of the 500 Arhats were recorded in *500 Arhats' Name Tablet* (see Volume 17 of *Jinshi Continuation*) by Gao Daosu of the Southern Song Dynasty; from the first Arhat to the five hundredth, none was missed. But this was actually the work of the Song people. The tablet was gone, and the tablet inscription was collected in the forty-third letter in *Jiaxing Xu Cang*, providing the basis of the names of the modern statues of 500 Arhats.

There was also the statue of Jigong in 500 Arhats Hall. Ji Gong (1148–1209) was a monk in the Southern Song Dynasty, whose former name was Li Xinyuan, from Taizhou, Zhejiang (now Linhai, Zhejiang). He became a monk in Lingyin Temple in Hangzhou, with the religious name of Daoji, and later he moved to Jingci Temple. According to legend, he did not keep precepts and was addicted to wine and meat, especially liking dog meat dipped in garlic. He was humorous, behaved crazily, and was known as the "Jidian Monk". Later, Chinese Buddhism deified him, saying he was the reincarnation of Xionglong Arhat, and thus called him "Ji Gong". According to legend, he was late to report to Arhat Hall, and had to stand in the aisle or squat on the beam. Ji Gong was a Chinese Arhat admired and loved by the people in ancient times, and was highly personalized. His legends and statues were the wonderful creations of the Chinese people, reflecting the differences from the Indian Buddhism. The novel *Ji Gong Biography* contained legends about him helping the poor and mocking officials.

8 Dhammasala (lecture room)

Zen called the lecture room "Dhammasala", and other sects called it the "lecture hall". It was the place to preach the Dharma and rituals, a main building second only to the main hall in temples. Zen master Baizhang advocated not setting up Buddha halls but only Dhammasala. Later Zen restored the Buddhist hall. As for the layout of Dhammasala, in addition to the Buddha statue, the throne was mainly set in the hall. The throne was a high platform, with a seat on it for preaching. Behind the throne hung the image of Sakyamuni preaching. In front of the throne was a podium with a small Buddha statue on it, standing for the Buddhas who listened to Dharma. Under the platform was the incense table, and on the two sides were the seats for listeners. There was also a large bell and drum in Dhammasala; the drum was on the right and the bell was on the left. When masters preached, the drum would be beaten and the bell would be rung. Ringing the bell was to gather the monks, and beating the drum was to persuade the monks. There were two drums in some Dhammasala, and the one in the northeast corner was called Dharma drum, while the one in the northwest corner was called the tea drum. The tea drum was beaten to call the monks to drink tea.

Notes

1 This section refers to the explanation of Zhou Shujia in "Fa Yuan Cong Tan – naming explanation of Buddha statues in the temple halls".
2 "Tusita": One of the so-called six heavens of the desire realm in Buddhism, with inner and outer yards. The outer yard was a part of the world, and the inner yard was the "Pure Land" in which Maitreya lived.
3 The "four major Arhats": Mahakasyapa, Kundapadhaniyaka, Pindolabharadvaja, and Rahula.
4 Buddhist scriptures did not state the sex of Avalokitesvara, Manjusri, or Samantabhadra; and some said they were daughters of Miaozhuangzhu, while some said they were princes of Wuzhengnianwang. In "A Dream of Red Mansions", Li Wan said, "Avalokitesvara had no biography", for a sentence in "The Four Books". Daiyu answered, "Although good, yet no biography". This answer meant the life of Avalokitesvara could not be tested. In fact, Manjusri, Samantabhadra, and other Bodhisattvas' lives could not be tested either.
5 "Kalyana-mitra": Those whohad profound Buddhist and moral knowledge, and were good at enlightening all beings.

7 Buddhist monuments in China

As an ancient saying goes, "the famous mountains in the world are mostly occupied by monks". In the Song Dynasty, Zhao Bian wrote in a poem, "Unfortunately, good mountain sceneries in the world mostly belong to monks" (one of the *Three Dragon Pictures of Ciyunfanshidao*, Volume 10 of *Complete Works of Mr. Zhao Qingxian*). Since ancient times, Buddhist temples seemed to have a natural connection to the scenic area, and some famous monasteries were mostly built in scenic famous mountains. In the list of national key cultural relic protection units published by the State Council in 1961, Buddhist grotto temples, halls, monument pagodas, and bronze Buddha statues accounted for about one-third. Enormous Buddhist monuments spread all over, like art palaces and expos, adding more color to the magnificent mountains and rivers of the motherland. Buddhist artifacts and nature add radiance and beauty to each other, forming harmony and unity between artificial beauty and the natural beauty of landscapes. This may be the reason Buddhist monuments lasted so long.

The god statues in Buddhist temples, the fictional legends, and the religious interpretations gave off an atmosphere of mystery, but also left an infinite burden of historical inheritance for people, causing believers' devout worship. However, as poet Meng Haoran of the Tang Dynasty wrote in his poem *Climbing Xian Mountain with Scholars*, "The world left famous historical site, we climb again and again". Traveling among famous mountains and rivers shall be a great pleasure of life. Visiting great landscapes helps to broaden people's horizons, expand their knowledge, lift morale, and improve their temperaments. In this respect, Buddhist monuments have clearly shown their special charm.

Next, let me focus on brief introductions to the formation, construction, evolution, and characteristics of Buddhist grottoes, famous mountains, ancestral temples, and lamaseries.

Three grottoes

Buddhist grotto temples make the most fascinating historical relics and tourist attractions of Chinese Buddhism. With the introduction and development of Buddhism, Buddhist grotto groups spread all over the vast majority of areas formed from west to east and from north to south in China. As the famous Buddhist artist Chang Renxia said in *Buddhism and Chinese Sculpture,*

> As Buddhism came to the east, its art also came with it. On the way of Buddhism's introduction to the east, it left grotto statues of Ancient Qiuci and Gaochang when it passed Xinjiang Uygur Autonomous Region; left Dunhuang Thousand Buddha Cave, Anxi Yulin Grottoes, Yongjing Bingling Temple, Tianshui Maijishan, and other grotto statues when it passed Gansu Hexi Corridor; as it went on eastward, it left large or small grotto statues like Shanxi Datong Yungang Grottoes, Henan Luoyang Longmen Grottoes, Shanxi Taiyuan Tianlong Mountain, Hebei Cizhou Xiangtang Mountain, He'nan Gongxian Grotto Temple, Shandong Yunmen Mountain, Liaoning Yixian Wanfotang Grotto, and so on, which were very magnificent. In regions south of the Yangtze River, there were Qixia Mountain Grotto statues, and in Sichuan, there were Guangyuan Grottoes and Dazu Grottoes, as well as grotto statues in Bazhong, Tongjiang and other places, widely distributed in large number.

Among the many grottoes, Dunhuang, Yungang, and Longmen are the three most famous, with extremely high historical value and strong artistic force, serving as tourist attractions for Chinese and foreign tourists.

1 Dunhuang Grottoes

Dunhuang Grottoes include Mogao Grottoes, West Thousand Buddha Cave, Yulin Grottoes, and Shuixiakou Small Thousand Buddha Cave, subordinate to the territory of Dunhuang in ancient times. Among them, Mogao Grottoes can be said to be the largest one with the most abundant content, so generally Dunhuang Grottoes refer to Mogao Grottoes.

Mogao Grottoes are commonly known as "Thousand Buddha Cave". They are located 25 kilometers southeast of Dunhuang County, Gansu Province, in the arms of Sanwei Mountain and Mingsha Mountain. They are surrounded by sand, but here many trees grow. The grottoes were chiseled into the cliff of the east side of Mingsha Mountain, five layers up and down, strewn at random, placed closely side by side, more than 1,600 meters long from north to south. As for the beginning of construction, according to the record of *Monument of Li Huairang rebuilding Mogao Grottoes* from the first year of Shengli in the Tang Dynasty (AD 698), in the second year of Jianyuan in the Former Qin Dynasty (AD 366), monk Lezun traveled west, and he arrived at the foot of Sanwei Mountain at dust, in the light of sunset; suddenly he saw a flash and golden light on the mountains, as if there were thousands of Buddhas, triggering his passion to chisel grottoes. So he chiseled the first grotto on the cliff opposite Sanwei Mountain. With the development of Buddhism, more and more grottoes were chiseled. To the reign of Wu Zetian in the Tang Dynasty, there had been more than 1,000 grotto rooms. Less than half are preserved now, including 492[1] grottoes with statues and murals of the Northern Liang Dynasty, the Northern Wei Dynasty, the Western Wei Dynasty, the Northern

Zhou Dynasty, the Sui and Tang Dynasties, the Five Dynasties, the Song Dynasty, and the Western Xia Dynasty to the Yuan Dynasty. Inside the grottoes, there is a total of more than 45,000 square meters of murals, more than 2,400 painted sculptures, five Tang and Song wooden structures, and thousands of lotus pillars and floral tiles. The grottoes are magnificent, gorgeous, and eye-catching. If arranged two meters high, the pictures could constitute a gallery up to 25 kilometers long. Mogao Grottoes fully reflect the development of social life of various nations and hierarchies, and the formative arts of various dynasties from the sixth century to the fourteenth century. It is a profound and comprehensive art hall composed of architecture, painting, and sculpture, and also the largest existing collection of Buddhist art treasures in China and even the whole world.

The structures of Mogao Grottoes included a Zen grotto and center pillar, a square Buddhist hall and bucket type. There were halls outside grottoes, as well as wooden corridors connected with the gallery road. The largest grotto was more than 40 meters long, covering an area of 30 square meters, and the smallest grotto was lower than 1 chi. The statues inside were painted sculptures made of mud, divided into single statues and group statues. The Buddha statue was in the middle, and from 3 to 11 disciples, Bodhisattva, Heavenly Kings, and Hercules, stood on the sides. The largest was 33 meters, and the smallest was 10 cm. The statue mostly embodied characters with exaggerated colors, in different and vivid styles. The mural contents were mainly divided into stories in Buddhist scriptures and simple Buddha statues. In addition, human portraits were painted and worshiped, as well as production and life scenes, such as farming, traveling, banquets, music, and dance. Murals of the Northern Dynasties mainly described the story of Sakyamuni's life to promote Kshanti and self-sacrifice. In the Sui and Tang Dynasties, the subject of sutra illustration became the main body, among which the most typical was to promote the pure land in the Western Paradise.

In 1900 (or 1899), the Library Cave in Dunhuang Grottoes (seventeenth Cave of Mogao Grottoes) was found, inside which there were 50,000–60,000 precious historical relics, such as historical books, silk paintings, and embroideries from the fourth century to the tenth century. In addition to Han books, there were also texts in Tibetan, Sanskrit, Uighur script, Khotanese, Kuchean, Sogdian, and other languages, as well as texts from the Song to the Jin Dynasty that had never been found, of extremely high value. Transcripts, ancient chorographies, poems, and songs were extremely important and valuable materials for studying the history and geography of the northwest, the history of middle and western traffic, the history of religion, and ancient languages and words. Unfortunately, more than two-thirds of Dunhuang's books were stolen and plundered by Britain, French, Russian, Japanese, and American "archaeologists" and "expeditions". The rich historical relics and art treasures in the grottoes caused great interest on the part of scholars at home and abroad, and the famous Dunhuang Studies were formed. China set up Dunhuang Art Institute in 1943 in Dunhuang, which was later renamed Dunhuang Institute of Cultural Relics. In the 1980s Dunhuang Research Institute was founded. The scholars of Dunhuang Research Institute are making more and more compelling contributions to the global study of Dunhuang.

2 Yungang Grottoes

Yungang Grottoes are located at the southern foot of Wuzhou Mountain (also known as Yunxi) 16 kilometers west from Datong City, Shanxi, and were chiseled in the mountain, stretching 1 kilometer. There are now 53 existing grottoes, of which 21 are the main grottoes, with more than 51,000 statues. Yungang is one of the largest grottoes in China. Among China's three major grottoes, Yungang sculpture statues are well known for their magnificent momentum.

Yungang Grottoes were chiseled from the first year of Heping during the reign of Emperor Wencheng in the Northern Wei Dynasty (AD 460), and the main grottoes were completed during the over 30 years before the eighteenth year of Taihe (AD 494), when Emperor Xiaowen moved the capital to Luoyang. At first it was presided over by the famous monk Tan Yao in Liangzhou, mobilizing tens of thousands of workers to chisel five grottoes – namely, "Five Tan Yao Grottoes" (the sixteenth to twentieth grottoes of Yungang Grottoes), chiseled by five emperors[2] for prayer after the Northern Wei Dynasty was founded. The carving and decoration were splendid, leading the world, and were very spectacular. After the Northern Wei Dynasty, Liao and Jin Dynasties chiseled the largest scale of grottoes. The early five grottoes' shapes were oval, with no back room. They were dominated by statues, and Buddha statues were tall. The outdoor Buddha statue in the twentieth grotto was in the posture of sitting, up to 13.7 meters high, with a plump face and broad shoulders, and the clothes were carved with beautiful flame patterns; it was the most magnificent and the representative of Yungang Grottoes. Later middle grottoes mostly had square shapes, with back rooms, and a large Buddha statue was carved in the middle. Walls, arches, and grotto tops were carved with small Buddha statues, Bodhisattva, Hercules, flying Apsaras, and other patterns, in a fine and beautiful style. The fifth and sixth grottoes and Wuhua Grotto of Yungang were colorful, rich, and magnificent, the essence of Yungang Grottoes art. The sitting Buddha in the center of the fifth grotto was dignified and magnificent; it was 17 meters high and 15.8 meters wide, and the middle finger was 2.3 meters long and a foot was 4.6 meters long. It was the largest among all the Buddha statues. A two-layer pagoda pillar was carved in the back room of the sixth grotto, which was about 16 meters high, straight to the top of the grotto. The area of the pagoda pillar was 62 square meters, under which there was a four-layer niche, surrounded by carved Buddha statues, which was very beautiful. Statues in Wuhua Grotto such as Acting Bodhisattva and Maitreya Buddha had a rich and colorful art style that was very unique, and were valuable images for studying ancient art, music, and architecture.

3 Longmen Grottoes

Longmen Grottoes, also known as "Yique Grottoes", are located on the two banks of the entrance of the Yi River, 13 kilometers south from Luoyang City. Here Xiangshan (Eastern Hill) and Longmen Mountain (Western Hill) stand facing each other, like a natural door in the distance, so they were called "Yique" in the ancient times. The landscape was magnificent. The famous, magnificent Longmen Grottoes are densely distributed on cliffs on both sides of the Yi River, dense like honeycombs, and 1,000 meters long from north to south.

Longmen Grottoes were chiseled from the eighteenth year of Taihe of the Northern Wei Dynasty (AD 494) around the transfer of the capital to Luoyang; later it went through the Eastern Wei, the Western Wei, the Northern Qi, the Northern Zhou Dynasty, Sui and Tang Dynasties, and the Northern Song Dynasty, more than 400 years. During that period, the large-scale construction of grottoes in the Northern Wei and Tang Dynasties lasted over 150 years, and the most niches and statues were built. After the Northern Song Dynasty, few were carved and chiseled. Now over 2,100 grotto niches, more than 40 pagodas, more than 100,000 statues, and 3,680 kinds of inscriptions remain in the two mountains. Longmen Grottoes were mostly related to emperors' prayers and offerings. In the Northern Dynasties, statues of Shakyamuni and Maitreya were mostly chiseled; in the Tang Dynasty, Amitabha and Maitreya were mostly chiseled, as well as Vairochana Buddha and Bhaisajyaguru, reflecting the rise of the Pure Land School in the Tang Dynasty and the secularization of grotto statues. Typical grottoes included Guyang Grotto, Binyang Grotto, and Lotus Grotto in the Northern Wei Dynasty, and Qianxi Temple, Myriad Buddha Hole, Fengxian Temple, and Kanjing Temple in the Tang Dynasty.

Guyang Grotto was the place where a group of nobility, senior generals who supported Emperor Xiaowen to move the capital, chiseled niches and statues; it was the earliest chiseled grotto with relatively rich contents. The statue, inscription, and calligraphy inside the grotto were rustic and ancient, and 19 works of the "Longmen Twenty Calligraphic Gems" were in this grotto. Binyang Grotto was built by Emperor Xuanwu of the Northern Wei for his parents, Emperor Xiaowen and Empress Wenzhao. On both sides of the wall was a large relief, divided into four layers: the exquisite "Wei Bo Bian", "Buddha's Story", "Emperor and Empress Paying Respect for Buddha", and "ten gods and kings' statues". Two pieces of the relief "Emperor and Empress's Buddha Hall" were masterpieces of the Northern Wei Dynasty, but were unfortunately stolen in 1934 and taken overseas, and they are now displayed in New York City Museum of Art and Nancouver Nelson Art Museum. Fengxian Temple was built from the third year of Xianheng in the Tang Dynasty (AD 672), taking four years to complete, and was the largest open niche in Longmen Grottoes. The Buddha niche was 36 meters wide from north to south, and 41 meters deep east and west, and contained 11 statues. The main statue of Vairocana Buddha was 17.14 meters high, the head was 4 meters high, and the ear was 1.9 meters long, with a full and beautiful face, long shoulders and eyes, and a slightly upturned mouth, looking kind and wise. Kasyapa was serious, Ananda was docile and devout, Bodhisattva was dignified, the Heavenly Kings frowned with an angry look, and the Herculeses were mighty and vigorous. The whole statue was in a rigorous layout and displayed exquisite carving skills. Statues in Fengxian Temple were the masterpieces of sculptures in the Tang Dynasty, embodying the artistic level and artistic style at that time. According to the statue record, Wu Zetian donated to the construction of this temple, and personally led officials to participate in the consecration ceremony of Vairocana Buddha.

Inscriptions of Longmen Grottoes, such as the prestigious "Longmen Twenty Calligraphic Gems" and the monument of Yique Buddha Niche written by the famous calligrapher Chu Suiliang in the Tang Dynasty, were representative of tablets of the Wei Dynasty and early Tang Dynasty regular script art.

The four famous mountains

Buddhists have always had the traditions of seeking masters and Dharma. Since the rise of Zen in the Tang Dynasty, it was stressed that there was no permanent master for study. Zen monks often left home, traveled all over the world, looked for masters, and visited friends, to seek Dharma and enlightenment. Because they walked for Zen meditation, they were called "walking monks". Zen master Zhaozhou in the late Tang Dynasty once walked to Wutai Mountain nine times, and he still went to various places on foot until the age of 80. There was no fixed place to go for Buddhist monks, but still temples were the main places of worship. To the end of the Tang Dynasty, there were a total of four places where Buddhists collectively worshiped: Wutai Mountain – Holy Land of Manjusri Bodhisattva, Sizhou Puguangwang Temple – Holy Land of the Great Sage of Sizhou, Zhongnan Mountain – Holy Land of Sanjiejiao, and Fengxiang Famen Temple – Holy Land of Buddha bones. During the reign of Ningzong in the Southern Song Dynasty, Minister Shi Miyuan applied to set the level of Zen temples, so the provision of "five mountains and ten temples" came into being. The five mountains referred to Xingsheng Wanfu Temple on Jingshan Mountain in Hangzhou, Lingyin Temple on Lingyin Mountain, Jingci Temple on Nanping Mountain, Jingde Temple on Ningbo Tiantong Mountain, and Guangli Temple on Ashoka Mountain. The ten temples referred to Yongzuo Temple in Hangzhou Zhongtianzhu, Huzhou Wanshou Temple, Jiangning Linggu Temple, Suzhou Baoen Guangxiao Temple, Fenghua Xuedouzisheng Temple, Wenzhou Longxiang Temple, Fuzhou Xuefeng Chongsheng Temple, Jinhua Baolin Temple, Suzhou Yunyan Temple, and Tiantai Guoqing Temple.

Limited to the conditions at the time, these mountains and temples mainly belonged to the Zen system, and were mainly concentrated in Zhejiang, Jiangsu, and Fujian. To the Ming Dynasty, most of the foregoing temples had been destroyed, and the Buddhist community lacked saints, so the fashion of worshiping other famous mountains appeared again among Buddhist believers. These famous mountains had all kinds of Buddhist legends, a magnificent temple building scale, and beautiful scenery. Later, from north to south, from east to west, they mainly concentrated on the four famous mountains: Shanxi Wutai Mountain, Zhejiang Putuo Mountain, Sichuan Emei Mountain, and Anhui Jiuhua Mountain. In the Ming Dynasty, there was a saying of "gold Wutai, silver Putuo, copper Emei, iron Jiuhua". The four famous mountains are still the Holy Lands for Buddhists and tourist attractions for general tourists.

1 Wutai Mountain

Wutai Mountain is in the northeast corner of Wutai County, Shanxi, winding from Mount Heng, and surrounded by five peaks. The whole mountain system covers 250 square kilometers. Five peaks stand tall, and the peak tops are broad and flat, like terraces, so they are called "Wutai Mountain". Wutai refers to Wanghai Peak in the east, Jinxiu Peak in the south, Guayue Peak in the west, Yedou Peak in the north, and Cuiyan Peak in the middle. As for the shapes of the five peaks, the former people compared the eastern peak to a standing elephant, the southern peak to a lying horse, the western peak to a peacock dance, the northern peak to a bird, and the middle peak to a lion. The eastern, northern, central, and western peaks form an arc, which are close to each other, while the southern peak is far away. Among the five peaks, the northern peak is the highest, with an altitude of more than 3,000 meters, earning the title of "the Roof of North China". Inside the five peaks is called Tainei, and outside the five peaks is called Taiwai. The center of Tainei is Taihuai Town, about 60 kilometers away in the northeast, with a lot of temples, making it a symbol of Buddhist sites of Wutai Mountain.

Wutai Mountain is also known as Qingliang Mountain, and is said to be the preaching Bodhimanda of Manjusri by Buddhism. *Pusazhichupin*, Volume 27 of the 60-volume *Buddhavatamsaka-mahavaipulya-sutra* translated in Jin, said, "There is a Bodhisattva residence in the northeast, named 'Qingliang Mountain'. In the past, Bodhisattvas often lived there, such as Manjusri and ten thousand Buddha dependents, who often preached there". It said Manjusri Buddha lived in Qingliang Mountain. In addition, *Manjusri Sutra* translated by Bodhiruci in Tang recorded the words of Vajra Trace Secret Spirits: "After I died, there is a country named Dazhenna in the northeast of Jambudvipa,[3] in the country there are mountains called Wuding, where Manjusri lived and preached for all sentient beings". It said Manjusri Buddha lived on Wuding Mountain. In the Tang Dynasty, Master Chengguan of the Huayan School lived in Grand Huyan Temple (now Xiantong Temple) on Wutai Mountain from the first year of Xingyuan (AD 784) to the third year of Zhenyuan (AD 787), lasting four years, and he wrote 60 volumes of *Annotation to Buddhavatamsaka-mahavaipulya-sutra*, clearly equating Qingliang Mountain in Buddhist scriptures with Wutai Mountain; *Pusazhichupin*, in Volume 47 of that annotation, said,

> Qingliang Mountain is exactly Wutai Mountain in Yanmen County, Daizhou, where there is Qingliang Temple now. There is ice all year round, in summer it still snows, no heat, so it is called "Qingliang". The five peaks stand tall, with no trees on the top, like terrace, so it's called "Wutai". It means the holy five wisdom has been achieved, five eyes have been cleaned, and the truths of five sects are integrated.

The five peaks are the five thrones of Buddha in five directions, also symbolizing that Bodhisattva had five buns, embodying the wisdom of Bodhisattva. In this way, based on the characteristics that Wutai Mountain had five tops and the weather was cold, it was called Qingliang Mountain, the preaching Bodhimanda of Manjusri. This inspired Buddhist believers who worshiped *Avatamsaka Sutra*, who came to Wutai Mountain and worshiped Manjusri Bodhisattva, which played a great role in making Wutai Mountain a Buddhist holy land.

After a long period of expansion, temples in Wutai Mountain gradually formed the largest and most Buddhist temple building group in China. Because of the worship of the emperors of the Northern Wei Dynasty, especially the development of Emperor Xiaowen, Wutai Mountain Buddhism flourished. In the Northern Qi Dynasty, as many as 200 temples were expanding in areas of Wutai Mountain. Emperor Wen of Sui ordered the building of a temple on each of the five tops. During the period of Kaiyuan in the Tang Dynasty, the "faith in Manjusri" centered on this mountain, making Buddhism reach its peak, and large temples stood in great numbers, on a grand scale. *Picture of Wutai Mountain* now remains in the sixty-first grotto of Dunhuang Mogao Grottoes and is more than 40 square meters, depicting a scene of monasteries and a crowd, which was the realistic portrayal of the grand occasion of temples in Wutai Mountain during the Five Dynasties. In the Song Dynasty, there were 72 temples on Wutai Mountain. The Yuan Dynasty specifically believed in Esoteric Buddhism, so temples of Esoteric Buddhism increased greatly on Wutai Mountain. Emperor Wuzong of Yuan built the temple on Wutai Mountain, and mobilized 6,500 sergeants to assist the construction. During the Wanli Period in the Ming Dynasty, Buddhist temples increased to more than 300. After Jiaqing's reign in the Qing Dynasty, the number gradually declined, but there were still more than 100 monasteries. Temples on Wutai Mountain were divided into two categories: one was the temples of Han monks, commonly known as "green temples"; the other was lamaseries, commonly known as "yellow temples". The Qing Dynasty transformed ten green temples into yellow temples, and green-clothing monks to yellow-clothing monks. Therefore, there were Han lamas. There are now 39 Tainei temples and 8 Taiwai temples on Wutai Mountain, and they are in constant recovery. Because the legends said Manjusri Bodhisattva appeared on Wutai Mountain, his statues are generally worshiped in temples.

There are a lot of famous temples on Wutai Mountain, and many sculptures, inscriptions, tomb pagodas, and Buddhist scriptures have high historical and artistic value. The most important is the monastery; there is Xiantong, Tayuan, Bodhisattva Top, Shuxiang, and Rahula, called "Five Zen Places" of Wutai Mountain. In addition, there is also Mimi Temple and Nanchan Temple.

> Xiantong Temple: According to legend, it was built by Emperor Ming in the Eastern Han Dynasty, which was the oldest temple on Wutai Mountain. It was initially called Dafu Lingjiu Temple, renamed Grand Yanhua Temple during the reign of Wu Zetian in the Tang Dynasty, and the present name was used from the Ming Dynasty. The existing buildings were rebuilt in the Ming and Qing Dynasties. There were more than 400 halls in the temple, among which Wuliang Hall, Copper Hall, and Copper Pagoda were the most prestigious. The world-famous Copper Hall was made of copper, imitating a wood structure. The doors and windows were cast

into floral patterns, and there were 10,000 copper Buddha statues in the hall, making it a fine work of ancient Buddhist arts.

Tayuan Temple: It originally belonged to Xiantong Temple. In the Ming Dynasty, it became independent when the stupa was rebuilt, and the name was changed to the present one. The white stupa was 50 meters high, with a perimeter of 83 meters. There was a copper plate on the stupa top, and bells were hung around. The particularly eye-catching white stupa stood tall among the green mountains and trees, and was the sign of Wutai Mountain. The white stupa and the magnificent Xiantong Temple added radiance and beauty to each other, making the most beautiful of scenery of Wutai Mountain.

Bodhisattva Top: It was also called Zhenrong Temple or Manjusri Temple because it was said in legends that Manjusri Bodhisattva lived here. There were 108 stone steps in front of the temple, which were said to refer to the original 108 counties in Shanxi. Monastery buildings imitated palace style, and the temple roof was paved with glazed tiles, resplendent and magnificent, like a palace. In the Qing Dynasty, Emperor Kangxi and Emperor Qianlong worshiped Wutai Mountain several times and lived here. They inscribed plaques and wrote inscriptions. A golden Bodhi tree painting was hung in the main hall, which was said to be personally painted by Emperor Qianlong.

Shuxiang Temple: It was so named because the statue of Manjusri was worshiped here. In Manjusri Hall, the Buddha altar was large, and Manjusri drove a lion, about 9 meters high. On the back of the niche, there were statues of Bhaisajyaguru, Sakya, and Amitabha, and the statues of 500 Arhats were on both sides. All the statues were beautiful and dignified, with fine craftsmanship.

Rahula Temple (Lama Temple): The fourth day of the fourth lunar month was said to be the birthday of Manjusri. Sakyamuni's son Rahula entertained with a "jumping ghost" to celebrate his birthday, which was why it was named. On that day, lamas wore bizarre dress, wore a ghost mask, and jumped with the beat. There was a lotus throne in the center of the temple's back hall, called "Giving Flower to Buddha".

Mimi Temple: In Buddhist legends, Mimi Temple was where Manjusri was cultivated, and Yongtai Zen Master lived in this place, known as the Mimi monk. There was the Hall of Three Saints in the temple, worshiping Buddha, Laozi, and Confucius, and the statue of Confucius was lost. Avalokitesvara Hole in the temple had three layers, with stone statues of Maitreya, Three Sages, and Guan Gong.

Nanchan Temple: It is located in the west of Lijiazhuang, 22 kilometers from Wutai County in the southwest. Its creation time is unknown, and it was rebuilt in the third year of Jianzhong in the Tang Dynasty (AD 782); it is the oldest existing wooden-structure monastery in our country now, standing alone over 1,200 years. There is a world-famous painted statue of the Tang Dynasty in the main hall.

Wutai Mountain Buddhism began to flourish since the Northern Wei Dynasty; to the Tang Dynasty, the Huayan School was the most popular, followed by the Pure Land and Vinaya Schools, and in the late Tang Dynasty, Zen prevailed. Because of the promotion of the Yuan Dynasty court, Esoteric Buddhism dominated on Wutai Mountain for a while. Since the Ming and Qing Dynasties, Green Temples of Wutai Mountain mostly belonged to Zen, among which the Linji School had the most, followed by the Caodong School; in addition, some also belonged to the Pure Land School. As for the Lama Temples, they belonged to Esoteric Buddhism.

Since the Tang Dynasty, Wutai Mountain began to become a well-known Buddhist holy site, and was China's earliest and largest international Buddhist Bodhimanda. In the first year of Fengyin in the Tang Dynasty (AD 676) Kasmira (now Kashmir area) came to Tang, specifically to see Manjusri Bodhisattva in the mountain. According to legend, he never came out after he went into the mountains. Yuan Ren, a famous monk in the Tang Dynasty, worshiped Buddha in Zhulin Temple on Wutai Mountain, connecting Wutai Mountain with the Japanese Buddhist community. In addition, monks from Nepal, Sri Lanka, Indonesia, and other nations came to visit and worship.

2 Putuo Mountain

Putuo Mountain is a small island in Zhoushan Islands in Putuo County, northeast of Zhejiang Province, formerly known as XiaoBaihua, and also known as Mei Cen Mountain. It was so named because there was an argument in *Avatamsaka Sutra* that Avalokitesvara lived on Putuo Mountain. The island is 8.6 kilometers long from north to south, and 3.5 kilometers wide from east to west. It occupies an area of nearly 12.76 square kilometers. It is surrounded by waves, and on the island are mountains and forests, known as the "Buddhist Kingdom on the Sea". According to legend, it was the Bodhimanda of Avalokitesvara Bodhisattva.

According to legend, in the first year of Dazhong in the Tang Dynasty (AD 847), an Indian monk came here and burned his fingers, and he witnessed Avalokitesvara appearing, so he built a hut here and said this was the place where Avalokitesvara appeared. A famous Japanese monk of the Rinzai School, Huie, came to Tang several times. In the second year of Zhenming in the Liang Dynasty during the Five Dynasties (AD 916), he brought the statue of Avalokitesvara from Wutai Mountain to Japan, and was hampered by the wind when he passed Putuo Mountain. According to legend, he prayed to Avalokitesvara and got the message that Avalokitesvara refused to go to Japan and was willing to stay in China, so he built "Bukenqu Avalokitesvara Temple" in the bamboo forest on Putuo Mountain, which was the beginning of this Bodhimanda.

In the third year of Yuanfeng in the Northern Song Dynasty (AD 1080), Wang Shunfeng was sent to Sanhan on a diplomatic mission, and met big waves; he kowtowed to Chaoyin Cave and prayed for safety. Later he appealed to the emperor, who gave the name of Baotuo Avalokitesvara Temple. Later, it got more and more famous, and people who went to Japan and Korea often stopped there to pray for peace. According to the legend of Chinese Buddhism, the birthday of Avalokitesvara was the nineteenth day of the second lunar month; she got enlightened on the nineteenth day of the sixth lunar month, and went into the mountain for cultivation on the nineteenth day of the ninth lunar month. Putuo Mountain became the largest international Buddhist Bodhimanda of modern Chinese Buddhism. In the first year of Shaoxing in the Southern Song Dynasty (AD 1131), Putuo Buddhist sects were attributed to Zen. Since then it was dominated by Zen. In the seventh year of Jiading (AD 1214), it was provided that the mountain was mainly to worship Avalokitesvara, and since then it continued. There were 216 temples, halls, and huts, and more than 3,000 monks and nuns in Putuo Mountain before the liberation. Puji, Fayu, and Huiji were called "Three Putuo Temples"; they were large, pagoda-like, and solemn, and were typical of the buildings in the early Qing Dynasty. There were over 200 halls in Puji Temple, which was magnificent and the main temple on the mountain to worship Avalokitesvara. In addition, there were more than 20 scenic spots on the island. The famous ones included Chaoyin Cave, where the grotto touches the tide day and night, making sounds like thunder. On the sides of Fanyin Cave, cliffs fit like doors, about 100 meters high and 100 meters deep. There was also Nantianmen, West Tianmen, and Qianbusha. The whole Putuo grotto is quiet, with bizarre rocks, waves, sand, mountains, and forests, and has always been a summer resort.

3 Emei Mountain

Emei Mountain is located 7 kilometers southwest from Emei County, Sichuan. It was named because the mountain meanders "like eyebrows, thin and long, beautiful and gorgeous" (*Emei County Annals*). Buddhism called it "Bright Mountain", and Taoism called it "Ling Xu Dong Tian" and "Ling Ling Tai Miao Tian". The main peak, Wanfoding, is over 3,000 meters above sea level, occupying an area of 2 square kilometers. It is over 50 kilometers from the foot to the peak, straight up to the sky. Mountains and valleys go up and down, with range upon range of mountains, flowing clouds, and waterfalls; like Li Bai of the Tang Dynasty said in his poem, "There are many mountains in Sichuan . . . Emei is unparalleled" (*Climbing Emei Mountain*). So there is the saying "Emei is beautiful in the world".

At first, Taoism was popular in Mount Emei, and Taoist temples were built from the Eastern Han Dynasty. To the Tang Dynasty, Buddhism became increasingly prosperous on Emei Mountain. It was said by the Song people that there was an old man who went to the mountain to gather herbs in ancient times, and saw Samantabhadra Bodhisattva there. In the sixth year of Qiande in the Song Dynasty (AD 968), Jiazhou repeatedly reported that Samantabhadra Bodhisattva showed up, so Zhang Chongjin was sent to build the statue of Samantabhadra. In the fifth year of Taiping Xingguo (AD 980), a huge statue of Samantabhadra was built and a hall was built to place it; in addition, Baishui Temple was renamed Baishui Samantabhadra Temple. Since then, Emei Mountain became the holy land of Samantabhadra. Buddhist temples on Emei Mountain reached their heyday in the Ming and Qing Dynasties, when there were nearly 100 large and small temples.

Ever since the Qing Dynasty, the temples have been dilapidated, and less than half remain. The main temples are as follows:

Baoguo Temple: There is a color-glazed porcelain Buddha statue from the reign of Yongle in the Ming Dynasty in the temple, 2.4 meters high. A 14-layer bronze Huyan pagoda was cast in the front hall, 7 meters high. There are more than 4,700 Buddha statues on the pagoda, engraved with all the scriptures of *Avatamsaka Sutra*.

Wannian Temple: It was built in the Jin Dynasty. It was called Baishui Temple in the Tang Dynasty, was renamed Baishui Samantabhadra Temple in the Song Dynasty, and was changed to Shengshou Wannian Temple in the Ming Dynasty. There is a copper statue of Samantabhadra riding a six-tooth white elephant cast in the Northern Song Dynasty in the hall, which is 7.3 meters high and weighs 62 tons. There are 24 Buddha statues cast in iron, and over 300 small Buddha statues cast in copper.

Hongchunping: It was called Thousand Buddha Temple in ancient times. There is a 1,500-year-old Hongchun tree near the monastery, so it was renamed Hongchunping. There is a lotus lamp carved in the Qing Dynasty in the temple, which is 2 meters high and 1 meter in diameter and carved with seven dragons, and hundreds of Buddha statues that are evidence of superb carving skills. The ancient temple stands under Tianchi Peak, with beautiful and pleasant scenery. "Light Rain in Hongchun" is one of the ten sceneries of Emei.

Puguang Temple: It was built in the Eastern Han Dynasty; due to frequent thunder fire, it was repeatedly built and repeatedly destroyed. The temple was built on the top of Emei's Golden Peak. There are three wonders: the sea of clouds, the sunrise, and Buddha's Light. When it is sunny in the afternoon, when people look down to the cliff from the Golden Peak, they can see a colorful halo floating in the clouds. In fact, this is a wonderful natural phenomenon formed when the sunlight penetrates the water vapor and is reflected.

Bailong Temple (Bailong Cave), Xianfeng Temple (Jiulao Cave), Fuhu Temple, Xixiang Pool, Leiyin Temple, Qingyin Hall, and other monasteries on Emei Mountain are also famous. In addition, there are Taoist sites and other attractions on Emei Mountain.

There were many monks on Emei Mountain, most of whom were Zen scholars. In the beginning, they were mostly monks of Qingyuan, and some belonged to the Caodong School and Yunmen School, while few belonged to the Linji School. Today, they mostly belong to Linji, followed by the Caodong School.

4 Jiuhua Mountain

Jiuhua Mountain is 20 kilometers southwest of Qingyang County, Anhui. The main peak is called Qianwang Peak and is 1,342 meters above sea level, occupying an area of over 100 square kilometers. There are 99 peaks on the mountain, among which 9 peaks, including Tiantai, Lianhau, Tianzhu, and Shiwang, are higher than clouds. Jiuhua Mountain was formerly known as Jiuzi Mountain. Li Bai compared the nine peaks to lotus and wrote in a poem, "Once I looked over the remote Jiuhua Peak on Jiujiang River, green water hanging, showing nine lotuses" (*Looking Over Jiuhua*). Then it was gradually called Jiuhua Mountain. The mountain is rich in streams, springs, waterfalls, rocks, grotto, pines, and bamboo. Water and mountains add radiance and beauty to each other, with historical sites throughout; the mountain is known as the "No. 1 mountain in the southeast".

According to Buddhist legends, 1,500 years after Sakyamuni died, Ksitigarbha was born in Silla as a prince, named Kim Gyo-gak, and called Ksitigarbha after he was tonsured. He sailed to China during the reign of Tang Gaozong, and built a hut to cultivate Jiuhua Mountain. Later he was found by Zhuge Jie, his fellow townsman, who saw him sitting alone in a stone room, eating food mixed with Avalokitesvara soil (a clay), and he admired his ascetic spirit very much. He also heard that he was a prince of Silla, and felt he should build a temple for him as the host. At that time, Jiuhua Mountain belonged to Min Gong, and it required Min Gong to offer the land to build a temple. When Min Gong asked Ksitigarbha how much land was needed, he replied, "A piece of land as large as a robe". Min Gong promised it. Unexpectedly, the robe was larger and larger and covered all of Jiuhua. It was said that Ksitigarbha lived on this mountain for decades. He died at the age of 99, on the night on the thirtieth day of the seventh lunar month in the first year of the reign of Emperor Xuanzong of the Tang Dynasty. His flesh did not rot, and his disciples encoffined him and placed him in the pagoda. According to legend, the famous "Flesh Hall" in the mountain was the place where Ksitigarbha became Buddha. Later generations recognized this day as the Chinese Nirvana Day of Ksitigarbha, when Ksitigarbha dharma assembly was held. Since the Ming Dynasty, Ksitigarbh was worshiped, and Jiuhua Mountain became the Holy Land of Ksitigarbh. During the Wanli Period of the Ming Dynasty, the temples increased to 100, and then increased to 150 by the early Qing Dynasty; Buddhist activities flourished, and the location won the title of "Buddhist City". After the Taiping Army went to Jiuhua Mountain, most of the temples were destroyed. Later they were renovated, and now 98 temples remain.

Famous temples on Jiuhua Mountain include Baisui Temple, East Cliff Temple, Jeta Temple, and Ganlu Temple. In addition, there is Huacheng Temple, Flesh Temple, and so on.

> Baisui Temple: It was built for the memorable Zen master Wuxia in the Ming Dynasty. Zen master Wuxia was cultivated hard all year round, and died when he was 100 years old, known as "Baisui Man". His flesh did not rot for three years after his death. Emperor Chongzhen of Ming thought that he was the reincarnation of Ksitigarbha, naming him "Nirmanakaya Bodhisattva". The flesh of Zen master Wuxia, worshiped in the temple, still remains. His head is not different from ordinary people, but the trunk has shrunk to the size of a child's.

East Cliff Temple: There was a huge stone near the East Cliff Temple, which was the place where Ksitigarbha sat according to legend. In the Ming Dynasty Wang Shouren traveled here and wrote verses of "sitting here on the rock all day". There was a hole in the east where Ksitigarbha lived. East Cliff Temple was the largest temple of Jiuhua Mountain before the War of Resistance against Japan.

Jeta Temple: It was built from the Jiajing period of the Ming Dynasty, and later it was expanded several times. It had the largest scale on Jiuhua Mountain. The main hall was majestic, the Buddha statue was spectacular, and incense flourished. It was called Shifang Temple in the Qing Dynasty.

Ganlu Temple: It was built in the early Qing Dynasty, and later it was reconstructed. The temple was built by the mountain, with five layers and shiny glazed tile roof. It was surrounded by bamboo forest, covering the sun, and surrounded by landscape, with beautiful scenery.

Huacheng Temple: It is in the center of Jiuhua Mountain, and was the first temple built on Jiuhua Mountain. According to historical record, it was built by Zhuge Jie and others in Qingyang, and Ksitigarbha was invited here. The temple was built by the mountain, and was imposing, solemn, and quaint. In the second year of Jianzhong in the Tang Dynasty (AD 781), it was developed into Bodhimanda of Ksitigarbha. Some emperors of the Ming and Qing Dynasties personally inscribed plaques and granted money for repairs. Today, imperial edict and scriptures of the Ming Dynasty are still collected in this temple. At the end of the Ming Dynasty, monk Ouyi (1599–1655) entered Jiuhua, lived in Huyan Temple in the south of Huacheng Temple, and worked on Buddhist activities.

Flesh Temple: It is commonly known as the flesh pagoda. According to historical records, Buddhists built it to commemorate Ksitigarbha. The existing pagoda was rebuilt in the Tongzhi Period in the Qing Dynasty. The temples are magnificent, and there is a seven-layer wooden pagoda, about 17 meters high. There are eight niches on each layer, and it worships a Ksitigarbha statue.

The ancestral temple of the eight schools

In the Sui and Tang Dynasties, eight Chinese Buddhist schools formed. They all had founders and a main heir, who were worshiped as ancestors. The temples of ancestors – namely, the temples they created or lived in – were known as the "ancestral temples". These ancestral temples were the birthplace of Chinese Buddhist schools, and had a very important position in the history of Buddhism; some of them were also well-known scenic spots and historic sites, and are still preserved so far, while the others are gone, or only the relics remain. The following is an introduction based on their different circumstances.

1   Tiantai Mountain – the ancestral temple of the Tiantai School

The birthplace of the Tiantai School, Tiantai Mountain, is located in the north of Tiantai County, Zhejiang. Peaks of Tiantai Mountain were beautiful in multiple shapes, making beautiful scenery. According to historical records, during the Three Kingdoms (238–251), there were monks building temples here. Since the Eastern Jin Dynasty, famous monks, such as Zhi Daolin, Tan Guang, and Zhu Tanyou, lived and practiced meditation here. The first ancestor of the Tiantai School, Huiwen, was in Hebei; the second ancestor, Huisi, lived in Nanyue, Hunan; and the third ancestor and the actual founder, Zhiyi, led over 20 disciples, such as Huibian, to live here in the seventh year of Taijian of Chen during the Southern Dynasties (AD 575), and built huts, where he preached for about ten years. He inherited the thought of Huiwen and Huisi, based on which he formed his unique ideological system and his own school, the Tiantai School. In the eighteenth year of the reign of the first emperor of the Sui Dynasty (AD 598), Prince Yang Guang of Jin inherited the unfulfilled wish of Zhiyi and built a temple in the foothills. In the first year of Daye in the Sui Dynasty (AD 605 years), the temple was named Guoqing Temple, and was the fundamental Bodhimanda of the Tiantai School. Later, after several generations of renovation, the existing building was built in the twelfth year of Yongzheng's reign in the Qing Dynasty (AD 1734). In 1973, a comprehensive renovation was implemented. This was a large building group containing 14 temples and more than 600 houses. A bronze Sakyamuni statue cast in the Ming Dynasty was set in the middle of Mahavira Hall, and was 6.8 meters high and weighed 13 tons. On both sides of the hall were arrayed the sitting statues of 18 Arhats carved in the Yuan Dynasty, with very fine work. On the eastern side of the hall was a small courtyard, where there was an ancient plum tree, which was said to be planted when the temple was built in the early Sui Dynasty. Precious cultural relics were collected in the temple, including the remains of Zhiyi, imperial Tripitaka in the reign of Yongzheng in the Qing Dynasty, and *Han Shan Poetry*, printed by a poetry monk in the Tang Dynasty.

A pagoda stood on the hill in front of Guoqing Temple, and was built in the Sui Dynasty and rebuilt in the Song Dynasty. It was about 6 meters high, with six planes and nine layers, in very good shape. There was also the tomb of Zen master Yixing of the Tang Dynasty in front of Guoqing Temple. To revise *Da Yan Calendar*, Yixing once went to Guoqing Temple to learn math from monks in the temple, and descendants built a tomb behind the seven-layer pagoda in front of the temple to commemorate him. According to historical record, when he came to the temple, it was windy and rainy on the North Mountain, and water in the mountain stream in the east of the front temple flooded, pouring into the west mountain stream. Today, there is a stone tablet beside Fenggan Bridge outside the temple, with the words "the water flows westward".

In the seventeenth year of the reign of the first emperor of the Sui Dynasty (AD 597), Zhiyi died. Descendants built a pagoda yard for him on Tiantai Mountain, called "wise master pagoda". This pagoda is now in Zhenjue Temple. The flesh pagoda of Zhiyi was set in the ancestral hall of the pagoda yard. The existing building was built in the Ming Dynasty, and was rebuilt in recent years. There were many temples on Tiantai Mountain, such as Gaoming Temple, also one of Bodhimandas of the wise master; Baoxiang Temple was the place where the wise master died. In addition, there was Huading Temple built by Master Dezhao in the Five Dynasties. They were all famous.

In the twentieth year of Zhenyuan in the Tang Dynasty (AD 804), Japanese monk Saicho came to China to seek dharma. He learned dharma of the Tiantai School from Daosui and Xingman on Tiantai Mountain, and founded the Tiantai School of Japanese Buddhism after returning home. After that, Japanese Tiantai monks often came here to visit the ancestral temple.

Tiantai Guoqing Temple, Nanjing Qixia Temple, Shandong Lingyan Temple, and Hubei Yuquan Temple were known as "The Four Temples in the World". Yuquan Temple was at the southeast foot of Yuquan Mountain, 15 kilometers west of Dangyang County, Hubei, and was also the ancestral temple of the Tiantai School. Zhiyi once taught *Exposition of the Deeper Meaning of the Lotus Sutra* and *Great Samadhiand Vipa'syana* in this temple. After repairs in the Tang, Song, and Ming Dynasties, this temple occupied an area of ten square li, known as "The Largest Temple in Jing Chu". Today, there is a large iron pot cast in the twelfth year of Daye in the Sui Dynasty (AD 616) in front of the main hall of this temple, weighing 1.5 tons, and there are also an iron bell and iron kettle cast in the Yuan Dynasty. There was a carved stone statue of Avalokitesvara on the side of the hall, with strong lines, which was said to be designed by Wu Daozi, the great painter of the Tang Dynasty. There was a Yuquan pagoda on the mound in the southeast, cast in the Northern Song Dynasty, containing 12 layers, reaching 17.9 meters high, and weighing 53.3 tons. The body was tall and straight, steady and exquisite, shiny and eye-catching.

2 Qixia Temple – the ancestral temple of the Three-Treatise School

The Three-Treatise School had many ancestral temples. The first ancestor, Senglang, and the second ancestor, Sengquan, lived in Nanjing Qixia Temple. Sengquan handed down to Falang, who lived in Xinghuang Temple in the Jinling suburbs, spreading *Madhyamika-sastra*, *Sata-sastra*, and *Dvadashanikaya-Shastra* of the Three-Treatise School. The actual founder of the Three-Treatise School, Jizang, followed Falang to become a monk at the age of seven, and learned from Falang for a long time; when the Chen Dynasty destroyed the Sui Dynasty, he went to live in Jiaxiang Temple in Kuaiji (now Shaoxing) for more than ten years. Later, he was invited by Emperor Yang of Sui to live in Riyan Temple in Daxing (now Xi'an), the capital of Sui. During this period, he completed the annotation to the Three Treatises, and wrote *Deeper Meaning of Mahayana* and *Deeper Meaning of Three Treatises*, giving special elaboration to the essence of the Three Treatises, and founded the Three-Treatise School. But now, in addition to Qixia Temple, other temples have been annihilated. The following is only an introduction to Qixia Temple.

Qixia Temple is located in Mount She, 22 kilometers northeast from Nanjing, Jiangsu. This mountain is rich in herbs, which can benefit the body and mind, and that's why it was so named. It was also known as Qixia Mountain because there was Qixia Temple on the mountain. During the period of Jianyuan of Qi in the Southern Dynasties (479–482), there was a lay Buddhist named Sengshao who lived in seclusion on this mountain, and there were often monks coming from Huanglong, forming a close exchange with Sengshao. After Sengshao died, a temple called Qixia was built. In the Liang Dynasty, Senglang from Liaodong was good at the "Three Treatises" and *Avatamsaka Sutra*, and was later known as the third ancestor of the Three-Treatise School. After Senglang died, his disciple Sengquan and Quan's disciple Huibu inherited this temple. During the reign of Tang Gaozu, the temple buildings increased to 49, and it was renamed Gongde Temple. Tang Gaozong made *Tablet of Sengshao*, and renamed the temple Yin Jun Qixia Temple; according to legend, the words "Qixia" were personally inscribed by Gaozong. The inscription was written by the famous calligrapher Gao Zhengchen, and placed on the left front side outside Qixia Temple, which was one of the ancient monuments in the regions south of the Yangtze River. This temple was destroyed by fire during Xianfeng's reign in the Qing Dynasty. In the thirty-fourth year of Guangxu (AD 1908), it was rebuilt by the temple monks, slightly restoring the old view.

There was a stupa inside the temple, built from the first year of Renshou in the Sui Dynasty (AD 601), and rebuilt during the Five Dynasties. The stupa had eight planes and five layers, and was 15 meters high and beautifully carved. There was Wuliang Hall in the east of the stupa, also called Large Buddha Hall. There was a statue of Amitabha in the middle of the hall. The statue was about 10 meters high, and the throne was 2 meters high. There were two Buddha statues on both sides, about 10 meters high. There was a Thousand Buddha Rock on the cliff behind Wuliang Hall. According to legend, Sengshao's son Zhongzhang adhered to his father's unfulfilled wish to carve Amitabha and two Bodhisattva statues on the cliff. Descendants continued to chisel. There were a total of 294 niches and 515 Buddha statues. The Buddha in the first grotto of the Thousand Buddha Rock was nearly 11 meters high, which was a famous grotto in the Southern Dynasties, as famous as Datong Yungang Grottoes.

3 Cien Temple and Xingjiao Temple – the ancestral temples of the Consciousness-Only School

(I) Cien Temple

Cien Temple was 4 kilometers south of what is now Xi'an, Shaanxi Province, and was originally Wulou Temple in the Sui Dynasty. In the twenty-first year of Zhenguan in the Tang Dynasty (AD 647), Prince Li Zhi (later Gao Zong) rebuilt it to pray for his mother Empress Wende, and named it "Cien". At that time, the building was large, with over ten Buddhist temples and a total of 1,897 houses, and was very gorgeous. It took Xuanzang as Sthavira. An office was set in the northwest of the temple for Xuanzang to translate scriptures. After Xuanzang died, his disciple Kuiji continued to live in this temple, so the Consciousness-Only School was also known as the Cien School. In order to place the scriptures brought back from India, in the third year of Yonghui (AD 652), Xuanzang built five pagodas modeled on the form of Western pagodas, called "Wild Goose Pagodas". According to Volume 9 of *Records on the Western Regions of the Great Tang Empire*, monks of Indian Hinayana Buddhism ate clean meat, and some people sought net meat but failed; when they saw a group of geese flying in the air, they joked, "Today the supplement for monks is not enough, and Bodhisattva shall know". Then a goose fell to the ground and died. The monks were ashamed, and no longer ate net meat, and they took the dead goose as the embodiment of Bodhisattva, and especially built a pagoda to bury it, named "Wild Goose Pagoda". It was estimated that the "wild goose pagoda" built by Xuanzang was named after this legend. It was named "Greater Wild Goose Pagoda" because it was relatively bigger than Jianfu Temple nearby, which was named "Small Wild Goose Pagoda". Greater Wild Goose Pagoda was rebuilt several times after it was built. The existing pagoda has seven layers, and the base and the pagoda are 64.1 meters high in total. Two tablets, *Da Tang San Zang Sheng Jiao Xu* written by Emperor Taizong of Tang and *Da Tang San Zang Sheng Jiao Xu Ji* written by Emperor Gaozong of Tang, were inlaid on the southern sides of the pagoda, inscribed by the great calligrapher of the Tang Dynasty, Chu Suiliang, and were famous tablets in the Tang Dynasty. Great poets of the Tang Dynasty, such as Du Fu, Cen Shen, and Gao Shi, had been to the Greater Wild Goose Pagoda, and each wrote their own poems.

(II)   Xingjiao Temple

Xingjiao Temple was located in Chang'an County, 20 kilometers southeast of Xi'an, where the remains of Xuanzang were buried. Xuanzang died in Yuhua Palace, buried on White Deer Plain on the east bank of the Chan River in the eastern suburbs of Xi'an, and later was moved to be buried here. At the same time, the temple was built as a memorial. Later, Emperor Suzong of Tang Li Heng traveled to this temple, and inscribed "Xingjiao" on the table of the pagoda. Since then, the temple was named "Xingjiao Temple". There were three pagodas in the temple, among which the middle was the highest – namely, Xuanzang's stupa – in five layers, about 23 meters, and there was a statue of Xuanzang at the bottom. The tombs of Xuanzang's disciples Kuiji and Yuance were on both sides, with stone carvings, pagoda inscriptions, and mud statues. During the reign of Tongzhi in the Qing Dynasty, in addition to these three pagodas, the rest of the buildings were destroyed by fire. In 1922 and 1939, it was rebuilt twice. Today, the main hall, Depository of Buddhist Sutras, and a rectangular pavilion outside the temple are modern buildings. There is a bronze statue and a statue of a white jade Maitreya sent by Burma in the main hall. The stone carving of Xuan Zang seeking dharma in India was embedded in the facade wall of the side hall, drawn from India.

4 Huayan Temple and Cottage Temple – the ancestral temples of the Huayan School

(I) Huayan Temple

Huayan Temple was on the slope of Shaoling Plateau in Chang'an County, Shaanxi. It was 15 kilometers from Xi'an in the north, occupy a commanding position, facing Zhongnan Mountain in the south, with a beautiful environment. The Huayan School's first ancestor, Du Shun, and second ancestor, Zhiyan, both lived in Zhixiang Temple on Zhongnan Mountain to preach *Avatamsaka Sutra*. The Huayan School's third ancestor and founder Fa Zang was buried in the south of Huayan Temple after death. Huayan Temple was built from the nineteenth year of Zhenyuan in the Tang Dynasty (AD 803), and was one of Bodhimandas of the Huayan School. During the reign of Qianlong in the Qing Dynasty, part of Shaoling Plateau collapsed, and all the halls of the temple were destroyed. There are two existing brick pagodas now. The east is the pagoda of Zen master Du Shun, the first ancestor of the Huayan School; it is square, in seven layers, and 13 meters high, and the upper stone is carved with "Yan Zhu". The west is the pagoda of the fourth ancestor of the Huayan School, Master Qingliang; it is hexagonal, in five layers, and 7 meters high, and there is a stone carving of "Pagoda of Master Qingliang in Tang Dynasty" on the pagoda. There used to be *Tablet of Monk Dushun* carved in the sixth year of Dazhong in the Tang Dynasty (AD 852) in the temple, which is now moved to Shaanxi Provincial Museum for preservation.

(II) Cottage Temple

Cottage Temple is at the foot of Guifeng Mountain, 20 kilometers southeast of Huxian County, Shaanxi. The fifth ancestor of the Huayan School, Zongmi, lived here and drafted *Yuan Jue Jing Shu*; later he entered Guifeng Lanruo in the south of Cottage Temple, chanting sutra and cultivating meditation. After he died, he was buried in the East Small Guifeng and was known as the "Gui Feng Zen Master". There was Guifeng's *Table of Zen Master Dinghui* set up in the ninth year of Dazhong in the Tang Dynasty (AD 855), written by Pei Xiu, who is quite famous. It was moved to the Drum Tower in Cottage Temple. According to legend, Cottage Temple was the place where Kumarajiva translated scriptures. It was named because the temple was built with grass. After Kumarajiva died, his cremation was held here. After the Tang Dynasty, it was repaired again and again. There was "Yao Qin Sanzang Kumarajiva Stupa" in the temple, in different modeling. The pagoda body was two meters high, octahedral, in 12 layers, and carved with white, brick green, black, yellow, pink, light blue, ocher purple, and gray jade. The embossed pattern and the carved Buddha statues were skillful, and commonly known as "Babao Jade Pagoda". There was a well in the northwest of the temple; in autumn and winter mornings, the water vapor rose and was known as the "cottage fog"; it was one of the eight ancient Guanzhong ("Eight Chang'an Sceneries").

5 Daming Temple – the ancestral temple of the Vinaya School

In the Tang Dynasty, Daoxuan lived in Fengde Temple on Zhongnan Mountain, Shaanxi, wrote *Sifenlvxingshichao*, and was the founder of the Nansong School, the mainstream of the Vinaya School. Dao Xuan's disciple's disciple Jian Zhen had traveled to Chang'an, Luoyang, and other places, and later lived in Daming Temple, Yangzhou, Jiangsu, to preach Vinaya. During the Tianbao Period in the Tang Dynasty he went to Japan to spread and carry forward Vinaya, taking the lead in Japanese Buddhism and culture. Jian Zhen built Tang Zhaoti Temple in Nara, Japan, and his tomb pagoda was in the backyard of this temple. Daming Temple was located in Yangzhou, Jiangsu; it was first built during the Daming Period of Song in the Southern Dynasties (457–464), which was why it was named Daming Temple. In the first year of Renshou in the Sui Dynasty (AD 601 years), Xiling Pagoda was built in the temple, and then it was renamed "Xiling Temple". Poets of the Tang Dynasty, such as Li Bai, Bai Juyi, and Liu Yuxi, went to the pagoda, and left famous poems. After Jian Zhen crossed the ocean to Japan, the temple went through several ups and downs. When the writer of the Song Dynasty, Ouyang Xiu, served as the prefecture chief of Yangzhou, he built Pingshan Hall. Poet of the Song Dynasty Su Shi built Gulin Hall behind Pingshan Hall to commemorate Ouyang Xiu, whose stone carved statues were hung on the wall. Emperor Qianlong of the Qing Dynasty cruised to Yangzhou and changed the title to "Fajing Temple". Today it is restored to the original name, Daming Temple. In 1973, Jian Zhen Memorial Hall was built in the east of Mahavira Hall, consisting of the main hall, tablet pavilion, and display room; it was designed by the famous architect Liang Sicheng based on the architectural style in the Tang Dynasty. The statue of Jian Zhen was in the hall, imitating the statue of him in Tang Zhaoti Temple in Japan.

6 Daxingshan Temple and Qinglong Temple – the ancestral temple of Esoteric Buddhism

(I) Daxingshan Temple

Daxingshan Temple was 2.5 kilometers south of Xi'an, Shaanxi Province. It was built from the reign of Emperor Wu of Jin, and renamed Daxingshan Temple in the reign of Emperor Wen of the Sui Dynasty. At that time, Indian monks Narendrayasas, Jnanagupta, and Dharmagupta came to this temple to translate Buddhist scriptures. During the Kaiyuan Period of the Tang Dynasty, Indian monks Subhakarasimha and Vajrabodhi and monk Amoghavajra from Simhalauipa (now Sri Lanka) – namely, "Three Kaiyuan Sages" – came here to translate Buddhist scriptures and spread Shastras. For a moment, it became one of the three translation sites of Buddhist scriptures in the city of Chang'an, and was also the birthplace of Esoteric Buddhism. Esoteric Buddhism took Vairocana as the first ancestor, Vajrasattva as the second ancestor, Nagarjuna as the third ancestor, Nagabodhi as the fourth ancestor, and Vajrabodhi as the fifth ancestor. Vajrabodhi handed down to his disciple Amoghavajra, who was the sixth ancestor. In fact, the Three Kaiyuan

Sages were the real founders of Chinese Esoteric Buddhism. Monk Yixing once served as abbot in this temple, and made outstanding contributions to astronomy and mathematical research. At present, the temple of the Tang Dynasty has been destroyed, and only the bluestone dragon head carved in the Tang Dynasty and the monuments remain. The existing monastery was built in the Ming and Qing Dynasties. Since 1956, it has been fully repaired, and the temple has been gradually restored to its original appearance.

(II) Qinglong Temple

Qinglong Temple was located in the northern highland in Tielumiao Village in the southeastern suburb of Xi'an. It was originally built in the second year of the first emperor of the Sui Dynasty (AD 582) and was named "Linggan Temple". In the Tang Dynasty it was repaired and named "Avalokitesvara Temple". In the second year of Jingyun (AD 711), it was named "Qinglong Temple", and was a famous monastery at that time, and the basic Bodhimanda of Esoteric Buddhism. Amoghavajra's Huiguo lived in the pagoda yard in the seat of this temple, and was called the seventh ancestor of Esoteric Buddhism. Huiguo's disciples included Bianhong from Kalinga (now Java, Indonesia) and Hui Chao from Silla. In the twentieth year of Zhenyuan (AD 804), Japanese monk Fakong went to Tang for Dharma, and inherited from Huiguo. He then handed down Diamond Realm and Womb Realm. After returning home, he set up Japanese Shingon Buddhism in Mount Kōya. After that, Japanese Tiantai monks Yuan Ren and Yuan Zhen and Shingon monk Zongrui came to Tang, and learned Shastras from Zifa. So "Qinglong Temple" was also the birthplace of Japanese Shingon Buddhism. The temple was destroyed in the Northern Song Dynasty. The Institute of Archaeology of Chinese Academy of Social Sciences began to explore the monastery site in 1979. Today, there is a monument on the site, and Memorial Hall for Huiguo has been built, which is still being actively explored and restored now.

7 Xuanzhong Temple, Xiangji Temple, and Donglin Temple – the ancestral temples of the Pure Land School

(I) Xuanzhong Temple

Xuanzhong Temple was located in Stone Wall Valley, 10 kilometers northwest of Jiaocheng County, Shanxi; it was surrounded by steep stone walls, so it was also known as "Stone Wall Temple", one of the birthplaces of the Pure Land School. It was built in the second year of Yanixng in the Northern Wei Dynasty (AD 472). At that time, master Tan Luan lived here to promote the faith in Pure Land. Dao Chuo of the Sui Dynasty and Shan Dao of the Tang Dynasty successively presided over this temple, basically completing the system of the Pure Land School of Tan Luan. Later the temple was renamed Stone Wall Yongning Temple. The main hall was destroyed in the Qing Dynasty, and rebuilt in 1955. The carved wooden statue in the temple was vivid and lifelike. The existing inscriptions from the Northern Wei Dynasty are precious cultural relics. In the east of the temple, there was a two-story octagonal white Qiurong Pagoda on Great Dragon Mountain. The Japanese Pure Land School and Shingon Buddhism, for taking Tan Luan, Dao Chuo and Shan Dao as the three ancestors of the Pure Land School, also worshiped the temple as the ancestral temple.

(II) Xiangji Temple

Xiangji Temple was in Xiangji Village, Chang'an County, Shaanxi Province, about 17 kilometers from Xi'an. It was built in the second year of Shenlong in the Tang Dynasty (AD 706) by Master Shan Dao's disciple Huaiyun and other people to commemorate Shan Dao. When it was first built, the hall was magnificent, with lush grass and flowers, and verdant trees. Emperor Gaozong of Tang (Li Zhi) granted Bai Bao Fan Hua, and Wu Zetian also came to worship. Poet Wang Wei wrote *Padding Xiangji Temple*, vividly depicting the scenery of the temple at that time. After the temple was destroyed, only Shandao Hall and Jingye Pagoda remained. The existing pagoda has been split into 11 parts and is 33 meters high. There was a small brick pagoda on its east side, which was said to be the tomb pagoda of Shan Dao. Xiangji Temple was rebuilt in 1980, and the appearance has been restored.

(III) Donglin Temple

Donglin Temple was at the northwestern foot of Mount Lu in Jiangxi, and was built by Huanyin for Huiyuan in the eleventh year of Taiyuan in the Eastern Jin Dynasty (AD 386). Hui Yuan promoted Amitabha Pure Land faith, and vowed to go to the Western Paradise with Liu Yimin and others. Later, it was said that Huiyuan invited 18 saints to set up the "White Lotus Association" in Mount Lu, so he was worshiped as the first ancestor of the Pure Land School. As an important place of Buddhism in the south after the Eastern Jin Dynasty, Donglin Temple once prevailed in history and was famous around the world. There was Shenyun Hall, Sanxiao Hall, Nianfo Hall, Manjusri Hall, Congming Spring, Shilong Spring, and Arhat Pine in the temple. The tablet with authentic work of the calligrapher of the Tang Dynasty, Liu Gongquan, was inlaid under the eastern window behind the hall. There was Huxi Bridge in front of the temple, and according to legend, Huiyuan never crossed this bridge when seeing off guests. Once he had a talk with the poet Tao Yuanming and Taoist Lu Xiujing, and then Hui Yuan took them out of the mountain. They talked while walking, and crossed Shigong Bridge; a "tiger" roared, and the three laughed. In fact, this was a reflection of the integration of Confucianism, Taoism, and Buddhism. Donglin Temple was surrounded by mountains, with quiet scenery. Ancient literati came here especially. Li Bai, Bai Juyi, Lu You, Yue Fei, and Wang Yangming all left famous masterpieces here. Before Monk Jian Zhen crossed the ocean to Japan, he came to Donglin Temple to invite monk Zhien to go to Japan with him, and Huiyuan's doctrine was also spread eastward, so the Japanese Donglin School also worshiped Huiyuan of Donglin Temple in Mount Lu as the first ancestor.

8 The ancestral temple of Zen

As mentioned earlier, Zen worshiped Bodhidharma as the first ancestor. Later Zen was divided into Northern and Southern Schools. The Northern School was very popular for a moment, but soon declined. There were various ancestors of the Southern School. Nanyue Huairang and Qingyuan Xingsi separated from the Southern School. The Linji School and Weiyang School separated from Nanyue. The Caodong, Yunmen, and Fayan Schools separated from Qingyuan. Huanglong and Yangqi separated from Linji later, and Yangqi also had two sects: Huqiu and Jingshan. So Zen had the most ancestral temples.

(1) Shaolin Temple

Shaolin Temple was at the foot of Wuru Peak, at the northern foot of Shaoshi Mountain, 13 kilometers northwest of Dengfeng County, Henan. It was so named because the foot of Shaoshi Mountain was covered with forests when the temple was built. It was built for Indian Zen Master Buddha in the nineteenth year of Taihe in the Northern Wei Dynasty (AD 495). According to legend, the Indian monk Bodhidharma came here to practice and teach Zen, so he was worshiped as the first ancestor of Zen; Shaolin Temple was also worshiped as the ancestral temple of Zen. When Emperor Wu of the Northern Zhou Dynasty wiped out Buddhism, Shaolin Temple was destroyed, and it was renamed "Zhihu Temple" during the Daxiang Period (579–580) after reconstruction. Later, Emperor Wen of Sui ordered the restoration of its original name. During the reign of Emperor Taizong of Tang, the monastery was rebuilt on a large scale, and there were more than 1,000 halls. To the late Tang Dynasty and the Five Dynasties, it gradually declined, but revived in the Southern Song Dynasty; it was rebuilt during the reign of Emperor Yongzheng in the Qing Dynasty. In 1928, in a warlord dogfight, the Hall of Heavenly Kings and Mahavira Hall were burned out. The existing building is the original main part. In Thousand Buddha Hall, there was a famous mural of the Ming Dynasty, called "Five Hundred Arhats Worshiping Vairocana Buddha", about 300 square meters. There were murals of the Boxing spectrum of Shaolin Temple in the Qing Dynasty and the story of 13 monks saving Li Shimin inside Baiyi Hall. Dharma Pavilion in the temple was said to be the place where Huike stood outside the door to wait for Dharma, and he did not move, although the snow accumulated to his knees, so it was also called "Li Xue Pavilion". More than 300 stone carvings since the Tang Dynasty were preserved in the temple, among which *Qin Wang Gao Shaolin Temple Tablet* and inscriptions written by Su Shi, Mi Fu, Cai Jing, Zhao Mengfu, Dong Qichang, and Japanese monk Shao Yuan were the most valuable.

There was Pagoda Forest of Shaolin Temple on the west side of Shaolin Temple, which was named because the pagodas were as dense as forests. In the Pagoda Forest were mostly tombs of famous monks of Shaolin Temple. There were a total of more than 220 pagodas, in different shapes, reflecting the different styles of pagoda-making in different times, which was an art treasure for comprehensive study of China's ancient masonry and sculpture.

There was a temple for the first ancestor on Wuru Peak in the northwest of Shaolin Temple; according to legends, Bodhidharma once faced the wall and meditated here for nine or ten years. The three characters "Mo Ran Chu" were engraved on the tablet in front of the cave. The four characters "Dong Lai Zhao Ji" were engraved in the north. The story of "facing the wall" in the verse "Facing the wall the ten years to break the wall" in Zhou Enlai's poem *Da Jiang Ge Ba Diao Tou Dong* came from here.

There was a temple for the second ancestor on Bomeng Peak 4 kilometers southwest of the temple; according to legends, the second ancestor, Huike, learned Zen from Bodhidharma, and healed his injury on this mountain after breaking his arm for standing in the snow, so his disciples built this temple to commemorate him. There was a hall and stele inside the temple, and three ancient pagodas outside the temple. There was Mixin Platform in the south of the temple, on which the view within 100 li could be seen.

Shaolin Temple was also the birthplace of Shaolin Boxing. Zen advocated meditation, but sitting for a long time caused muscular numbness, and one needed to get up to stretch the body; over time, this stretching action became fixed, known as boxing. At the beginning of the Tang Dynasty, the monks of Shaolin Temple were able to own 500 temple soldiers to serve Taizong, which brought military tactics and many weapons. Later Shaolin Boxing became more prestigious and spread widely. Boxing was an important kind of martial art, and there was a saying "the martial arts in the world came from Shaolin". The martial art and the temple became famous for each other, and Shaolin Temple was thus known as the "No. 1 Temple in the World".

(II) Valley Temple

Valley Temple was also known as Qianyuan Zen Temple or Third-Ancestor Temple. It was located in the village area on Tianzhu Mountain in Qianshan County, Anhui. According to legend, in Liang of the Southern Dynasties, Zen master Baozhi came to the mountain to build a temple, and later the third ancestor of Zen, Zen Master Seng Can, traveled here and expanded the monastery, where he preached and spread Dharma, making it famous. Jueji Pagoda stood in the temple and was also known as Three-Ancestor Temple Pagoda. It had seven layers and eight planes and was 33 meters high. The pagoda was hollow, and there were steps to climb to the top of it. There was Niushigu Cave in the west of the temple, where Huang Tingjian, litterateur of Song, had studied; he was fond of the beauty of its landscape, and thus called himself "Valley Taoist".

(III) Fourth-Ancestor Temple

Fourth-Ancestor Temple was on Poe Mountain (Western Hills), 15 kilometers west of Huangmei County, Hubei Province, and was Bodhimanda of Tongxin, the fourth ancestor of Zen. The original temple was magnificent, but was destroyed several times in war. Now Fourth-Ancestor Hall and Ci Yun Yue remain. There was Pilu Pagoda on the slope in the west of the temple, which was the tomb pagoda of Daoxin. The pagoda was made of brick, imitating a wooden structure, and about 15 meters high, with a slightly square platform. The modeling was stable and imposing. There was Luban Pavilion on the hillside in the northwest of the temple, which was said to be built by the ancient architect Luban; in fact, it was built in the Tang Dynasty, with the architectural style of the early Tang Dynasty. There was Lingrun Bridge on the stream, built in the Yuan Dynasty. The words "Bi Yu Liu" were engraved on the rock under the bridge, written by Zongyuan. There was also a poetic inscription of people of Huangmeishan in the Yuan Dynasty and poets of the Ming and Qing Dynasties. Around Fourth-Ancestor Temple, there was a temple, pagoda, pavilion, and bridge, adding radiance and beauty to each other.

(IV) Dongshan Temple

It was so named because it was located on Dongshan, 12 kilometers east of Huangmei County in Hubei Province. Because Dongshan was also known as Shuangfeng Mountain, it was also known as "Shuangfeng Temple", where the fifth ancestor of Zen, Hongyi, taught Zen and carried forward dharma-paryaya of Dongshan, also commonly known as "Fifth-Ancestor Temple". The temple was built from the Sui Dynasty, and expanded in the Tang Dynasty, with more than 1,000 halls. It was 3 kilometers from the foot of the mountain along the trail to the top of the mountain. There were many monuments inside and outside the temple. There was a pagoda in front of the temple, built in the Northern Song Dynasty. The pagoda was dignified and carved elegantly. There was Shifang Pagoda beside the road under the Floral Bridge of the temple, made of blue gravel; it was octagonal, in seven layers, and 6.36 meters high. There was a niche, in the middle of which was placed a Buddha statue, with a handsome appearance and rigorous structure. There was Feihong Bridge in the temple, built in the Yuan Dynasty and made of stone stripes, across the valley stream like a rainbow. There was White Lotus Pool outside the temple. Seen from the peak, the ancient temple was hidden, and Mount Lu was not far. Great poets of the Tang Dynasty, such as Du Fu, Liu Zongyuan, Song Zhiwen, and the litterateur of the Song Dynasty, Ouyang Xiu, all came to this temple and wrote excellent verses.

(V) Nanhua Temple

It was 20 kilometers south of Shaoguan City, Guangdong Province. It backed the Yu Ling Mountains, and faced Caoxi, the tributary of the North River, which was quite beautiful. It was first built in the third year of Tianjian of Liang in the Southern Dynasties (AD 504), and was named "Baolin Temple". In the first year of Yifeng of the Tang Dynasty (AD 676), Hui Neng was tonsured in Xingfa Temple in Qianing, Guangzhou. Xingfa Temple was now Guangxiao Temple. There was Sixth-Ancestor Hall inside the temple, formerly known as "ancestor hall" – namely, a building in memory of the sixth ancestor of Zen, Hui Neng. Yifa Pagoda in the temple was said to be built to commemorate Hui Neng, who was tonsured here and buried his hair under the bodhi tree. There was also a Sleeping-Buddha Hall in the temple, also known as "Wind-Streamer Hall", which was said to be the place where Hui Neng preached the theory that the wind and flag did not move but the hearer did. In the second year of Yifeng (AD 677), Hui Neng presided over the Baolin Temple and founded the Southern School of Zen. He was worshiped as the sixth ancestor of Zen, and the temple also became a famous ancestral temple of Zen. In the Tang Dynasty, it was named "Zhongxing Temple" and "Faquan Temple", and in the early Song Dynasty, it was named "Nanhua Temple", which is still in use today. Nanhua Temple had the reputation of "No. 1 temple in East Guangdong". The temple buildings have gone through several ups and downs, and a statue of the sixth ancestor is worshiped in the temple, which is said to be the statue of Hui Neng. In addition, there are statues of the 500 Arhat, in vivid forms. A lot of precious cultural relics, such as a golden embroidered Thousand Buddha robe, imperial edicts in the past dynasties, and a crystal bowl, are collected in the temple.

(VI) Nanyue Prajna Temple (Fuyan Temple) – the ancestral temple of Nanyue of Zen

Nanyue Prajna Temple is located at the foot of Zhengbo Peak of Mount Heng in Hunan Province, and was built in the first year of Guangda in Chen of the Southern Dynasties (AD 567). In the second year of Xiantian in the Tang Dynasty (AD 713), Huairang came here after worshiping Hui Neng, and lived in Avalokitesvara Hall of Prajna Temple to promote Zen, founding Nanyue Sect. It was expanded in the Song Dynasty, and renamed "Fuyan Temple". It was rebuilt again in the Qing Dynasty after destruction. The words "Tian Xia Fa Yuan" were engraved on the stone plaque on the temple gate, and the words "ancient temple over the Six Dynasties, Bodhimanda of the seventh ancestor" were engraved on the stones on two sides. There was a copper statue of God Yue cast in the Southern Dynasties in the temple, weighing 6.3 tons, and there were also three Buddha statues, weighing 5 tons each. There was "Jigaoming Platform" next to the temple, with the handwriting of Liqin "Ji Gao Ming" in the Tang Dynasty on it. There was "Sansheng Pagoda" not far from the temple, which was the tomb of Zen master Huisi, the third ancestor of Tiantai. There was a mirror-grinding platform nearby. According to historical records, Huairang said that grinding brick can make a mirror state that meditation could not make people become Buddha, to enlighten Zen master Daoyi. Later Zen master Daoyi lived in Kaiyuan Temple in Zhongling (now Jinxian County, Jiangxi) and carried the doctrine of Huairang, known as the Hongzhou School.

(VII) Qingyuan Mountain Jingju Temple – the ancestral temple of the Qingyuan Sect of Zen

Qingyuan Mountain is 15 kilometers southeast of Ji'an County, Jiangxi Province. Jingju Temple on Qingyuan Mountain was Bodhimanda of Xingsi, the founder of

Qingyuan Sect of Zen. Later, the Caodong, Yunmen, and Fayan Schools separated from the Qingyuan Sect, worshiping Xingsi as the seventh ancestor of Zen. "Qingyuan Mountain" in Wen Tianxiang's handwriting was engraved on the front door of Jingju Temple. The halls inside the temple were in neat formation, with a lot of monuments. Literatis and poets like Yan Zhenqing and Su Shi had all traveled here and written.

In the second year of Tianbao in the Tang Dynasty (AD 743), Xingsi's disciple Xiqian (stone monk) was invited to live in Nantai Temple on Mount Heng, Hunan, which was made Bodhimanda to promote Zen of Xingsi. There was Xiqian Pagoda in the temple. A relevant Japanese tablet inscription said that Japanese monk Liuxiu was the forty-second-generation grandson of Xiqian. The Japanese Buddhism Caodong School of Japanese Buddhism worshiped Nantai Temple as the ancestral temple.

(VIII) Chengling Pagoda of Linji Temple – the ancestral temple of the Linji School

Linji Temple is in Linji Village, 1 kilometer southeast of the city of Zhengding; it was first built in the second year of Xinghe in the Eastern Wei Dynasty (AD 540). In the eighth year of Dazhong in the Tang Dynasty (AD 854), Yi Xuan founded Linji Zen Temple here, opened Bodhimanda, widely accepted disciples, promoted Zen, and founded the Linji School, flourishing at the moment. Its style was famous for "blow and shout". In the eighth year of Xiantong in the Tang Dynasty (AD867), Yixuan died, and his disciples built a mantle pagoda to bury him, which was named Chengling Pagoda, also known as Green Pagoda. The pagoda was 33 meters high and octagonal, with nine layers. The overall structure was compact, and the outline was beautiful and clear. The Linji School was introduced to Japan in the Southern Song Dynasty, and had many believers, and this temple was worshiped as the birthplace of the Linji School.

In addition, Wanfu Temple on Huangbo Mountain in Yuxi Town, Fuqing County, Fujian Province, was worshiped as the ancestral temple by the Japanese Huangbo School. In the fifth year of Zhenyuan in the Tang Dynasty (AD 789), Hui Neng's inheritor Zen master Ganzheng founded Prajna Temple, which was later renamed Jiande Temple and Wanfu Temple. Zen master Xiyun of the Linji School lived in Wanfu Temple, and the mountain was named Huangbo at first. Later this mountain became a large monastery of Zen. In the ninth year of Chongzhen in the Ming Dynasty (AD 1636), Zen master Yinyuan Longqi lived on this mountain for more than 20 years. In the eleventh year of Shunzhi in the Qing Dynasty (AD 1654), Yinyuan was invited to go to the southeastern suburbs of Kyoto, Japan, to build "Huangbo Mountain Wanfu Temple", which became the fundamental Bodhimanda of the Huangbo School in Japanese Buddhism. Wanfu Temple in Fujian Province was also worshiped as the ancestral temple. Zen master Yinyuan crossed the ocean to spread Zen at the age of 63 and founded the Huangbo School. He continued the course of Jian Zhen 900 years ago, who crossed the ocean to spread Dharma at the age of 66 and founded the Vinaya

School; they added radiance to each other, promoting the exchange of Chinese and Japanese culture.

(IX) Mount Wei and Mount Yang – the ancestral temples of the Wei Yang School

In the late Tang Dynasty, Lingyou lived on Mount Wei, and his disciple Huiji lived on Mount Yang. The master and disciple founded a new school called Weiyang. Mount Wei was 70 kilometers west of Ningxiang County, Hunan Province. There was Miyin Temple on the mountain, in which Lingyou lived. Lingyou lived here alone for seven years, and was worshiped by the premier minister, Pei Xiu. Many monks came to this mountain to study, known as "Weishan Lingyu". On the top of Mount Wei was a wide field. Ancient monks who lived here farmed on the mountain, known as "Arhat Field". There were tombs of Pei Xiu of Tang and Zhang Shi, the Neo-Confucianist of the Song Dynasty. Mount Yang was 40 kilometers south of Yichun, Jiangxi. There was Qixia Temple on the mountain, which was renamed Taiping Xingguo Temple in the Song Dynasty. Huiji set up a lot of hanging banners here, and often enlightened learners with a gesture known as "Yang Shan Men Feng".

(X) Mount Dong, Mount Cao, and Tiantong Temple – the ancestral temple of the Caodong School

1 Mount Dong and Mount Cao: Zen master Liangjia of Tang lived on Mount Dong, and disciple Benji lived on Mount Cao; they founded the Caodong School together. Mount Dong was 25 kilometers northeast of Yifeng County, Jiangxi Province, and there was Puli Temple on the mountain. At the end of Dazhong (847–859) in the Tang Dynasty, Liangjia carried forward Zen here, and was known as "Liangjia of Mount Dong". They created the theory of five monarchs and ministers, which was quite prosperous. Mount Cao was in Yixian County, Jiangxi, formerly known as Jishui Mountain, which was renamed by Benji to commemorate Hui Neng. There was Heyu Temple on the mountain, where Benji promoted Zen.

2 Tiantong Temple was at the foot of Taibai Mountain, 30 kilometers east of Ningbo, Zhejiang. In the first year of Yongkang in the Jin Dynasty (AD 300), monk Yixing came here and built a hut. The temple was built from the Kaiyuan Period in the Tang Dynasty. In the second year of Zhide in the Tang Dynasty (AD 757), monk Zongbi Temple moved the temple to the present site. Later, the emperor named it Tiantong Linglong Temple, and later named it Tianshou Temple again. In the Northern Song Dynasty, it was named Jingde Zen Temple. In the twenty-fifth year of Hongwu in the Ming Dynasty (AD 1392), the name Tiantong Temple was set. In the third year of Jianyan in the Southern Song Dynasty (AD 1129), Zen master Zhengjue lived here and promoted the Caodong School, setting up "Mozhao Zen". In the first year of Baoqing (AD 1225), Rujing presided over this temple. The Japanese monk Taoyuan came to Song and learned from Rujing, and

he founded the Japanese Caodong School after returning to Japan; his followers worshiped Tiantong Temple as their ancestral temple. The existing buildings of Tianto0ng Temple were rebuilt in the Qing Dynasty, and were renovated in 1979. The temple was large and surrounded by mountains and overlapping peaks, with a deep landscape.

(XI)   Yunmen Temple – the ancestral temple of the Yunmen School

Yunmen Temple was 6 kilometers away from Ruyuan Yao Autonomous County, Guangdong. It was founded in the first year of Tongguang in the Later Tang Dynasty of the Five Dynasties (AD 923). It was formerly known as Guangtai Temple, later known as Dajue Temple, and also known as Yunmen Temple. During the Five Dynasties, Zen master Wenyan carried forward Zen here, and founded the Yunmen School, which was the birthplace of the Yunmen School. This school was very prosperous in the Northern Song Dynasty, and tended to decline to the Southern Song Dynasty. Two valuable tablets, *Tablet of Late Master Kuangzhen of Guangtei Temple in Yunmen Mountain in Shaozhou in Han Dynasty* carved in the first year of Dabao in the Southern Song Dynasty (AD 958), and *Tablet of Master Hongming of Dajue Temple in Yunmen Mountain in Shaozhou in Han Dynasty* carved in the seventh year of Dabao (AD 964), are now preserved in the inner wall of the temple door. The existing halls were reconstructed from 1934 to 1950 by the abbot Xuyun with donations. The temple was surrounded by scenic spots.

(XII)   Qingliang Temple – the ancestral temple of the Fayan School

Qingliang Temple was on Qingliang Mountain in Hanzhongmen in Nanjing, Jiangsu. It was called Xingjiao Temple in Yangwu of the Five Dynasties and Ten Kingdoms, and Qingliang Bodhimanda was built in the Southern Tang Dynasty. After the first emperor of the Southern Tang Dynasty, Libian, founded the country, he invited Wen Yi to Jinling to live in Baoen Zen Temple, who was known as Zen master Jinghui. Then he moved to Qingliang Temple, held three rites, and carried forward the style of a new school. He had quite high prestige and many disciples, and founded the Fayan School (Fayan was the official title of Wenyi), which was spread for about 100 years. According to legend, Qingliang Temple was the summer palace of the Li family; emperor Li Yu often stayed here. The original temple was destroyed. The existing Buddhist temple was built in the late Qing Dynasty, and a well of the third year of Baoda of the Southern Tang Dynasty (AD 945) is still preserved. It was said that monks drank water from this well for their whole lives, and their hair did not turn white when they got old.

(XIII)   Huanglong Mountain – the ancestral temple of the
Huanglong School

Huanglong Mountain was in Wuning County, Jiangxi. In the Tang Dynasty, Shi Chaohui founded Yong'an Temple on this mountain, which was named "Chong

En Zen Temple" by Emperor Zhenzong of the Northern Song Dynasty. During the reign of Emperor Renzong of the Northern Song Dynasty, Zen master Hui Nan created the doctrine of "Huanglong San Guan" in Chong En Zen Temple on Huanglong Mountain, promoted the force of Zen, and was known as "Huanglong Huinan". He created another school under the Linji School of Zen, and established the Huanglong School.

(XIV)   Yangqi Mountain – the ancestral temple of the Yangqi School

Yangqi Mountain was in Pingxiang City, Jiangxi Province. According to legend, it was named Yangqi Mountain because the pre-Qin philosopher Yang Zhu traveled southward and got lost here, unable to distinguish the fork roads, and then he burst into tears. In the Tang Dynasty, Yangqi Temple was built here, also known Putong Zen Temple. Master Chengguang lived on Mount Xi. After his death, the poet and philosopher Liu Yuxi wrote *Table of Late Zen Master Guang in Yangqi Mountain, Pingxiang County, Yuanzhou* for him. In the Northern Song Dynasty, Huinan's fellow Fanghui lived here and carried forward Dharma; he also created a new faction under the Linji School, and became the orthodoxy of the Linji School. It took the name of the mountain and was named the Yangqi School. Fanghui was also known as a Yangqi Zen master. The ancient temples were destroyed in the Cultural Revolution, and the tablet written by Liu Yuxi, the pagoda of Master Zhen Shu, and the pagoda of Zen Chengguang survive. The famous "Tang cypress" is 14 meters high and more than 2 meters in diameter, and still proudly stands in the temple now.

(XV)   Tiger Hill – the ancestral temple of the Tiger Hill School

Tiger Hill was on Shantang Street, Changmenwai, Suzhou City, Jiangsu Province, about 3.5 kilometers from the city. In the Spring and Autumn Period, King Fuchai of Wu buried his father, He Lv, here. In the Jin Dynasty, Situ Wangxun and Wangmin built a villa, and the back house was a temple, called Tiger Hill Temple. In the Song Dynasty, it was reconstructed into Yunyan Temple, and in the Qing Dynasty, it was renamed Hufu Temple. Between the Jin and Song Dynasties, Daosheng once preached here, leaving a legend of "rocks nodding in approval". In the fourth year of Shaoxing in the Song Dynasty (AD 1134), the fifth ancestor of Yangqi of the Linji School, Shaolong, lived here, and founded the Tiger Hill School, which became the mainstream of the Linji School later. There were many cultural relics in Tiger Hill, which was magnificent with beautiful scenery. Tiger Hill Pagoda was also known as Yunyan Temple Pagoda, and was built in the Five Dynasties, in octagonal planes and seven layers. The brick of the pagoda was decorated with colorful paintings, with exquisite designs, which were some of the early architectural paintings in China. Yunyan Temple at the foot of Tiger Hill had two gates, also known as "Duanliang Temple" and "Shuangliang Temple", which were built in the Yuan Dynasty and very beautiful. The ancients highly praised Tiger Hill:

pagoda came out of the forest, the mountain hid in the temple. It had the reputation of "No. 1 scenic spot in Wu".

(XVI) Mount Jing – the ancestral temple of the Jingshan School

Mount Jing was 25 kilometers northwest from Yuhang County, Zhejiang Province, and it was named because there were two paths on the mountain, 5 kilometers long, winding straight up to Tianmu Mountain. There was Nengren Xingsheng Wanshou Temple on the mountain, referred to as Jingshan Temple for short. In the seventh year of Shaoxing in the Song Dynasty (AD 1137), the fellow of Shailong, the fifth ancestor of the Yangqi School, Zonggao lived here, and founded "Kanhua Zen" (Huatou Zen). It was known as the Dahui School (Dahui was the title of Zonggao), and also known as the Jingshan School. There were seven peaks, such as Lingxiao on Mount Jing, with quiet scenery. There was Jingshan Temple, which is now destroyed.

In addition, the White Horse Temple, about 12 kilometers east of Luoyang City, Henan, was known as the "No. 1 ancient temple in China", and was also worshiped as the ancestral temple and "source" (the birthplace of Buddhism) by the majority of Buddhists. According to the traditional argument, the White Horse Temple was founded in the eleventh year of Yongping in the Eastern Han Dynasty (AD 68), with a history of more than 1,900 years. This temple played an important role in the early translation of Buddhist scriptures and the communication of doctrine. The monastery was large, and its back part, Qingliang Platform, was said to be the place where Emperor Min of Han read books, and was the site in which two Indian eminent monks, Kaśyapamatanga and Dharmaratna, translated Buddhist scriptures and preached. The existing statues in the temple now are works of the Yuan, Ming, and Qing Dynasties. The statues of Buddhas of Three Worlds, two Heavenly Generals, 18 Arhats, and the "dry lacquer" of the Yuan Dynasty in Mahavira Hall were vivid, making a group of art treasures with high cultural value and reputations at home and abroad. There are more than 40 existing inscriptions, also having important artistic and historical value. There was a round tomb in the southeastern and southwestern corner of the temple, respectively carved with tombstones of Kaśyapamatanga and Dharmaratna. There was White Horse Temple Pagoda in the southeast of the White Horse Temple, also known as "Qi Yun Pagoda" and "Sakyana Stupa". The pagoda had 13 layers and was about 25 meters high. It was exquisite, tall, straight, and beautiful. According to the monument of the Song Dynasty in the temple, this pagoda was built in the twelfth year of Yongping in the Eastern Han Dynasty (AD 69), and could be described as China's first ancient pagoda. The existing temple pagoda was rebuilt in the fifteenth year of Dading in the Jin Dynasty (AD 1175), with a history of more than 800 years.

Famous lamaseries

In addition to Potala Palace – the Dalai Lama's residence – among lamaseries of Shamanism in China, the largest ones include Tashilhunpo Monastery, Drepung

Monastery, Sera Monastery, and Ganden Monastery in Tibet, Taer Monastery in Huangzhong, Qinghai, and Labrang Monastery in Xiahe, Gansu, which had the highest status; these were known as the six main monasteries of Shamanism. In addition, Outer Eight Temples in Chengde, Hebei, and Yonghe Lamasery in Beijing also very famous. The following is a brief introduction.

1 Potala Palace

Potala Palace was on Mountain Maburi, in the northwest of Lhasa. Potala was a Sanskrit transliteration, meaning "Buddhist holy land". According to legend, in the seventh century, Srongtsen Gampo, Zanpu of Tubo, first built the palace here to welcome Princess Wencheng of Tang. Later it was repeatedly repaired. To the middle of the seventeenth century, after the fifth Dalai Lama was canonized by Emperor Shunzhi of the Qing Dynasty, he greatly expanded it, and it took nearly 50 years to be built to today's size. The palace's main building had 13 layers and was 117.19 meters high, 360 meters long from east to west, and more than 500 meters wide from north to south. All of the building was made of stone and wood. There were nearly 10,000 buildings, which could accommodate more than 20,000 monks. Inside there was the palace, Buddha hall, study room, bedroom, pagoda hall, courtyard, and so on. Dalai Lama's very luxurious eight pagodas were wrapped in gold and inlaid with precious jade. The walls of the palace were painted with colorful and vivid murals. There were also a large number of precious historical relics preserved in the palace. All the buildings were built by the mountains. The buildings overlapped and the temples were lofty and imposing. Potala Palace was a huge complex of palace and monastery, the essence of ancient Tibetan architecture; it was the winter palace of Dalai Lama in the past dynasties, and also the ruling center of the former Tibetan political and religious unity, where major religious and political ceremonies were held.

2 Tashilhunpo Monastery

It was at the foot of Niseri Mountain in the south of Shigatse County in Tibet. In Tibetan, Tashilhunpo meant "Auspicious Sumeru Mountain". In the fourteenth year of Zhengtong in the Ming Dynasty (AD 1447), it was built by Gendun Drup, the disciple of Tsongkhapa, the founder of Gelugpa in Lamaism (Shamanism). After the fourth Panchen Lama Luosangqujian came into power at the end of the Ming Dynasty, Tashilhunpo Monastery became the enthronement place of Panchen Lama. Later, it became the center of the religious and political activities of Panchen Lamas. Tashilhunpo Temple was near the mountain and by the river, towering and solemn. There were four Dratsang (college) and dozens of halls in the monastery. There was a statue of Byams-pa in the monastery, 26.8 meters high; according to records, 110,000 kg of bronze and 250 kg of gold were used to construct this statue, which was a very rare gold-plated Maitreya Buddha. There were also pagodas of Panchen Lamas in the monastery, wrapped in silver skin. In addition, there were a large number of other precious historical relics.

3 Drepung Monastery

Drepung Monastery was located on the hillside 5 kilometers northwest of Lhasa, Tibet. In the fourteenth year of Yongle in the Ming Dynasty (AD 1416), it was built by Jiaxiangqujie, Tsongkhapa's disciple. The monastery's construction area was 250,000 square meters, with tens of thousands of houses and four Dratsangs, and the monk quota was 7,700. The monastery could accommodate 8,000 people, and was the largest lamasery in China. It was called "Three Major Lhasa Temples" together with Sera Monastery and Ganden Temple. Gandan Podrang (palace) in the monastery was the place where the second to fifth Dalai Lamas lived. All Dalai Lamas took this monastery as the mother monastery, whose status was extremely important. Monks in Lhasa who learned scripture mostly went to Guomang Dratsang of this monastery. The collection of historical relics and arts and crafts in this monastery was very rich, and there were numerous books, among which the three Kangyur scriptures were particularly valuable.

4 Sera Monastery

Sera Monastery was at the foot of a mountain 3 kilometers north of Lhasa, Tibet. In the seventh year of Yongle in the Ming Dynasty (AD 1409) Tsongkhapa's disciple Byams-chen chos-rje went to the capital on behalf of Tsongkhapa, and was later conferred the title of Dacifawang. In the sixteenth year of Yongle in the Ming Dynasty (AD 1418), Byams-chen chos-rje built this monastery to worship the Buddha statue and Buddhist scriptures granted by the emperor. There were three Dratsangs in the monastery, and the monk quota was 5,500. The statues of Maitreya and Bodhisattva in the main hall were cast in copper and were in beautiful shape. There was one "Tripitaka" and a set of chandana-carved statues of 16 Sthaviras brought back by Byams-chen chos-rje from Beijing in the monastery; in addition, there was an image of Dacifawang made of fine silks and gold thread by the inland in the Ming Dynasty. All of these were extremely valuable cultural relics.

5 Ganden Monastery

Ganden Temple was on Wangguer Mountain in Dazi County, 60 kilometers east of Lhasa, Tibet. It was built by Tsongkhapa, the founder of Tibetan Shamanism, which was regarded as the ancestral temple of Shamanism. Tsongkhapa's heir, Gelugu leader Ganden Tripa, lived in this monastery. The monastery was founded in the seventh year of Yongle in the Ming Dynasty (AD 1409), and it was so large that it was the equivalent of three Potala Palaces. There were two Dratsangs, and the monk quota was 3,300. The hall in the monastery could accommodate more than 3,000 lamas chanting at the same time. There was the flesh pagoda of Tsongkhapa in Sidongtuo Hall. Chiduoka in the monastery was the place where Tsongkhapa lived. The monastery was destroyed, and is now in active renovation.

6 Taer Monastery

Taer Monastery was in Lushaer Town, Huangzhong County, Qinghai Province, 25 kilometers away from Xining City. It was built to commemorate Tsongkhapa, the first ancestor of Shamanism, in the thirty-ninth year of Jiajing in the Ming Dynasty (AD 1560) in his birthplace. After 400 years of construction and repair, it reached today's size. The whole monastery went up and down with the mountain. Large and small buildings, such as Dajinwa Temple, Xiaojinwa Temple, Xiaohua Temple, Large Scripture Hall, Large Kitchen, Nine Hall, Dalalang, Ruyi Pagoda, Taiping Pagoda, Bodhi Pagoda, and Guomen Pagoda, composed the complete complex. There were both Han-style palace and Tibetan-style flat-top buildings, embodying the integration of Han and Tibetan architectural traditional art. It was impressive and dazzling. The Butter Sculpture, mural, and barbola in the monastery were known as the "three unique skills" of the monastery, and had a unique style and high artistic value. Four Dratsangs were set under large and small scripture halls of the monastery, studying argumentation, the doctrine of Esoteric Buddhism, Indian classical logic, astronomy, mathematical astronomy, divination, technology, medicine, imprison spells, and so on. Four major Dharma assemblies were held in the first, fourth, sixth, and ninth lunar months every year, and two small Dharma assemblies were held in the second and tenth lunar months. Especially the Lantern Festival on the fifteenth day of every first lunar month attracted tens of thousands of people of all ethnic groups to visit, pay respects, and worship by showing the Butter Sculpture, mural, and Buddha statue (hanging up the Buddha statue on the hillside), which made the monastery a center of Buddhist activities in the northwest and a famous tourist attraction, acquiring a great reputation in the country and Southeast Asia.

7 Labrang Monastery

Labrang Monastery was formerly known as Zhaxiqi Monastery and was located 1 kilometer west of Xiahe County. It was built from the forty-eighth year of Kangxi's reign in the Qing Dynasty (AD 1709), which used to be the political, religious, and cultural center of the Tibetan region at the junction of Gansu, Qinghai, and Sichuan, ruling 108 monasteries, and up to 20,000 lamas. The monastery building was magnificent and splendid. The main buildings included six Dratsangs, 18 Lakang (Buddha temples), 18 Nangqian (Living Buddha's office), one bema, one scripture printing institute, one depositary of Buddhist sutra, and more than 10,000 monks' dorms. There were more than 3,000 monks at its peak. A large number of precious pagodas, Buddha statues, and other precious cultural relics, as well as more than 65,000 volumes of Tibetan books, Tibetan history, Tibetan medicine, calendar, music, art, Tibetan scriptures, the *Buddhist Encyclopedia*, and other books were preserved in the temple. The richness of its Tibetan books is among the best of the lamaseries in the nation.

8 The Outer Eight Temples

The Outer Eight Temples were a large temple group dominated by lamaseries, located outside Emperor Kangxi's Summer Mountain Resort in Chengde City,

Hebei Province, so they were called the Outer Eight Temples. They were built in the Qing Dynasty to receive Mongolian and Tibetan leaders, contact the nobility, and achieve national unity. The Outer Eight Temples became another Lamaist center apart from Lhasa, Tibet. They were continuously repaired from the forty-second year of Kangxi (AD 1703) to the fifty-fifth year of Qianlong (AD 1790), and finally built into the Temple of Sumeru Happiness and Longevity, lasting 87 years. There used to be 11 temples, 7 of which exist now: Puren Temple, Pule Temple, Anyuan Temple, Puning Temple, Putuo Zongcheng Temple, Shuxiang Temple, and Temple of Sumeru Happiness and Longevity. This group of large temples was built by the mountains and strewn at random, with a changing layout and magnificent temperament. The temple modelings were not limited to one type, and architectural arts of Tibet, Mongolia, Han, and other nations shone together. The Outer Eight Temples mostly faced the Summer Mountain Resort, symbolizing national unity in the world. In Puning Temple, there was a carved wooden statue of a Thousand-Arm and Thousand-Eye Buddha in "Mahayana Hall". It was 22.28 meters from the throne to the forehead and the waistline was 15 meters; it was carved with pine, cypress, aspen, elm, and linden, and is currently one of the largest carved wooden Buddha statues in China. Putuo Zongcheng Temple was modeled on Potala Palace in Tibet, enjoying the title of small Potala Palace, and was the largest among the Outer Eight Temples. Dozens of red and white platforms in the temple were arranged in a crisscross pattern; they were well proportioned, sparkling, brilliant, and eye-catching. Temple of Sumeru Happiness and Longevity was commonly known as the temporary imperial palace, and was modeled on Tashilhunpo Monastery in Shigatse, Tibet. This was specifically built by the court of the Qing Dynasty for the third Panchen Lama, who came to congratulate Emperor Qianlong on his seventy-fifth birthday.

9 *Yonghe Lamasery*

Yonghe Lamasery was in the east of Yonghe Lamasery Street in Dongcheng District, Beijing. It was originally the mansion of Emperor Yongzheng of Qing before he ascended the throne, and was named the Mansion of Prince Gong. In the third year of Yongzheng's reign (AD 1725), it was renamed Yonghe Lamasery, and became the place where emperors of the Qing Dynasty worshiped the ancestors. In the ninth year of Qianlong's reign (AD 1744), it was transformed into a lamasery, and was the largest lamasery in cities in mainland China. The buildings of Yonghe Lamasery were magnificent, with five parts of a courtyard, red walls, and yellow tiles, in bright colors; they were very solemn. The statue of Maitreya in Wanfu Pavilion (Wanfo Building) of the palace was 18 meters high, and 8 meters of it was buried underground; in total it was 26 meters tall, with symmetrical proportions and a magnificent body. It was carved from sandalwood obtained by the seventh Dalai Lama in Tibet and given to the Emperor Qianlong. There was a flower basket on the left and right arms of the Buddha statue, and the lotus inside the baskets were in bud. The gesture of the Buddha statue symbolized the determination of Maitreya to inherit Sakyamuni and become the Buddha of the Future. The copper statue of Tsongkhapa in Falun Hall was tall and arrogant. In the first lunar month of each year, a costume dance to expel the evil spirit was held in Yonghe Lamasery, embodying expelling evil spirits and praying for happiness, quite like the Buddhist activities in the Mongolian and Tibetan regions, called "Exorcising Demons in Yonghe Lamasery" by Beijing residents.

Notes

1 In recent years, 243 grottoes were unearthed from Mogao Grottoes, so that the number of grottoes in Mogao Grottoes increased to 735.
2 According to legend, the Buddha statues simulated the images of the five emperors of the Northern Wei Dynasty: Daowu, Ming Yuan, Tai Wu, Jing Mu, and Wencheng.
3 "Jambudvipa": One of four continents in ancient Indian myths. Buddhism also used this argument that this was the place where humankind lived.

8 The source of basic characteristics of Chinese Buddhism

Since Buddhism was introduced into China from India, it rooted and grew in the soil of the autocratic society in China, produced its own unique structure, formed a national sectarian system, and became an integral part of the superstructure of China's autocratic society, as well as an important part of ancient Chinese ideology and culture.

Indian Buddhism developed from Hinayana to Mahayana, formed Madhyamika with the main classics of *Pancavimsatisa-hasrika-prajnaparamita* and *Madhyamaka Shastra*, and the Consciousness-Only School with the main classics of *Sandhinirmocanavyuhasutra* and *Yogacara-bhumi-sastra*, and achieved a peak of the development of ideas. Chinese Buddhism was different, and, through the systematic interpretation and introduction of the famous translation masters Kumarajiva and Tang Xuanzang, directly inherited the Chinese Three-Treatise School and the Cien School formed from Madhyamika and the Consciousness-Only School of Indian Mahayana; but it did not experience independent development at first. The speculative form of Madhyamika and Buddhist logic of the Consciousness-Only School were not particularly important in the history of Buddhist thought in China. Mahayana Esoteric Buddhism in late Indian Buddhism did not experience significant development through its introduction to China by Vajrabodhi and Amoghavajra during the Kaiyuan and Tianbao Periods in the Tang Dynasty. On the contrary, some classics with no great impact in India – *Nirvana Sutra, Vimalakirti-nirdesa-sutra, Saddharmapundarika Sutra, Avatamsaka Sutra, Surangama Sutra*, and *Amitabha* – were particularly welcomed by our country and widely disseminated in the community. The Tiantai, Huyan, and Pure Land Schools, based on one of these classics, experienced huge development, not to mention typical Chinese Buddhism – Zen. Chinese Buddhism was from India, but it was different from India, showing China's temperament and characteristics. Although both Chinese and Indian Buddhism were Buddhism, they were very different in terms of content and image.

Chinese Buddhism had its own different characteristics in different historical stages. The characteristics of Chinese Buddhism we will discuss here are the special phenomena and natures of Chinese Buddhism that are different from those of Indian Buddhism, particularly the new theories and new cultivation methods. To study the characteristics of Chinese Buddhism, it is necessary to clarify the social and ideological roots of the formation of characteristics, combined with the evolution process from the production, development, prosperity, and decline of Chinese Buddhism, combined with the characteristics of Chinese Buddhism in different historical stages, comprehensively reveal the general characteristics of Chinese Buddhism that are different from Indian Buddhism, and examine some regular phenomena of the nationalization of foreign Buddhism that come from the basic characteristics of Chinese Buddhism.

The root of the basic characteristics of Chinese Buddhism

Buddhism was a seed from India that was introduced to China from far away, rooted, grew, blossomed, and yielded fruit in a vast country with a highly centralized autocratic system, highly developed Confucianist and Taoist culture, extremely scattered small peasant economy, and multiple nations. The foundation of Chinese Buddhism was in China but not in India. The root of the formation of Chinese Buddhist characteristics was comprehensive, which could be divided into two major categories: the social root and the ideological root. Between these two categories of roots, the primary was the social root. In other words, the characteristics of Chinese Buddhism were first constrained and determined by the characteristics of Chinese society, and they were a direct or indirect reflection of China's society, economy, and politics. The birth, prosperity, and decline of Chinese Buddhism happened in the historical stage of the autocratic society in China, and were consistent with the historical pace of China's autocratic society from development to decline; therefore, to explore the social root of the characteristics of Chinese Buddhism was essentially to explore the impact, constraint, and even determination of China's autocratic social structure on the formation of the characteristics of Chinese Buddhism. The next root is the ideological root. As a foreign religion introduced into China, there was also a problem of how to meet and adapt to the thoughts, psychology, feelings, habits, and requirements of the Chinese people for Buddhism. When Buddhism was introduced into China, China already had a mature traditional ideological system, and Chinese Buddhism continued to form its own characteristics in its conflict and reconciliation with the inherent ideological culture in China. The ideological root also included the important role of Chinese language and culture for the formation of the characteristics of Chinese Buddhism in the translation of Indian Buddhist scriptures.

Important aspects of the social roots of the formation of characteristics of Chinese Buddhism are as follows:

1 The strict rule of an autocratic centralization system. Since the Qin and Han Dynasties, until the demise of the Qing Dynasty, no matter whether in national unity or as a separatist state, Chinese society was under autocratic state power. The emperor and his bureaucratic rulers were the ruling class – the concentrated embodiment of the interests of the landlord class, holding absolute political power. This power was supreme and indivisible, and a higher leader or similar papalism above the emperor was not allowed. The decree

and decision of the emperor were an imperial edict that any person, including religious believers, must not violate. Nobody, including religious believers, was allowed to belittle the emperor's status. Indian Buddhism believed that monks were higher than secular people. At home, parents must pay homage to their son who became a monk, saying that this was not worshiping their son but worshiping Buddha's disciple. The monks did not bow when they saw kings. In China, it was believed that monks must bow to the king, and they would be punished if they refused. Chinese emperors had absolute power, so the fate of Buddhism, to a certain extent, was determined by the secular majesty. This was something that some Buddhist leaders knew. For example, Faguo, who was given the title of Sramana leader by Tuoba Gui of the Northern Wei Dynasty, flattered Tuoba Gui that he was "wise and kind", the Buddha of that time, and Sramana should worship him. He also said, "Those who can carry forward Dharma become emperors. I am not worshiping the emperor, but paying respect to the Buddha" (*Wei Shu – Shi Lao Zhi*). Dao'an also realized from his personal experience, "The religious rites would fail if they did not rely on the emperor" (Volume 5, *Dao'an Biography*, of *Memoirs of Eminent Monks*). These were all clear indications of the importance of the secular majesty and the dependence of Buddhism on it.

The emperors of the autocratic society in China often advocated and fostered Buddhism for the purpose of preserving the autocracy, and restricted or even destroyed Buddhism for the same purpose. The basic attitude of the overwhelming majority of supreme rulers toward Buddhism was to make Buddhism serve their own rule, but not allow Buddhism to develop too much – namely, the policy of using and restricting. The feudal rulers used Buddhism mainly because the unique doctrines of karmic retribution and heaven and hell, and a set of methods of religious cultivation of Buddhism, helped to slacken and devastate the fighting will of the people, and maintain and consolidate their own long-term stability.

Chinese autocratic rulers, in order to control the development of Buddhism, mainly took two measures: eliminate monks and nuns and recognize monk officials. On the first item, even Shi Hu of the Later Zhao Dynasty and Fu Jian of the Former Qin Dynasty, who strongly worshiped Buddhism, once decided to "eliminate" or "reduce" Buddhist monks, and Emperor An of the Eastern Jin, Emperor Xiaowu of Song in the Southern Dynasties, Emperor Wu of Qi, and Emperor Gaozu of Tang also eliminated monks and nuns. The "eliminating" and "reducing" of monks and nuns were to reduce the Buddhist temples and take other measures to limit the development of Buddhism. On the second item, the creation of monk officials firstly started from the Hongshi Period of the Later Qin, whose purpose was to "promote the rules, to rule decadence" – namely, to manage Buddhist monks. In the Southern and Northern Dynasties and Sui and Tang Dynasties, monk officials were also set up, the positions of which were held by monks. At the same time, organs in the charge of secular people to manage Buddhist affairs were gradually set up in the central bureaucracies to further strengthen the control of Buddhism. Unlike Indian Buddhism, Chinese Buddhism must be governed by secular law. Tang Xuanzang once proposed to Emperor Taizong of Tang that management of monks may not comply with secular law for the religious privilege that Chinese monks were governed by the monk law, but he was rejected. This showed that the crown had total supremacy over religious power.

In history, every time the power of Buddhism excessively expanded, the supreme autocratic rulers took compulsive measures using state power to destroy Buddhism. From the Northern Wei Dynasty to the Later Zhou Dynasty, there were four events of destroying Buddhism: in the seventh year of Taipingzhenjun in the Northern Wei Dynasty (AD 446), Emperor Taiwudi destroyed Buddhism; in the third year of Jiande in the Northern Zhou Dynasty (AD 574), Emperor Wu destroyed Buddhism in the fifth year of Huichang in the Tang Dynasty (AD 845), Emperor Wuzong destroyed Buddhism; and in the second year of Xiande in the Later Zhou Dynasty (AD 955), Emperor Shizong destroyed Buddhism. This was the most dramatic manifestation of the conflict between the development of Buddhist power and the interests of autarchy in Chinese history. When Emperor Wu of Liang was in power, he tried to elevate Buddhism to the status of state religion, but he finally gave up due to the opposition of some forces in the bureaucratic ruling group, while the foregoing four times of destruction of Buddhism were implemented. Although the destruction of Buddhism could not completely prevent the continuous development of Buddhism, it was a heavy blow to Buddhism, and had a very profound impact on the survival and development of Buddhism. In fact, after the decisive blow in the period of Emperor Wuzong of Tang, many Buddhist sects were indeed depressed. History has shown that Buddhism did not have the power to fight the rulers' destruction of Buddhism. Even when Buddhism was of great renown and influence, it could only crouch under the monarchy of absolutism, blessing the monarchy. Historical facts forced the upper Buddhist monks to think deeply about how to adapt to the needs of the autocratic rulers of China in all respects to ensure the survival of Buddhism. From this we can draw this conclusion: the Buddhist policy formulated by the autocratic rulers for the purpose of protecting the autocratic centralized system had determined the fate, direction, track, and characteristics of Chinese Buddhism to a great extent.

2 Ethical relations based on the family patriarchal system. In the long history of autocratic society, the family patriarchal system was stubborn, powerful, and well governed. In ethical relations based on this system, the cardinal guides and constant virtues of emperors and subjects, fathers and sons, husbands and wives, and brothers formed, and became a set of moral norms to maintain the autocracy's order, which people could not violate, overstep, or destroy absolutely. The whole society worshiped heaven, earth, sovereign, parent, and teacher. And the "heaven, earth, and teacher" were in the foil

position; their core was to truly embody the "sovereign" and "parent" in the patriarchal system. Because of this, "loyalty" and "filial piety" also became the two highest banners in the political and moral areas of autocratic society, and the highest standards of people's lives and behavior. Such a deep network of ethical relations and the strong moral concept of China's autocratic society were the core powers to resist the spread of Buddhism, as well as the ablation agent to melt Buddhist belief.

The patriarchal system also brought profound influence to the inheritance system of Chinese Buddhism. Adapting the inheritance of the secular patriarchal clan system, Buddhism established a set of heir systems and monastic property inheritance regulations. The relationship between master and disciple in various factions was like the relationship between father and son, handing down from generation to generation, forming the hereditary system. In order to draw up the genealogy and history of this faction, the ancestors of the school were arranged from generation to generation, and age-old ancestors were even fabricated. Indian Buddhist believers did not attach importance to their exact past years, while Chinese Buddhist sects made up a history, and introduced it as the western ancestor of the school. The members inside the Chinese Buddhist sects trampled each other and framed their opponents to get inheritance and monastic property, and the sects attacked each other in order to compete for the orthodox status of Buddhism. This was a tortuous reflection of the patriarchal system among Buddhist monks.

3   Political unity and the integration of nations. China's autocratic society was different from that of India, and the national politics was unified in the vast majority of the historical period; while the divisive historical period was short, especially in the Sui and Tang Dynasties, the feudal dynasty had unified politics, a strong military, a prosperous economy, and a developed culture. Reflected in Buddhism, such a situation also required the unity of Buddhism. The unprecedented integration of the Chinese nations in the Sui and Tang Dynasties promoted the exchange of northern and southern cultures, which helped Buddhism to get rid of the difference between the north and the south and form a unified Buddhism. Buddhist sects and their teachings with international influence formed in the Sui and Tang Dynasties were direct reflections of this situation.

4   The vicissitudes of the ruling class and the frequency of peasant uprisings. When Buddhism was introduced into China, the landlord class had been highly developed, and its political rule had been consolidated. As far as the landlord class members were concerned, the vast majority of them would not give up real political and economic interests and become monks unless they were frustrated with their official career or life, or had other special reasons. It was also difficult for Buddhism to convert most secular landlords into monk landlords. Buddhism was conducive to rule consolidation of the landlord class, but the excessive expansion of Buddhist monastery economic forces would inevitably damage the real interests of the landlord class, and

caused strong opposition from the landlord class. Its concentrated performance was the destruction of Buddhism. For the landlord class members, Buddhist belief and religious life were more of a luxury and embellishment. For example, some landlords of two Jin Dynasties and the Southern and Northern Dynasties did believe in Buddhism, but mostly it was related to metaphysics, which was flashy without substance, and lacked true Buddhist characters. To the Sui and Tang Dynasties, fewer people of the landlord class really believed in Buddhism. At the same time, the intelligentsia landlords tended to decline, and humble landlords gradually rose. The social basis of Buddhism changed, which would certainly influence and restrict the development of Buddhism and made it form new features.

There were a large number of farmers in the autocratic society in China. They couldn't bear oppression and exploitation from the landlord class, and some directly went to Buddhist monasteries to escape the corvée, while some risked danger in desperation, resulting in repeated vast uprisings, but eventually they all failed. Farmers could do nothing in reality, but naturally turned to religion for comfort. Farmers' culture was backward and they lived dispersedly and undertook heavy labor, so it was hard for them to understand difficult Buddhist theory; they neither grasped the cumbersome religious cultivation methods nor had time to often engage in religious activities for long. Zen, which pointed directly to the nature and advocated sudden enlightenment to become Buddha, and the Pure Land School, which chanted the name of Amitabha, had a wide effect among the farmers because of their simplicity.

Important aspects of the ideological roots of the formation of characteristics of Chinese Buddhism were as follows:

1   The orthodox position of Confucianism. Confucianism was the main part and representative of traditional Chinese thought and culture. It basically included two parts: the world view and the political and moral theory, of which the latter part was more important. The Confucian political and moral theories were founded by the ancient Chinese ruling class thinkers, and adapted to China's land ownership, autocratic centralization system, and the social ethical relations based on the patriarchal system. In short, it conformed to the fundamental interests and demands of the landlord class. Due to the long-term advocacy and propaganda of the ruling class, Confucianism's humanistic thought and moral theory became the most characteristic content of traditional Chinese thought. Buddhism promoted abandoning home and becoming monks, which was equal to advocating no king and no father, forming a sharp contrast with Chinese Confucianism. In the autocratic patriarchal society in China, any religious belief would get the strongest opposition if it slandered or opposed Confucian political ethics. Therefore, Chinese Buddhism always compromised and coordinated with Confucianism, and strove to emphasize the consistency of Buddhism and Confucianism, and the coordinating role of Buddhism in Confucian ethical doctrine. At the

same time, in a certain sense, Buddhism was the moral theory of life; its detailed analysis of human psychology and the central spirit of Confucian humanities could also complement each other, and increasingly integrated the theories of Confucianism and Buddhism, thus becoming similar or even common theory.

2 The profound influence of Taoism. Taoism ranked only second to Confucianism in traditional Chinese thought, with an important influence of Taoist philosophical thought in particular. Taoism promoted that "Tao" ("no") was the ontology, and pursued the spiritual realm coinciding with "Tao", often regarded as the same as Buddhist thought of life by the early Chinese. The vast majority of Chinese Buddhist scholars were often influenced by Confucian doctrine before becoming monks, and then got edified by Taoism, and studied, explored, and accepted the theory of Buddhism. The level, procedure, and structure of knowledge formation must profoundly influence these monks' understanding of Buddhism. This situation was particularly prominent among Buddhist scholars in the Southern and Northern Dynasties. For example, the famous monk Zhi Dun admired "Laozi and Zhuangzi", and the *Zhuangzi – Enjoyment in Untroubled Ease* annotated by him prevailed for a moment and gained a prestigious reputation. For another example, Huiyuan said when he tracked down his own change of thought, "When I saw *Laozi* and *Zhuangzi*, I realized that religion was virtual. When I look back down, I know it's fun" (Volume 27 of *Detailed Anthology of Hong Ming*). Huiyuan began to believe in *Laozi* and *Zhuangzi* from Confucianism, and later he was converted to Buddhism, in which the potential impact of Taoism was great. Sengzhao also said, I read *Moral Chapter* of Laozi, and sighed, 'it was beautiful, but it was not perfect'. Here, *Laozi* was affirmed as an important guiding book in the pursuit of the ideological mysterious realm, but it was not perfect, and could not eliminate ideological restraints, achieving only spiritual relief. In the Eastern Jin Dynasty, the six schools of seven sects of the Prajna School of Buddhism used metaphysics – the opinion of different factions of new Taoists to analyze the meaning of "emptiness", it was a direct reflection of the penetration of Chinese Taoist thought into foreign Buddhism.

3 The restrictive role of traditional religious superstition. Before the introduction of Buddhism to China, the religious belief characterized by the worship of God and ancestral gods had formed in China, whose contents were very complicated, including the five elements, five virtues, five emperors, spirits and gods, immortals, divination, and other superstitious ideas. Accompanied by necromancies, such as divination, astrology, and observing air currents and wind angles, various sacrificial rites prevailed. Taoism formed in the Han Dynasty. Taoism integrated ancient primitive witchcraft and immortal necromancy. Although it lacked a systematic theological theory, it was an indigenous religion of Han nationality. It was native and reflected the characteristics of national culture in some respects. When Buddhism was first introduced into China, the Chinese people looked at it with inherent

religious belief – namely, they regarded Buddhism as a kind of immortal necromancy. The early Buddhist monks who came to China also absorbed some characteristics of traditional Chinese religious belief to meet the social habits of China, and took the popular method of supernatural beings and alchemists to attract the masses. Later, Huisi of the Tiantai School even tried to break the barrier between Buddhism and Taoism and integrated becoming Buddha and becoming immortal. As for the sculptures integrating Buddhism and Taoism still preserved in some Buddhist temples, they also show the profound influence of inherent religious belief on Chinese Buddhism.

4   Changes caused by differences in language and thinking in the process of spread and integration. The source of Chinese Buddhism was basically based on the interpretation and study of Indian Buddhist Confucianism as a medium. Chinese monks also had to study after getting Indian Buddhist scriptures. In this series of processes, Chinese characteristics and thinking characteristics in China also directly affected the understanding and acceptance of Indian Buddhism, which led to changes in Buddhist doctrines. China's language and thinking limited the spread of Buddhist thought on the one hand, but on the other hand, they absorbed and melted this foreign thought, thus creating a new type of Chinese-style Buddhist vocabulary. For example, the concept of "Ru Xin" in Indian Buddhism, which meant "as it is", had no equal word in Chinese. It was translated as "BenWu", and later translated as "Zhen Ru", regarded as the origin of all things, which was far away from the original idea of the Sanskrit and Buddhist idea. Foreign Buddhism was melted in the thinking form of ancient Chinese through the spread of Chinese translation, and the original quality of Indian Buddhism also disappeared. Kumarajiva was deeply aware of this and said, "Once Sanskrit was translated, it lost its meaning, like chewing rice to feed people, which not only lost the taste, but also made people sick" (Volume 2, *Kumarajiva Biography*, of *Biographies of Eminent Monks*). In fact, this change was also a creation, which was a doctrine combining two different ideas of China and India, different from both the traditional Chinese ideas and Indian thought, thus creating a nearly new ideological realm.

The basic characteristics of Chinese Buddhism

Important characteristics of Chinese Buddhism included reconciliation, absorption, and simplicity.

1   Reconciliation

After Buddhism was introduced into China, although it had differences, contradictions, conflicts, and struggles with the inherent religious belief, ideas of sovereignty, and Confucian and Taoist doctrine, it mainly took a reconciled position, and it was generally in the subsidiary position of traditional Chinese ideology and culture, except in the Sui and Tang Dynasties, when the situation was different.

The so-called reconciliation of Chinese Buddhism referred to the compromise, compliance, greeting, and attachment to different ideas or even different views outside Buddhism, naturally including the approval, admiration, absorption, and integration of certain similar or consistent views. The reconciliation of Buddhism to external thought was basically compatible with the changes of ancient social thought in China, so there were different priorities in different historical stages.

In the Eastern Han Dynasty and Three Kingdoms Period, Buddhism was attached to Taoist priests and necromancy, which could be seen as the reconciling period of Buddhism and Taoism. Between the Qin and Han Dynasties, immortal necromancy prevailed in China. First Emperor of Qin and Emperor Wu of Han were convinced that the medicine for immortal life could be made and they could become immortal. The social impact of such religious belief was very extensive and far-reaching. When Buddhism was first introduced to China, Buddha was regarded as similar to God and immortal in traditional Chinese belief by the Chinese, while Buddhism was regarded as one of the 96 kinds of Taoist magic arts, the religious ritual for praying to God. At this time, a set of practice methods of Buddhism Zen was also considered to be connected to Taoist necromancy to keep in good health and become immortal, such as "eating qi", "inducing qi", "single-mindedness", and was attached to the School of Huang-Lao and immortal necromancy in order to be spread. In order to survive in China and expand their impact, some of the foreign monks who came to preach also paid attention to learning about Chinese necromancy belief and divination superstition as a convenient way to missionize – for example, the first Chinese translator of Buddhist scriptures, An Shigao, "mastered seven luminaries, five elements, medicine, necromancy and even the sound of birds and animals" (Volume 1, *Anqing Biography* of *Biographies of Eminent Monks*), and Dharmakala "mastered constellation and divination" (*Dharmakala Biography* of *Biographies of Eminent Monks*). This was necessary for Buddhism to become Chinese people's faith.

It is noteworthy that Buddhist scholars at that time also tried to reconcile Buddhism and Confucianism and master them by translating or editing Buddhist scriptures. For example, An Shigao consciously or unconsciously adjusted the translation so as not to conflict with the then Chinese social and political ethics in the translation of Buddhist scriptures. In the Volume 1 of *Srgalavadasūtra* translated by him, "Liu Fang" referred to the ethical relationship between parent and child, brothers, master and disciple, husband and wife, lord and servant, relatives and friends. The original meaning in the book was that both parties were equal and free; taking the relationship between the lord and servant as an example, the lord respected the servant, and the servant loved the lord, but it was cut from the translation by An Shigao to be consistent with the custom in Chinese society that slaves absolutely obeyed their lords. For another example, the translator of the Three Kingdoms Period, Kangsenghui, collected relevant Buddhist scriptures into *Six Paramitas Sutra*, and said the highest principle of Buddhism was to "govern people for the heaven with benevolence". The "benevolence" was that the country was peaceful, people were rich, the emperor did not hurt people for his own interest, people did not suffer hunger and cold, and the territory was peaceful. He also used the Buddhist doctrine of "impermanence" and "karma" to persuade the emperor to believe in Buddhism and implement "benevolence". This "benevolence" was the same social and political ideal as the "benevolent government" of Mencius in essence. Kangsenghui took the Confucian political ideal as the highest principle of Buddhism, and used Buddhism to serve the implementation of Confucian governance, which clearly embodied the harmony of Buddhism and its political tendency to adapt to and coordinate with Chinese autocratic rule.

As mentioned earlier, the book *Master Mou's Treatise Dispelling Doubts* also fully demonstrated the attitude of China's inherent culture to foreign Buddhism, reflecting the understanding of Chinese Buddhist intellectuals of foreign Buddhism at that time, and was an important record of the formation and development of Chinese Buddhism. The basic position of this book was to reconcile Confucianism, Buddhism, and Taoism to dispel opposition. The author said when he explained the cause for the book, "I am determinedly devoted to Buddhism and Taoism, and research *Laozi* . . . Read *Five Classics*", and firstly stated that the three religions can stand in parallel. When this book discussed the relationship among the three religions, it vigorously promoted Buddhism and tried to defend it. Interestingly, it often quoted Confucian and Taoist thoughts to explain Buddhism in the exposition of Buddhist doctrine – for example,

> "What is called as Tao and what is Tao?" Mouzi said, "Tao means guidance, which leads to inaction. It will not go forward if it's pulled, not go backward if it's dragged, not go upward if it's lifted, and not go downward if it's dropped. It cannot be seen or heard. It winds outwards, detailed, related, which is called Tao".

"Tao", mentioned in early Indian Buddhism, originally referred to the method, not the origin of all things talked about by Laozi and Zhuangzi. The highest level that Buddhism pursued was called "Nirvana", referring to the realm of relief where trouble is elimination, going beyond life and death. As for Taoist "inaction", Laozi meant "discarding knowledge", clear and natural, not the same thing as the "Nirvana" of Buddhism. Explaining "Nirvana" with "inaction" was incompatible, but this was determined by the time, and it is also the embodiment of Chinese Buddhism. *Master Mou's Treatise Dispelling Doubts* also tried to meet Confucian thought with Buddhist doctrine, preached that the Buddhist precepts "were no different from" Chinese "ancient rites", and said that the Buddhist standards of good and evil were consistent with Confucian ethical norms. *Master Mou's Treatise Dispelling Doubts* said that the basic ideas of Buddhism, Taoism, and Confucianism were consistent, but was critical of the original Taoism and belief in immortals, saying that it was impossible for a person to become immortal, which again reflected the fundamental divergence of Buddhism and Taoism.

During the Wei, Jin, and Northern and Northern Dynasties, metaphysics began to emerge. Correspondingly, Chinese Buddhist scholars also got rid of the idea that Buddhism was Taoist, and began to approach Buddhism with the opinion of metaphysicians, realizing that Buddhism was a religion that contained argumentation.

It was in such historical context that the main doctrine of Buddhism, the Doctrine of Prajna, reconciled with metaphysics. The words "Geyi" emerging at that time compared classic nouns, concepts, and categories with China's inherent terms, concepts, and categories, especially the nouns, concepts, and categories of Laozi and Zhuangzi's philosophy – for example, Kang Falang and Zhu Faya created the method of Geyi. This method of translating Buddhist scriptures purely with traditional Chinese academic ideas reflected the attachment of Buddhism to metaphysics. As for the "six schools and seven sects", different factions regarding the empty nature theory of Prajna were a direct result of different schools of Wei Jin metaphysical thought. The central issue of Wei Jin metaphysics was to explore the relation between the beginning and the end, while the theoretical core of the Doctrine of Prajna was also to elucidate the existence or lack of existence of all beings, which were similar topics. "Six schools and seven sects" were doctrines formed by Chinese Buddhist scholars to understand and clarify the theory of Prajna with different metaphysical views; among them some of the Buddhist scholars also had a strong reputation of idle talk, such as Zhi Daolin, the representative of the Jise School, who loved raising horse and cranes, poetry, and writing, and was respected by celebrities.

In the late period of the Eastern Jin Dynasty, Hui Yuan, a Buddhist leader, consciously reconciled Buddhism with inherent Chinese religious ideas and Confucianism in the promotion of various Buddhist doctrines. Early Indian Buddhism was ambiguous and contradictory regarding the concept of the soul, but after Buddhism was introduced in China, it quickly absorbed the concept of the immortality of the soul in China, and also absorbed the theory of "vitality" to promote the "immortality of the soul". For example, it was said in Volume 8, *Cha Wei Wang Jing*, of *Buddhist Scripture of Six Fixed Ways for Saints* translated by Kang Senghui, "the soul combines with vitality, repeatedly, endlessly". *Master Mou's Treatise Dispelling Doubts* also said while affirming the concept of ghosts and gods, "the soul is solid immortal, but the body decays". Huiyuan especially wrote *Shamen Bujingwangzhelun-Xing Jin Shen Bu Mie* to systematically elucidate the theory of the "immortality of the soul". He paid particular attention to citing ancient Chinese idealist opinion, such as the words of the Yellow Emperor, "the body ends but the soul does not, the change is infinite" (*Wenzi – Shou Pu*), also comparing the end of the body and immortality of the soul with the Eternal Flame. This was all part of the development of Indian Buddhism. Huiyuan preached the "immortality of the soul" to prove the theory of karma. The idea of karma had great influence from Buddhism on the common people; Hui Yuan promoted it by combining it with China's inherent resignation of "the Doctrine of Fatality": "the weal and woe today came from the past, the retribution leads to different fates" (*Sanbaolun*). It stressed that karma was inevitable and inescapable. Hui Yuan also connected the Confucian feudal ethical code to karma:

> Teach to love with geniality, make people know the natural grace; teach to respect with strictness, make people know the natural weight. Karma did not lie in the present, but should find its origin. Punish crime to make people fear

and then be cautious; reward with heaven, make them pleased and then move. This is the impact of Karma, make it clear in teaching, rather than change its nature.

(Shamen Bujingwangzhelun)

Promoting filial piety and respecting for the monarch conformed to karma. Huiyuan also directly put forward the theory of the "combination of Buddhism and Confucianism" and the "combination of internal and external Tao" (ibid.): "If the combination has its basis, then all the schools tend to be the same" (*Letter to Liu Yimin*); this more vividly embodied the harmonious color.

Real social needs also directly encouraged Chinese Buddhist scholars to put forward creative Buddhist theories based on China's inherent thinking. Between the Jin and Song Dynasties, the governance of hereditary gentry increasingly strengthened, and the community was extremely unequal, so that people were concerned about whether there were differences in the issue of becoming a Buddha. Zhu Daosheng spoke out first before *Nirvana Sutra* was introduced, saying that people can also become a Buddha with icchantika. Later, *Nirvana Sutra* was introduced, which really proved this proposition. The new theory of Zhu Daosheng was based on the thought that becoming a Buddha lay in enlightenment, and said that all beings had the Buddhist nature, and "icchantika" was no exception. This was the result of the enlightenedness of thorough exploration of the logos and the intrinsic character of Chinese Buddhism and the thinking inspiration that everyone could become Yao and Shun. Zhu Daosheng also directly explained *Saddharmapundarika Sutra* with the "thorough exploration of the logos and the intrinsic character": "thorough exploration of the logos and the intrinsic character meant immeasurable yoshisada" (*Lotus Sutra*). As for Zhu Daosheng's way of thinking, such as "perspective thinking", "translate the content rather than the form", and "forget the means by which the end is attained", it came from Taoism and metaphysics. Zhu Daosheng's Buddhist theory contained important thoughts of Confucianism and Taoism in China.

In the Southern Dynasties, Emperor Wu of Liang was deeply influenced by Confucian doctrine when he was young. At the beginning, he believed in Taoism, and later he was converted to Buddhism, becoming the only emperor who tried to make Buddhism the national religion in Chinese history. Although he took the lead in worshiping Buddhism, he also put forward the theory of three religions with the same source, that Laozi, Zhou Gong, and Confucius were the disciples of Buddha Sakyamuni, that Tathagata, Laozi, and Confucius were master and disciple, and that Confucianism and Taoism were derived from Buddhism. He proclaimed that Confucianism and Taoism pursued the good for the world, and were unable to make people Buddha like Buddhism, but the pursuit of the good of the world was also important. He compared Buddhism to the moon in the dark night, and Confucianism and Taoism to stars. The three had distinctions, but also contrasted with each other. Sometimes he called Sakyamuni, Laozi, and Confucius the "three saints". Emperor Wu of Liang attached great importance to the role of Confucianism, personally discussing Confucian classics. He wrote *Xiao Si Fu*, saying that

Confucianism attained both loyalty and filial piety, built "Great Love Temple" to return the grace of parents, and also used Confucian classics such as *Ji Yi*, *Li Yun*, and *Yue Ji* as weapons to defend the theory of the immortality of the soul of Buddhism. In fact, although Emperor Wu of Liang took Buddhism as the first among three religions, Buddhism, he preached, had Confucian color.

During the Wei and Jin Dynasties and Southern and Northern Dynasties, some famous scholars were also keen to reconcile the relationship between Buddhism and Confucianism. For example, the famous litterateur of the Jin Dynasty, Sun Chuo, once wrote a monograph, comparing monks to the famous celebrities at that time, who had a certain social impact. He directly equated Confucianism and Buddhism: "Zhou Gong and Confucius were Buddhas . . . Buddha was Zhou Gong and Confucius" (Volume 3, *Yu Dao Lun*, of *Anthology of Hong Ming*). "Zhou Gong and Confucius corrected the wrong . . . Buddhism clarified it" (Volume 3, *Yu Dao Lun*, of *Anthology of Hong Ming*). Between the Jin and Song Dynasties, the great poet Xie Lingyun firmly believed in Buddhism, and he inherited Zhu Daosheng's thought, writing *Bian Zong Lun*. The so-called Bian Zong was to discuss the way to become a Buddha or saint. Confucianism mostly believed that people could not become saints, and it was difficult to achieve through learning, and Buddhism believed that people could become a Buddha, and could achieve through learning (progressive). Xie Lingyun removed the gradual progress of Buddhism, and adopted Buddhism's theory that one could become a Buddha. He removed Confucianism's theory that one could not become a saint, took the Confucian opinion of realizing the universe suddenly, and reconciled Confucianism and Buddhism, further promoting the opinion of inseparable ontology and sudden enlightenment. Another example was Yan Tuizhi of the Southern Dynasties, who wrote *Yan's Family Instructions*. In *Convert Chapter* he said that "both internal and external religions are integrated as one"; the five precepts of Buddhism conformed to the five ethical norms of Confucianism to strengthen secular ethics.

In the Sui and Tang Dynasties, Chinese Buddhist factions were successively founded; this was the heyday of Chinese Buddhism. Buddhist sects could be divided into two categories: one basically inherited the prototype of Indian Buddhism, and rarely combined with traditional Chinese thought, so the idea was rarely changed – for example, the Three-Treatise School, founded by Jizang, the Consciousness-Only School, founded by Tang Xuanzang and his disciple Kuiji, and Esoteric Buddhism, founded by Subhakarasimha, Vajrabodhi, and his disciple Amoghavajra. The Three-Treatise School inherited the doctrine of Madhyamika of India Mahayana Buddhism, and promoted the dual negative way of thinking. The Consciousness-Only School was characterized by trivial analysis, blindly abided by the teachings of the Indian Buddhist scriptures, and insisted that there was a type of person that could not become a Buddha. These two schools were not adapted to the needs of China at that time, which was understood by fewer and fewer people, and almost intangibly disrupted. Esoteric Buddhism, especially Shastras, was directly contradictory to Confucian ethics, and thus its spread was limited, but it became popular in Tibet, China. The other category was schools founded by combining traditional Chinese ideas, such as the Tiantai School,

Huayan School, and Zen. These sects had very strong signs of sinicization, especially Zen. The Pure Land School was founded by inheriting the idea of Indian Buddhist scriptures, but it was not founded in India, so it was a special Chinese sect. These four sects, especially the former three sects, could be considered the mainstream of Buddhism in the Sui and Tang Dynasties, and the main body of Chinese Buddhism, occupying the most important position in the history of Chinese Buddhism.

The Tiantai School took its own way, with a unique style. It's characterized by promoting *upaya dharma-paryaya* to reconcile China's inherent Confucianism and Taoism, so as to found an ideological system combining Chinese and Indian ideologies.

Saddharmapundarika Sutra-upaya said,

> Sariputta! Why did every Buddha appear in the world due to one great karma? The Buddhas wanted to make all beings understand the Buddha, so they appeared in the world; they wanted to show all beings the perception of Buddha, so they appeared in the world; they wanted to make all beings understand the perception of Buddha, so they appeared in the world; Sariputta! So very Buddha appeared in the world due to one great karma.

"Tathagatajnana-darsana" referred to the wisdom and insight of the Buddha. It meant that the Buddha appears in the world due to one great karma, with the purpose of educating (enlighten, show, understand, enter) all beings, and made them own "Tathagatajnana-darsana" to become a Buddha. Followers of the Tiantai School thus deduced that the Buddhist scriptures were upaya, the means to teach all to become a Buddha. They took upaya dharma-paryaya as an excuse to reconcile Indian Buddhism and Chinese Confucianism and Taoism. The pioneer of the Tiantai School, Huisi, set out from the Buddhist standpoint and incorporated blind faith in immortality into Buddhism. He said in *Nanyue Sida Zen Master Vow Text* that he hoped to "achieve immortality":

> I now go into the mountains to practice asceticism, confess breaking precepts and other sins. This life and the past life were a crime confession. I pray for long life. I wish all saints help me get ganoderma lucidum and elixir, to cure severe illness and remove hunger and thirst. I often practice Zen, and wish to stay in quiet places in the mountains. Cultivate inner elixir with outside elixir. If I wish to pacify all beings, I shall pacify myself first. With my own constraint, I can relieve others' constraint. I am willing to practice in the mountains to get ganoderma lucidum and elixir, become immortal, and then become a Buddha. I take becoming immortal as a step that I must take to become a Buddha.

People of the Tiantai School also of the people also incorporated Taoist theories, such as an elixir field and refining Qi, into their own doctrine – for example, Zhiyi said, "the place 1 cun below the navel is called Udamacronna – namely, the elixir field. If one can restrain the heart and keep this, after long his diseases can be cured" (*Xiu Xi Zhi Guan Zuo Chan Fa Yao*). Zhanran said,

> The sun's grass is called sealwort, which brings longevity; the sun's essence is called Gelsmium elegans, which brings death. . . . As for elixir, at the beginning of making up the mind, one becomes the Buddha and the immortal.
> (*Zhi Guan Fu Xing Chuan Hong Jue*)

It can be seen that the Tiantai School contained quite rich Taoist meaning. The Tiantai School also reconciled *samatha-vipassana* with the Confucianist theory of human nature– for example, Zhanran said, "the three truths were the natural virtues. . . . It was inherent, not gained" (*Shi Zhong Xin Yao*). All beings were born with the "virtues" of the three truths. Thus samatha-vipassana dharma-paryaya of Buddhism was said to be a theory and practice similar to Confucianism's theory of exploring thoroughly the logos and the intrinsic character, and restoring human nature.

The Huayan School was founded by Fa Zang under the direct support of Empress Wu Zetian. The Huayan School took *Avatamsaka Sutra* as the scripture sutra of the school, but it was different from the thought of *Avatamsaka Sutra*, which focused on emphasizing that everyone is equal according to the same human quality, while the Huayan School focused on carrying forward the theory of endless origin from "nature", fully affirmed the value of the reality of a social basis through propaganda of the doctrine of Everything Going with No Obstacle, and said that the world in the Wu Zhou Dynasty was harmonious and enjoyable. There was the argument of "spiritualism in Triloka" in *Avatamsaka Sutra*, emphasizing starting from the "heart" – namely, a human's state of consciousness – to get relief, but not showing and realizing everything from the "heart", while followers of the Huayan School distinguished the main and auxiliary with opposition, regarded the "heart" as the lord of all things, and clearly promoted idealism. Followers of the Huayan School attached importance to absorbing the ideas of Chinese scholars, such as inheriting the proposition of "Li was irresistible" of the original Chinese Buddhist Zhu Daosheng, who paid attention to the status of "Li", and took it as the ontology of "Things".[1] Yanhua scholar Li Tongxuan, contemporary of Fa Zang, studied the philosophy of "Yi" when he was young, and later he was devoted to writing *New Discussion on Avatamsaka Sutra*, explaining *Avatamsaka Sutra* with the thought of *Zhou Yi*. Cheng Guan also absorbed the argument of Li and later Esoteric Buddhism matched the "four virtues" (Yuan, Heng, Li, Zhen) of *Zhou Yi* with the "four virtues" (Nitya-Sukha-Atma-Subha) of Buddha, and even matched the "Five Relationships" with the "five precepts", and the trend of reconciling Confucianism became more and more intense.

Zen was a unique school inheriting traditional Chinese thought and Chinese Buddhist thought. It openly challenged the authority of all Indian Buddhism classics, and worshiped Hui Neng's record as *Sutra*, calling it *Altar Sutra*, which was the only work written by Chinese monks that was called sutra. Followers of Zen also called those that focused on systematically promoting Buddhist doctrines in the past "Jiao", and called themselves "Zong" to show the difference. Opposing "Jiao" with "Zong" was also unprecedented in the history of Buddhism. The thinking method of Zen was not to pay attention to and even ignore the role of language, and even deny the proposed hypothesis, with particular emphasis on mystery and intuition and pursuit of sudden enlightenment. It can be seen that although Zen was also inspired by Indian Buddhist thought, such as "the meaning is profound and delicate and cannot be expressed by words", "dharmata and animitta", "no way", "the one and only way", fundamentally it was a product inheriting the Chinese ideological line of "having a tacit understanding", and "forgetting the means by which the end is attained".

The development of everything declined right after they flourished. The argumentation of Buddhism began to decline in the late Tang Dynasty. In the Song, Yuan, Ming, and Qing Dynasties, although some Buddhist sects revived, the general trend was deteriorating. In this long historical stage, some philosophical ideas of Buddhism had been learned by Neo-Confucianism (New Confucianism), and suffered an eclipse, losing the value of independent existence. Some important Buddhist scholars paid more attention to reconciling traditional Chinese thought in order to seek the survival of Buddhism, and directly gave in to the powerful Confucian thought, sticking in the mud.

We can see how Buddhism in the Song, Yuan, Ming, and Qing Dynasties was more Confucianized from the following examples.

Zhiyuan (976–1022), scholar of the Tiantai School in the Northern Song Dynasty, called himself "Zhongyongzi" for compromising between Confucianism and Buddhism. He clearly declared what he did in his later years "was based on Confucianism" (Volume 22, *Xie Wu Si Cheng Zhuan "Preface of Xian Ju Bian"*, of *Xian Ju Bian*), because "without Confucianism, the country cannot be ruled, families have no peace, and the individual is not safe", and "if the country cannot be ruled, families have no peace, and the individual is not safe, how can Buddhism play its role!" (ibid., Volume 19, *Biography of Zhongyongzi*). He also said that "Confucianism advocated cultivation . . . Buddhism advocated managing the mind" (ibid.), and Buddhism and Confucianism "were the outside and the inside" (ibid.), and he opposed "putting Confucianism above Buddhism or putting Confucianism above Buddhism" (ibid.). Zhiyuan stressed "cultivating with Confucianism", and was "Confucianism-based", tending to put Confucianism above Buddhism, which reflected the significant decline of Buddhism.

Qi Song (1007–1072), a famous Buddhist monk in the Northern Song Dynasty, wrote a lot, focusing on the full praise of Confucian doctrine, and promoting the integrity of Confucianism and Buddhism. He wrote three parts of *Fu Jiao Pian*, saying, "There were ancient sages, Buddhism, Confucianism, and a hundred schools. The mind was uniform, while the traces were different" (*Fu Jiao Pian – Middle Part – Guangyuan Jiao*). Among them, Confucian scholars ruled the world, while Buddhist scholars advocated getting out of the world. Confucianism and Buddhism cooperated with each other. Qi Song wrote one chapter of *On Filial Piety* (*Fu Jiao Pian – Part Three*), and systematically demonstrated the relationship between Buddhism and Confucian filial piety, saying that Buddhism paid the most attention to filial piety: "filial piety was prior to precepts". He wrote five parts of *Zhong Yong Jie*, and greatly praised the Golden Mean of Confucianism. He proclaimed the Confucian theory of "exploring thoroughly the logos and the intrinsic character" and the Doctrine of Fatality, and praised the "Five Classics" and rituals of Confucianism. Qi Song believed that many truths "came from Confucianism, but their wide spread is attributed to Buddhism" (Volume 8, *Memorial to Emperor Renzong*, of *Tan Jin Collection*). In fact, he attributed Buddhist theories to Confucian doctrines. This fully shows the harmonicity of Buddhism.

Famous Zen Master Wansong Xingxiu (1166–1246) inherited the Zen of Qingyuan Caodong School, and his works were very rich. His ideas integrated Confucianism, Buddhism, and Taoism, and he often advised his disciple Yelu Chucai, a minister at that time, to rule the country with Confucianism and manage his mind with Buddhism, which was appreciated by Chucai. He also praised his master: He inherits from the Caodong School, but also has the fineness of the Yunmen School and sharpness of the Linji School. To rule the country with Confucianism and manage the mind with Buddhism was an important theory of reconciling Confucianism and Buddhism.

Zhuhong, Zhenke, Deqing, and Zhixu were the most influential four Buddhist scholars in the Ming Dynasty, known as the four Buddhist masters of the Ming Dynasty. One of their common features was to promote the integrity of Confucianism and Buddhism. Zhuhong (1535–1615), the master of the Pure Land School, converted to Buddhism from Confucianism, and believed that Confucianism and Buddhism "do not harm each other but support each other"; "Confucian scholars ruled the world, while the Buddhist scholars advocated getting out of the world" (*Yun Xi Fa Hui – Shou Zhu*). Buddhism could "help with what the king can't do", and Confucianism could "help with what Buddhism can't do". He also believed that Confucianism, Buddhism, Taoism "came from the same origin" (ibid.); "there is no difference in Li". The three religions were essentially the same. Zhenke (1543–1603) was originally a butcher, and later became a famous Zen master, with the title "Zibai". He believed that Confucianism, Buddhism, and Taoism stressed the mind; the outside was different but the essence was the same. The "five virtues" of Confucianism – namely, benevolence, righteousness, courtesy, wisdom, and trust – corresponded to the Five Dhyani Buddhas, whose names were different, but the essence was the same. Zen master Deqing (1546–1623) was also known as Han Shan. He read the Four Books, Zhou Yi, and ancient poetry, and was proficient in Confucianism, Buddhism, and Taoism. In addition to Buddhist writings, he also wrote one volume of *Direct Exploration of the Great Learning* and *The Doctrine of the Mean*, one volume of *Chun Qiu Zuo Shi Xie Fa*, two volumes of *Exploration of "Laozi"*, one volume of *Influence of Laozi and Zhuangzi*, four volumes of *Annotation to Zhuangzi*, and so on. He tried to reconcile Confucianism, Buddhism, and Taoism, saying,

> Three keys are needed for study: if one does not know Spring and Autumn, it's hard for him or her to survive in the world; if one is not proficient in Laozi and

Zhuangzi, it's hard for him or her to forget the world; if one does not practice meditation, it's hard for him or her to get out of the world.
(Volume 39, *Shuo – Xue Yao*, of *Collection of Master Hanshan*)

He also propagated that the "five virtues" of Confucianism were the "five precepts" of Buddhism; he even said the "self-restraint" and "return to kindness" of Confucius were "meditation" and "sudden enlightenment" of Buddhism, and regarded Confucius and Loazi as the incarnation of the Buddha, saying that they were both Buddhas, which actually replaced Buddhism with Confucianism and Taoism. Deqing also explained Confucianism and Taoism with Buddhism, such as explaining the Great Learning with Zen, comparing Laozi with the Consciousness-Only theory. Deqing completely connected Buddhism to Confucianism and Taoism in theory, thought, and moral practice. Zhixu (1599–1655) was also known as "Dabudaoren", and was called "Ouyilaoren" in his late years. He wrote *Zen Explanation of Zhou Yi*, "going into Confucianism with Zen, leading Confucianism to know Zen". He wrote Ouyi's understanding of The Four Books, explaining Confucian classics with Buddhism. He also wrote texts like *Xiao Wen Shuo* and *Guang Xiao Xu* to vigorously promote filial piety, saying that "all the principles in the world take filial piety as their basis" (Volume 4–2, *Xiao Wen Shuo*, of *Ling Feng Zong Lun*). "Confucianism took filial piety as its basis . . . Buddhism took filial piety as its purpose" (ibid., Volume 7–1, *Ti Zhi Xiao Hui Chun Zhuan*). He even said, "Every time I say only Buddhism can rule the world, so Sambo can protect the world; Confucianism can get out of the world, so all the kings, ministers, the elders and lay Buddhists can often remember the Buddha" (ibid., Volume 7–3, *Xuan Su Kai Shi Jie Mao Xiu Zhi Guan Zhu Yuan Shu*). "People can only learn Buddhism and then know Confucianism, and only true Confucianism is able to learn Buddhism" (ibid., Volume 7–4, *Fu Xian Kai Shou Xi Zhu Yuan Shu*). This was to break the boundary between "governance" and "getting out of the world", cancel the differences between Confucianism and Buddhism, and integrate the two. Zhixi also said, "These saints [referring to Confucius, Lao Tzu] were the incarnations of Bodhisattva, dispatched by Tathagata" (ibid., Volume 3–3, *Two Answers and Questions – Xing Xue Kai Meng Da Wen*). Confucius and Laozi were representatives of Buddha in China. This was the idea of three religions with the same source. Zhixu put forward this idea out of the opinion of "self-heart", saying, "Self-heart was the source of the three religions, from which the three religions came. . . . The heart is enough to build the three religions" (Volume 7–4, *Jinling Sanjiaoci Chongquan Shiguan Shu*, of *Ling Feng Zong Lun*). "The saints of the three religions just don't violate their true intention" (ibid., Volumes 2–3, *Fa Yu San – Shi Pan Gong Zhen*). The fundamental tenet of Confucianism and Taoism was "self-heart" or "true intention". Not violating the heart meant conforming to the three religions, and violating the heart meant not conforming to the three religions. "Self-heart" was fundamental. Zhixu unified the three religions based on "self-heart".

2 Absorption

The aforementioned reconciliation was for the relationship between Buddhism and traditional Chinese ideology and culture, and the absorption here was for the internal relationship in Buddhism – that is, Chinese Buddhism absorbing all the Buddhist classics and doctrines, and unifying the characteristics of the style of study of Buddhism in various places. This was particularly prominent in Buddhist sects in the Sui and Tang Dynasties, especially the Tiantai School and Huayan School; famous Buddhist scholars after the Tang Dynasty also continued to exert the characteristics of absorbing beliefs of all the Buddhist factions. This will be discussed ahead.

(1) Unity of the style of study of various factions in various places

The ancient history of China and India was different, but the unified situation was the mainstream. Political unity required ideological unity; for Buddhism, it also required the establishment of a unified Buddhist. In the feudal unified dynasties of Sui and Tang, national strength was great, the economy was prosperous, and the culture was developed. Buddhist sects formed at this time were the most important period of Chinese Buddhism, and also the increasingly mature period. One of the basic characteristics of the Buddhist sects in the Sui and Tang Dynasties was their unity, and the different styles of study of various Buddhist factions in various places in the past were unified, which shows the high degree of absorption of Chinese Buddhism.

After Buddhism was introduced into China in the Han Dynasty to the Sui Dynasty, it experienced a split period; especially the opposition of the regime in the Southern and Northern Dynasties and the different political, economic, and cultural backgrounds of the two regions made Buddhism tend to differentiate. The content of Buddhism included Sila, Samadhi, and Panna. Sila and Samadhi referred to the practice of religious cultivation; Panna referred to wisdom, meaning that the religious ideology system included both theory and practice. During the period of the Southern and Northern Dynasties, generally Buddhism in the north focused more on religious rituals and activities, such as sitting in meditation, practice, Dāna, and building statues and monasteries, while Buddhism in the south focused more on idle talk of profound theory. Zen was widely popular in the north, while Buddhist schools were more developed in the south. After the Sui Dynasty unified the whole country, exchange between the north and the south was very convenient; monks in the two regions communicated with each other, a variety of theories communicated with each other, and a variety of doctrines gradually tended to be consistent. Buddhism of the Sui and Tang Dynasties, such as the Tiantai School, Consciousness-Only School, Huayan School, and Zen, all paid equal attention to theory and practice, emphasizing Samadhi and Panna. The Tiantai School was originally a school of Zen, which also attached importance to theory. "Fahua Samadhi" of this school reflected the unity of Zen and theory. According to historical record, the ancestor of the Tiantai School, Zen master Huiwen, realized "three views in one mind" based on *Mahaprajnaparamita Upadesha* and *Mahaprajna-paramita-sastra* and passed on to Huisi. Hui Si went from the north to the south, and paid equal attention to both Zen and Buddhist argumentation. Huisi's disciple Zhiyi was the actual founder of the Tiantai School, and established the principle of practicing both Samadhi and Panna. The formation of the style of the Tiantai School that paid equal attention to theory and practice marked the change in styles of study that the north focused on Zen while the south focused on argumentation. The Consciousness-Only School inherited the opinion of Indian Mahayana, made tedious and delicate arrangements of material and psychological phenomena, forming a complex idealist ideology system. At the same time, there was Yogacara – namely, making the so-called truth directly present in front through meditation, without language as the intermediary, with Buddhist "wisdom". In *Chapter of Consciousness-Only* of *Dachengfayuanyilinzhang*, one of the founders of the Consciousness-Only School, Kuiji, also put forward five layers of a consciousness-only view from wide to narrow, from shallow to deep, from coarse to fine, as a unique view. Kuiji's master was Xuanzang, a great master, who learned widely. After returning from India, he was always busy presiding over translation, which made him regret his lack of meditation in his later years. For another example, the Huayan School had a set of theories of "endless origin" centered on "one-true dharma realm"; at the same time, its "view of dharma realm" was also Zen. The first ancestor of the Huayan School, Du Shun, was a Zen master; the second ancestor, Zhiyan, learned Zen from Du Shun, and re-explained samatha-vipassana with the doctrine of *Avatamsaka Sutra*. The real founder of the Huayan School, Fa Zang, put forward the "view of dharma realm" and "ten layers of consciousness-only view". The "ten layers of consciousness-only view" was to absorb the five layers of consciousness-only view of the Consciousness-Only School and combined with the view of dharma realms, which advocated integrating the dharma realm in one heart – namely, regarding all things as a concept in the mind, and achieving a harmonious situation in speculation. As for Zen, although it advertised "no writing", it attached great importance to practice; in fact, it also had its bright and delicate theory.

(II)   Systematic interpretation of the consistent position of Buddhist codes of different factions – "religious interpretation"

There was originally simple religious interpretation in India – for example, *Avatamsaka Sutra* was divided into Mahayana and Hinayana, *Lankavatarasutra* was divided into sudden enlightenment and gradual enlightenment, *Sandhinirmocanavyuhasutra* was divided into bhava, sunya, and antara, and *Nirvana Sutra* was divided into five tastes. In China, the theory of religious interpretation occupied a particularly important position in the various sects theoretically, and the content was very different from the religious interpretation of India – even against it. In a certain sense, religious interpretation was an inevitable phenomenon and a unique problem of Chinese Buddhist sects after the introduction of Indian Buddhism into

China. It embodied the digestion and absorption of foreign Buddhism by Chinese Buddhist scholars, and the absorption of Buddhist sects.

As mentioned earlier, the source of Chinese Buddhist doctrine basically relied on translation and lectures as media. Translation was not conducted simply in accordance with the occurring and developing order of Indian Buddhist doctrine, but mixing up doctrines of different factions of Mahayana and Hinayana. These were actually different from and conflicted with different doctrines of Buddhist theorists of different factions in different times of India, but all in the name of Sakyamuni, saying that they were the words of Buddha, and were confessed and sacred. There was a problem of how to eliminate content conflicts and reconcile ideological contradictions. Chinese Buddhist sects used the method of religious interpretation in order to justify this phenomenon and make the sect have a seemingly penetrating theoretical system. The so-called religious interpretation was to divide and organize all Buddhist theories – namely, not to deal with the relationship among the thoughts and beliefs of various factions with a simple confronting and even negative attitude, but to regard the thoughts of various factions as the preaching of Buddha at different times to different audiences, so that there were a variety of differences – namely, to distinguish the different grades as different arguments of a complete unified ideological system, and make systematic arrangements of thoughts of various factions in accordance with the theoretical system of the faction, and give a certain position, more importantly, to put the doctrine of their own faction above other factions. In the process of division and religious interpretation, the traditional Chinese thought understood by the author was often added, or even like Zen, which regarded original Chinese Buddhist thought as the supreme theory of all Buddhism.

The doctrine of religious interpretation in the Southern and Northern Dynasties was summarized as ten types by descendants, called "three Southern and seven Northern". "Three Southern" referred to the three types of the south, dividing Buddha's words into sudden enlightenment, gradual enlightenment, and indetermination. Among them, "gradual enlightenment" had different views, divided into "three times", "four times", and "five times", and took the "five times" of Huiguan as the most important. Huiguan referred to *Nirvana Sutra – Shengxingpin* on the basis of "four times", took the process from the cow giving milk → making cheese → raw junket → mature junket → finest cream as an example, compared the five tastes of milk to the five layers of Buddhist dharma, and divided Buddhist scriptures into five times: the first was the first scripture teaching, mainly referring to *Agama* of Hinayana; the second was the scripture teaching to triniyanani, mainly referring to *Prajna Sutra*; the third was the scripture teaching to Mahayana and Hinayana, referring to *Vimalakirti-nirdesa-sutra* and *Ses acintabrahmapariprccha*; the fourth referred to *Saddharmapundarika Sutra* of triniyanani; the fifth was the last scripture teaching that said Tathagata dharma-kaya was often the most perfect – namely, *Nirvana Sutra*. The "five-time" argument had a great influence in the south, and became the basis of some religious interpretations that later appeared. "Seven Northern" was also seven different arrangements of Buddhist scriptures in the order of Mahayana and Hinayana. For example, Bodhiruci established the semi-word and full-word teaching, saying that semi-word shall be taught first and then the full word when enlightening children. Semi-word was Hinayana, and the full word was Mahayana. For another example, Buddhasanta and Huiguang of Dilun Shi divided Buddhism into four schools: the first was the theory of karma of Hinayana – namely, "karma school"; the second was Pramacronjñapti of Chengshi Shi – namely, "prajnapti school"; the third was that everything was empty, said by *MahAvagga* and *Three Theses*; the fourth was *Nirvana*, *Avatamsaka Sutra*, and so on.

When the Tiantai School was founded, Zhiyi criticized the religious interpretation of "three Southern and seven Northern", and put forward the interpretation of "five times and eight schools". The "five times" referred to the order of Buddhist doctrines. *Avatamsaka Sutra* was preached the first time, Hinayana was preached the second time, general Mahayana was preached the third time, such as *Da Ji* and *Bao Ji*, *Prajna* was preached the fourth time, and *Avatamsaka Sutra* and *Nirvana* were preached the fifth time. The Tiantai School worshiped *Avatamsaka Sutra* as the highest classic, so making it the last time. The "eight teachings" divided Buddhism into eight categories according to form and content. For the way of enlightenment, they referred to "four teachings of rite": sudden enlightenment, gradual enlightenment, guhya, and indetermination. Sudden enlightenment and gradual enlightenment opposed each other, and indetermination opposed each other. People had different understandings after listening to Buddhist Dharma; if they did not know each other, it was guhya, and if they knew each other, it was indetermination. And then regarding the content of teachings, Zang (referring to Hinayana, for *Mahaprajnaparamita Upadesha* criticized that Hinayana knew only trinipitakani, specifically referring to *Agama*), Tong (through triniyananiby, referring to *Prajna*), Bie (Mahayana was different prior to Hinayana, referring to *Vimalakirti*), and Yuan (complete, referring to *Avatamsaka Sutra*, *Nirvana*, and *Saddharmapundarika Sutra*, among which *Saddharmapundarika Sutra* was purely complete), called "four teachings". The five times and eight teachings focused on the "four teachings", centered on *Saddharmapundarika Sutra*, which were the unique claim of the Tiantai School, so it was also known as "Tiantai four teachings". The five times and eight teachings of the Tiantai School, on the one hand, said that there was difference between the five times and the four teachings; on the other hand, they advocated that the five times and four teachings could not be limited by time and even by scripture teachings – namely, all the scriptures absorbed each other, so as to justify the different standpoints of various schools. In this way, even if the various teachings had distinctions, they could still parallel each other, which reflected the absorption of the Tiantai School. At the same time, it was different from the classics especially respected by Indian Mahayana Buddhism, which proposed *Avatamsaka Sutra*, *Nirvana*, and *Saddharmapundarika Sutra* as the most important classics, embodying the creative spirit of Chinese Buddhist scholars. The claim of religious interpretation of the Tiantai School had a great influence on the development of Chinese Buddhism – for example, the Huayan School absorbed part of the doctrine of religious interpretation of the Tiantai School as a basic view of its own religious interpretation.

The claim of religious interpretation of Jizang, the founder of the Three-Treatise School, was to believe that all the teachings of Buddha were equal, with no distinction of high and low, but Buddhist teaching could be divided into two categories: from dharma, there was Bodhisattva-pitaka and sravaka-pitaka; from human beings, there was Mahayana and Hinayana. Mahayana was divided into three categories: the first was *Avatamsaka Sutra*, the second was *Prajna*, and the third was *Saddharmapundarika Sutra* and *Nirvana*. These were arguments of different objects, but they were not attributed to the end. Jizang's claim was not exactly the same as the religious interpretation generally only for elevating the status of this school, and he put *Nirvana* above *Saddharmapundarika Sutra*, which also reflected that he did not fully agree with the religious interpretation of the Tiantai School.

The religious interpretation of the Consciousness-Only School was mainly based on the theory of three times of *Sandhinirmocana Sutra*, and held that the teaching of the Buddha was as follows: at the beginning, it talked about the "four truths" – suffering, origination, cessation, and path – and then talked about no self-nature (empty), and finally about the three self-natures (existence). This argument was basically consistent with the evolution of Indian Buddhism.

The Huayan School learned from the religious interpretation of predecessors and reorganized it, and Fa Zang proposed the five teachings of small, beginning, end, complete, and sudden. Small, beginning, end, and complete were equivalent to Zang, Tong, Bie, and Yuan of the Tiantai School, and sudden in the "four teachings" was taken. Fa Zang combined religious interpretation of the Tiantai School originally from form and content into five teachings, resulting in confusion in classification. Later in *Huayan Jinshizi Zhang*, Fa Zang attempted to start from the origin and uniformly described the meaning of five teachings. He pointed out that karma belonged to Hinayana, and no self-nature belonged to the beginning teaching of Mahayana, confirming that illusion belonged to the end teaching of Mahayana, the end of emptiness and existence was sudden teaching, and emotion ending was complete teaching. The theory of the Biyan School was characterized by integrating the difference of all things in the universe and promoting universality and harmony, and its religious interpretation also reflected the school style of absorption.

(III) The absorption of theories and beliefs of various Buddhist sects

The absorption of Chinese Buddhism was also reflected in the mutual integration of various sects after the Tang Dynasty, which was more and more significant and closer. In general, firstly it was the mutual integration of Zen Buddhism, followed by integration of other sects with the Pure Land School, and then it was the great integration of various sects centered on Zen. Many famous monks studied various religions, and thus gradually lost the character of the past sects.

It was Zongmi of the Tang Dynasty that took the lead in vigorously eliminating Zen confrontation and promoting the inconsistency of Zen. Zongmi was the fifth ancestor of the Huayan School as well as the four-generation disciple of Heze Association of Zen. He believed that the intention of Buddha was completely consistent with the teachings of Buddha, and said that there were only three teachings of one Tripitaka, and only three schools that practiced Zen; but these three schools corresponded to three teachings. The three teachings corresponded to the Consciousness-Only School, Three-Treatise School, and Huayan School. The three schools referred to the Northern Zen master, the Niutou School, and the Hongzhou and Heze Schools. The foregoing three schools and teachings corresponded to each other and absorbed each other; thus "three teachings and three schools are integrated". In the Song Dynasty, Yanshou (904–975) of the Fayan School of Zen Buddhism was worried about Zen scholars who did not understand teachings and became mixed up. He inherited and developed Zongmi's idea of unity of Zen Buddhism, emphasizing that "sutra was the Buddhist word . . . Zen was Buddha's will",[2] clearly promoting the view of paying equal attention to Zen and teaching. He also convened the scholars of the Consciousness-Only School, Huayan School, and Tiantai School at that time to live separately and read widely, question each other; finally based on meditation, to unify the doctrines of various school, he compiled 100 volumes of the *Mirror of Orthodoxy*, which had a great impact since the Southern Song Dynasty.

Tiantai, Huayan, and other schools of Buddhism originally had their own method of practice of observing the mind; to the Song Dynasty, many masters often contacted people with the Pure Land faith and advocated the practice of Buddhism, and Zen people also advocated practicing both Zen and the Pure Land School. Dharma-paryaya of the Pure Land School actually became the common faith of all schools. As Zen and the Pure Land School were the two most popular schools since the Song Dynasty, it became the mainstream of the development of Buddhist thought to advocate practicing both Zen and the Pure Land School as well as other schools. Taking "Four eminent monks of the Ming Dynasty" as an example, Zhuhong was not only the master of the Pure Land School but also an eminent monk of the Huayan School; at the same time, his attainment of Zen was also very deep. He believed that the various schools were not antagonistic:

> If people kept precepts, which is the Buddhist system, just call the name of Buddha; if people read the scripture, which is the words of Buddha, just call the name of Buddha; if people sit in meditation, which is the Buddha heart, just call the name of Buddha.
> (Volume 3 *Pu Quan Nian Fo Wang Sheng Jing Tu of Yunxi Posthumous Manuscript*)

He advocated the common chanting of all the schools and returning to the Pure Land. Zhenke had no specific master, and his thinking was not limited to one school or faction. *Buddha-Worship Ceremony* (see Volume 4 of *Anthology of Venerable Zibai*), compiled by him, in addition to vowing to worship all Buddhas, taught people to worship the religious interpretation of the west and the east, which was actually to reconcile the thoughts of various schools. Deqing once concentrated on the Pure Land School, and he was also known as the reviving ancestor of the Caoxi School for the restoration of Caoxi, the ancestral temple of

Zen. He also inherited the Huayan School's legacies, tried to advocate the consistency of Zen and the Pure Land School, and paid tribute to the Huayan School. He combined Zen, the Pure Land School, and the Huayan School, and put forward new opinions about Zen meditation and buddhanusmrti, believing that "Zen is another name of the heart . . . if the quietus of heart is understood, and the body does not move, why is movement restrained?" (Volume 15, *Da Xu Jianhu Jin Yi*, of *Collection of Master Hanshan*). He also said, "The Buddha whose name we call now is Amitabha . . . the Pure Land pursued is the ideal bliss. If people cannot forget, Amitabha appeared, step to the bliss home, why shall they pursue the Pure Land?" (ibid., Volume 2, *Showing Upasaka buddhanusmrti*). Actually this was to govern various schools with the original heart. Zhixu's thought was to combine Zen, sastra, and vinaya and to return to Pure Land. He believed that the theory and practice of the Tiantai School should govern Zen, the Vinaya School, the Pure Land School, and the Consciousness-Only School; at the same time he explained the doctrine of the Tiantai School with Consciousness-Only – namely, converging the two schools theoretically. He thought that buddhanusmrti was meditation – namely, he advocated the integration of Zen and the Pure Land School in practice. He advocated the unity of Zen, sastra, and vinaya, and governed all Buddhism with the Pure Land School. Zhixu said,

> Zen was the heart of Buddha, sastra was the words of Buddha, and vinaya was the act of Buddha . . . People shall not seek for Zen, sastra and vinaya outside the heart, all seek for self-heart outside Zen, sastra and vinaya, for this, they sit in meditation all day, reading sastra, learning vinaya.
> (Volume 2–3 *Fa Yu San of Ling Feng Zong Lun*)

He attributed Zen, sastra, and vinaya to one mind, which was the characteristic of Zhixu's thought, and also the typical performance of the evolution of late Buddhism that various schools tended to unite.

3 Simplicity

Some of the sects of Chinese Buddhism, such as the Tiantai School, Consciousness-Only School, and Huayan School, all had the nature of complex scholasticism, whose system was huge and complex, whose argument was complicated and trivial, and whose discussion was abstruse. Among them, the Consciousness-Only School was spread for decades and declined; the Tiantai School and Huayan School centered on heart in theory, advocated gradual enlightenment in religious practice, and excluded the complex religious practice method of Indian Buddhism, and thus it was spread longer than the Consciousness-Only School. What really stretched long and unbroken in Chinese Buddhism was Zen and the Pure Land School that did not exist in India; especially Zen was the mainstream of Buddhism after the Tang Dynasty. Zen was actually the synonym for Chinese Buddhism after the Tang Dynasty. Although the simplicity of Zen was based on a profound theoretical basis – namely, to grasp the theoretical core of Buddhism to expound directly, and accordingly put forward a set of simple methods of practice – and the simplicity of the Pure Land School was based on faith, the simplicity of teachings and practice methods was after all the common point of the two schools, and thus simplicity also became an important feature of Chinese Buddhism, distinguishing it from Indian Buddhism. The following is a brief description.

1. Seeing the original nature and becoming the Buddha. The Zen theme was to emphasize the spirit of comprehending, direct at the heart, see the original nature and become the Buddha This purpose took the pure nature and self-realization as a theoretical premise, and Hui Neng thought that Buddha nature is often pure, and everyone had it. Buddha nature was human nature. At the same time, everyone had a congenital Bodhi wisdom (the so-called Buddha wisdom), to realize the nature and become a Buddha. The reason all beings failed to be a Buddha was confusion – namely, having no consciousness to their own nature. If they believed in Buddhism and adhered to practice, once the improper thought was exterminated and the true wisdom was revealed, they would get enlightened inside and outside, understand the nature, and achieve becoming a Buddha. Hui Neng said, "if the self-nature is confused, the Buddha is all beings; if the self-nature is enlightened, all beings were the Buddha" (Dunhuang version of *Altar Sutra*). Dispel the clouds and see the sun; the nature could be seen in a clear heart, and the self-nature was Buddha. Hui Neng advocated that everyone could become a Buddha, but confusion and enlightenment had their orders, and were different from Indian Hinayana Buddhism, which recognized only Sakyamuni Buddha, which was also different from later Indian Mahayana Buddhism, which believed that some people could not become a Buddha, with strong Chinese color. Hui Neng turned the Buddha outside the heart into the Buddha inside the heart, and thus denied the external Buddha; it was to turn the Buddha into a common ordinary human, or elevate ordinary humans to the same status as the Buddha, reflecting the idea that humans and Buddhism were different only in confusion and enlightenment, but were actually equal. Although this theory had a nature of distinctive mysterious intuitive experience, it was simple and concise, consistent with traditional Chinese ideas; it was undoubtedly adopted to both the will of the upper rulers of autocratic society to pursue a happy life in the afterlife and the desire of lower-class people to get rid of real suffering, and was thus widely circulated.

2. Sudden enlightenment to become a Buddha. Buddhism believed that the key to becoming a Buddha lay in "enlightenment", and there were two ways of enlightenment: one was gradual, and the other was sudden. Gradual enlightenment was to achieve the consciousness of Buddhism via long-term practice. Sudden enlightenment meant there was no need for long-term practice; once the Buddhist "truth" was grasped, one could suddenly get enlightened. In the Eastern Jin of the Southern Dynasties, Zhu Daosheng once advocated sudden enlightenment. Hui Neng further developed sudden enlightenment based on the thought of Daosheng. It promoted that humans could suddenly become

a Buddha with a moment of enlightenment; it also emphasized not writing text – namely, humans did not need language to help them understand, but could suddenly get enlightened, with more mysterious intuition. Hui Neng said, "If the mind was confused, one became an ordinary person ... if the mind was enlightened, one became Buddha". "Confusion lasts long, and the enlightenment is in an instant" (Dunhuang version of *Altar Sutra*). This completely denied the set of levels of practice in Indian Buddhism and denied the endless practice, which was a highly fast method to become a Buddha. Besides, Zen not only met the traditional Chinese ideas but also corresponded to China's customs. Normally, Zen required meditation, but later it even canceled meditation. It believed that sudden enlightenment did not require one to leave real life. "Being contented or insatiable, stay in Taoist rites often; both the mood and feeling return to nature" (Wang Wei: tablet inscription for the sixth ancestor). "Carrying water and chopping wood were wonderful ways". Every move could not leave the temple; whether it was intentional or emotional, it would be attributed to the nature and achieve Buddha. In other words, humans could also get enlightened and became a Buddha in the daily life of labor. Zen's doctrine of sudden enlightenment most fully demonstrated the simplicity of Chinese Buddhism.

3 Easy way of practice and chanting sutra by Buddha's name. Tan Luan (476–542) of the Northern Wei was the pioneer of the Pure Land School; he once created the doctrine of difficult and easy ways of practice in *Wang Sheng Lun Zhu*, and believed that in the so-called Buddha-free world, the world was chaotic, relying only on "self-power", with no "other-power" (Buddha's power), and practicing to become a Buddha was as hard as walking on the ground and very painful; it was called the difficult way of practice. On the contrary, in the rebirth in Amitabha's Pure Land with the power of Amitabha's, it was like taking a boat in water; it was very happy and called the easy way of practice. Later, Daochuo (562–645) of the Tang Dynasty inherited the thought of the Pure Land of Tan Luan, and divided Buddhist teachings into the sage paths and the Pure Land. He promoted that the sage path was far from the saints, with deep understanding, and could not be enlightened by general beings; only the Pure Land was easy, and could lead to the Pure Land with the power of Amitabha Buddha. Daochuo's disciple Shan Dao (613–681) was the true founder of the Pure Land School, and advocated calling the name of Buddha as the internal cause, the power of Amitabha Buddha as the outer karma, corresponding inside and outside, leading to the Pure Land. As mentioned earlier, there were three dharma-paryaya of buddhanusmrti: the one was chanting sutra by Buddha's name, such as Nama Amitabha, reciting endlessly; the second was Vipasya – namely, concentrating on Buddha's beautiful appearance and the solemn scene of the location of Buddha; the third was dharmata buddhanusmrti – namely, watching dharma-kaya of Buddha. Buddhanusmrti, advocated by Tan Luan, included the foregoing three types; through Shan Chuo and Shan Dao, it turned to focus on chanting sutra by Buddha's name, and advocated chanting

sutra by Buddha's name about 70,000 or 100,000 times. It was believed that mechanically repeated recitation of the Buddha's name could help people go to the Pure Land with the power of Amitabha. This dharma-paryaya of Pure Land was popular in the ancient Chinese countryside and towns with its simplicity and convenience, and was generally worshiped by the civilians who lacked culture but had faith.

In addition, paying attention to the self-nature, paying attention to real problems, and being concerned about the real society were important features of Chinese Buddhism.

In short, Buddhism came from India, and went through a long history of evolution in China, forming a religion with Chinese characteristics. From the characteristics of Chinese Buddhism, we can roughly see some of the regularity of nationalization of foreign Buddhism.

After the introduction of Buddhism in China, from the perspective of the history of religious thought and culture, externally, it had differences with and opposition to traditional Chinese thinking; internally, there were differences and contradictions among doctrines of various Buddhist schools, and each sect itself had to try to adapt to the need for faith of the majority of farmers with cultural backwardness and urban civilians from teaching and practice. The history of Chinese Buddhism over the past 2,000 years shows that after Buddhism was introduced into China, it soon reconciled with traditional Taoist alchemy and Confucian ethics, and then attached to the metaphysics of the Wei and Jin Dynasties. In the Sui and Tang Dynasties, the founders of Buddhist sects also learned traditional Chinese thought to build the ideological system of their own school. After the Song Dynasty, the forces of Buddhism were declining, and various schools focused on combining Confucianism and Buddhism, preaching the three teaching homology theory, reconciling Confucianism and Taoism to maintain their own survival. The reconciliation between Buddhism and inherent Chinese thinking had been continuous, was more and more comprehensive, and more and more intense, lost the original features of Indian Buddhism, and almost belonged to Confucianism, becoming the Confucianized Buddhism. Moreover, the classics of Indian Mahayana Hinayana were introduced into China together; until the Southern and Northern Dynasties, the factions basically peacefully coexisted, and were carried forward in parallel. To the Sui and Tang Dynasties, Zen had only the strongest status, with a distinctive sectarian and exclusive style, but it also absorbed the classics and doctrines of other sects through the way of religious interpretation, and constituted a system with different levels in theory. After the Song Dynasty, in order to coordinate internally and avoid internal friction, all the schools put more emphasis on mutual absorption, harmony, and consistency. Zen and the Pure Land School, established in the middle of the Tang Dynasty, both had very simple teachings and practice methods, and could be adapted to the habits and needs of the general public; thus they were spread for a long time. Chinese Buddhism generally evolved along the track of external reconciliation first, followed by internal absorption, from cumbersome to simple, thus constituting the basic appearance of the development of Chinese Buddhist thought, showing the typical characteristics of Chinese Buddhism.

Buddhist belief and thought were not immutable. Chinese Buddhism had characteristics different from Indian Buddhism in morphological and theoretical systems. This change was rooted in the economic, political, and cultural soil of Chinese society, in the awareness, methods of thought, and customs of the nation. Here we should stress that the traditional Chinese ideology and culture and the potential national psychological consciousness formed under the long-term propaganda, education, and influence of Confucian orthodox ideology had the power of transforming foreign ideas. Thus, the spread, rise, and decline of the Buddhist sects were often directly related to whether they had a national character. In general, the less national nature the sect had, the faster it declined, and the more national nature the sect had, the longer it could stay prosperous.

The increasing sinicization of Buddhism was also the process of constantly being absorbed and transformed by the inherent thinking and culture of China. At the same time, it should be mentioned that both the Tiantai School and Huayan School created philosophical systems with a large structure, which was unprecedented in the history of Chinese thought, and also inspired the Neo-Confucianist system of Zhuxi later. The impact of Zen thought on the "School of the Mind" of Lu Xiangshan and Wang Yangming later was very obvious.

It also shows that China's inherent culture was not replaced when facing the importation and challenge of foreign Buddhist culture. It effectively absorbed the achievements of Buddhist thought and transformed it into a part of Chinese culture, which shows that China's inherent culture was fully open, highly resilient, and good at digesting, and embodied the Chinese nation's strong and distinct subject consciousness.

P.S.: Regarding the basic characteristics of Chinese Buddhism, after nearly 20 years of thinking, the author believes that they can be summarized as paying attention to self-nature, reality, simplicity, and harmony, and I will have a detailed discussion in the future.

Notes

1 Cheng Guan said, "Dust and sand can be counted . . . Li is irresistible". See Volume 13, "Taisho Tibetan", of "Dafang Guangfo Huayanjing Shu", Volume 35, 593 pages.
2 "The Mirror of Orthodoxy", "Taisho-pitaka", Volume 1, page 418.

9 The external influence of Chinese Buddhism

In the formation and development of Chinese Buddhism, the two systems of Han Buddhism and Tibetan Buddhism were constantly spread outward. In the Sui and Tang Dynasties, Buddhism was spread to Korea and Japan in East Asia, and Vietnam in Southeast Asia; in modern times, it was spread to Malaysia, Singapore, and the Philippines in Southeast Asia. Tibetan Buddhism was spread northward to Mongolia and the Soviet Union, as well as southward to Bhutan and other places. Chinese Buddhism was introduced into countries in East Asia and Southeast Asia, and some countries in South Asia, where Buddhist faith went deep in the people; Buddhist thought and power permeated a wide range of fields, such as politics, ethics, philosophy, literature, art, and customs of these countries, and had a tremendous impact on their historical development.

The influence of the Buddhist sects of the Sui and Tang Dynasties on Korea

In the fourth century AD, Buddhism was introduced to Korea[1] from China. Fu Jian of the Former Qin Dynasty sent messengers and monk Shun Dao to send Buddha statues and Buddhist scriptures to Goguryeo in the eighth year of Jianyuan (AD 372). In the tenth year of Jianyuan (AD 374), A Dao, monk of Qin, went to Goguryeo. Later Goguryeo built Buddhist temples for Shun Dao and A Dao to live, which was the beginning of Goguryeo Buddhism. In the ninth year of Taiyuan in the Eastern Jin Dynasty (AD 384), monk Malananda went to Baekje from the Eastern Jin Dynasty, and founded Buddhist temples, which was the beginning of Baekje Buddhism. Buddhism was introduced into Silla early; in the third year of Taiqing during the reign of Emperor Wu of Liang (AD 549), messengers were sent with monk Juede of Silla, who came to China to send Buddha relics to Silla. In the sixth year of Tianjia (AD 565) in the reign of Emperor Wen of Chen, messengers were sent to Silla to send more than 1,700 volumes of Buddhist scriptures.

During the Sui and Tang Dynasties, there were many Korean monks studying in China, especially in the late seventh century, when Korea was closer to the Tang Dynasty in the unified era of Silla, and most of the Buddhist sects of the Sui and Tang Dynasties were introduced into Korea.

Three-Treatise School: In the second year of Zhenguan (AD 628) in the Tang Dynasty, Korean monks Hui Guan and Dao Deng came to China successively, and inherited the argumentation of "Three-Treatise" from Jizang, the founder of the Three-Treatise School. Later they spread the Three-Treatise School in Japan.

Consciousness-Only School: Silla natives Shenfang and Yuance were the chief disciples of Xuanzang. Yuance's disciple Dao Zheng returned to Silla from Tang in the second year of Changshou (AD 693) during the reign of Wu Zetian, elucidating and promoting the theory of Consciousness-Only. Zhifeng, Zhiluan, and Zhixiong came to Tang from Silla to learn the argumentation of Consciousness-Only from Zhizhou, Kuiji's disciple, and later they went to Japan to carry forward the Consciousness-Only School.

Huayan School: Famous Silla monk Yixiang came to Zhixiang Temple on Zhongnan Mountain in Shaanxi, learning *Avatamsaka Sutra* from Zhiyan, the second ancestor of the Huayan School with Fa Zang. Later he returned to Silla and carried forward the argumentation of the Huayan School, and was worshiped as the first ancestor of Huayan in the East China Sea. Fa Zang once entrusted someone to send his own works to Yixiang, who ordered disciples to study them after reading, and claimed that "Master Fa Zang broadens me", becoming a much told tale of Chinese and Korean monks carrying forward the "Huayan School". At the same time, Silla monk Yuanxiao was also proficient in scriptures of Huayan with a lot of writing.

Vinaya School: Silla monk Cizang came to China to study Vinaya, and later he returned to the motherland with Tripitaka, which was the beginning of Korea owning Tripitaka. After Cizang returned home, he was given the title of Daguotong, and vigorously promoted Dharma. He also changed the imperial/official dress of Silla to Tang rites, which was the beginning of Silla adopting Chinese clothing rituals.

Zen: After the introduction of Chinese Zen sects into Korea, nine sects of Zen were founded in the time of Silla, in full flourish. Silla monk Daoyi came to Tang to learn Southern Zen, and lived there 37 years before returning home, where he was worshiped as the national master. After several generations of spreading, the Kaji san School Faction formed, and Daoyi was regarded as the first ancestor of the Kaji san School in the East China Sea. Hongzhi came to China to study Zen, practiced the Silsangsan School after returning home, and was the first ancestor of the Silsangsan School. Hui Zhe came to Tang and studied for 25 years, and founded the Tongni san School after returning home. Wuran studied *Avatamsaka Sutra* first after coming to China, and later he learned koan from Mazu's disciples Ruman and Shiche; he was worshiped as the national master after returning home, enjoying the courteous reception of the six generations of kings. He had 2,000 disciples and founded the Songju san School. Fanri came to Tang and learned from Zen master Ji'an, the disciple of Mazu, and he returned home during the Huichang Period, founding the Sagul san School. Daoyun, who returned home in the same year as Fanri, had a disciple called Zhezhong, who lived on the Lion Hill, to carry forward Zen, and founded the Saja san School. According to legend, the Silla monk Falang came to Tang and learned Zen from Daoxin, the fourth ancestor of Zen, and carried forward after returning home. When it was handed down to Daoxian, he founded the Huiyang san School. Silla monk Xingji was the first to learn from Xingsi of the Qingyuan School after coming to Tang, and he had more than 500 disciples after returning home. Shunzhi came to Tang to learn from Huiji of Mount Yang, returned home after learning Dharma, and first spread the Weiyang School in Silla. Xuan Yu came to China and returned home after learning Dharma, and he had a disciple called Shenxi. Later the followers who inherited Xuan Yu and Shenxi's Zen became the Pongnim san School. Qingyou and Jiuwei successively came to China, learned from Daoying of the Yunju School, and spread the Caodong School after returning home. At that time, Liyan and Lian also learned from the Yunju School, and the four were known as the Catasso Appaman Nayo of the East China Sea. Li Yan came to China during the reign of Emperor Zhao of Tang; after learning Dharma from Daoying of the Yunju School, he returned home in the first year of Qianhua during the reign of Emperor Taizu of Liang (AD 911), and he built Guangzhao Temple in Sumeru Mountain in the northwest, founding the Sumisan School. In the eighth year of Dade in the Yuan Dynasty (AD 1304), Zen monk Shaoqiong went to Korea by sea to carry forward Zen, and was welcomed by the king of Korea. There were many Korean monks learning Zen, and Shao Qiong implemented *Baizhang Regulations*. Another Korean monk, Zichao, came to China in the Yuan Dynasty to learn Zen, and returned home in the sixteenth year of Zhizheng (AD 1356) to carry it forward. At this time, China was in the end of Yuan and beginning of Ming, while in Korea the Ly Dynasty was replacing the Goryeo Dynasty, and Zichao was worshiped by the first emperor of Korea as the imperial master for Zen. Zen, with its nine mountains of many martial arts, became the mainstream of Korean Buddhism. With various sects under the nine schools of Silla, Zen became the mainstream of Buddhism in Korea. Among the nine schools, eight were in Silla, and the Sumisan School was in Goryeo. Among the nine schools, Huiyang san School belonged to the sect of Daoxin, and the others all belonged to the sect of Hui Neng. Among the eight schools of the sect of Hui Neng, in addition to the Sumisan School, the remaining seven schools all belonged to the sect of Mazu of Jiangxi. In addition to the nine schools, Shunzhi introduced the Weiyang School, which also belonged to Mazu's sect.

Esoteric Buddhism: Silla monk Minglang came to China in the sixth year of Zhenguan in the Tang Dynasty (AD 632) to learn Esoteric Buddhism. Three years later, he returned home and built Jinguang Temple, becoming the first ancestor of the Haidong Shenyin School. Since then,

Korean monks continuously came to China to study Esoteric Buddhism and carried it forward after returning home. In the Tang Dynasty, monk Yi Lin learned *garbha* from Subhakarasimha, and later went to Silla to spread Esoteric Buddhism.

Tiantai School: According to legend, Silla monk Xuanguang came to China to learn Fahua Samadhi from Huisi. After 120 years, Yitian came to China to learn Tiantai teachings. Yitian was the fourth son of Emperor Wenzong of Korea, and became a monk when he was young. He learned argumentations of the Huayan School, and was given the title of Youshisengtong. In the eighth year of Yuanfeng in the Song Dynasty (AD 1085), he came to China to seek dharma, where he learned Tiantai teachings from Cibian of Tianzhu Temple, and learned argumentations of the Huayan School in Dazhong Xiangfu Temple in Hangzhou. After he returned home, he carried forward teachings of the Tiantai and Huayan Schools.

With the introduction of Buddhism, Chinese Buddhist cultural relics also entered Korea. For example, in the early Song Dynasty, the new carving of *Tripitaka* was completed in Chengdu; in the second year of Duangong in the Song Dynasty (AD 989), it was gifted to Emperor Chengzong of Goryeo. Later there were presents from time to time. In northern China, in the ninth year of Qingning of the Liao Dynasty (AD 1063), the newly printed *Qidanzang* was gifted to Emperor Wenzong of Goryeo. The Goryeo Dynasty also started carving and printing *Tripitaka* with the Shu version as the master copy – namely, the famous *Gaolizang*. Later it was proofread and corrected according to the Shu version, Khitan version, and first *Gaolizang*, and was re-carved, which had an important academic value.

After the introduction of Buddhism in Korea, it went through the period when Goryeo, Baekje, and Silla existed at the same time, the period of Silla until the era of Goryeo (918–1392). During 1,000 years, Buddhism was extremely prosperous. In the Goryeo Dynasty, the king believed in Buddhism, and princes and royal families struggled to become monks. Many monks were worshiped as imperial masters and national masters, and served as the advisor of the king, and Buddhism reached the peak of its prosperity. Korean civil and military affairs, various systems, ideology, and culture were impacted by Buddhism. To the Ly Dynasty, Confucianism, especially Zhuxi's doctrine, became the national religion, and Buddhism tended to decline. In the 1950s, Buddhism regained rapid development in South Korea, and is now the largest religion there.

The wide impact of Buddhist sects in the Sui and Tang Dynasties on Japanese Buddhism and culture

As Chinese Buddhism was spread to foreign countries, Japan was most deeply affected. In the sixth century, Buddhism was introduced via Baekje in the southern part of the Korean Peninsula to Japan. At that time, Japan believed in polytheism, and thought that the gods blessed and protected human beings, but also punished and destroyed them. The image of Sakyamuni Buddha and the Buddhist doctrine of compassion seemed to bring the gospel of mercy and salvation. The Japanese welcomed this foreign religion in awe and joy. In the period of the introduction of Buddhism, Yamato was evolving from a power structure composed of several tribes into a central government. Regent Prince Shotoku decided to make use of Buddhism as a political tool and required all subjects to convert to Sambo, so Buddhism developed greatly, and Buddhist temples became the symbol of power and wealth of the ruling class, as well as a symbol of the new culture.

As Chinese monks went to Japan to carry forward Dharma and Japanese monks came to the Sui and Tang Dynasties to study, in the Nara Era (708–781), Japanese Buddhism gradually formed different sects:

> Three-Treatise School: Goryeo monk Huiguan, disciple of Jizang, the founder of the Chinese Three-Treatise School, went to Japan to spread "Three Treatises" in 625, and founded the Three-Treatise School. Jizang's disciple, Goryeo monk Dao Deng, also went to Japan and lived in Yuanxing Temple, where he spread Madhyamika. Huiguan's disciple Fu Liang, Fu Liang's son Zhizang, and Zhizang's disciple Daoci had been to the Tang Dynasty to study "Three Treatises", and spread the teaching after returning home.
> Dharma Character School: In AD 653, Japanese monks Daozhao and others came to Chang'an, and learned from Xuanzang. After they returned home, they carried forward the doctrine of the Consciousness-Only School, which was the first spread of the Japanese Dharma Character School. Later, Japanese Sramana continued to study in China, and formed Yuanxing Temple (south) and Xingfu Temple (north) after they returned home.
> Huayan School: In AD 736, Tang monk Dao Rui was invited to Japan to carry forward the argumentation of the "Huayan School", which was the first introduction of the Huayan School in Japan. Later, Shenxiang from Silla, the disciple of Fa Zang, the founder of the Chinese Huayan School, went to Japan to preach *Avatamsaka Sutra*, and was the first ancestor of the Huayan School in Japan. Since then, the Huayan School gradually flourished.
> Vinaya School: At the invitation of Japanese Sramana Rongrui and Puzhao, Jian Zhen, master of Sramana in Yangzhou Daming Temple, experienced five setbacks, went blind, and finally arrived in Japan on his sixth try in the twelfth year of Tianbao in the Tang Dynasty (AD 753). A precept platform was built in the East Temple in Nara, where 430 people, including the emperor and queen of Japan, accepted Bodhisattva precepts. Later, Tang Zhaoti Temple with a precept platform was built, where 40,000 people or more accepted precepts. Jian Zhen was worshiped as the first ancestor of the Japanese Vinaya School, and he also introduced the literature, medicine, craft, and cultural relics system of the Tang Dynasty to Japan, making great and far-reaching contributions to Japan's cultural development.

In addition, Goryeo monk Huiguan also preached *Satyasiddhi-sastra* in Japan, and thus formed the Satyasiddhi School attached to the Three-Treatise School.

Daozhao and others learned *Abhidharmakosa-sastra* from Xuanzang; after they returned home, they preached it, and thus also formed Kusha-shū inside the Dharma Character School. The foregoing were the six sects formed in the Nara Era introduced to Japan from the Sui and Tang Dynasties. At that time, the Three-Treatise School and Dharma Character School were the most prosperous.

In AD 794, Japan's capital was moved from Nara to Heian. In the Heian Period (782–1191), the Tiantai School and Zhenyan School (Esoteric Buddhism) of Chinese Buddhism were introduced into Japan. Japan's famous monk Saicho (Master Chuanfa) and Kukai (Master Hongfa) went to Tang in 804. In China, Saicho learned the doctrine of the Tiantai School from Daosui and Xingman, disciples of Zhanran, the ninth in China of the Tiantai School, and later he also learned Zen of the Niutou School and Esoteric Buddhism; the next year he returned home and greatly carried it forward, and founded the Tiantai School in Mount Hiei. Kukai went to Chang'an and learned from Huiguo of Esoteric Buddhism in Qinglong Temple; in AD 806, after he returned home, he carried forward Esoteric Buddhism, and founded Shingon Buddhism in Mount Kōya. Saicho's disciples Ennin and Enchin and Kukai's disciples Changxiao, Yuanxing, Huiyuan, and Zongrui all went to Tang for Dharma, and they and the masters sought a large number of books and cultural relics from China and then returned to Japan, which greatly promoted the development of Buddhism in Japan; they were called "eight masters to Tang" in the Buddhist history of Japan, and were very famous. The Tiantai School and Shingon Buddhism both took "protecting the country" and "accumulating blessing and eliminating disaster" as missions. In the Heian Period, they were deeply respected by the royal family and nobility, and were the most dominant and prevailing, known as the "Two School of Heian Period". So far they still have a large number of believers.

During the Kamakura Period of Japan (1192–1333), Zen was introduced from China, and the Pure Land School and Nichiren, based on the spread of Chinese Buddhism, were especially prosperous, and made Buddhism popular. Japanese monk Eisai came to China twice in the fourth year of Qiandong (AD 1168) and fourteenth year of Chunxi (AD 1187) in the Southern Song Dynasty to learn koan of Linji from Zen master Huaihcang, and practice "kan hua Zen". After he returned, he formally founded the Linji School. Dogen, a disciple of Eisai's disciple, came to China to learn from Zen master Rujing, and practice "Mo Zhao Zen". After he returned home, he founded the Caodong School. Since the Southern Song Dynasty, Japanese Zen monks came to China to study and Song monks crossed to Japan to carry forward Zen (especially the Yangqi School) very frequently. In 1199, Japanese monk Junreng came to Hangzhou to learn Dharma from Yuansong, the sixth ancestor of the Yangqi School, and spread into Japan. In 1246, Daolong of Lanxi crossed to Japan to carry forward Zen of the Yangqi School, which promoted the great development of Zen in Japan. During the Kamakura Period, there were 24 schools of Japanese Zen, among which 20 schools belonged to the Linji and Yangqi Schools, advocating a tranquil and hard style.

Dharma-mukha of chanting the name of Buddha of the Pure Land School of Shandao, introduced in the Tang and Song Dynasties, later evolved into a number of schools in Japan – for example, Honen established the teachings of purely chanting sutra by Buddha's name and going to the Pure Land with other-power, and founded the Pure Land School. Honen's disciple Shinran did not pay attention to diligent practice and chanting the name of Buddha, but stressed the firm faith in Amitabha inside the heart, and carried the school with his wife, permitting people to eat meat. He founded Jodo Shinshu. This school was later divided into 15 schools, such as Otani and Honganji. Nichiren worshiped the Chinese translation of *Saddharmapundarika Sutra*, and believed that only promoting *Saddharmapundarika Sutra* and chanting "Nam-Myo-Ho-Len-Ge-Kyo" of *Saddharmapundarika Sutra* could save all beings; he was worshiped as the ancestor of Nichiren. Later this school was divided into a number of schools. None of Zen, the Pure Land School, and Nichiren had complicated doctrines and rituals, and they all advocated that humans could become a Buddha without practice for life, and were thus widely spread among the Samurai and middle- and lower-class people. Among them, the Pure Land School and Nichiren were the most closely related to Japanese folk beliefs and customs, and had the distinctive characteristics of the Japanese nationalities, with the most rapid development; they are still schools with the most believers of Japanese Buddhism now.

In the middle of the seventeenth century, Yinyuan Longqi of Fuzhou Huangboshan was invited to go to Japan, and founded Huangboshan Wanfu Temple in Uji, promoting the Huangbo School and advocating practicing Zen and chanting the name of Buddha. They used Chinese daily, and their life was sinicized. For a while, Zen monks of the Japanese Caodong and Linji Schools all joined him. Temples of the Japanese Huangbozong School still maintain the style of the Zen temple in China's Ming Dynasty.

After Buddhism was introduced into Japan, its system, doctrine, thought, and culture penetrated broad fields of politics and culture in Japanese society, into all the corners of the Japanese people's life, and had a profound impact on social life, family life, education, charity, kendo (Bushido), the tea ceremony, calligraphy, literature, painting, sculpture, architecture, and so on.

Buddhism was closely connected to the state power of Japan, and strongly affected the country's political life. Prince Shyotoku made Buddhism the national religion. In the Nara Era, Emperor Shōmu mobilized national strength to establish East Temple and Kokubunji Temple. Bureaucrats and nobles of the Heian Period, generals of the Kamakura Era, and aides and staff of the Edo Era also believed in Buddhism. Most of the affairs of the country were handled by the monks, and ancient Japanese politics had a strong Buddhist color. Since the middle of the nineteenth century, the Japanese Buddhist community had reformed Buddhism to adapt it to the capitalist society. Emerging groups in the Buddhist community formed – for example, the Soka Gakkai Society and Rissho Kosei-kai of Nichiren Shu were very famous. The Komeito Part established by the Soka Gakkai Society played an important role in the Japanese House and Senate and had an important influence on Japan's political life.

Buddhism went deep into all social strata, and almost every family in Japan had Buddha statue and Buddhist altar for daily worshiping for a while. Shinran advocated "household Buddhism", so Buddhism tended to stay in the household. Buddhism became an important part of the spiritual life of Japanese people, and had a profound impact on their way of life.

Buddhism had long built a large number of schools, nursing homes, and orphanages, playing an important role in social education and charity. Now in Japan, there are 12 Buddhist universities set up by some Buddhist sects – namely, Taisho University, Otani University, Ryukoku University, Kenshin University, Komatsau University, Buddhist University, Garden University, Takano University, Kyoto Women's University, Doho University, Shuchiin University, and Aichi Gakuin University. In addition to teaching Buddhism, these universities offer other disciplines. This has a profound impact on people's cultural, educational, and even social life.

Zen had a direct and significant impact on Bushido. Samurai traveled in the world in danger, and they were stubborn and tough, so they needed an ideology and cultivating method adapted to this state of mind and lifestyle. Zen's simple and concise teachings, its simple life with few desires and hard physical and mental practice, its fashion of paying attention to loyalty, and its ideas regarding death as a dream all had a great impact on the spirit of Samurai. Zen's teachings became the spiritual weapons of Samurai. In the view of Samurai, people who did not practice meditation were not qualified to talk about Bushido. Samurai had to practice meditation to temper the spirit and achieve the so-called realm of "Anatta".

In the twelfth century, monk Eisai took tea seed from China. At first he planted it in the courtyard of the temple, and since then, a fashion of drinking tea and the tea party formed in the temple, which was later gradually spread to Samurai society. Japan also adopted the etiquette of the "tea feast" of Chinese Buddhism: grind the tea, and then pour water to brew the tea dust into a paste to drink. This kind of tea ceremony is still popular.

Calligraphy was a kind of art unique to Chinese and Japanese characters. When Jian Zhen traveled to Japan, he took a volume of *Calligraphy of Wang Xizhi of Jin* and copybooks of *Authentic Work of Wang Xianzhi*. For a moment, it became popular in Japan to study Wang Xizhi's calligraphy, which once played a leading role in Japanese calligraphy. Monk Kukai, Juyishi, and Emperor Saga were called "three calligraphers" in the history of Japanese calligraphy, among whom Monk Kukai and Juyishi both had studied in the Tang Dynasty. Monk Kukai studied Chinese calligraphy when he was in China, following Yan Zhenqing, and he was good at seal script, clerical script, regular script, semicursive script, and cursive script; he was also the ancestor of Japanese calligraphy. Kukai also created gojūon of Japanese symbols with cursive script of Chinese characters – namely, the so-called hiragana. Since the Song Dynasty, Zen monks also played an important role in the dissemination of calligraphy art.

Since the Song Dynasty in China, Zen monks often studied Confucianism, too. In the Yuan Dynasty, Zen monk Yishan Yining began to take the Zhuzi School to Japan, where a number of Zen monks studying Confucianism appeared. From the late Kamakura Era to the late Muromachi Era, five schools of Zen in Kyoto and

Kamakura became the places where Zen, Confucian, and other Chinese publications were pressed and published. The Zen monks of the five schools painstakingly learned Chinese and wrote Chinese poetry, forming brilliant "five-school literature", having a very important position in the history of Japanese literature, and directly promoting the rise of Edo sinology.

Kukai wrote *WenJingMiFuLun* in the early ninth century AD, which marked the large-scale introduction of Chinese literature and literary theory into Japan. As Buddhism was spread eastward, Tang poetry was also spread to Japan. In the minds of the Japanese, Tang poetry was regarded as their own country's classic. Until now, a lot of Chinese poetry and Chinese fables are compiled in the textbooks of Japanese primary and secondary schools.

As Buddhism was spread eastward, China's architectural art was also introduced to Japan. Monk Jian Zhen was an architect enthusiastic to build monasteries, and also took architectural art to Japan. He built Tang Zhaoti Temple in Nara, which imitated Tang architecture, and had such a great impact that Heijyokyo and Heian kyo built in Japan were exactly the same as Chang'an City and the palace of the Tang Dynasty in city planning and palace construction.

People often say China and Japan have the same culture and species. In the aspect of the same culture, it can be said that Buddhism has played the important role of the bridge. This has been well documented in the foregoing examples.

The close relationship between Zen and the Pure Land School and Vietnamese Buddhism

China borders on Vietnam, so transportation is convenient. Vietnam is also the intersection of the Sino-Indian sea route, so Buddhism has long been introduced to Vietnam. According to legend, at the end of the second century, Mou Rong, a Chinese scholar of the Eastern Han Dynasty, moved to live in Cochin (now Hanoi, Vietnam) from Guangxi to run away from social upheaval, and he wrote *Lihuolun* to promote Buddhism. Since then, Chinese monks continued to spread Buddhism in Vietnam. Since the sixth century, Zen and the Pure Land School of Chinese Buddhism were introduced into Vietnam and widely circulated, forming a number of schools. In Vietnam, Buddhism was made the national religion by the Ly Dynasty (1010–1224) and the Chen Dynasty (1225–1405). By the fifteenth century, Vietnamese rulers worshiped Confucianism, and Buddhism was weakened. At the end of the seventeenth century, Buddhism began to revive and formed a further combination of Zen and the Pure Land School.

> Vinitaruci Zen School: Vinitaruci was from southern India, and he learned from the third ancestor of Zen, Seng Can, after coming to China. In 580, he went from China to Vietnam, and founded the Vinitaruci School of Chinese Zen in Fayun Temple in Vietnam. According to legend, Vinitaruci's disciple Faxian took *Lankavatarasutra* as essentials of the mind, and Faxian's disciple Qingbian took *The Diamond Sutra* as the eyes. The school was spread to the thirteenth century and then tended to decline.

Wuyantong Zen School: Zen master Wuyantong was Cantonese, and became a monk in Shuanglin Temple in Wuzhou, Zhejiang (now the Jinhua area). He used to learn from Zen master Baizhang Huaihai. In the fifteenth year of Yuanhe in the Tang Yuan Dynasty (AD 820), he went to Vietnam, and founded the Wuyantong Zen School in Jianchu Temple in Tiên Dug County, Bac Ninh Province, promoting the Southern Zen of Zen master Baizhang. The school's fourth generation of master Khuông Việt was given the title of monk commander in the Dinh Dynasty, in charge of government affairs, and later was promoted as imperial tutor. In the heyday of the Ly Dynasty, talents of this school came forth in large numbers. The Wuyantong Zen School was handed down in Vietnam, stretching constantly, and is still the mainstream of Vietnamese Zen now.

Caotang Zen School: Zen master Caotang was Chinese and the disciple of Xuedou Zhongxian of the Yunmen School of Zen. He went to Vietnam to preach, and was respected by the emperor and ministers of the Ly Dynasty of Vietnam, where he lived in Kaiguo Monastery and held Dharma feasts, promoting "100 rites of Xuedou" and forming his own school.

Zhulin Zen School: After the Ly Dynasty, the Chen Dynasty also worshiped Buddhism. Emperor Taizong of Chen was taught by Zen master Tianfeng going from China to Vietnam, and he also learned from Zen master Decheng of the Song Dynasty. It was handed down among three generations to Emperor Renzong of Chen, who believed more firmly in Zen, and became a monk with the title Master Zhulin. He practiced Zen meditation and wrote books, educated more than 1,000 disciples, and founded the Zhulin Zen School. Because the Bodhimanda was located in Huayan Temple in Anzi Mountain, it was also known as the "Zhulin Anzai Zen School". This school mainly promoted the Linji School of Chinese Zen.

Zhulin Lianzong School: At the end of the seventeenth century, a new school was differentiated from the Zhulin Zen School. Monk Baimeilinjiao of the Zhulin Zen School founded the Zhulin Lianzong School in Shenglong City (now Hanoi). He absorbed the doctrine of the White Lotus School advocated by Cizhaoziyuan of China in the Southern Song Dynasty, combined Linji Zen with Amitabha Buddhism, and promoted the dual practice of Zen and sastra, taking sastra as the eye of Buddha, and Zen as the heart of Buddha; in fact, it centered on chanting Amitabha. This school was widely spread among Vietnamese peasants in the north, and even became the mainstream of Vietnamese Buddhism later.

Vietnamese Buddhism was deeply influenced by Chinese Buddhism, and the buildings of the monasteries and pagodas retained the color of China. Vietnamese Buddhist scriptures also used Chinese characters; monks and other Buddhists always used Chinese Tripitaka, and the ceremony of accepting precepts was also the same as Chinese Buddhism. As for modern Vietnamese Buddhism, it was a mixture of Chinese Mahayana Buddhism, Confucianism, Taoism, and Vietnamese folk beliefs, showing a unique form of mixed faith.

The spread of Tibetan Buddhism

At the end of the thirteenth century, the Yuan Dynasty formally made Tibetan Buddhism the national religion, and Tibetan Buddhism was gradually spread among the upper aristocrats and the lower people in Mongolia. The upper nobles built Buddhist temples and invited lamas from Tibet to translate Tibetan scriptures into Mongolian. In 1641, the son of Tüsiyetü Khan, the feudal lord of Khalkha, was declared the Mongolian living Buddha, with the Buddhist name of Jebtsundamba. The Qing Dynasty also stipulated that every banner of Mongolia should build a lamasery, and each family that had more than two men must have one man become a monk. After the demise of the Qing Dynasty in 1911, the living Buddha Jebtsundamba became an authoritarian emperor with political and religious powers in Mongolia. Lama serf owners had a large number of slaves and livestock. Until 1924, before the constitutional monarchy of the living Buddha Jebtsundamba was abolished and Mongolian People's Republic was established, there were more than 105,000 lamas in Mongolia, accounting for 44 percent of the total Mongolian adult male population, or one-seventh of the total population.

Tibetan Buddhism was also spread in current Siberia and other places. Since the seventeenth century, tsarist Russia had been adopting the policy of fostering Buddhism, and built many large lamaseries in the areas bordering on Mongolia. There are now about 500,000 Buddhists, divided into three sects: one is Buryat, distributed in the Buryat Republic in Siberia, Irkutsk Province, and Chita Province; one is Calmuc, distributed in the southwest of the Volga River Delta; and one is Tuva, distributed in Tuva Autonomous Province on the Sino-Russian border.

At about the end of the twelfth century, Lama Anjia Wang Nanmojialuo, eminent monk of Kagyu of Tibetan Buddhism, went to Bhutan to spread Kagyu. Later he introduced Nyingma. In Bhutan, Tibetan Buddhism was worshiped as the national religion, the reincarnated lama was the supreme ruler of the country, and the main temple of Lamaism in various places was the headquarters of all levels of government agencies. At the beginning of the twentieth century, lamas confirmed Bhutan as a monarchical state, and later terminated the system of the reincarnated living Buddha. Now every village in Bhutan has a monastery, and there are 5,000 lamas nationwide, whose cost of living is provided by the government.

At the beginning of the seventeenth century, Lama Lacong Qinbo, eminent monk of Tibetan Buddhism, went to Sikkim with his disciples to spread Ningma. In the eighteenth century, Sikkim built the main temple of Kagyu. Nyingma and Kagyu became the dominant sects in Sikkim Buddhism. In 1642, the Buddha gifted the title of "Zuojiayaluo" to the king of Sikkim, meaning divine right of kings, and Sikkim became a kingdom with political and religious unity.

The introduction of modern Chinese Buddhism into Southeast Asia

In modern times, as a large number of Chinese migrated to Southeast Asia to be engaged in business and reclamation, Chinese Buddhism was also introduced to Malaysia, Singapore, and other countries.

The ancient Malay Peninsula was strongly influenced by Indian culture, and most of the inhabitants believed in Buddhism and Hinduism. In the fifteenth century, the Kingdom of Malacca declared Islam as the national religion, Buddhist temples were destroyed, and Buddhism was close to extinction. Since the nineteenth century, a large number of Chinese monks and Buddhists went to Malaysia and constructed Buddhist temples, and believers gradually increased. The two Buddhist centers of the county, Penang and Kuala Lumpur, formed. About 70 percent of the Chinese in Penang believed in Mahayana Buddhism.

At the beginning of the nineteenth century, people from Fujian and Guangdong went to settle in Singapore, and Buddhist monks also went there to build temples, found Buddhist schools, and spread Buddhist doctrine. In 1926, Master Tai Xu went to Singapore from China to organize the Xingzhou Scripture Seminar, and later he organized the Singapore Chinese Buddhist Association. Three-fourths of the residents in Singapore were Chinese, and mainly believed in Buddhism and Taoism. Singapore had one temple in two lanes, three temples on a street, which meant that there were many temples, some of which were also large. Buddhist monks were divided into Fujian and Guangdong factions, and most of the two factions believed in Zen of Chinese Buddhism and the Pure Land School.

In addition, modern Chinese Buddhism was introduced into the Philippines, mainly because some overseas Chinese and ethnic Chinese believed in Buddhism from mainland China in order to eliminate disasters, and there were nearly 50,000 Buddhists, mainly concentrated in the capital, Manila.

Note

1 At that time, Korea was in the Three Kingdoms Period (also known as the Three Koreas). The three kingdoms were Goguryeo in the north, Baekje in the southwest, and Silla in the southeast. The Three Kingdoms Period lasted from the first century BC to the seventh century AD.

Index

Note: Page numbers in *italics* indicate figures.

20 Skandha 104, 113n2

Abhidhamma Pitaka 74, 88
Abhidharma, term 26n2
Abhidharmacarya: classics scholars and in Southern and Northern Dynasties 39–41; Sarvativadavinaya 42; scholars and, in Northern Dynasties 42–43; scholars and, in Southern Dynasties 41–42
Abhidharma Shi 39, 40–41
Amitabha Pure Land, ideological trend of praying for 35
Amoghavajra 126, 166, 167, 183, 195
Amognarajra 55, 56, 80
An (Emperor) 28, 185
Anathapindika 10, 144
anatman 90; theory of 112–113
ancestral hall 131, 145
ancestral temples: Cien Temple and Xingjiao Temple (Consciousness-Only School) 163–164; Huayan Temple and Cottage Temple (Huayan School) 165; Qixia Temple (Three-Treatise School) 162–163; Tiantai Mountain (Tiantai School) 161–162; Xuanzhong Temple, Xiangjui Temple and Donglin Temple (Pure Land School) 167–169; of Zen 169–177; *see also* Buddhist monuments in China; lamaseries; Zen
animals 5, 91, 191: Buddhism *vs* Brahmanism for killing 12; eating 49; worshipping 67
animism 67
An Shigao 28, 191
anti-reincarnation 97–98
Arhat Hall 131, 145
Arhats (16) 139–140

Arhats (18) 140
Asaga 38; Yogacara of Buddhism 19
Asoka 13
Asura 7, 91
authenticity of universe, theory of Buddhism on 108–111
Avalokitesvara Hall 131, 142–143

Bai Juyi 166, 168
Baishui Temple, Emei Mountain 157
Baisui Temple, Jiuhua Mountain 159
Baiyun School 63
Baizhang (Zen master) 146
Baizhang Regulations (Haihai) 115, 119–120, 127n3, 214
Baizhang Regulations, Imperial Revised 124, 127n3
Baoguo Temple, Emei Mountain 158
beast 3; Bangsheng 91; *see also* animals
Benji 60, 174
Benwu School 35, 36
Bhavaviveka and Buddhapalita, Madhyamika faction of Buddhism 18
Bhiksu 116–118, 126n1, 136, 144
Bodhidharma 43, 169–170
Bodhimanda, Qingyuan Sect of Zen 172–173
Bodhiruci 38, 42
Bodhisattva 42, 141
Bodhisattva Hall 141–144; Avalokitesvara (Hall of Great Mercy) 142–143; Ksitgarbha hall 143–144
Bodhisattva Top, Wutai Mountain 155
Bon-Religion 67–68
Brahma, god 2–3
Brahmanism 2–4, 26; Buddhism *vs* 12–13, 111–112; Esoteric Buddhism

226 *Index*

and 55; goal of relief 7–8; people of 52; reincarnation 97–98; view of self in 110
Buddha 155; birthday 123–124; Five Dhyani Buddhas 138–139; statue of Sakyamuni 135–137; Tathagatajnana-darsana of 196; term 4; thirty-two appearances 106, 114n3; three statues 137–138
Buddhabhadra 33, 34, 39
Buddhacinga 31
Buddhasanta 41, 44, 204
Buddhas of Three Worlds 137–138
Buddhism 115; in Sixteen Kingdoms 30–32; appellation of believers 115–116; beginning of introduction into China 27–29; Buddhist categories 115–116; creation and prosperity in Sui and Tang Dynasties 45–62; in Eastern Jin Dynasty 32–33; five precepts of 11; Four Noble Truths of 39; initial spread in Three Kingdoms and Western Jin 29–30; Mahayana 17–22; opposition to Brahmanism 12–13; Pratitya-samutpada 109–110; process of joining 116–118; prosperity in Sixteen Kingdoms in Eastern Jin Dynasty 30–36; rulers supporting 11; state power of Japan and 218–219; theory of anatman 112–113; theory of impermanance 110–111; theory on authenticity of universe 108–111; *see also* doctrines of Buddhism; Indian Buddhism; Sui and Tang Dynasties
Buddhism and Chinese Sculpture (Chang Renxia) 148
Buddhism rituals, Dudie and the monk and temple registers 118
Buddhist classics: importance of 74–75; writings of Chinese monks 81–82
Buddhist Ghost Festival 124–125
Buddhist monuments in China 147–182; ancestral temple of the eight schools 160–177; Dunhuang Grottoes 148–149; Emei Mountain 152, 157–158; famous lamaseries 177–182; famous mountains 152–160; Jinhua Mountain 152, 158–160; Jiuhua Mountain 158–160; Longmen Grottoes 150–152; Putuo Mountain 152, 156–157; Wutai Mountain 152, 153–156; Yungang Grottoes 150; *see also* ancestral temples; lamaseries
Buddhist rituals 115; bathing of the Buddha 123, 124; Buddhist Ghost Festival 124–125; confession method 121–123; daily recitation 120–121; Daqi and 123; feeding Yankou 125, 126; Shui Lu Rites 125–126
Buddhist scriptures: Avalokitesvara 142–143, 146n4; Bodhisattva 141; catalog of 86–88; Chinese translation of 76–80; collection of 75–76; Dai translation of 81; structure of 88–89; Tibetan translation of 80; translation in Southern and Northern Dynasties 37–38; translation in Sui and Tang Dynasties 47; translation of 28–29; *see also* Tripitaka
Buddhist system 115; process of joining Buddhism 116–118; regulation 119–120; temple 118–119
Buddhist temple hall: ancestral hall 145; Arhat Hall 145; Bodhisattva hall 141–144; configuration of temple 131; Dhammasala (lecture hall) 146; eastern and western side halls 144–145; evolution of monastery construction 128–130; Hall of Heavenly Kings 132–135; Mahavira Hall 135–141; Sangharama Hall 144; three-door hall 131–132
Bu Zhen Kong Lun (Seng Zhao) 36

caityas 129, 130
calligraphy, Japan and China 219
Cambodia 24, 26, 37
Caodong School 64, 65, 158, 199, 214; Japan 218; Mount Dong and Mount Cao of 174; Tiantong Temple of 174–175
Caotang Zen School, Vietnamese Buddhism 221
caste system, India 1–3, 12–13
Chengling Pagoda of Linji Temple, ancestral temple of Linji School 173–174
China: Buddhism in 24–25; Buddhist monuments in 147–182; *see also* Buddhist monuments in China
Chinese Buddhism: absorption in 201–207; autocratic centralization system 184–186; characteristics of 183–184; doctrine of religious interpretation 202–205; ethical relations 186–187; history of 210–211; influence of Sui and Tang Dynasties on Korea 212–215; influence of Taoism 189; introduction of modern, into Southeast Asia 222–223; orthodox position of Confucianism 188–189; political unity 187;

reconciliation in 190–200; role of traditional religious superstition 189–190; root of basic characteristics of 184–190; ruling class, landlords and peasant uprisings 187–188; simplicity in 207–211; spread and integration of 190
Chongning Regulations 120
Chongningzang, wood engraving of Tripitaka 84
Cien School 183
Cien Temple, Consciousness-Only School 163–164
confession method 121–123; Daqi and 123; five repentances 121–122, 127n4; practicing Samath 122–123; ritual of 122
Confucianism 32, 74, 188–189, 194–195; Buddhism and 210; Taoism and 210
Confucius 4, 41, 155, 194–195, 200; Confucius Temple 131
confusion, Hinayana vs Mahayana Buddhism 21
Consciousness-Only School 20, 48, 53, 65, 183; absorption of theories 207; Cien Temple 163–164; founding of 195; influence on Korea 213; unity of study 201–202; Xingjiao Temple 164; Xuan Zang and 50–53
cosmology 16, 19, 106, 109
Cottage Temple, Huayan School 165

Dalai Lama 69, 71, 72, 181; Potala Palace 177, 178
Daming Temple, ancestral temple of Vinaya School 166
Dao An 30–32, 35, 40, 54, 77–78, 115, 121, 122
Daochang Temple 32–33, 34
Dao Chuo 56–57, 209
Dao Deng (monk) 213, 216
Daowu (Emperor) 37, 182n2
Dao Xuan 44, 53–54, 166
Daoyi (Master Ma) 59–60, 172, 213
Daxingshan Temple, ancestral temple of Esoteric Buddhism 166–167
Dazhong, issue of Dudie 118
Dehuito (Zen master) 120
Deqing 199–200
Deva 40; Madhyamika faction of Buddhism 18
Dhammasala (lecture room) 131, 146
Dharma 37, 38, 43; term 26n3; westing movement for 34
Dharma Character School: influence on Japan 216; Three-Treatise School and 217

Dharma Ending Age 49
Dharmagupta 47, 166
Dharmaguptavinaya 30, 34, 53–54, 104
Dharmaguptavinaya Shi 43
Dharmakala 30, 191
Dharmaksema 38–40, 135
Dharmapala (King) 22, 23
Dharmaraksa 29–30
Dharma Semblance Age 49
Dharmata Nirvana 100–101
Dilun Shi 39, 42–43, 51, 204
doctrines of Buddhism 90–113; 12 karmas 95–97; essence of humanity 92; ideal realm of life 99–102; kinds of sufferings 93–94; nature and value of life 90–95; Noble Eightfold Paths 102–103; position of man in universe 90–92; retribution and reimbursement 97–99; root of suffering of life 95–99; "Six Mortals" 91; Six Perfections 107–108; Three Practices of precept, meditation, and wisdom 103–106; value of life 92–95; way of life relief 102–108
Donglin Temple, ancestral temple of Pure Land School 168–169
Dongshan Temple, ancestral temple of Zen 171
Dongta School of Dongta Huaisu 54
Drepung Monastery 179
Dritarashtra, Heavenly King Hall 132–134
Dudie, monk and temple registers 118
Du Fu 128, 164, 171
Du Shun 54, 165, 202

East Cliff Temple, Jiuhua Mountain 160
Eastern Han Dynasty 27–28; Chinese translation of scriptures 77
Eastern Jin Dynasty: Buddhism in 32–33; Chinese translation of scriptures 77–78; prosperity of Buddhism in Sixteen Kingdoms 30–36
"eight holy paths" 102–103
Emei Mountain 152, 157–158
Esoteric Buddhism 22–23, 25, 26, 67, 73n10; auspicious sitting 136; Daxingshan Temple of 166–167; influence on Korea 214–215; Lotus sitting 136; Qinglong Temple of 167; Tang Dynasty 55–56; Wutai Mountain 154
Esoteric Pitaka 88, 89
"Evam Maya Srutam" 74, 76, 89n1
Exoteric Buddhism 22–23, 67, 73n10
Exotic Buddhism 23

factions, Sectarian Buddhism 14, *15*, 16–17
Fa Lang 41, 50
Fangzhang 120, 128n2
Fa She (Buddhist organization) 44
Fa Tai 35, 41
Fa Xian 33, 34, 38, 39
Fayan School 64; Qingliang Temple of 175
Fa Zang 197, 202; Huayan School 54–55, 213
Fengshen Romance 131, 134, 141
Fengxian Temple 151
Five Dynasties: Buddhism on decline since 62–66; historical evolution of Buddhist sects since 64–66; Huayan School 66; Pure Land School 65; Tiantai School 65; trend of Buddhism's development since 62–64; Vinaya School 66; Zen 64–65
five repentances 121–122, 127n4
Flesh Temple, Jiuhua Mountain 160
Foguang Temple 129
Four Noble Truths of Buddhism 39
Four Sage Bodhisattvas 142
Four Temples in the World, Tiantai School 162
Fourth-Ancestor Temple, ancestral temple of Zen 170–171
Fu Jian 31–32, 185, 212
Futian clothing, monks 117
Futu Temple 129, 130

Ganden Monastery 179
Ganlu Temple, Jiuhua Mountain 160
Gaozong (Emperor) 45, 82, 164, 168, 185
Gaozu (Emperor) 45, 185
Garbhadhatu 56
Gelug (Shamanism) 70–72, 73n10
ghost 91
Green Pagoda 173
grotto temples 130; Dunhuang Grottoes 148–149; Guyang Grotto 151; Longmen Grottoes 150–152; Mogao Grottoes 148–149; Yungang Grottoes 150
Guangxu 64, 163
Gunabhadra 38, 43

hall *see* Buddhist temple hall
Harivarman 39–40
heaven 3, 35, 67, 91, 124, 185
Heavenly Kings, Hall of 131, 132–135, 169; four Heavenly Kings 91, 130, 132–135, 149, 151; Maitreya Buddha 134; Skanda 134–135
hell 3, 91, 93, 94, 125, 143, 185
Hinayana Buddhism 29; difference from Mahayana Buddhism 20–22, 100–102, 203–205, 208; Nirvana in 139; theory 34

Hinduism 22, 23, 26, 55, 133, 223
Hongchunping, Emei Mountain 158
HongFa Zang, wood engraving of Tripitaka 84
Honglu Temple 128
Hongwunanzang, wood engraving of Tripitaka 85
Huacheng Temple, Jiuhua Mountain 160
Huaihai 60, 115, 119–120
Huang-Lao School 28
Huanglong Mountain, ancestral temple of Huanglong School 175–176
Huanhua School 35
Huayan School 122; absorption of theories 206–207; Cottage Temple 165; development since Five Dynasties 63, 66; Fa Zang and 54–55; founding of 197; Huayan Temple 165; influence on Japan 216; influence on Korea 213; unity of study 201–202; Vairocana 136; Wutai Mountain 153; Wutai Mountain Buddhism 156
Hui Guan (monk) 32, 33, 38–40, 213
Hui Ke 38, 43, *61*
Hui Neng 58–59; *Altar Sutra* 81, 82; disciples of 59; Huairang and 59–60; sudden enlightenment 208–209; Xingsi and 60; Zen and 57–62, 81, 119, 145, 171–172, 197–198, 208; Zen and Korea 213–214
Hui Si 44, 202
Huiyuan 32–33, 35, 40, 50, 56, 122
human 91; essence of humanity 92

impermanence: term 90; theory of 110–111
India, caste system of 1–3
Indian Buddhism 183; early development of 4–13; Esoteric Buddhism 22–23, 25, 26; historical background of Shakyamuni's creation of 1–4; Mahayana Buddhism 17–22, 208; outward spread of 24–26; profile of introduction to the north 24–25; profile of introduction to the south 25–26; revival movement of 23–24; routes for introduction to China 27–28; Sectarian Buddhism 13–17; Shakyamuni's creation of 4–13; Tao in early 192
Indian Buddhist Center 23

Jainism 3, 8, 26n1
Jambudvipa 131, 153, 182n3
Japan: Buddhism in 24–25, 218–219; Buddhist universities in 219; impact of

Buddhist sects in Sui and Tang Dynasties on Buddhism in 215–220; Jodo Shinshu 218; Kamakura Period of 217
Jeta Temple, Jiuhua Mountain 160
Jian Zhen (monk) 166, 168, 173, 216, 219, 220
Jian Zhen Memorial Hall 166
Jiaxingzang, wood engraving of Tripitaka 85
Jingshan School, Mount Jing as ancestral temple of 177
Jise School 35, 36, 193
Jiuhua Mountain 152, 158–160
Ji Zang 41, 44; Three-Treatise School and 49–50, 205
Jnanagupta 47, 166
Jushe Shi 40–41

Kadam 70, 72n9
Kagyu (white religion) 69–70
Kaibaozang, wood engraving of Tripitaka 84
Kangxi (Emperor) 71, 155, 180–181
karma: 12 karmas 95–97; Hinayana *vs* Mahayana Buddhism 21
Kingdoms *see* Sixteen Kingdoms
Korea: Buddhism in Korean Peninsula 24, 215; Consciousness-Only School and 213; Esoteric Buddhism and 214–215; Huayan School and 213; influence of Buddhist sects of Sui and Tang Dynasties 212–215; Three Kingdoms Period 223n1; Three-Treatise School and 213; Vinaya School and 213; Zen sects in 213–214
ksana 111, 114n5
Ksitigarbha 159–160
Kublai Khan 25, 63, 69, 88
Kuiji 50–53, 82, 164, 195, 202, 213
Kumarajiva 30–32, 36, 40, 50, 77, 183

Labrang Monastery 178, 180
Lamaism 66, 129; historical development of 66–68; Mongolian (Nyingma) 68–69; *see also* Tibetan Buddhism
lamaseries: Drepung Monastery 179; famous 177–182; Ganden Monastery 179; Labrang Monastery 180; Outer Eight Temples 180–181; Potala Palace 177, 178; Sera Monastery 179; Taer Monastery 180; Tashihunpo Monastery 177, 178; Tibetan 130; Yonghe Lamasery 181–182; *see also* ancestral temples; Buddhist monuments in China
Lankavatarasutra 38, 43, 45, 58–59, 202, 220

Laozi 28, 155, 189, 192–194, 199–200
Liangjia 60, 174
Li Bai 157, 159, 166, 168
life: 12 karmas 95–97; ideal realm of 99–102; retribution and reimbursement 97–99; root of suffering of 95–99; value of 92–95; way of life relief 102–108
Li Jing 61, 133
Lingji School, Chengling Pagoda of Linji Temple 173–174
Linji School 25, 60, *61*, 64–65, 156, 158, 169, 173, 199, 217–218, 221
Liu Yimin 33, 168, 194
Liu Yuxi 166, 176
Longxing Temple 143

madhyamapratipad, Sakyamuni's doctrine 8–13
Madhyamika faction, Mahayana Buddhism 18–19
Mahasanghika 14–17
Mahavira Hall 131; 16 Arhats 139–140; 18 Arhats 140; configuration of 135; Five Dhyani Buddhas 138–139; Island Avalokitesvara 141; one statue 135–137; seven Buddhas of the past 139; three sages 141; three statues 137–138
Mahayana Buddhism 17–22; difference from Hinayana Buddhism 20–22, 100–102, 203–205; Esoteric 26; introduction to China 29; Madhyamika faction 18–19, 23; meditation and 105–106; precepts 104–105; process of joining 117; Six Perfections 107–108; Thailand and 25; theory 33; Yogacara faction 19–20, 23
Maitreya Buddha 19, 132, 134
Maitreya Pure Land, ideological trend of praying for 35
Malay Peninsula 27, 223
Malaysia 24, 26, 212, 222–223
Manjusri Buddha, Wutai Mountain 153
Marpa, Kagyu (white religion) by 69
Master Ma (Daoyi) 59–60
Medicine Buddha, hall of 131
meditation, one of Three Practices 105–106
Mei Cen Mountain 156
Mimi Temple, Wutai Mountain 155
Ming (Emperor) 28, 29, 37, 182n2
Min Gong 144, 159
monastery construction, evolution of 128–130
monks: categories of 116; Chinese system 115, 116; issue of Dudie 118; Pravarana

Day 124–125; procedures for becoming 117; temple and 118–119; Tian Xiang style 117
Mount Dong and Mount Cao, ancestral temples of Caodong School 174
Mount Jing, ancestral temple of Jingshan School 177
Mount Wei and Mount Yang, ancestral temples of Wei Yang School 174

Nagarjuna 100–101; Madhyamika faction of Buddhism 18
Nalanda Temple 22, 51, 52
Nanchan Temple 129, 154, 155
Nanhua Temple, ancestral temple of Zen 171–172
Nanyue Prajna Temple (Fuyan Temple), ancestral temple of Nanyue of Zen 172
New Chinese Tripitaka Catalog (Lv Cheng) 88
New Confucianism 198
Nirvana: of Buddhism 192; doctrine 44; goal of relief 8; Hinayana *vs* Mahayana Buddhism 21, 100
Nirvana Shi 39–40, 48
Noble Eightfold Paths 102–103
Northern Dynasty *see* Southern and Northern Dynasties
Nyingma (Mongolian Lamaism) 68–69

Outer Eight Temples 178, 180–181
outside schools 74, 75
Ouyang Xiu 166, 171

pagoda temples 130; *see also* ancestral temples
pain, theory of suffering 7; *see also* suffering of life
Pancavidy 106, 114n4
Paramartha 19, 37–38, 41, 50
People's Republic of Mongolia 25, 222
permanence 95, 101, 110
Phagspa (monk) 69, 88
Piluzang, wood engraving of Tripitaka 84
Potala Palace 177, 178
Pratitya-samutpada: of Buddhism 19; foundation of Buddhist doctrine 109–110; theory of anatman from 112–113
Pravarana, two-day confession rally 9
Pravarana Day 123, 124–125
precept, one of Three Practices 103–105
Pudgala 16, 26n1
Puguang Temple, Emei Mountain 158
Puningzang, wood engraving of Tripitaka 84

Pure Land: faith of 44; Hinayana *vs* Mahayana Buddhism 21; ideological trend of praying for 35
Pure Land School 49, 119, 122, 123; absorption of theories 206–207; Ambassador Buddha 136–137; basis of 57; development since Five Dynasties 62, 65; Donglin Temple 168–169; founding of 196; Sui and Tang Dynasties 56–57; Wutai Mountain Buddhism 156; Xiangji Temple 168; Xuanzhong Temple 167–168; Zen and Vietnamese Buddhism 220–221
Putuo Mountain 152, 156–157

Qianlong (Emperor) 140, 181
Qidanzang, wood engraving of Tripitaka 84
Qingliang Mountain 153–154; *see also* Wutai Mountain
Qingliang Temple, ancestral temple of Fayan School 175
Qinglong Temple, ancestral temple of Esoteric Buddhism 167
Qingyuan Mountain Jingju Temple, ancestral temple of Qingyuan Sect of Zen 172–173
Qingzang, wood engraving of Tripitaka 85
Qishazang, wood engraving of Tripitaka 84
Qi Song (monk) 198–199
Qixia Temple, Three-Treatise School 162–163

Rahula, Madhyamika faction of Buddhism 18
Rahula Temple (Lama Temple), Wutai Mountain 155
Ralpacan 67–68
Ratnamati 42, 44
reincarnation 97–98; theory of retribution and 98–99
Rituals of Three Refuges 117
Rupadharma, five elements 56

Sakyamuni: Buddhist founder 115–116; Buddhist scriptures 89; disciples of 9; Hinayana *vs* Mahayana Buddhism 20–21; life and mission of 89; lotus postures of Buddha 136; retribution and reimbursement 97–99; sacredness of 16; statue of 135–137; wandering and mendicity 9; *see also* Shakyamuni
Sangharama, temples in India 128–129
Sangharama Hall 131, 144
Sanjie Jiao (Pufa School) 48–49

Sarvastivada 14, *15*, 16
Sarvastivadavinaya, school of 42
Satyasiddhi School, Three-Treatise School and 216
Sautrantika 14, 16–17
Sectarian Buddhism 13–17; cosmology and 16; factions of 14, *15*, 16–17; Northern Buddhism 14; philosophical theory 16; religious ideals 15–16; religious practice 14–15; Southern Buddhism 14; term 14
Seng Can (Zen master) 43, 58, *61*, 170
Seng Lang 41, 50
Seng Zhao 32, 36, 41
Sera Monastery 179
settling period 9–10
Seven Elements, theory of 4
Shakyamuni 1; aspects of creating Buddhism 6–13; attaining Buddhahood 6; founder of Buddhism 4; historical background of Buddhism creation 1–4; marriage and family 5; as monk 5; religious discipline 5–6; theory of madhyamapratipad 8–13; theory of relief 7–8; theory of suffering 7, 95, 97; *see also* Sakyamuni
Shamanism 129; Gelug in Tibetan Lamaism 70–72; lamaseries 177–180
Shan Dao 56–57, 209
Shaolin Boxing 170
Shaolin Temple, ancestral temple of Zen 169–170
Shihan School 35
Shiva, god 2
Shizong (Emperor) 62, 186
Shui Lu Rites (Yang E) 126
Shun Dao (monk) 212
Shunzhi (Emperor) 178
Shuxiang Temple, Wutai Mountain 155
Singapore 212, 222, 223
"Six Mortals" 91
Six Perfections 107–108
Six Realms of Samsara 7
"six schools" 35–36
Sixteen (Kingdoms 30; Buddhism in 30–32; *Bu Zhen Kong Lun* (Seng Zhao) 36; characteristics of Buddhist activities in 33–36; formation of "six schools and seven sects" 35–36; ideological trend of praying for Pure Land 35; translation of Buddhist scriptures 33–34; westing movement for Dharma 34
Skanda 132, 134–135

Southeast Asia: Buddhists in 26, 124; introduction of modern Chinese Buddhism into 222–223
Southern and Northern Dynasties: Chinese translation of scriptures 78; different characteristics of Buddhism in 43–45; rulers flattering and exterminating Buddhism 36–37; scholars and Abhidharmacarya in 38–43; translation of Buddhist scriptures 37–38
Sramanera precepts 116–117
Srongtsen Gampo 67, 178
Sthaviravada 14–17, 23, 25–26
Subhakarasimha 55, 166, 195, 215
suffering of life: doctrine of 93–95; Hinayana *vs* Mahayana Buddhism 21–22; root of 95–99; Sakyamuni's doctrine 7–8; theory of 7–8
Sui and Tang Dynasties: Chinese translation of scriptures 78–80; Esoteric Buddhism 55–56; Fa Zang and Huayan School 54–55; Hui Neng and Zen 57–62; impact of Buddhist sects on Japanese Buddhism 215–220; influence of Buddhist sects on Korea 212–215; Ji Zang and Three-Treatise School 49–50; Pure Land School 56–57; rulers' use, advocacy, and restriction of Buddhism 45–46; Sanjie Jiao (Pufa School) 48–49; translation of Buddhist scriptures 47; Vinaya School 53–54; Xuan Zang and Consciousness-Only School 50–53; Zhiyi and Tiantai School 47–48
"sunyata theory", Pratityasamutpada 19
"supernatural Buddha" 15
"superworld Buddha" 15
Sutra Catalog 86–88
Sutra Pitaka 74, 75, 82–83, 88
Suzong (Emperor) 164

Taer Monastery 178, 180
Taichang Temple 128
Taiping Xingguo 157
Taisho Tripitaka (Japan) 88
Taiwu (Emperor) 37, 182n2
Taiwudi (Emperor) 186
Taizong (Emperor) 45, 50, 52, 80, 164, 169, 170, 186, 221
Taizu (Emperor) 44, 62, 214
Tang Dynasty *see* Sui and Tang Dynasties
Tang Gaozong 159, 163
Tan Guang (monk) 161
Tang Xuanzang 14, 139, 183, 186

Tan Luan 43, 44, 56–57, 209
Taoism 18, 31, 36, 62, 63, 133, 157, 189, 192
Tashilhunpo Monastery 177, 178
Tayuan Temple, Wutai Mountain 155
temple: Buddhist 118–119; evolution of monastery construction 128–130; registers 118; term 128; *see also* Buddhist temple hall
Thailand, Buddhism in 25–26
theory of impermanence 110–111
theory of madhyamapratipad, Sakyamuni's doctrine 8–13
theory of relief, Sakyamuni's doctrine 7–8
theory of suffering, Sakyamuni's doctrine 7
Three Kingdoms: Korea in 223; spread of Buddhism in 29–30
Three Practices 103–106; meditation 105–106; precept 103–105; wisdom 106
Three-Treatise: Buddhist scholars of 41; doctrine 44; masters of 39
Three-Treatise School 183; founding of 195; influence on Japan 216; influence on Korea 213; Ji Zang and 49–50; Qixia Temple of 162–163; religious interpretation of Jizang 205
Three-Treatise Shi 41, 48
Tiantai Mountain, ancestral temple of Tiantai School 161–162
Tiantai School 122–123; absorption of theories 206–207; development since Five Dynasties 62, 65; five books of 48; founding of 195, 196, 202; influence on Korea 215; practice of observing the mind 206; religious interpretation of Jizang 204; Taoist meaning in 196–197; three-body Buddha 137; Tiantai Mountain as ancestral temple of 161–162; unity of study 201–202; Zhiyi and 47–48, 122–123, 144
Tiantong Temple, ancestral temple of Caodong School 174–175
Tian Xiang, style for monks 117
Tibetan Buddhism 25, 27; first and second propagation of 66–68, 72n9; formation and development of 66–72; Ganden Monastery in 179; Gelug (Shamanism) 70–72; Kagyu (white religion) 69–70; lamaseries 130; monks in 116; Nyingma (Mongolian Lamaism) 68–69; Sakya (floral religion) 69; spread of 222; translation of scriptures 80
Tiger Hill Temple, ancestral temple of Tiger Hill School 176–177

Tripitaka: Chinese 221; engraving scriptures 83–85; new carving of 215; origin meaning of 74; printing scriptures 85–86; purpose of 89; stone engraving of 83; Tibetan 80; transcribing scriptures 82–83; wood engraving of 84–85; writings of Chinese monks 81–82
Trisong Detsen 67–68
Tsongkhapa, founder of Gelug 70–71
Tusita 134, 146n2

Vaishravana, Hall of Heavenly Kings 133–134
Vajrabodhi 55, 166, 183, 195
Vajradhatu 56, 71
Valley Temple, ancestral temple of Zen 170
Vasubandhu 38, 42; Yogacara of Buddhism 19
Vatsiputriya 14, 16
Vedas, Brahmanism and 2–3
Vietnam: Buddhism in 25; relationship between Buddhism, Zen, and Pure Land School 220–221
vihara, site at temple 129
Vinaya Pitaka 74, 75, 88
Vinaya School 30, 119; absorption of theories 207; Daming Temple as ancestral temple of 166; Dao Xuan and 53–54; development since Five Dynasties 66; influence on Japan 216; influence on Korea 213; Wutai Mountain Buddhism 156
Vinitaruci Zen School, Vietnamese Buddhism 220
Virudhaka, Hall of Heavenly Kings 133–134
Virupaksha, Hall of Heavenly Kings 133–134
Vishnu, god 2

Wang Wei 140, 168, 209
Wang Yangming 168, 211
Wannian Temple, Emei Mountain 158
Wansong Xingxiu 199
Wei Yang School: Mount Wei and Mount Yang as ancestral temples of 174; Mount Wei and Mount Yang of 174
Wen (Emperor) 44, 87, 117, 122, 154, 166, 169, 212
Wencheng (Emperor) 37, 150, 182n2
Wencheng (Princess) 67, 178
Wenyan 60, 175

Wenzong (Emperor) 215
Western Jin Dynasty, spread of Buddhism in 29–30
Wheel-Turning King 4–5
White Horse Temple 128, 129, 177
White Lotus Association 168
White Lotus Pool 171
White Lotus School 63
wisdom, one of Three Practices 106
Wu (Emperor) 27, 36, 44, 58, 117, 122, 125, 129, 185, 186, 191, 194–195, 212
Wutai Mountain 152, 153–156; temples of 154–155
Wuyantong Zen School, Vietnamese Buddhism 221
Wu Zetian (Empress) 54, 148, 151, 197, 213
Wuzong (Emperor) 119, 129, 154, 186

Xian Chun Regulations 120
Xiangbu School of Fa Li 54
Xiangji Temple, ancestral temple of Pure Land School 168
Xiantong Temple, Wutai Mountain 154–155
Xiaowen (Emperor) 37, 150, 154
Xiaowu (Emperor) 185
Xingjiao Temple, Consciousness-Only School 164
Xingsi, Hui Neng and 60, 173
Xinwu School 35, 36
Xiqian (stone monk) 173
Xuan (Emperor) 37, 44, 48, 122
Xuanwu (Emperor) 37
Xuanzang 41, 43, 47, 202; Consciousness-Only School and 50–53; disciples of 52; known as Tang Sanzang (Tang Monk) 51; translation field by 79
Xuanzhong Temple, ancestral temple of Pure Land School 167–168
Xuanzong (Emperor) 49, 87

Yang (Emperor) 48, 50, 117
Yangqi Mountain, ancestral temple of Yangqi School 176
Yangqi School 64
Yaoxing (King) 115
Yi (Emperor) 83
Yican 60–61
Yique Grottoes (Longmen Grottoes) 150–152
Yi Yi (Buddhist organization) 44
Yogacara faction, Mahayana Buddhism 19–20
Yonghe Lamasery 178, 181–182

Yonglebeizang, wood engraving of Tripitaka 85
Yonglenanzang, wood engraving of Tripitaka 85
Yongtai (Zen master) 155
Yongzheng (Emperor) 169
Yuan (Emperor) 47
Yuanhui School 36
Yuanjeuzang, wood engraving of Tripitaka 84
Yuan Ren (monk) 156, 167
Yuan Zhen (monk) 167
Yunmen School 65, 158
Yunmen Temple, as ancestral temple of Yunmen School 175

Zen: ancestral temples of 169–177; *Baizhang Regulations* 119–120; Chengling Pagoda of Linji Temple 173–174; Daqi of 123; development since Five Dynasties 62, 64–65; division of Southern Zen 57; Dongshan Temple 171; five schools of 57; Fourth-Ancestor Temple 170–171; genealogy of *61*; Huanglong Mountain, as ancestral temple of Huanglong School 175–176; Huayan School 55; Hui Neng and 57–62, 81, 119, 145, 171–172, 197–198; influence on Korea 213–214; Lanka Zen 58; mainstream of Buddhism 207–208; meditation and 105–106; Mount Dong, Mount Cao, and Tiantong Temple of Caodong School 174–175; Mount Jing, as ancestral temple of Jingshan School 177; Mount Wei and Mount Yang of Wei Yang School 174; Nanhua Temple 171–172; Nanyue Prajna Temple (Fuyan Temple) 172; Niutou Zen 58; Northern and Southern Dynasties 44–45; Qingliang Temple of Fayan School 175; Qingyuan Mountain, Jingju Temple 172–173; relationship with Pure Land School and Vietnamese Buddhism 220–221; Shaolin Boxing 170; Shaolin Temple 169–170; sudden enlightenment doctrine 209; in Tang Dynasty 62; Tiger Hill Temple, as ancestral temple of Tiger Hill School 176–177; Valley Temple of 170; Yangqi Mountain, as ancestral temple of Yangqi School 176; Yunmen Temple of Yunmen School 175; Zhiyi and Tiantai Schools 47–48

Zhaochengzang, wood engraving of Tripitaka 84
Zhaozhou (Zen master) 152
Zhenke 199, 206
Zhenzong (Emperor) 176
Zhi Daolin (monk) 35, 161
Zhida Regulations 120
Zhixu 199, 200, 207
Zhiyi 50; confession method 122–123; death of 161–162; Tiantai Schools and 47–48, 144, 202; Zen and 202
Zhongzong (Emperor) 54

Zhuangzi 192, 193
Zhu Daosheng 40, 194, 208
Zhuhong 199, 206
Zhulin Lianzong School, Vietnamese Buddhism 221
Zhulin Zen School, Vietnamese Buddhism 221
Zhu Tanyou (monk) 161
Zichao (monk) 214
Zifuzang, wood engraving of Tripitaka 84
Zong Mi 55, 205–206